THE TRUE CHRONICLES OF
JEAN LE BEL, 1290–1360

The chronicles of Jean le Bel, written around 1352–61, are one of the most important sources for the beginning of the Hundred Years' War. They were only rediscovered and published at the beginning of the twentieth century, though Froissart begins his much more famous work by acknowledging his great debt to the 'true chronicles' which Jean le Bel had written. Many of the great pages of Froissart are actually the work of Jean le Bel, and this is the first translation of his book.

It introduces English-speaking readers to a vivid text written by a man who, although a canon of the cathedral at Liège, had actually fought with Edward III in Scotland, and who was a great admirer of the English king. He writes directly and clearly, with an admirable grasp of narrative; and he writes very much from the point of view of the knights who fought with Edward. Even as a canon, he lived in princely style, with a retinue of two knights and forty squires, and he wrote at the request of John of Hainault, the uncle of queen Philippa. He was thus able to draw directly on the verbal accounts of the Crécy campaign given to him by soldiers from Hainault who had fought on both sides; and his description of warfare in Scotland is the most realistic account of what it was like to be on campaign that survives from this period. If he succumbs occasionally to a good story from one of the participants in the wars, this helps us to understand the way in which the knights saw themselves; but his underlying objective is to keep 'as close to the truth as I could, according to what I personally have seen and remembered, and also what I have heard from those who were there.' Edward may be his hero, a 'gallant and noble king', but Le Bel tells the notorious story of his supposed rape of the countess of Salisbury because he believed it to be true, puzzled and shocked though he was by his material.

It is a text which helps to put the massive work of Jean Froissart in perspective, but its concentrated focus and relatively short time span makes it a much more approachable and highly readable insight into the period.

Nigel Bryant read History and French at Balliol College, Oxford. He worked for many years as a theatre director and radio drama producer for the BBC, and was head of drama at Marlborough College and Lecturer in Drama at the University of Manchester. He has translated five major Arthurian romances from medieval French; this is his first translation of a historical work.

Other translations by Nigel Bryant

The High Book of the Grail:
A translation of the thirteenth century romance of Perlesvaus

Chrétien de Troyes, *Perceval: The Story of the Grail*

Robert de Boron, *Merlin and the Grail*

The Legend of the Grail

Perceforest

THE TRUE CHRONICLES OF JEAN LE BEL, 1290–1360

Translated by Nigel Bryant

THE BOYDELL PRESS

First published 2011
The Boydell Press, Woodbridge
Paperback edition 2015

ISBN 978 1 84383 694 0 hardback
ISBN 978 1 78327 022 4 paperback

The Boydell Press is an imprint of Boydell & Brewer Ltd
PO Box 9, Woodbridge, Suffolk, IP12 3DF, UK
and of Boydell & Brewer Inc.
668 Mount Hope Ave, Rochester, NY 14620–2731, USA
website: www.boydellandbrewer.com

The publisher has no responsibility for the continued existence or accuracy of
URLs for external or third-party internet websites referred to in this book,
and does not guarantee that any content on such websites is,
or will remain, accurate or appropriate

A CIP catalogue record for this book is available
from the British Library

This publication is printed on acid-free paper

Contents

List of maps   xiii

INTRODUCTION

'True Chronicles'   1
Chivalry   4
Honour and Blame   9
Stations   11
Style   13
Dates   14
Further Reading   17

JEAN LE BEL'S CHRONICLE

Prologue   21

EDWARD III'S ACCESSION

I   The genealogy of the noble King Edward, and how he was   22
         driven out of England.
II   How Sir John of Hainault took the Queen of England and her   26
         eldest son back to England.
III   How the Earl of Arundel and Hugh Despenser the Elder were   29
         captured and executed.
IV   How the king and Lord Hugh the Younger were captured and   30
         Lord Hugh sentenced to a foul death.
V   How the king was condemned and deprived of his crown and   32
         the government of the realm.
VI   How King Edward was crowned King of England at the age   33
         of sixteen.

THE CAMPAIGN IN THE BORDERS 1327

VII   How King Robert of Scotland defied the young King Edward   34
         and began to ravage England.
VIII   How the Hainaulter pages came into conflict with the English 36
         archers.
IX   How the king and all his army left the city of York to march 38
         against the Scots.
X   The nature of the Scots and their methods in war.   39
XI   How the King of England pursued the Scots who were burning   40
         and laying waste his land.

XII   How the English searched for the Scots and didn't know   42
where they were.

XIII   How young King Edward laid siege to the Scots, who were   45
burning and laying waste his land, on a mountain.

XIV   How the noble King Edward was married to the daughter of   50
the Count of Hainault.

'THE BLACK DOUGLAS'

XV   How the good King Robert of Scotland entrusted Sir James   52
Douglas with carrying his heart to the Holy Sepulchre.

XVI   How Sir James Douglas set out on his journey from Scotland.   53

THE CLAIMS TO THE FRENCH CROWN

XVII   How King Charles of France died and Lord Philip of Valois,   54
by common accord, was crowned King of France.

XVIII How King Philip of France defeated the Flemings at the hill of   56
Cassel.

XIX   How Lord Robert of Artois was forced into exile from France.   56

XX   How King Edward ordered the executions of his uncle the   58
Earl of Kent and Lord Mortimer.

WAR WITH SCOTLAND

XXI   How young King Edward resumed war against the young   59
King David of Scotland, his brother-in-law.

XXII   How King Edward invaded Scotland and burned and laid   61
waste the land and captured cities and castles.

XXIII How the noble King Edward laid siege to the good city of   62
Berwick.

XXIV   How the young Count of Namur and his brother crossed the   63
sea to England and were captured.

THE WAR WITH FRANCE BEGINS

XXV   How the noble King Edward sent the Bishop of Lincoln to the   65
Count of Hainault to discuss war with France.

XXVI   How a man named Jacob van Artevelde held sway in   69
Flanders.

XXVII How these English lords went to Flanders to secure the aid of   70
the Flemings and especially of Jacob van Artevelde.

XXVIII How the King of England crossed the sea and landed at   71
Antwerp, trusting in the promises made to his ambassadors
by a number of lords.

XXIX   How the Margrave of Jülich went to the Emperor to seek aid   73
          and guidance for King Edward against the French.

XXX   How the Emperor, through the Margrave of Jülich,   75
          commissioned King Edward to be his Vicar and lieutenant.

XXXI   How King Edward and his allies marched into the Cambrésis   77
          because Cambrai had turned to the King of France.

XXXII   How King Edward first entered France and ravaged a large   79
          part of the Thiérache before the eyes of the French king.

XXXIII   How and why the King of England took the name and the arms   82
          of France and called himself King of France and England.

XXXIV   How the King of France sent an army into the land of Hainault   83
          around Chimay.

XXXV   How the Duke of Normandy took a great army to besiege,   84
          capture and burn the mighty castle of Thun in the Cambrésis.

XXXVI   How King Edward of England, on his way to help the Count   85
          of Hainault, defeated the King of France's admiral.

XXXVII   How the King of England and other great lords of his alliance   87
          besieged the city of Tournai.

XXXVIII   How the King of France came within two leagues of Tournai   89
          to raise the siege, but a settlement was made and agreement
          reached.

XXXIX   How a truce was made between the two kings at the siege of   92
          Tournai, through the mediation of my lady of Hainault, sister
          of the French king and mother of the Queen of England.

1340–58

XL   How the kings of Spain and Portugal defeated three heathen   95
          kings who had entered Spain and were besieging a great
          city.

XLI   How Lord Charles of Bohemia was crowned King of   98
          Germany.

XLII   How a great conflict arose between Duke Wenceslaus and the   101
          Count of Flanders over the duchy of Brabant.

XLIII   How Leuven and the other cities, with one accord, took   103
          Duke Wenceslaus as their lord in opposition to the Count of
          Flanders.

XLIV   How the Count of Hainault made peace between the Count   105
          of Flanders and the people of Brabant, and how the Emperor
          came to hold a great court at Metz.

XLV   How Count William of Hainault went insane, losing his wits   107
          and his reason.

THE WAR OF THE BRETON SUCCESSION

XLVI   How the Count of Montfort seized the land of Brittany after   108
            the death of his maternal half brother and found great wealth
            at Limoges.

XLVII   How Lord Charles of Blois went to Brittany and won back a   113
            large part of the country by force of arms and captured the
            Count of Montfort.

EDWARD AND THE COUNTESS OF SALISBURY

XLVIII   Here the book returns to its proper story and recounts the   118
            great feats of arms and high prowess performed by the Scots
            against the English.

XLIX   How the Countess of Salisbury sent Sir William Montagu to   124
            King Edward for help against the King of Scotland who was
            besieging her.

L   How King Edward came to Wark Castle, expecting to find the   125
            Scots, but they had already gone; and how he fell in love with
            the beautiful Countess of Salisbury.

LI   How King Edward left Wark Castle with all his army and   127
            pursued the Scots to the forest of Jedburgh.

THE WAR IN BRITTANY

LII   Here the book returns to the adventures in Brittany, to tell how   128
            Lord Charles of Blois laid siege to the city of Rennes.

LIII   How the Countess of Montfort sent to England, pleading for   129
            help from the king, who sent her Sir Walter Mauny.

LIV   How the citizens of Rennes surrendered the city to the lord of   130
            Blois in defiance of their captain.

LV   How Lord Charles of Blois held two castles under siege.   133

LVI   How Sir Walter Mauny came with a mighty company to   134
            Hennebont, where the Countess of Montfort was besieged.

LVII   How Lord Louis of Spain left Hennebont and went to besiege   136
            and capture two towns, Guémené-sur-Scorff and Guérande.

LVIII   How Sir Walter Mauny and his companions pursued Lord   139
            Louis of Spain across the sea and defeated him.

LIX   How the French lords took the town of Carhaix and then laid   142
            siege to Hennebont.

LX   How Lord Louis wanted to behead two knights who were   143
            valiantly rescued by Sir Walter Mauny.

LXI   How the King of England held a great feast in London, and   146
            the Countess of Montfort came to ask him for help.

LXII   How King Edward came to Brittany and laid siege to three   149
         cities in a single day.

LXIII   You have heard how Sir Olivier de Clisson was beheaded in   152
         Paris; here are details of others who suffered the same fate.

EDWARD AND THE COUNTESS OF SALISBURY

LXIV   How King Edward had Windsor Castle restored and   153
         announced a great feast to be held there.

LXV   How King Edward committed a great wrong when he raped   154
         the Countess of Salisbury.

THE WAR IN GASCONY

LXVI   How a feast was held at Windsor in the year 1344; and of the   157
         men-at-arms sent by King Edward to Gascony and Brittany.

LXVII   How the worthy Earl of Derby arrived in Gascony and won   158
         many towns and castles there.

LXVIII   How the Duke of Normandy went to Gascony with a very   160
         great army and won back several places there.

LXIX   Of the outstanding deeds of arms and feats of high prowess   164
         reported at the siege of Aiguillon.

CRÉCY AND CALAIS

LXX   How King Edward left England and sailed to Normandy and   167
         laid waste the land.

LXXI   How King Edward conquered numerous towns and castles in   171
         Normandy, namely the isle of Guernsey, Saint-Lô, etc.

LXXII   In which you may hear of the astonishing battle of Crécy, where 179
         the greatest lords of France were defeated and captured.

LXXIII   How the King of England with a great army besieged the   184
         mighty city of Calais.

LXXIV   Here we return to Aiguillon, and how the Duke of Normandy   185
         and the others abandoned the siege and went back to the King
         in France.

LXXV   How the Earl of Derby left Bordeaux and went to Poitou and   187
         took Poitiers and Saint-Jean-d'Angély.

LXXVI   How the King of Scotland was captured and defeated in battle   189
         while King Edward had been before Calais, etc.

LXXVII   How King Edward tried to arrange the marriage of his   192
         daughter to the young Count of Flanders, but the count would
         not consent.

LXXVIII How Bishop Engelbert of Liège quarrelled with the people of   194
         the region and fought a fierce battle at Vottem and another at
         Tourinne.

LXXIX   How Lord Charles of Blois was defeated and captured in battle   196
          before La Roche-Derrien in Brittany, and taken to England.

LXXX   How the King of France advanced close to Calais to counter   198
          the King of England's siege, but could go no further.

LXXXI   How six burghers of Calais, stripped to their shifts and with   202
          nooses at their necks, delivered the keys of the city to the King
          of England.

LXXXII   How bands of brigands assembled and pillaged towns and   205
          castles in Brittany and elsewhere.

LXXXIII   How King Edward personally saved the castle of Calais,   206
          treacherously sold by its castellan to Sir Geoffroi de Charny.

KING JOHN'S REIGN BEGINS

LXXXIV   How King Philip and his son remarried, and King Philip died   209
          soon after and the Duke of Normandy was crowned king.

LXXXV   How the English and Gascons defeated the French outside   210
          Saint-Jean-d'Angély.

LXXXVI   How thirty French agreed to do battle against thirty English   212
          and Germans in Brittany, and the English and Germans were
          defeated.

LXXXVII   How King John of France ordered the beheading of the worthy   214
          Count of Eu and Guînes, Constable of France, even though he
          was a prisoner of the English.

LXXXVIII The reason for the hostility that arose between King John of   215
          France and the King of Navarre and his brother.

LXXXIX   How King John of France created an order of knights in the   216
          manner of the Round Table, and it was called the Company of
          the Star.

XC   How the King of France made a pact with the King of Navarre,   217
          and how King Edward crossed the sea to Calais and ravaged
          the country.

XCI   How King Edward besieged the city of Berwick, captured by   221
          Sir William Douglas and the Scots, and won it back.

THE PRINCE OF WALES'S CAMPAIGNS

XCII   How the Prince of Wales led a great and bold expedition   222
          through Languedoc, destroying and laying waste the country
          between Narbonne and Carcassonne.

XCIII   How King John, with his own hands, arrested the King of   223
          Navarre and the young Count of Harcourt at a castle where
          they were dining with his son.

XCIV   Of the amazing fortune and adventures of the valiant Prince   225
          of Wales who, with only a small army, left Bordeaux in the
          year of grace 1356 and advanced through Gascony, Limousin

and Berry, burning and laying waste the land almost as far as Orléans and Paris; and how King John followed him to Poitiers, where the French were defeated and the said king was captured.

XCV   How peace was made between the King of England and the   230
King of Scotland, who had been held captive in England for
ten years.

XCVI   How the Duke of Lancaster besieged and took the city of   230
Rennes in Brittany.

PLUNDER AND UPRISING

XCVII   Of a knight who, after the King of France was captured,   231
gathered men from every land and plundered Provence.

XCVIII How the kingdom of France was governed by the three estates,   231
that is to say the clergy, the nobility and the bourgeoisie, while
King John was a prisoner in England.

XCIX   How robber bands ravaged the kingdom of France, and how   233
the Provost of the Merchants of Paris had two of the Duke of
Normandy's counsellors killed.

C   How there was a rising of leaderless men bent on killing   235
noblemen, ladies and damsels, and of the atrocities they
committed.

CI   How knights and squires who had taken refuge at Meaux in   237
Brie killed a great number of the commons.

CII   How the Duke of Normandy laid siege to Paris and the   238
Provost was killed inside the city, which prompted the King
of Navarre to defy Paris and wage war upon the kingdom.

CIII   Of the terrible plunder committed by robber bands in the   242
most noble kingdom of France, and how they were finally
destroyed.

EDWARD'S LAST CAMPAIGN

CIV   How peace was agreed and sealed by the kings of France and   247
England, but the French would not observe it, so the King of
England made ready to come to France once more.

CV   How King Edward entered France with a greater force than   251
ever before, determined to secure an honourable peace or
never to return to England.

CVI   How the King of Navarre hatched a plot in Paris to have the   253
Duke of Normandy murdered by a knight, who was executed
for it.

CVII   Here you can see which parts of the kingdom of France the   254
King of England wasted and held to ransom, and how long he
stayed there unchallenged.

CVIII   How peace was made between the two kings, and how King   256
           Edward returned to England and sent home King John of
           France.

CIX   How the Marquis of Montferrat led the Great Companies into   261
           Lombardy.

Index   263

List of Maps

1. France in the fourteenth century   xiv
2. The Scottish Borders   xv
3. The Low Countries   xvi
4. Brittany   xvii
5. Gascony   xviii
6. The Crécy Campaign 1346   xix
7. Champagne   xx

FRANCE IN THE FOURTEENTH CENTURY

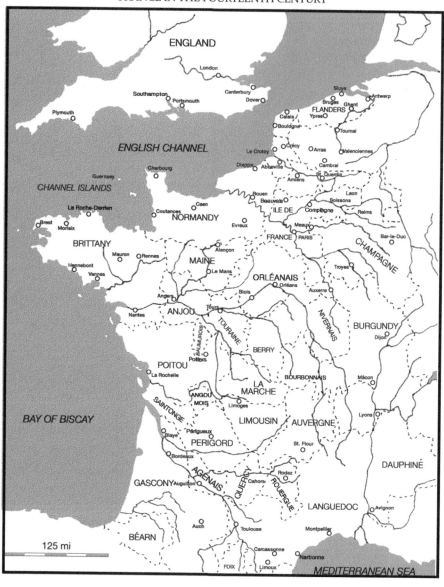

ENGLAND

London

Southampton Portsmouth Canterbury Dover Sluys
Plymouth Bruges Ghent Antwerp
Calais Ypres FLANDERS
Boulogne Tournai

ENGLISH CHANNEL

Le Crotoy Crécy Arras Valenciennes
Dieppe Abbeville Cambrai
Cherbourg St. Quentin
Guernsey Amiens
CHANNEL ISLANDS Rouen Laon
Beauvais Soissons
La Roche-Derrien Caen ÎLE DE Compiègne Reims
Coutances NORMANDY Meaux
Brest Evreux FRANCE PARIS Bar-le-Duc
Morlaix CHAMPAGNE
BRITTANY Alençon
Mauron Rennes MAINE Troyes
Hennebont Le Mans ORLÉANAIS
Vannes Orléans Auxerre
Angers Blois
Nantes ANJOU Tours NIVERNAIS BURGUNDY
TOURAINE Dijon
BERRY
POITOU BOURBONNAIS Mâcon
La Rochelle
LA Lyons
ANGOU MARCHE
MOIS Limoges
SAINTONGE LIMOUSIN AUVERGNE
BAY OF BISCAY Blaye Périgueux St. Flour
PERIGORD DAUPHINÉ
Bordeaux Rodez
GASCONY Auguilton Cahors
AGÉNAIS QUERCY ROUERGUE LANGUEDOC Avignon
Auch Toulouse Montpellier
125 mi BÉARN
Carcassonne Narbonne
FOIX Limoux MEDITERRANEAN SEA

THE SCOTTISH BORDERS

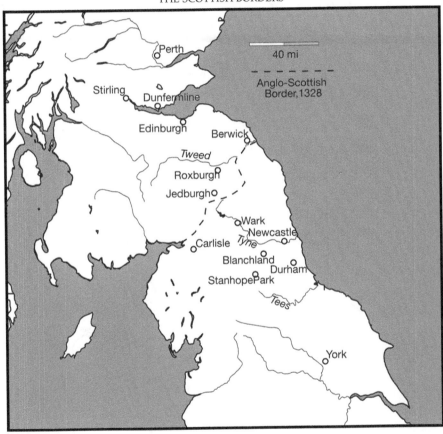

40 mi

Anglo-Scottish
Border, 1328

Perth

Stirling
Dunfermline

Edinburgh
Berwick

Tweed

Roxburgh

Jedburgh

Wark
Newcastle
Tyne
Carlisle

Blanchland
Durham
StanhopePark

Tees

York

THE LOW COUNTRIES

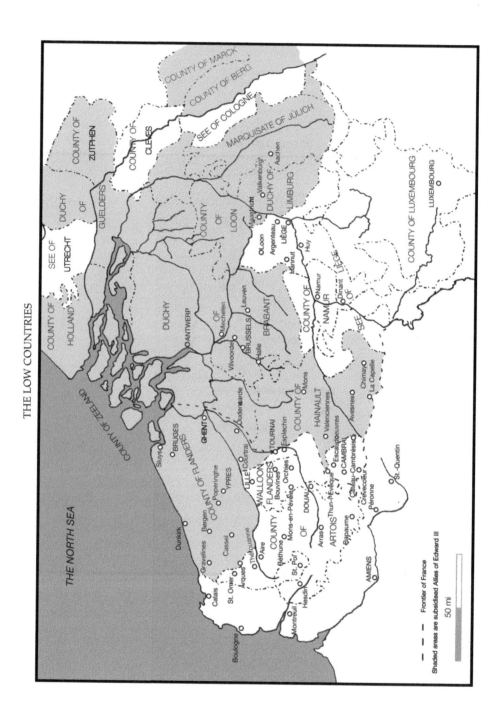

--- Frontier of France

Shaded areas are subsidised Allies of Edward III

50 mi

THE NORTH SEA

COUNTY OF ZEELAND

COUNTY OF MARCK

COUNTY OF BERG

SEE OF COLOGNE

MARQUISATE OF JÜLICH

COUNTY OF CLEVES

COUNTY OF ZUTPHEN

DUCHY OF GUELDERS

SEE OF UTRECHT

COUNTY OF HOLLAND

COUNTY OF LOON

DUCHY OF LIMBURG

Valkenburg
Aachen
Maastricht

Loon
Argenteau
LIÈGE
Huy
Hannut

COUNTY OF LUXEMBOURG

LUXEMBOURG

DUCHY OF BRABANT

Leuven
Mechelen
BRUSSELS
Halle
Vilvoorde
ANTWERP

SEE OF LIÈGE

Namur
NAMUR
Dinant

Oudenaarde

GHENT
BRUGES
Sluys

COUNTY OF FLANDERS

Bergen
Popreinghe
YPRES

Dunkirk

Gravelines
Cassel
Aire
Thérouanne
Béthune

Calais
St. Omer
Arques

Boulogne
Montreuil
Hesdin
St. Pol

LILLE
Courtrai

WALLOON FLANDERS

COUNTY OF DOUAI

Mons-en-Pévèle
Orchies
DOUAI

Bouvines
Esplechin
TOURNAI

COUNTY OF HAINAULT

Mons

Valenciennes
Escaudœuvres
CAMBRAI
Cateau-Cambrésis
Crèvecoeur

Avesnes
Chimay
La Capelle

ARTOIS
Thun-l'Évêque
Arras
Bapaume

Péronne
St.-Quentin

AMIENS

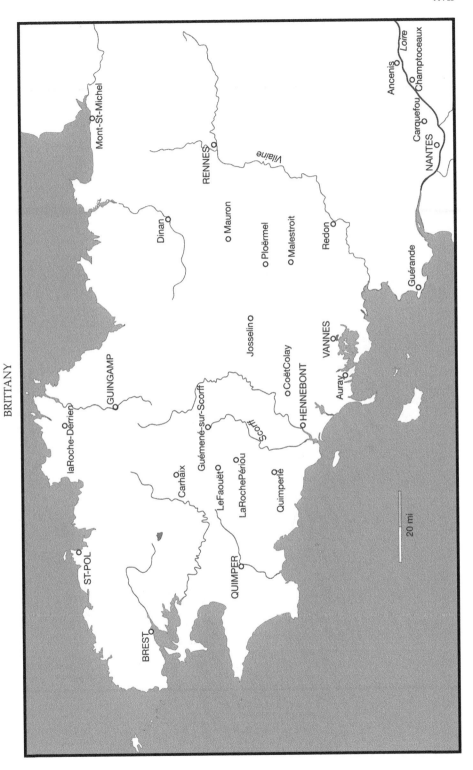

BRITTANY

GASCONY

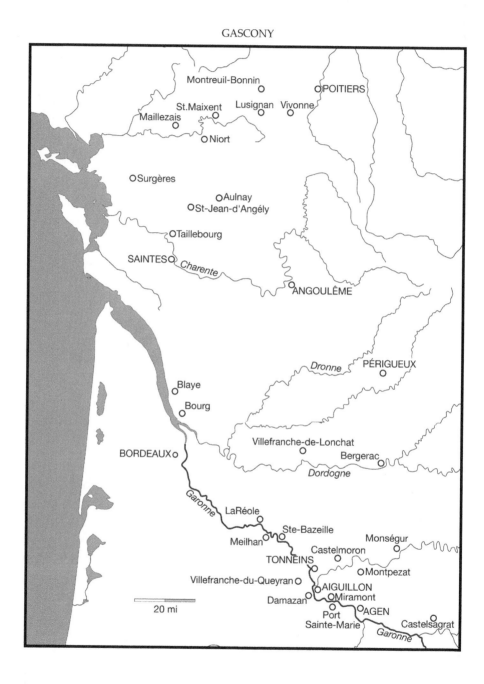

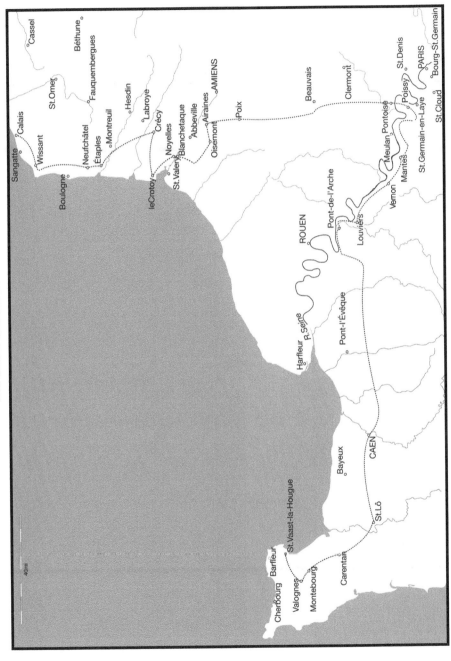

THE CRÉCY CAMPAIGN 1346

CHAMPAGNE

Crécy-sur-Serre

Pierrepont

LAON

Sissonne

Oise

Coucy

Montaigu

Rethel

Compiègne

Attigny

Aisne

Vailly

Roucy

Soissons

Pont-Arcy

Cormicy

REIMS

Saponay

Rosnay

Hans

Château-Thierry

Troissy

Damery

Meaux

Épernay

PARIS

Marne

Châlons

Lucy

Vertus

Seine

Aube

Provins

Pont

Nogent-sur-Seine

Conflans

Bray

Rosnay-l'Hôpital

Joinville

TROYES

Seine

Bar-sur-Aube

20 mi

Tonnerre

AUXERRE

For Maurice Keen

Introduction

'True Chronicles'

This title is not Le Bel's own. It's a quote from the far more famous chronicler Jean Froissart, who in his very first pages acknowledged his debt to Le Bel by declaring:

> I wish to base my work on the example of the *true chronicles* previously written and assembled by that venerable and astute gentleman Jean le Bel, canon of Saint-Lambert[1] at Liège. He applied great care and diligence to the task, which he continued throughout his life with all the precision that he could. It cost him a good deal to acquire the information, but he neither cared nor complained about the expense, for he was a man of wealth and power and was perfectly able to meet the cost, and he always spent his money freely, being a man of generosity, courtesy and honour. Moreover, he was a dear and close friend of that most noble and respected lord Sir John of Hainault,[2] who is rightly well remembered in this book, for he was a driving force and principal player in many illustrious events and very closely connected with kings, so that in his company the aforementioned Jean le Bel was able to witness and learn directly of many of the exploits that follow.[3]

It's only right that Froissart should have acknowledged his debt, for many of the early passages in his Chronicle for which Froissart is justly praised were lifted directly from Le Bel.[4] Indeed, the main reason why Le Bel's work was for a long while little known and little copied – only one manuscript survives, and it wasn't found until the second half of the nineteenth century – is that Froissart absorbed sections of it into his own Chronicle which, because he then went on to recount the events of later years, made Le Bel's work seem redundant.

Froissart may also be indebted to Le Bel (and the title 'True Chronicles' justified) for a second reason: he was very much influenced by his predecessor's insistence upon accuracy and veracity. According to another Liégeois chronicler, Jean d'Outremeuse, it was at John of Hainault's behest that Le Bel wrote his Chronicle, and John wanted him to write 'the pure truth ... without favour to any party ... [and] without attributing blame or honour to any who have not deserved it... And when it was complete he was to show it to Sir John and others who had

---

[1] The cathedral.
[2] John (1288-1356) was the brother of Count William I of Hainault (1286-1337).
[3] Besançon MS 864, folio 1 v.
[4] That is not to say that the texts are identical. At some points subtle alterations and changes of emphasis – which become more marked in Froissart's later revisions – are important in revealing the chroniclers' differing intentions. See Gerald Nachtwey, "Scapegoats and Conspirators in the Chronicles of Jean Froissart and Jean le Bel" in *Fifteenth-Century Studies 36*, ed. Gusick and Heintzelman (Woodbridge, 2011), pp.103-25.

been present at the events described so that it could be corrected according to their truthful guidance, without any fiction...'[1] At the beginning of his Chronicle, Le Bel writes scathingly about

> the great book written in verse that I've seen and read, which some imaginative soul has concocted in rhyme, full of nonsense and wild invention... littered with errors and lies... [and] with a good deal of contrivance and repetition to embellish the verse, and such an abundance of feats of prowess attributed to certain knights and other persons that they test credulity, bordering on the impossible! Such a fanciful versified history is unlikely to please or appeal to people of wit and reason...[2]

It may be that these lines sobered and influenced Froissart as he embarked upon his work, because Froissart confesses to a change of method after composing a piece of his juvenilia:

> I have consistently done all I can to seek and request true accounts of the wars and events that have taken place, especially since the great battle of Poitiers...; for before that I was young both in age and in thinking, and undertook rather presumptuously, having only just left school, to compose an account of the aforementioned wars in verse...[3]

At all points, Le Bel was determined to base what he wrote solely on 'what I've witnessed myself or have heard from those who've been present when I have not; and I mean to do so as truthfully as I can'.[4] Indeed, he will sometimes even break off his account of events at dramatic and crucial moments with phrases such as 'I can't describe it in detail so I'll leave it at that'[5] or 'I won't tell you exactly how it was done, as I wasn't there'.[6] If, then, his version of an event ever differs from someone else's (as it sometimes does), we may depend at least on Le Bel's honest intention and desire to be accurate and authoritative. Some of his remarks about the battle of Crécy, for instance – not least his assertion that King Philip at no point entered the fray[7] – may raise eyebrows, but he can very credibly assure us that

> I've described this as accurately as I can, following the account given to me from his own lips by my lord and friend Sir John of Hainault...and ten or twelve knights and companions of his household; they'd been in the press with the noble and valiant King of Bohemia and had their horses killed beneath them. From the other side I've heard similar accounts from several English and German knights who were there.[8]

[1] Outremeuse, *Ly myreur des histors*, ed. A. Borgnet, Brussels, 1864-1880, vol. 6, pp.322-3. Outremeuse also tells that Le Bel had two copies made, one of which he kept and the other he gave to Sir John.
[2] Below, p.21.
[3] Besançon MS 864, folio 1 v.
[4] Below, p.22.
[5] p.157.
[6] p.215.
[7] See p.181 and footnote 1.
[8] p.181.

Certainly, as Outremeuse said, Jean le Bel was well placed to acquire good eye-witness reports. He was a canon of Liège Cathedral in an age when bishop-dukes and bishop-counts led armies into battle. And a vivid description of Le Bel by yet another Liégeois writer, Jacques de Hemricourt, makes the chronicler's status very clear. In his *Miroir des nobles de Hesbaye*[1] Hemricourt assures us that Le Bel was rather special. The cathedral of Saint-Lambert, he says, had never had a man of finer character than 'Johan le Beal'; he was 'tall and of fine stature' and notably well-dressed 'in the manner of a banneret,[2] his shoulders trimmed with ermine', wearing clothes 'of samite or silk depending on the weather'; whenever he went to church he 'never had an escort of fewer than sixteen or twenty persons ... and often as great a company as the Bishop of Liège himself, having fully fifty or at least forty followers, all of whom stayed to dine with him!' His household in fact was instructed to be ever-ready to entertain eminent visitors to Liège: 'whenever they saw any worthy stranger, be he a prelate or a knight or a squire, they invited him to dinner or supper ... and if any prince arrived in the city he would certainly be dining at his side'.[3]

This description endorses Froissart's remark that Le Bel incurred considerable (nay, probably lavish) expense in gaining his information; and it helps to explain why, being so fabulously well connected, Le Bel was able to compose his remarkably wide-ranging story – his Chronicle covers, after all, events in most of Western Europe, from Scotland to Spain, from Brittany to Germany – without ever apparently drawing on any written sources: it is, in a sense, a quite exceptional piece of oral history.

Le Bel's exclusive reliance on orally transmitted information leads to some curious imbalances. In dealing with Edward III's Scottish wars, for example, he doesn't so much as mention the major pitched battle of Halidon Hill (is he, one wonders, aware that it ever happened? – he surely would have made some reference had he been drawing on any other written sources), but devotes considerable space and detail to a relatively trivial clash at Boroughmuir. The reason is almost certainly that he happened to know and to have spoken to no one present at the former, while the latter involved a contingent from his native Low Countries, 'young knights and squires eager to gain experience in arms and test themselves and win honour [who had] set out to serve the noble English king whose fame was increasing by the day',[4] led by the young Count John of Namur and his two brothers Sir Guy and Sir Philip. One or more of these 'young knights and squires' will presumably have been his source – though with his typical unwillingness to make assumptions and his commitment to recording only what he's been told by reliable informants, Le Bel adds that 'I could never discover whether the lords of Namur were kept in captivity or for how long or if they were ever released'.[5]

---

[1] Hesbaye was the name of the region centred upon Liège.
[2] A wealthy and eminent knight who led his own company of troops into battle.
[3] Hemricourt, *Le Miroir des nobles de Hesbaye*, ed. Borman & Bayot (Brussels, 1910), p.226.
[4] Below, p.63.
[5] p.64.

It might be argued, however, that such imbalances and omissions are compensated for by Le Bel's aim for integrity, by the sense that he has at least personally assessed the reliability of what he is recording.

Chivalry

Jacques de Hemricourt's description of Le Bel gives another extremely important insight. He tells us that he 'had been engaged in arms in his younger days and taken part in the tournament, and was in the household of Sir John of Hainault, lord of Beaumont and Chimay'.[1] Indeed, Le Bel accompanied John of Hainault when he crossed the sea to England to support the young Edward III against the Scots in 1327, and his direct, first-hand account of this shambolic campaign in the Borders (not to mention the terrifying clash between English archers and their Flemish allies in the streets of York) is one of the most gripping and atmospheric passages in the Chronicle. But Le Bel's experience in arms is much more significant than that. Throughout his work it is clear that he is entirely wedded to the values of the chivalric class. The armies of Edward III and all the other great princes of his time may be wreaking death, destruction, havoc and misery on an epic scale, but, says Le Bel, 'these things happen in war and they have to be accepted'[2] and he idolises the glamour of knighthood. He loves display and pageantry, classifies fighting men according to their armour, and deplores the fact that standards are slipping:

> At that time the great lords took no account of men-at-arms unless they had crested helms, whereas now we count any with lances, cuirasses, hauberks and iron caps. In my own time things have changed a lot, it seems to me: the splendid caparisoned horses and crested helms of old, and the shining plate and heraldic coats, are gone, replaced by cuirasses, gambisons and iron caps. These days a humble page is as well and as finely armed as a noble knight.[3]

He is clearly steeped in chivalric literature: some passages read uncannily like episodes from Arthurian romance. When, for example, John of Hainault hears of the plight of Queen Isabella and the young Edward, in exile and afraid to return to England,

> Sir John began to weep fervent tears of pity, and said: "Lady, behold your knight, who will defend you with his life, truly, even if all others fail you. I shall do everything in my power to escort you and your son to England and restore you to your rightful stations, ... and I and all those I can rally will stake our lives upon the enterprise..."

---

[1]   *Le Miroir*, p.226. There was nothing at all unusual about a churchman being engaged in arms; not only did bishop-counts and bishop-dukes lead armies, but see, for example, p.91 below, where a clash between opposing forces near Tournai involves 'Henry d'Asse, a canon of Saint John at Liège, whose prowess had often been witnessed, and Thierry de Mohalt, canon of Huy... [and] the rector of Winchekus, who acquitted himself splendidly and received a cut across the nose and face...'

[2]   Below, p.173.

[3]   p.68.

Only the most hard-hearted man would have failed to feel deep pity if he'd seen how that fair and tearful lady stood then, ready to fall at the feet of the noble knight and thank him for the mighty pledge he'd made. But he wouldn't allow it; and when she couldn't do as she wished – that is, fall at his feet – she flung her arms about his neck and kissed him joyously, saying to the noble knight:

"A thousand thanks! If you'll do as you've so courteously promised, my son and I will be your servants evermore..."

And this good knight, then in his prime, replied: "My dear lady, if I didn't mean to carry it out I wouldn't have made the promise..."

Having promised to escort the lady to her kingdom, he wouldn't fail her were it to cost him his life; and he would rather die, if die he must, with that exiled lady than elsewhere, for all knights should do everything in their power to aid and comfort ladies and maidens who are deprived and distressed, especially when requested.[1]

And straight from the pages of a romance, one could be forgiven for thinking, is the passage in which 'the valiant Countess of Montfort', besieged at Hennebont, desperately awaits the arrival of 'the valiant knight Sir Walter Mauny', who has been locked in a forty-day storm at sea. In cliffhanging fashion she is alone in still believing he's on his way, and her supporters are on the very point of surrendering her stronghold, when

the valiant countess, looking out to sea from a castle window, began to shout in jubilation, crying with all the strength she could summon: "I see the aid I've desired so long!"

All the people in the city ran to the walls to see what she had seen; and there, as plain as could be, they beheld a vast fleet of vessels, great and small, heading for Hennebont.[2]

Le Bel's references to things Arthurian are, in fact, numerous and striking: for him Carlisle is 'the castle and city which the Welsh call Cardueil and which was formerly held by King Arthur';[3] Blanchland Abbey is 'an abbey of white friars, known in King Arthur's time as the Blanche Lande';[4] the engagement at Boroughmuir is fought in the ruins of 'an old city which had been known in the days of King Arthur's Round Table as the Castle of the Maidens';[5] and he is full of admiration for Edward III whose 'noble heart inspired him not only to restore and improve the castle at Windsor, which King Arthur had built and where the Round Table was first established in honour of the worthy knights of that time, but also to create a counterpart to that Round Table for the greater honour of his own knights'.[6]

It may be interesting, indeed, to consider whether John of Hainault was moved to commission Le Bel's Chronicle by the example of such orders of chivalry

[1] p.27.
[2] p.134.
[3] p.39.
[4] p.45.
[5] p.63.
[6] p.153.

as Edward's Order of the Garter, who solemnly recorded the deeds of their members. In the more-or-less contemporary romance of *Perceforest* (in which King Perceforest's 'Order of the Franc Palais' may well have been the inspiration for Edward's Garter), a clerk named Cresus is commissioned 'to keep a record of all the events that have happened in this kingdom, and all the deeds that befall the noble knights of the Franc Palais, for their renown must never die';[1] likewise, Le Bel tells us, when in 1351 John II of France founded his ill-fated Company of the Star (probably in imitation of both *Perceforest* and the Garter), it was decided that at a plenary court held once a year each member

> would recount all the adventures – the shameful as well as the glorious – that had befallen him since he'd last been at the noble court; and the king would appoint two or three clerks who would listen to these adventures and record them all in a book, so that they could annually be brought before the companions to decide which had been most worthy, that the most deserving might be honoured.[2]

It was probably in the following year (1352) or thereabouts that Le Bel's Chronicle was commissioned by John of Hainault,[3] and the intention appears to have been very similar: on one extremely important level the Chronicle is just such a catalogue of honourable deeds, an attempt to record worthy feats of arms and prowess to assess which knights – and indeed kings – were most deserving of lasting credit and renown. Almost the whole of Le Bel's Prologue, in fact, is an expression of this aim, and in the first thirty-nine chapters, covering the years 1326-40, it is very noticeable that John of Hainault and his Hainaulter companions are themselves major players: Jean le Bel may be setting out to write the 'history of the worthy and noble King Edward', but the opening section of his Chronicle is also very markedly a record of the worthy deeds of the nobility of Hainault. The county might not have had a chivalric order like England's Garter or France's Company of the Star, but it would have an equivalent book of deeds.[4]

The great paladin Geoffroi de Charny earns several mentions from Le Bel as 'a most worthy and valiant knight', and in the 'manual' of chivalry that Charny wrote for the Company of the Star[5] he has an oft-repeated catchphrase: '*Qui plus fait, mieux vault*' ['Who does more is of greater worth']. It is a knight's – and a king's – *deeds* that count for Charny, and for Le Bel. Nowhere is this seen more clearly than in his comparison of the worth of Edward III and Philip VI:

[1] *Perceforest*, tr. N.Bryant (Woodbridge, 2011), p.260.
[2] Below, p.217.
[3] For a discussion of the dates of composition, see below, pp.14–15.
[4] In addition to the focus placed upon the deeds of Sir John and his companions in Chapters 1-39, every chance is later taken to record the prowess of the Hainaulter Walter Mauny, and a remarkable amount of attention is given to listing men from Hainault and Hesbaye (Le Bel's home ground) who participate in a minor skirmish outside Tournai. This accidental clash on a foggy morning is described in more detail (including a wound to a rector's nose) than the mighty battle of Sluys: see below, pp.90–1.
[5] Available in translation as *A Knight's Own Book of Chivalry*, tr. Elspeth Kennedy, Philadelphia, 2005.

Some people, when they hear this story read, may wonder why I call the King of England 'the noble King Edward' but the French king simply 'King Philip of France'; they might well imagine I'm biased or partisan. Saving the grace of all listeners, it's not a question of taking sides; I do this to honour the one who behaved most nobly in this story, and that's King Edward, who cannot be honoured too highly, for in all his deeds he always followed sound advice, and loved his men and knights and squires, and honoured each man according to his degree, and defended his land well against his enemies (and won a good deal from them), and bravely put his life at stake alongside his men both at home and abroad, and paid his troops and allies well and gave generously of his own wealth; for these reasons all should be glad to serve him and he deserves to be called 'noble king'. None of this can be said of King Philip of France, who allowed his land in many parts to be ravaged and laid waste, and stayed ensconced around Paris in comfort and safety, and always followed the poor advice of clerics and prelates, especially those who said:

"Dear sire, don't fret, and don't go putting yourself at risk!"[1]

In King Edward's case, the list of his deeds is endless. Having just won Calais after a year-long siege,

it should be considered a sign of great honour and a great blessing from God, as indeed it was, that, as well as this, he and his men had destroyed and laid waste the whole land of Scotland between the city of Perth and the great forest of Jedburgh, and won the city of Berwick and all the surrounding fortresses; and elsewhere his men had ravaged and laid waste most of Gascony almost as far as Toulouse, and, nearer at hand, had ravaged and wasted all of Poitou and won many major towns and strong castles such as Lusignan, Saint-Jean-d'Angély and the city of Poitiers, and likewise the great land of Brittany; and he personally had destroyed and laid waste the lands of the Cotentin and Normandy and the county of Évreux as far as Paris, and crossed the great River Seine at the bridge of Poissy and ravaged and wasted the country around Amiens and Beauvais and the county of Ponthieu, and had then stood arrayed for battle, with a small army in open fields, without ditches or fortifications, to face the entire might of France, and had held the field for two whole days and vanquished, captured and killed all the greatest lords in the kingdom of France, the Empire and Germany, and then laid siege to the mighty city of Calais and stayed there for a year without once returning home, and at the end of that year had taken it as you've heard. It seems to me that such great and lofty exploits are not without high honour, and that one cannot praise, esteem or honour too much the very noble king whom God so clearly wished to help.[2]

Meanwhile what has King Philip done, but repeatedly decline to do battle with the destroyer of his lands? 'I just don't understand it,' says Le Bel. 'To put it bluntly, he never had the stomach or the courage to fight.'[3]

Of all deeds, the famous 'Battle of the Thirty' in Brittany in 1351 – a formal and pre-planned engagement between two teams, fought on an appointed day

[1] Below, pp.167–8.
[2] pp.204–5.
[3] pp.174–5.

according to tourney-like rules but with lethal weapons (hence the death rate of one in four, not to mention the maimed who died later) – might seem to the modern mind to have been an extravagant folly; but for Le Bel – and, presumably, his audience – it was a glorious affair, and he lavishes praise on all involved. It was, he writes, 'an extraordinary deed of arms which should certainly not be forgotten... I've never heard of any other battle of this kind being proposed or taking place, and all its survivors should be treated with special honour wherever they go.'[1]

That's not to say that Le Bel's admiration for knights who perform courageous deeds blinds him to good sense on a battlefield; he is fully aware, for instance, of the foolishness of the knights of the Company of the Star at the battle of Mauron, where

> all those French who rushed to engage too soon and too recklessly were
> routed and slaughtered. No fewer than eighty-nine knights of the Star were
> killed there, and all because of their vow about not retreating: had it not been
> for that vow, they would have been perfectly able to withdraw. Many others
> died, too, on their account: men they might well have saved had it not been
> for this vow of theirs and their fear of reproach by the Company.[2]

Or *is* he aware of the folly? Depending on the delivery when read aloud, this passage could express regret and amazed admiration rather than censure.

There is certainly no censure involved in Le Bel's ubiquitous descriptions of the collateral damage wrought in France by 'the noble King Edward'. Land is wasted and villages, towns and cities are razed to the ground on a breathtaking and chilling scale; and although Le Bel is honest in cataloguing the rape and slaughter of women and refers to such acts several times as 'a grievous pity', and although on one occasion he takes the reader aback by for once acknowledging that 'the country was ravaged and laid waste by both parties, and it was the poor people who paid for it',[3] there is an overwhelming sense that the world is the fighting class's playing field, a place for a man to enforce his rights and prove his prowess, and devastation is merely a regrettable consequence.

But it might well be added that Le Bel hides nothing. His commitment to writing 'true chronicles' leads him to admit that even 'the noble King Edward' has committed a most unworthy deed in his alleged rape of the Countess of Salisbury. Now, the veracity of Le Bel's story of Edward and the Countess has been much debated, and some of the names and details he gives certainly appear confused;[4] but we can depend, if nothing else, on the honesty of Le Bel's intentions: he was anything but an anti-Edward propagandist, and is not at all inclined to prurience, so we can at least safely assume that someone had told him it had happened and he deemed his source to be a credible informant, so he'd felt it his duty as a 'truthful' chronicler to record it. And it's a duty that he doesn't shirk: he describes the rape in quite shocking detail, and despite his overwhelming

[1]   pp.212, 214.
[2]   p.217.
[3]   p.196.
[4]   See below, footnote 1, p.146.

admiration for the 'noble king', declares it to have been 'an unworthy act...much to his discredit', and 'all the lords of England were deeply upset and angry, and the king was reproached by everyone'. Le Bel even boldly cites the Countess's husband's words to Edward: "You should be utterly ashamed: it will stay as a black mark against you forever, and all your fine deeds will be stained and tarnished by this base act."[1]

For Le Bel and the knightly class of his time it was what people *do* that matters – '*qui plus fait, mieux vault*'. Deeds are all-important and should be recorded for posterity. But it is strange, to a modern sense of history, that for Le Bel, exactly *where* and *when* the deeds happen are not particularly important. Le Bel's geography isn't all it might be, especially in regions of which he has no personal knowledge, and this can lead the modern reader to a conundrum or two in trying to make sense of campaign-routes and place-names in Brittany, for instance, and Aquitaine. His chronology, too, can sometimes be off-beam, with dates in short supply. Anyone expecting clear accounts of itineraries or the dispositions of armies on precisely identified battlefields is going to be disappointed. Astonishingly (to the modern reader), many of the battles he describes are not even given names, even those as important as Río Salado or Neville's Cross, let alone Mauron or Tourinne. But curiously, none of this diminishes the essential trustworthiness the reader is likely to feel towards Le Bel. The fact that he will never, it seems, venture a guess as to what happened, but will only put on record what he has seen or (in his view) reliably heard leads to strikingly direct, succinct accounts, and one is inclined to respect their accuracy with few exceptions; those romanticised or fanciful passages which raise serious doubts are all the more glaring for being untypical.

Honour and Blame

But it does, of course, depend on what one means by 'accuracy'. If he's not interested in time and place, what *is* he being 'accurate' about? According to Jean d'Outremeuse, John of Hainault required Le Bel not merely to 'write the pure truth' but specifically 'without favour to any party... [and] without attributing blame or honour to any who have not deserved it'. And that is the crux. Honour and credit (or dishonour and discredit) are the real issues, not geography or chronology or exact manoeuvres or numbers.

So, then, how 'accurate' is his judgement of honour and shame? How balanced and unprejudiced is Le Bel? It can't be said that he hides his personal feelings. True, he rarely gives direct comments such as his view that Robert le Coq, Bishop of Laon, was 'ever a devious man'.[2] But one visualises gritted teeth as Le Bel describes the mead-brewer Jacob van Artevelde rising above his station and holding thuggish sway in Flanders.[3] He lets slip a number of 'national'

---

[1]   pp.154, 156.
[2]   p.236.
[3]   p.69.

and regional prejudices: his dislike of craven, double-dealing men of Brabant is all too clear, in particular the 'haughty pride' (and subversive tendencies) of the citizens of Brussels;[1] Frenchmen 'have always promised well and paid poorly';[2] and as for the knights of neighbouring Germany, imposing reasonable ransom demands 'hasn't been the custom hitherto among the Germans! ... When Germans capture Christian men-at-arms they have no more pity or mercy upon them than they do upon dogs.'[3] Nor can Le Bel suppress his ill feelings towards the Francophile Avignon papacy: two French royal marriages 'were clearly against the commandments of Holy Church, but Pope Clement gave his consent to them, not daring to do otherwise';[4] he can't quite resist a dig at Papal legates who live off the fat of the land: 'in the year 1359, the two cardinals sent to England by the Pope to broker peace between the kings, from whose conflict the whole of Christendom had suffered, left England with nothing achieved – even though they'd been there for two years and more in great comfort and at vast expense'[5] – the same kind of expense that Le Bel clearly resents when the Cardinal of Boulogne is sent on a peace mission and arrives 'in greater pomp than Saint Peter, so beloved of God, ever travelled the Earth: it was said he came with seven hundred horses, all paid for by the churches of France';[6] and (depending once again on one's oral delivery of Le Bel's terse prose) it's hard not to read into the closing lines of his Chronicle the utter contempt he feels for Pope Innocent as he buys off the terrorising Great Companies with 'a huge sum of money paid to each one' to induce them to 'leave the country around Avignon and Pont-Saint-Esprit and go with the marquis [of Montferrat] to Lombardy to fight the Milanese. But that's not all: the Pope also gave them pardon for all their misdeeds and absolution and remission from Purgatory.'[7] But since the veracity of his Chronicle was to be checked by John of Hainault and his fellow lords, these views were, we must assume, considered fully justified.

And for the most part, Le Bel does leave the 'blame or honour' due to men to be judged not by his commentary but by their deeds. He clearly wants us to share his admiration for the chutzpah of 'the noble King Edward' as he invites a captured French knight to "inspect our battalions; he can make a note of what troops we have and go and tell his lord the king";[8] and this is on an expedition in which 'King Edward had no more than three thousand cavalry and six thousand archers, yet he wanted to do battle with the King of France and his whole army in his own land'.[9] How different he is, Le Bel plainly wants us to observe, from Philip VI, who earns no honour with his pusillanimous (and repeated) reluctance to risk pitched battle – rather like the Duke of Brabant, who, Le Bel witheringly

[1]   p.94.
[2]   p.133.
[3]   p.229.
[4]   p.209.
[5]   p.247.
[6]   pp.215–6.
[7]   p.261.
[8]   p.220.
[9]   p.219.

notes, 'had no desire to do battle that day – not that he ever did, anywhere'.[1] But Le Bel is not being crudely anti-French in his depiction of King Philip's lack of valour; each man individually is to be judged for his deeds, and Philip's son John II is given full credit for his valiant display at Poitiers, after which Le Bel reports the Prince of Wales saying to John:

> "It seems to me you should be of good cheer, even though the battle has gone against you, for you have earned a reputation for high prowess and surpassed the finest of your army in the way you fought today. I'm not saying this to flatter you! All your companions agree with me in awarding you the prize and the laurels if you'll accept them."[2]

On the other hand, John earns blame for another action, in a striking lack of courtesy: having finally been released from his long captivity after the battle, he processed through France to Paris and, says Le Bel, 'everywhere he passed he was showered with handsome, splendid gifts, but not a word of thanks ever crossed his lips'.[3] This is not the behaviour Le Bel (and his audience) expects and deems fitting in a chivalrous prince.

Stations

For Le Bel judges men essentially by how well they behave according to their station. Just as he names remarkably few battles, so he names astonishingly few people: princes, counts, earls, dukes, margraves and bishops he almost invariably identifies purely by their titles; the kings of Spain and Portugal aren't graced with names, nor is a significant figure in his story, the King of Navarre; not even Edward III's mother Isabella or – even more surprisingly, perhaps – his wife Philippa of Hainault, is ever named: they are simply 'the queen'; so there's certainly no hope for the non-noble Étienne Marcel, who uniformly appears on these pages as 'the Provost of the Merchants of Paris' – his near-counterpart in Ghent, Jacob van Artevelde, is remarkably fortunate in this respect. What interests Le Bel is the position, the attendant duty, and how well that expected duty is accomplished.

And meanwhile what behaviour does he expect from the commons? Being a man of his station, and given his audience, it is unsurprising to find Le Bel rather simple and straightforward in his view of the lower classes, and notably aghast at the uprisings known (after the contemptuous aristocratic nickname for the peasants) as the Jacquerie. Those involved are, for Le Bel, purely 'wicked people', their captain is 'a perfect villain', and it was a 'chaotic madness', a 'devilry', and 'it's truly bizarre that [they should have been] gripped by the same fever in many different, far-flung places all at the same time...' But 'God in His mercy intervened, for which all good people should give Him thanks'.

---

[1] Referring to his non-involvement in the battle of Tourinne, below, p.195.
[2] p.228.
[3] p.260.

This divine intervention takes the form of mass slaughter, and one can hear the unquestioning assumption of where right and wrong lie as Le Bel writes:

> Then [the lords of the region] attacked these pernicious bands from every side, and killed them and hung them from the nearest trees; and when they asked them why they'd behaved in this appalling way they said they didn't know, except that they'd seen others do it and decided to do the same, and really thought they could wipe out the gentry.[1]

Even here, however, it should in all fairness be noted that Le Bel does attempt a measure of more probing analysis. He acknowledges the outrage the commons felt towards the feudal lords who had so lamentably failed in their duty to protect them: 'they declared that the nobles, knights and squires were a disgrace and bringing the kingdom to ruin, and that it would be a good deed to destroy them all'.[2] And he questions whether the uprisings might have been 'instigated by some of those controllers and collectors of taxes who didn't want to see peace take hold in the kingdom and thereby find themselves kicked out of office. Some people suspected the involvement of the Bishop of Laon [Robert le Coq] and the Provost of the Merchants [Étienne Marcel], being of one mind as they were and colluding with the King of Navarre.'[3] And, exploring this possibility further, Le Bel says that 'when the lord of Coucy, summoning help from wherever he could find it, attacked the mob in his region and destroyed them and hanged and butchered so many that it would be amazing to relate, the captain of these miscreants ... tried to suggest that the Bishop of Laon had put him up to it, because he was one of his men. And indeed, the lord of Coucy was no friend of the bishop.'[4]

But it may be over-generous to describe this as 'probing analysis' by Le Bel. In context, the commons' view that it would be 'a good deed to destroy' the nobility is surely intended to strike the reader or audience as an outrageous inversion of the social order, and Le Bel's suggestion that such men as Marcel, Le Coq and Navarre had instigated the uprisings – of which the peasantry by implication would have been incapable on their own – is another facet of his world-view, in which events are determined and driven by the mighty deeds of notable individuals: in Gerald Nachtwey's words, Le Bel 'strongly desired to establish negative exemplars throughout his account: he wanted to lay the blame for the Jacquerie on specific nobles ... [For him] the "dyablerie" of the Jacquerie was the result of the singular malice of a few men.'[5]

So how 'true', in the end, are Le Bel's chronicles? In the prefaces to the first two volumes of his great narrative history of the Hundred Years War, Jonathan Sumption writes that 'being essentially journalists, the chroniclers were also snobs. They rarely showed much interest in events in which no duke, earl or count participated... These sources need to be approached with the same caution

---

[1] p.236.
[2] Below, p.235.
[3] p.236.
[4] p.237.
[5] Nachtwey, op. cit., pp.121-2.

which one brings to reading newspaper accounts of modern wars...'; and being a QC as well as an historian, Sumption is well qualified to add that 'those who work daily in the law courts will know how fallible even eye-witnesses can be'.[1] These are important observations; and should we not especially doubt the self-interested and self-serving judgements of Le Bel's aristocratic eye-witnesses? Oddly, no. We may in fact have better cause than usual to trust them – if nothing else, in the credit or discredit they award to deeds of arms. Their devotion to the demigods Prowess and Honour (without which their behaviour on battlefields is incomprehensible, as is the trust on which their system of parole for captives depended) makes their judgements and their rolls of honour and shame well worthy of note and credence. After all, one of the qualities expected of a noble knight was modesty, and Le Bel would have assumed his sources to be mindful of principles such as that expressed, for example, in the contemporary romance of *Perceforest*:

"The man who speaks well of another enhances his own honour; and in deeds of arms a worthy knight should always keep silent about his own achievements and record the feats of others."[2]

For all his shortcomings – notably his shaky grasp of (or lack of interest in) chronology and geography – Jean le Bel's achievement in assembling accounts of major events over a wide expanse of land and time is quite remarkable, and his 'true chronicles' can for the most part be treated with large measures of confidence in one respect at least: they vividly reveal the perceptions, responses and mindset of the aristocracy in this singularly dramatic and traumatic period.

Style

His Chronicle can be read also with great enjoyment for the quality of his writing. Le Bel's 20th-century editors, Viard and Déprez, suggest in their Introduction that 'a great many of his passages can figure in the ranks of the finest pages in French literature';[3] they quote Henri Pirenne's view that 'this chronicle appears today to be one of the most remarkable pieces of literature of the fourteenth century';[4] and in an enthusiastic study of his technique Diana Tyson has written of Le Bel: 'Far from being an annalist chronicling events without literary taste or pretension, Jean le Bel is a writer whose work should be read not only for its valuable historical information but also for the sheer pleasure it gives the reader.' Tyson observes that Le Bel's hallmarks are 'intelligence, clarity and order', and that he gives 'many vivid pictures of people, places and events... [There are] many instances throughout the work of thumbnail sketches which instantly conjure up a vivid

[1] Sumption, *The Hundred Years War, Vol. 1, Trial by Battle* (London, 1990), p. x; *Vol. 2, Trial by Fire* (London, 1999), p.xii.
[2] *Perceforest*, tr. N. Bryant (Woodbridge, 2011), p.570.
[3] *Chronique de Jean le Bel*, ed. Jules Viard and Eugène Déprez, 2 vols. (Paris, 1904-5), p.xxxi.
[4] H. Pirenne in *Biographie Nationale XI* (Brussels, 1890-1891) col. 518-25.

image or convey an atmosphere... [And] his account, like all good writing, draws in the reader, makes him think, judge, choose, applaud or condemn.'[1]

Jacques de Hemricourt's description of his fellow Liégeois concludes by telling us that Le Bel was 'light-hearted, jovial and good-humoured and able to compose songs and *virelais*, and keen on all manner of sports and pleasures... God favoured him with prosperity and rude health all his life, and he was eighty or more when he died';[2] and he left behind 'a pair of sons, named Johan and Gilhes, by a damsel of good extraction... The elder is now a knight and lord of Hemricourt, and Gilhes is a chantry priest and canon of Saint-Martin at Liège.'[3]

Le Bel left behind also a document of enormous value, an outstandingly readable, absorbing and revealing record of what is essentially aristocratic oral history.

Dates

The only surviving manuscript of Jean le Bel's Chronicle was discovered in 1861 at a library in Châlons-sur-Marne. The handwriting is typical of the first half of the fifteenth century (it is unquestionably not Le Bel's own: the scribe who made the copy clearly had frequent difficulty in interpreting proper names). The text was edited by Jules Viard and Eugène Déprez and published in Paris in 1904-5 by the Société de l'Histoire de France. An unabridged facsimile of this edition (in two volumes, like the original) was made available in 2006 by Elibron Classics (ISBN 0-543-95301-7 and 0-543-95295-9).

As for the date of its composition, it is worth observing that Le Bel's work is not really a chronicle at all – not in the strict sense of being a register of events in the order of their occurrence and, usually, as they occur. It is rather, to quote from the opening page of Le Bel's prologue, a *'petit livre'* telling *'la vraye hystoire du proeu et gentil roy Edowart'*. He wrote it as a 'little book', much of it a fair while after the events described, and most readers would probably agree that the first part, down to the end of Chapter 39, reads very much as if it was written more or less in one go. There are a number of useful indicators of the dates of composition of different sections of the 'Chronicle':

Chapters 1-39: as mentioned earlier, Jean d'Outremeuse tells us that Le Bel began the Chronicle at the prompting of John of Hainault, and delivered one copy to him. Since John died in March 1356, the Chronicle was clearly begun before then; and, as Jules Viard argues in his Introduction to the edition,[4] if those chapters were indeed written more or less in one go it was probably started after – or not long before – the death of the abbess of Fontenelle (the widow of Count William I of Hainault) in March 1352, because in Chapter 39, when he is

[1] Diana B. Tyson, 'Jean le Bel, Annalist or Artist? A Literary Appraisal', *Studies in Medieval French Language and Literature*, ed. Sally Burch North (Geneva 1988), pp. 217-26.
[2] Le Bel died in February 1370; if Hemricourt is right, he was therefore born in 1290 or a little earlier.
[3] Hemricourt, op. cit., pp.226-7.
[4] *Chronique*, ed. Viard & Déprez, pp.xiv-xvi.

recounting events of 1340, Le Bel speaks of her as someone already deceased.[1] It is interesting, too, that this chapter ends with phrases which could imply that Le Bel intends to take a break and feels he needs more time and information before continuing his work.[2] It seems that the copy delivered to John of Hainault before his death can only have been the first part of the Chronicle: those first thirty-nine chapters, covering the years 1326-40.

Chapters 40-94: the likelihood is that these chapters (relating to the years 1340-58) were written during 1358. This section begins with an odd (and untypical) jumble of contemporary and other digressions before Le Bel returns to the war in Brittany in the early 1340s and 'the book returns to its proper story'[3] – the 'history of the worthy and noble King Edward'. Among these digressions, in Chapters 44 and 45, he refers to events which took place at the very end of 1357 and in the course of '58. He is clearly writing Chapter 70 (in which he discusses events in 1346 and the relative merits of kings Edward and Philip) after the 1356 battle of Poitiers, because he speaks of King John as 'now a captive'.[4] And chapter 94 ends with a particularly significant aside: writing of the peace agreed by Edward III and John II at Windsor in mid-1358, Le Bel says that 'the exact terms and conditions of the peace were still not generally known when these words were written; I'll say no more about them until they are'.[5]

Chapters 95-109: the final chapters of the Chronicle, covering the years 1358-61, appear to have been written more or less as events unfolded or shortly after. In Chapter 103, referring to the capture of the Count of Porcien and his imprisonment at Roucy in the spring of '59, Le Bel says: 'He was still there at the time of writing, in the month of May 1359.'[6] And a little later he writes that (in the summer of that year) 'the Duke of Normandy set out from Paris with a great company and went to lay siege to Melun. He stayed there till August: he was still there as I was writing this, and I'll say no more until we see the outcome.'[7] The proximity of Le Bel's writing to the events described may well explain why there are far more indications of date here (and a clearer sense of chronology) than he gives in the earlier chapters of his book.

For a book – rather than a chronicle – it really is. And despite its many digressions it is principally, as he says, a 'true history of the worthy and noble King Edward'. As for whether the adjective 'true' is justified, in the end it should probably be said that, although Le Bel declares his intention at the outset to write 'as truthfully as I can', truth and falsehood are not exactly the issues in the factual sense that most modern historians and readers might expect and understand them. Le Bel is essentially a chivalric writer, and he is concerned first and foremost, like the clerk Cresus in the romance of *Perceforest* and the clerks of John II's Company of the Star, with recording 'adventures, the shameful as well as the

---

[1]   See below, p.93.
[2]   p.95.
[3]   p.118.
[4]   p.168.
[5]   p.230.
[6]   p.244.
[7]   p.245.

glorious', so that the reader or listener can 'decide which had been most worthy, that the most deserving might be honoured'. As he says after setting forth the conflicting claims of the French and English in the 1339 stand-off at La Capelle:[1]

'Everyone who hears these claims can judge for himself where the honour lay, according to reason and chivalry.'

---

[1]   Below, pp.81–2.

Further Reading

Ainsworth, Peter, *Jean Froissart and the Fabric of History* (Oxford 1990)

Chareyron, Nicole, *Jean le Bel: Le Maître de Froissart, Grand Imagier de La Guerre de Cent Ans* (Brussels 1996)

Chareyron, Nicole, 'L'Amour d'Edouard III d'Angleterre pour la Comtesse de Salisbury: Histoire, Conte de Fées ou Tragédie?', *Revue de Littérature Comparée* 70 (1996), pp.341–56.

Chareyron, Nicole, 'Crimes et Châtiments dans la Chronique de Jean le Bel," in *La Violence dans le Monde Médiéval* (Aix-en-Provence 1994), pp.107-20.

de Medeiros, Marie-Thérèse, *Jacques et Chroniqueurs: Une étude comparée de récits contemporains relatant la Jacquerie de 1358* (Paris 1979)

Nachtwey, Gerald, 'Scapegoats and Conspirators in the Chronicles of Jean Froissart and Jean le Bel', in *Fifteenth-Century Studies 36*, ed. Barbara I. Gusick and Matthew Z. Heintzelman (Woodbridge 2011), pp.103-25.

Tyson, Diana B., 'Jean le Bel: Portrait of a Chronicler,' *Journal of Medieval History* 12 (1986), pp.315–32.

Tyson, Diana B., 'Jean le Bel, Annalist or Artist? A Literary Appraisal', in *Studies in Medieval French Language and Literature*, ed. Sally Burch North (Geneva 1988), pp.217-26.

THE TRUE CHRONICLES OF
JEAN LE BEL 1290–1360

Translated by Nigel Bryant

Prologue

Here begins the true and remarkable history of the recent wars and events that have taken place between the years 1326 and '61 in France, England, Scotland, Brittany and elsewhere, in particular the high deeds of King Edward of England and the two kings Philip and John of France.

Anyone who wishes to read and hear the true history of the noble and valiant King Edward, presently reigning in England, should read this little book I've begun, and ignore the great book written in verse that I've seen and read, which some imaginative soul has concocted in rhyme,[1] full of nonsense and wild invention: the first part of it, down to the beginning of the war that the said king undertook against King Philip of France, is littered with errors and lies. Thereafter it's a mixture of truth and falsehood, with a good deal of contrivance and repetition to embellish the verse, and such an abundance of feats of prowess attributed to certain knights and other persons that they test credulity, bordering on the impossible! Such a fanciful versified history is unlikely to please or appeal to people of wit and reason; for, by writing so extravagantly, it's possible to claim such outlandish deeds of prowess by certain knights and squires that their valour is diminished, for their true feats are less likely to be believed. That's a great shame for them; and it's why it's essential to speak with as much accuracy and precision as possible. For in my view it's a story of such nobility and such illustrious prowess that it eminently deserves to be recorded with all possible veracity, following reliable information kindly given to me.

Since that noble king was crowned in England in the year of grace 1326,[2] so many notable and perilous adventures have occurred, so many pitched battles and other deeds of arms and prowess, that he and all who've been with him in those battles and exploits – or who've accompanied his men when he hasn't been present in person, as you'll hear in due course – should be deemed and reputed worthy. Indeed, many of them should be deemed outstandingly so: the noble king himself, his son the Prince of Wales (considering his youth), the Duke of Lancaster, Sir Reginald Cobham, Sir Walter Mauny, Sir Frank van Hale and a good number of others – I can't name them all. In all the battles in which those I've listed have fought, both on land and at sea, they've been victorious and displayed such valour that they should be deemed worthy men indeed, supremely so. But those who've fought alongside them should not be overlooked, for, truth to tell, all should be considered worthy who in such fierce and perilous

---

[1] This has not survived, but in the late 19th century some fragments – just 36 lines in all – of a verse history in octosyllabic rhyming couplets were discovered which may well have belonged to the work so scathingly dismissed here by Le Bel. But it was not the only such work: an inventory of Charles V's library referred to three poems (now lost) relating to events in the reigns of Philip VI and John II. See Léopold Delisle, *Fragment d'un poème historique du XIVe siècle*, in Bibliothèque de l'école des chartes 60 (1899), 611-6.

[2] Old style. Edward III's coronation took place on 1 February 1327.

battles – of which there have been a good number – have had the courage to stand firm to the last, ably doing their duty. It should be enough to say: 'this knight fought best in that battle' (and name the knight and the battle) and 'this other knight performed well, too, as did this other one', without attributing to anyone prowess beyond the credible powers of man! So should be recorded all the battles and exploits worthy of mention, because, as we all know, when armies meet in pitched battle Fortune abruptly switches back and forth, but there are always some who perform better than others and their deeds should be recorded along with their names when they're known.

And whereas in those verse histories one finds heaps of nonsense, I intend to take pains wherever possible to set down in prose what I've witnessed myself or have heard from those who've been present when I have not; and I mean to do so as truthfully as I can, according to the memory God has granted me, and as concisely as I can without doing anyone a disservice. And if I'm unable to complete it, let someone do so after me, and may God grant him grace.

Chapter I

Here follows the genealogy of the noble King Edward, and how he was driven out of England.

Before I begin, it should be noted that it's a commonly held view among the English – and it's often been seen in England since the days of King Arthur – that between two worthy English kings there has always been one of less wisdom and prowess. Such is the case with the noble King Edward, now reigning, on whose account this history is begun; for the truth is that the good king his grandfather, Edward by name,[1] was wise, worthy, bold, enterprising and most fortunate in war: he had much to do against the Scots and conquered them three or four times; they were never able to defeat or resist him as long as he lived. But after his death he was succeeded by his son of his first marriage[2] – the father of the present noble King Edward – who resembled him neither in wisdom nor in prowess; he governed and ruled most irresponsibly and under the influence of others – and suffered severely for it in the end, as you can hear in due course if it please you. He hadn't been crowned long before the noble Robert Bruce, king of the Scots, who'd often been a concern for the aforementioned worthy King Edward, reconquered all of Scotland and the fine city of Berwick with it; twice he burned and ravaged a great swathe of the kingdom of England within a four or five days' ride, and defeated this king and all the barons of England in a pitched battle at a place called Stirling.[3] The pursuit continued for two days and two nights, the King of England fleeing all the way to London with very few of his men. But that's not what concerns us, so I'll say no more.

[1]   Edward I (reigned 1272-1307).
[2]   Edward II (1307-27).
[3]   i.e. at Bannockburn, 23 June 1314.

This king, the noble King Edward's father, had two half-brothers,[1] one known as the Earl Marshal, ruthless and devious in his ways, and the other named Edmund, Earl of Kent, a worthy, generous, kindly gentleman much loved by the good.

This king was married to the daughter of King Philip the Fair of France.[2] She was one of the most beautiful ladies in the world – and is so still for her age – and she had by him two sons and two daughters: the elder son is the noble King Edward whose story is here begun, and the other's name was John of Eltham and he died quite young; the elder daughter[3] was married at a fairly young age to the young King David of Scotland, son of the worthy King Robert of whom we spoke above, and the other[4] was married to Reginald of Guelders, who later became Duke of Guelders, and he had by her two sons who are still alive, the elder being the present Duke of Guelders and the other is named Lord Edward.[5]

Along with the daughter who was married to the aforementioned King of England, King Philip the Fair had three sons, and they were fine sons indeed: the eldest was named Louis, who in his father's lifetime was King of Navarre[6] and was called the Quarreller;[7] the second was named Philip the Tall;[8] the third was named Charles;[9] and all three became kings of France after their father's death, one after the other by right of succession, for none of them sired a male heir. And after the death of King Charles the twelve peers[10] and the barons of France did not give the kingdom to their sister, the Queen of England, because they claimed and insisted – as they still do – that the kingdom of France is so great that it should not pass to a female and consequently to the King of England, her eldest son; for, in their view, the son of the female cannot have right of succession through his mother, the mother herself having no right to succeed. For these reasons the twelve peers and the barons of France, by common accord, gave the kingdom of France to Lord Philip,[11] son of the late Lord Charles of Valois, who had been the brother of the aforementioned King Philip the Fair, thus rejecting the Queen of England and her son, who was a male heir, son of the sister of the last king, Charles.

---

[1] Thomas of Brotherton, Earl of Norfolk, and Edmund of Woodstock, Earl of Kent, sons of Edward I by his second wife, Margaret of France.
[2] Edward II married Isabella, daughter of Philip IV (the Fair), on 25 January 1308.
[3] Joan of the Tower.
[4] Eleanor of Woodstock.
[5] The elder son was named Reginald after his father; his younger brother in fact took the duchy from him in 1361.
[6] Louis, later to reign as Louis X of France (1314-16) became King of Navarre on the death of his mother, Joan of Navarre, in April 1305.
[7] 'le roy Hustin'– in Spanish his soubriquet was 'el Obstinado'.
[8] The text accidentally repeats 'le Bel'; Philip V (reigned 1316-22) is usually known as 'le Long'.
[9] Charles IV (reigned 1322-8).
[10] The highest ranking members of the French nobility, six clerical and six lay: the arch-bishop-duke of Reims, the bishop-dukes of Laon and Langres, the bishop-counts of Beauvais,Châlons and Noyon, the dukes of Burgundy, Normandy and Aquitaine and the counts of Toulouse, Flanders and Champagne.
[11] Philip VI, cousin of the three previous kings, who was to reign from 1328-50.

Thus it was that the kingdom passed from rightful succession – so it seems to many people. And it led to many wars and widespread destruction of land and people in the kingdom of France, as you'll hear in due course, for that is the basis of this history. And to record the great exploits and deeds of arms that have resulted – such mighty martial adventures have not been seen in the kingdom of France since the time of the good King Charlemagne – I shall return to my main theme and leave this subject until due time and place.

The King of England, father of the noble King Edward who now reigns, governed most irresponsibly and committed many outrageous acts in the land by the advice and at the prompting of Lord Hugh Despenser, who had been raised with him from early childhood. This Lord Hugh had contrived to make himself and his father – likewise named Hugh – the greatest barons of England in both power and wealth. They always had commanding positions in the royal council and sought to hold sway and lord it over all the magnates of England. It brought the country – and themselves – much trouble and suffering, for after the disaster at Stirling where the King of Scotland routed this King of England and all his barons as you heard earlier, resentment and discontent spread among the magnates and the royal council, especially against Despenser. They declared that his decisions had led to their defeat: happily for the King of Scotland, they said, he'd given the king such ill advice and worked so counter to English interests that the Scots had recaptured the good city of Berwick, twice set the land ablaze within a four or five days' ride, and finally inflicted that crushing defeat. The barons, with the king's uncle, Thomas Earl of Lancaster, at the forefront, repeatedly discussed what they should do.

This led to Despenser telling his lord the king that these barons were conspiring against him and would drive him from his land and his kingdom unless he took action. So earnest were his promptings that at last the king arrested all these lords where they were gathered together, and had thirty-two of the foremost beheaded without delay or trial:[1] the least of them was a banneret.[2] And the first to be beheaded was Thomas, Earl of Lancaster, his uncle – a most worthy and saintly man, they said: indeed, great miracles later occurred on the site of his execution. It brought Despenser deep hatred from all the land, including the Queen and the aforementioned Earl of Kent, the king's brother. But it didn't stop him urging the king to further wrongs: when he saw how the Queen and the Earl of Kent were against him he sowed such discord between the king and queen, by way of mistresses[3] and shady acquaintances, that he wouldn't go anywhere near her. This rift lasted a fair while, and intensified to the point where the Queen had to leave England along with her eldest son, Lord Edward, for fear of their

---

[1]   Le Bel is referring here to the baronial revolt – the 'Despenser War' – which culminated in a royal victory at the battle of Boroughbridge in March 1322 and a round of summary executions.

[2]   A wealthy and eminent knight commanding his own body of troops in battle, under his own rectangular banner rather than a triangular pennon.

[3]   There is a suggestion that Edward II was even involved with Despenser's wife – a relationship not merely adulterous but incestuous, as Eleanor was his niece. See Ian Mortimer, *The Perfect King* (London, 2006), pp.33, 445.

lives.[1] She fled to France, to her brother King Charles who then reigned, taking with her the Earl of Kent, Lord Mortimer[2] and several other knights who dared no longer stay in England, being allies of Mortimer and therefore much hated by Despenser.

When he saw he'd achieved a good part of his ambition – he'd eliminated the greatest barons of the land, driven the Queen and her eldest son from the kingdom and brought the king under his control – Despenser then had so many good people executed without trial or sentence on the slightest suspicion, and committed so many outrageous acts with his overweening pride, that the remaining barons and the rest of the country could abide him no longer. Some formed a secret alliance and sent covert word to their lady the Queen – who by this time had been in Paris for three years[3] with her eldest son Edward, banished from her land and kingdom as you've heard – saying that if she could find a way of raising about a thousand men-at-arms[4] and brought her son and such forces back to England, they would all rally to her and to him and obey him as their lord, for they could no longer tolerate the deviant wrongs the king was committing in the land at the instigation of Hugh Despenser and his party.

When the Queen received this message she went in secret to seek the guidance of her brother King Charles of France. He was delighted by the news and advised her to proceed with confidence, for he would willingly support her and lend her whatever manpower, gold and silver she required. With that the Queen left him and made due provision, seeking the aid of those magnates of France whom she most trusted and who were most sympathetic to her cause. Feeling very assured, she sent back secret word of this to the English barons.

But it couldn't be kept secret from Despenser! And before the Queen could act, he sent such messages, gifts and promises that King Charles of France was urged by his Council to summon his sister, and to dissuade and bar her in the strongest possible terms from pursuing her plan. The lady was obviously shocked by this. She realised her brother was being pressurised, for nothing she could say was of any use, and she left and returned to the house where she was staying, most downcast and dismayed.

But she continued to make her preparations, and when her brother learned of this he was furious and, following his Council's promptings, decreed that any

---

[1] This is not strictly accurate. Queen Isabella did not flee the kingdom; she was sent by Edward II to negotiate with her brother King Charles and settle the dispute in Aquitaine known as the War of Saint-Sardos, and her son Edward followed her to pay the French king homage for the county of Ponthieu. It is true, however, that she would not then return to England for fear of Despenser.

[2] Roger Mortimer had been imprisoned following a revolt against Edward II in 1321-2. In August 1324 he had escaped from the Tower of London and taken ship to Dunkirk.

[3] Again this is not quite right: Queen Isabella landed in France in March 1325 and returned to England in September 1326. In August 1326 her son Edward was betrothed to Philippa, daughter of Count William of Hainault.

[4] 'armeures de fer'. Throughout the text I have used either 'heavy cavalry' or simply 'men-at-arms' (especially if they are dismounted) as a translation of Le Bel's unusual term 'armeures de fer' ('iron-clads'), by which he indicates mounted troops in full armour. He later classifies other troops as 'brigandines' because of their lesser armour: see for example below, p.222.

man in his kingdom who joined forces with his sister the Queen would forfeit his life and possessions. Hearing this, the lady was even more alarmed than before, and little wonder. She didn't know what to do or think: everything was going against her as it had been for a long while, and ill counsel was now depriving her, it seemed, of the one who should have been her greatest aid in her hour of need – and the time agreed with her supporters in England was fast approaching. She was left bereft of comfort or guidance, not knowing what to do or what would become of her.

Then she was told that, unless she behaved, her brother would detain her son but have her taken back to England and delivered to her husband the king, for King Charles was no longer happy to have her estranged from her husband. Now she was more distressed than ever: she would rather have been killed and dismembered than placed at the mercy of her husband and Hugh Despenser who wished her nothing but ill. She left with all possible speed and secrecy, along with her fifteen-year-old son.

Accompanied by the Earl of Kent, Lord Mortimer and all the other English knights who'd gone into exile with her, she rode swiftly to a small town near Cambrai where she took lodging at the house of a poor knight[1] who welcomed her with such comfort and honour as his limited means allowed; and there she stayed the following day, weary fugitive that she was.

News of this reached Sir John of Hainault, lord of Beaumont,[2] a gentleman then in his prime, and he went to her at once and, with typical courtesy, paid her all possible honour and respect. The lady, so heavy-hearted, wept piteously and told him of her distressing plight and misfortunes: how she and her son had been driven from England and taken refuge in France, trusting in her brother the king, and how she'd expected – at her brother's own suggestion – to be provided with French troops so that she could return in strength and make her son King of England as her supporters had proposed; and how her brother had then been counselled otherwise, as you've heard; and how, and with what difficulty, she'd escaped with her son, not knowing where or from whom to find support and sustenance.

Chapter II

*How Sir John of Hainault took the Queen of England and
her eldest son back to England.*

At this Sir John of Hainault began to weep fervent tears of pity, and said: "Lady, behold your knight, who will defend you with his life, truly, even if all others fail you. I shall do everything in my power to escort you and your son to England and restore you to your rightful stations, with the help of the friends you tell me are across the sea; and I and all those I can rally will stake our

---

[1] Froissart identifies this as the castle of Bugnicourt, near Douai.
[2] Jean de Beaumont (1288-1356), son of Count Jean II of Hainault and brother of Count William I.

lives upon the enterprise, and if it please God we shall have men-at-arms enough without the aid of the French."

Only the most hard-hearted man would have failed to feel deep pity if he'd seen how that fair and tearful lady stood then, ready to fall at the feet of the noble knight and thank him for the mighty pledge he'd made. But he wouldn't allow it; and when she couldn't do as she wished – that is, fall at his feet – she flung her arms about his neck and kissed him joyously, saying to the noble knight:

"A thousand thanks![1] If you'll do as you've so courteously promised, my son and I will be your servants evermore; and we shall place the kingdom of England entirely at your legitimate disposal."

And this good knight, then in his prime, replied: "My dear lady, if I didn't mean to carry it out I wouldn't have made the promise. But made it I have, and I shan't fail to keep it, whatever may befall me: I'd rather die."

The matter thus resolved, the noble knight bade the lady and her company mount at once and escorted them to Valenciennes, to his brother the noble Count William,[2] who greeted them with all warmth and honour possible, which in his case was much.

The lady stayed there for eight days, making her preparations, while Sir John of Hainault sent heart-felt letters to the knights and most trusted friends he had in Hainault, Brabant and Hesbaye,[3] urging them as strongly as he could, in the name of friendship, to join him in this enterprise. A good number came from each of these lands out of love for him, but a good many more did not come despite his entreaties. And indeed, Sir John met with deep disapproval from his brother and members of his own council: they thought the enterprise so grave and perilous, in view of the current strife and bitter hatred among the barons and commons of England (and the animosity the English generally show towards any defeated foreigners, especially in their own country), that they feared Sir John and his companions had no chance of ever returning. But for all their rebukes and attempts to dissuade him, the noble knight wouldn't change his mind: having promised to escort the lady to her kingdom, he wouldn't fail her were it to cost him his life; and he would rather die, if die he must, with that exiled lady than elsewhere, for all knights should do everything in their power to aid and comfort ladies and maidens who are deprived and distressed, especially when requested.

Once the noble lady and her forces had made their preparations she left Valenciennes and set out under the knight's protection and escort, riding on until they came to Dordrecht in Holland. There they mustered all the vessels they could find – ships and boats both great and small – and took aboard their horses, their equipment and provisions and, commending themselves to Our Lord's protection, put to sea.

---

[1]   Literally 'five hundred'!
[2]   Count William I of Hainault (1286-1337).
[3]   'Hesbaing' (from the Latin 'Hesbania' used in many medieval documents). Hesbaye (or Hasbain) was part of the land centred on the city of Liège.

They were prevented from landing at their intended port by a mighty storm, which carried them so far off course that after two days they didn't know where they were. But this was a great stroke of luck and a blessing from God, for if they'd landed where they'd planned or thereabouts they'd have been lost indeed: they'd have fallen into the hands of their enemies who were well aware of their approach and were waiting there, ready to slaughter them all including the Queen and the young king. But God would not permit it and diverted them by a veritable miracle as you've heard.

After two days the storm abated, and the mariners caught sight of the English coast and headed towards it joyfully. They made landfall on an open beach, not in a harbour or a proper port, and they stayed there on the strand for three days, very short of provisions, discharging their horses and equipment. They didn't know where in England they'd landed, or whether it was the territory of friend or foe. On the fourth day they placed themselves in God's hands and set out. They'd suffered much from cold and hunger and fear, and fear was with them still. They journeyed high and low, this way and that, through hamlets and villages, until they came upon a great abbey of black friars named St Edmund's;[1] they took lodging at this abbey for three days, resting and recovering.

News spread through the country and reached those whose assurances and messages had brought the lady back to England. They prepared with all speed to come to her and her son whom they wished to have as their lord. The first to arrive, and the most heartening presence to all involved, was Henry Earl of Lancaster, the crook-necked, who was brother of Thomas Earl of Lancaster who'd been beheaded as you've heard, and father of the Duke of Lancaster[2] who is currently one of the finest, worthiest knights alive, both in arms and otherwise. He brought with him a great company of men-at-arms, and after him came earls, barons, knights, squires and so many troops that all felt they were out of danger. Day by day, as they made their advance, more and more men-at-arms rallied to them.

The Queen and the knights who'd joined her decided to make straight for Bristol with their whole army: that was where the king had set himself, for it was a fine, great and prosperous city, very strongly fortified, with a splendid sea port and a mighty castle overlooking the sea, which washes all around it. There sat the king, along with Hugh Despenser the Elder (then close to four score years and ten), his son Lord Hugh who was the king's chief adviser and had prompted all his wicked deeds, the Earl of Arundel, who'd married the daughter of Hugh the Younger,[3] and a number of knights and squires who resided with the king and his court as high-ranking men are pleased to do with their lord. The Queen and all those barons, knights and lords of England headed that way; and at every town they entered they were greeted with honour and celebration, and right and left,

---

[1]   Bury St Edmunds.
[2]   Henry of Grosmont, 1st Duke of Lancaster, c.1310-61.
[3]   Edmund Fitzalan, 9th Earl of Arundel; it was not he but his son Richard who married Despenser's daughter.

from every side, people flocked to them. On they marched until they reached the city of Bristol and laid close siege to it.

Chapter III

How the Earl of Arundel and Hugh Despenser the Elder
were captured and executed.

The king and Hugh Despenser the Younger were happily ensconced inside the castle. Old Lord Hugh the father and the Earl of Arundel were below in Bristol town with others of their party. When they and the townsfolk saw the lady's mighty and ever-growing army, supported by almost the whole of England, and realised the threat of clear and imminent disaster, they decided to surrender themselves and the city in exchange for their lives, limbs and possessions. But the Queen and her council would not accept their surrender unless she could do as she wished with Hugh the Elder and the Earl of Arundel: she hated them exceedingly and had come there for them. When the townsfolk realised there was no other way of making peace and saving their lives and possessions, they reluctantly agreed and opened the gates, and the Queen and all the barons and Sir John of Hainault took such lodgings as they pleased in the city, while those who could find no lodging within lodged without. Lord Hugh was taken prisoner there along with the Earl of Arundel, and they were led before the Queen for her to deal with exactly as she wished. Her other young children – John her son and her two daughters – were found in the keeping of Lord Hugh, and they too were brought to her; the lady was overjoyed, as were all those opposed to the Despensers.

As great as their joy was the anguish of the king and Despenser: from their mighty castle they could see disaster poised to strike and the whole country turning against them and rallying to the Queen and her eldest son. There's no need to ask if they were despondent, aghast.

Once the Queen and her supporters had arranged comfortable lodgings, they laid the closest possible siege to the castle. Then the Queen had Lord Hugh the Elder and the Earl of Arundel brought before her and her eldest son and all the barons present, and told them that she and her son would pass fair and rightful judgement upon them befitting their deeds and just deserts. Lord Hugh replied:

"My lady, may God grant us a fair judge and fair judgement; if we don't have them in this world, may He grant them to us in the next."

Then Sir Thomas Wake, marshal of the Queen's army, a good knight, wise and courteous, stood and read out a full account of their deeds and works, all set down in writing; then he turned to one of the knights present and bade him declare on oath what sentence should be passed on persons who had committed such deeds. This knight consulted with other knights and barons, and returned with a swift decision: that they fully deserved death for the terrible crimes they'd heard recounted there which they took to be true and manifest; and in view of their wide-ranging crimes they deserved a threefold execution: they should first be drawn, then beheaded and their bodies then hung upon a gibbet. And they were indeed executed according to this sentence, right outside Bristol Castle, in full view of the king and Hugh the Younger and all the others inside, who were maddened by the sight, you can be sure. This took place in the year of grace 1326, in the month of October.

Chapter IV

*How the king and Lord Hugh the Younger were captured and
Lord Hugh sentenced to a foul death.*

After these executions the king and Hugh Despenser, seeing they were closely and hopelessly besieged with no possibility of relief, boarded a little boat one morning with a few retainers and put to sea behind the castle, planning to sail to the kingdom of Wales if they could, hoping to find refuge there. But God would not allow it, burdened by sins as they were, and a great marvel and miracle occurred: for fully nine days they were in that boat, struggling and straining to sail away, but the wind, ever against them by the will of God, blew them back towards the castle at least once or twice a day, so that they were in constant sight of the Queen's forces who could see exactly who they were. At last some companions from Holland who'd come with Sir John of Hainault and were able sailors boarded some boats and skiffs they found and sailed after them with all speed; the king's crew couldn't sail fast enough, and were overtaken and captured along with their boat, and led back to the city of Bristol.[1] They were delivered as prisoners to the Queen and her son, who rejoiced with all their supporters – and with good reason, for with God's help they had accomplished and entirely fulfilled their desires.

So it was that the Queen reconquered the whole kingdom of England for her eldest son, with the support and guidance of the noble knight Sir John of Hainault and his company; and he and all his companions were held in high esteem for their great enterprise, for when they set sail from Dordrecht as you've heard they numbered only three hundred mounted men-at-arms, but they carried out this daring venture for love of the Queen, taking ship and crossing the sea with so few to conquer such a kingdom as England in the face of its very king and all his supporters.

And so, as you've heard, this bold enterprise was accomplished. Through the support and guidance of the worthy knight Sir John of Hainault and his companions, that noble lady won back her position and destroyed all her enemies. The king himself, as you've heard, was taken captive in this débâcle, to the unanimous joy of the whole country – except the few supporters of the aforementioned Lord Hugh.

---

[1] This is a colourful but somewhat fanciful account of their capture. They had escaped to South Wales (after an unsuccessful attempt to put to sea from Chepstow), but were captured by the Earl of Lancaster near Llantrissant.

When the king and Lord Hugh were brought back to Bristol, the barons and knights decided to send the king to a strong castle – I'm not sure of the name[1] – and entrusted him to the keeping of men of good standing who would know how to guard him well and decently, until such time as the people of the land had resolved how to proceed.

Meanwhile Lord Hugh was delivered to Sir Thomas Wake, marshal of the Queen's army. As the Queen and all her company set off for London, the capital of England, Sir Thomas had Lord Hugh Despenser thoroughly, tightly bound on the smallest, scrawniest, most wretched horse he could find, and had him clad in a specially made tabard festooned with his coats of arms; and he was dragged along in shame behind the Queen's escort through every town they passed accompanied by fanfares to humiliate him all the more, until they reached a fine city named Hereford. There the Queen and all her company were nobly received with great solemnity, and a great feast was held to celebrate All Saints, which was that very day.

The feast day past, Lord Hugh, who was little loved there and rightly so, was led before the Queen and all the assembled knights and barons, and reminded of all he'd done. He said not a word in reply, so he was promptly sentenced by all the knights and barons to death by the execution you're about to hear. Thus did Lord Hugh fall from such great eminence, and all his line with him.

First he was dragged on a hurdle, amid fanfares of trumpets, from street to street right through the city of Hereford, and led to a great square in the centre where all the people had gathered and a huge fire had been lit. There he was tied to a tall ladder so that everyone could see him. Once he was so bound, they first cut off his penis and testicles because he was alleged to be a pervert and a sodomite – above all with the king himself, which was why the king, at his urging, had driven the Queen away. His severed penis and testicles were thrown on the fire and burnt; then they sliced open his belly and tore out his heart and threw it in the flames to burn, because it was a false and treacherous heart, and it was through his treacherous advice and promptings that he'd brought shame upon the king and disaster to his kingdom; he was responsible for the beheading of the greatest lords of England, who should have been the kingdom's support and defence. Moreover he had worked upon the king until he couldn't and wouldn't see the Queen or his eldest son, their lord-to-be, and had driven them from the kingdom in fear of their lives.

When they'd done the aforementioned to Lord Hugh they cut off his head and sent it to London, and his body was quartered and sent to the next four principal cities of England.

Once Hugh Despenser had been executed as you've heard, the Queen and all the barons and knights, and commoners too, set off for London, that fine city which was England's capital. They made their way swiftly and arrived in a mighty company, and all the people of London, the highest and the lowest, came out together and greeted the Queen and her eldest son, their rightful lord-to-be,

---

[1] Edward II was taken first to Kenilworth.

with great celebration and reverence, and the whole company likewise; and they presented splendid gifts to the Queen and those who seemed most deserving.

After they'd been thus gloriously received and had had a chance to rest, the companions who'd crossed the sea with Sir John of Hainault were all keen to return to their own lands. They felt their mission had been well achieved and that they'd earned much honour, as indeed they had, and they took their leave of the Queen and the barons. The Queen and all the lords asked them to stay a little longer to see what decision would be made about the king, who, as you've heard, had been imprisoned; but such was their desire to go home that these prayers were vain. Then the lady and her council begged Sir John of Hainault to stay till after Christmas and to keep with him such companions as he could. The noble knight didn't wish to fail in his service: he wanted to complete his mission and see it through to the end. So he accepted the request and courteously agreed to stay as long as the Queen wished. He kept with him as many of his companions as he could, but they were very few: most had no desire at all to stay, which upset Sir John greatly. Nonetheless, when the Queen and her council saw there was no persuading them, they paid them all possible honour and respect, and the Queen awarded them silver and gifts a-plenty to repay their expenses and their service, each according to his station. They had good reason to be pleased, and indeed they made her generosity widely known. What's more, she repaid them the value of the horses they'd left behind, at such a high rate that there was no cause to haggle! And it was all paid in silver, in pure English sterling, so that they all departed with great joy, great honour and great profit, and crossed the sea between Dover and Wissant[1] and returned safe home well furnished with English sterling.

But that noble knight Sir John of Hainault, at the Queen's request, stayed behind with just a small band of companions, and the English treated him with all possible honour. So did the ladies of the land: there were many in attendance, countesses, ladies and maidens who had come to accompany the Queen; and they came daily to pay him their respects, for they felt the noble knight had well deserved it, as he most certainly had.

Chapter V

How the king was condemned and deprived of his crown and the government of the realm.

When the companions from this side of the sea had left London and Sir John had stayed behind, as you've heard, the Queen gave leave to those of her land to return to their homes and their own affairs, except for a number of barons and knights whom she kept behind to counsel her. But she bade all return to London on a certain day at Christmas when she planned to hold a great court.

When the day came and she held the promised court, all the earls, lords and knights, together with aldermen of all the cities of the land, gathered there. At

[1]   On the coast between Calais and Boulogne.

that great feast and assembly it was decreed that, since the land couldn't long remain without a lord, a record should be made of all the ill-advised deeds and actions the king had committed, and of his conduct and behaviour, and how he'd ruled the country, so that it could be read in open court and the wisest in the land could debate and decide how and by whom the kingdom should thenceforth be governed. This decree was duly carried out; and when all that the king had done and consented to, and details of his conduct and behaviour, were read out and fully understood, the barons and knights and aldermen of the cities withdrew to discuss how to proceed; and the majority by far – especially the greatest lords and high nobility, along with the cities' aldermen – agreed that, from the account they'd heard and what they knew of most of the king's actions and conduct, such a man was unfit ever to wear the crown or to be called king. And they all agreed that his eldest son, his rightful heir who was present there, should be crowned forthwith in his father's place,[1] and should appoint around him good counsellors, wise and trustworthy men, so that the country might thenceforth be better governed than it had been thitherto; and that the father should be securely but decently kept, in a manner befitting his station, for as long as he should live.

Chapter VI

How King Edward was crowned King of England at the age of sixteen.

The decision of the lords and the cities was duly carried out, and in the year of grace 1326,[2] at the age of sixteen, the noble, worthy King Edward, the present King of England, was crowned at London before the whole country with great joy and splendour. At the ceremonial entry to the coronation the noble knight Sir John of Hainault was highly honoured by all the princes and knights of the land, noble and non-noble, and he and the companions who'd remained with him were presented with splendid gifts and finery.

He stayed there, enjoying the joyful and generous attention of all the lords and ladies present, until after the day of Epiphany. Then he heard that the noble King of Bohemia and his brother the Count of Hainault and a great many lords of France were gathering for a tournament at Condé-sur-l'Escaut. No plea then would make him stay, such was his desire to be at the tourney and to see his noble lord and brother and all the others, especially the worthiest king there ever was – that is, the noble, courteous, generous King of Bohemia, who held Sir John in great affection. When the noble King Edward and the Queen and all the lords saw he would stay no longer and that entreaties were useless, they gave him leave with heavy hearts. And the young king, on the advice of his mother the Queen, granted him an heritable annuity of four hundred marks (in sterling, at a silver penny to the *denier*),[3] to be held in fee and paid each year in the city

---

1   Edward II's abdication was announced on 24 January 1327.
2   Old style. The coronation took place on 1 February 1327 new style.
3   Le Bel may be emphasising the generosity and value of this: there were 240 English pennies to a pound just as there were 240 *deniers* to the *livre*, but by the time Le Bel was writing his Chronicle the high quality and stable value of English currency and the repeated devalua-

of Bruges; and to Philippe du Chastel, his principal squire and counsellor, he granted an annuity of a hundred marks to be paid in the same way. Then the king had ample money delivered to Sir John to defray his expenses and those of his company on the journey home, and arranged for a great escort of knights to accompany them to Dover and ensure their safe and free passage. And the ladies, notably the countess of Warenne,[1] sister of the Count of Bar, and several others gave him abundant gifts at his departure.

When Sir John arrived at Dover, he and his companions took ship at once, eager to arrive on time at the tournament at Condé. He took with him fifteen hundred fine young knights from England, to accompany him in the tourney and to introduce them to the lords and companions who were due to attend. He showed them all possible respect and companionship; and when they arrived they took part twice in the splendid tournament at Condé.

But I'll say no more about that noble knight until due time; for the moment I'll return to King Edward.

Chapter VII

How King Robert of Scotland defied the young King Edward and began to ravage England.

After Sir John of Hainault had left young King Edward and my lady the Queen, the king and lady governed the land with the guidance of the Earl of Kent and Lord Roger Mortimer, who had great estates in England, the revenue from his lands being fully eight thousand pounds (at a penny to the *denier*).[2] Both these lords had been in exile with the Queen and the young king as recounted above. They often sought the advice, too, of Sir Thomas Wake and a number of others accounted the wisest in England, though this caused resentment in some quarters. (Indeed, it's said that envy was never dead in England – and it thrives in many other lands!) Winter passed by, and so did Lent, and Easter came, and in that time the king and my lady his mother enjoyed peace.

Meanwhile King Robert, who'd been a worthy adversary but suffered many defeats and reverses in the days of the good King Edward (the young King Edward's grandfather), had grown very old and was suffering, it was said, from the unclean sickness.[3] But when he heard the news from England – that the king had been imprisoned and deposed and his counsellors tried and executed as you've heard – he decided to defy the young king. With him being young and the English barons by no means in agreement (as he'd been led to believe perhaps by some resentful malcontent), he thought he had a good chance of conquering

---

tions of French coinage had made a pound sterling worth four or five *livres*. But in view of the similar comment about Roger Mortimer's income (below, p.34), it may simply be that Le Bel was expressing a relative value to his audience in the Low Countries.

[1]   Joan of Bar (1295–1361), granddaughter of Edward I. She was the wife of John de Warenne, 8th Earl of Surrey, but their unhappy marriage was annulled in 1315.

[2]   See note 3, p.33..

[3]   'la grosse maladie': the traditional assumption is that Robert suffered from leprosy.

part of England. So he followed his hunch and around Easter sent a message of defiance to King Edward and all his land, declaring that he would burn and lay waste as far as he'd done after the disastrous defeat at Stirling.[1] When the young king and his council heard this challenge they sent word throughout the kingdom that all nobles and non-nobles should prepare, each according to his station, and come in all possible strength to the fine city of York on Ascension Day following; and he sent large numbers of men-at-arms to defend the Scottish border. He sent messengers, too, to the noble knight Sir John of Hainault with heartfelt pleas that he should come and aid and support him in this emergency, and join him in York on Ascension Day with as many men-at-arms as he could muster.

As soon as the noble knight received the call he sent messengers and letters to everyone likely to lend support in Flanders, Hainault, Brabant and Hesbaye, appealing to them in the most earnest terms to follow him, as well equipped and mounted as possible, and meet at Wissant to make the crossing to England. Everyone willingly came to join him – not only those he'd summoned but many more, unbidden – thinking they'd return with as much money as the others had who'd accompanied him on his first foray into England! Before Sir John arrived at Wissant there were more men there than he'd expected – more, perhaps, than he'd have wished!

When he and the whole company had gathered they found all the ships ready to sail, and they swiftly boarded with all their gear and horses and made the crossing to Dover; then they rode night and day without stopping, passing through the good city of London and reaching York three days before Pentecost. The king and my lady his mother were there with a great company of barons to advise and attend upon the young king, waiting as all the men-at-arms, archers and common folk arrived from the towns and villages. As they came flocking in they were billeted in hamlets for two or three leagues[2] around York, and were ordered to press on next day towards the border.

It was at this point that the noble knight Sir John of Hainault and his great company arrived at York. That he was joyfully welcomed and received is beyond question: he and his men were given quarters in the finest parts of the city – and none of them had to share! Sir John was provided with lodging for himself and his staff in an abbey of white friars.[3]

In the said knight's company there came from Hainault the lord of Enghien, then named Sir Walter;[4] the lord of Fagnolle;[5] Sir Henry d'Antoing; Sir Fastré du Roeulx; the lord of Havré, castellan of Mons;[6] Sir Alard de Briffeuil; Sir Jean de Montigny the younger and his brother; Robert de Bailleul, lord of Fontaine l'Évêque and Morialmé; and several more I can't recall. From the land of

[1] Bannockburn, as above, p.22.
[2] The league was a notoriously vague medieval unit of measurement, not least because it varied from country to country. The English league was about three miles, the French league just over two.
[3] Presumably the Carmelite friary near the River Foss.
[4] Gauthier d'Enghien.
[5] Hugues, lord of Fagnolle and Wiège.
[6] Gérard d'Enghien, castellan of Mons and lord of Havré.

Flanders came Sir Hector Vilains, Sir Jehan de Rodes, Sir Wulfart de Ghistelles, Sir Guillaume de Straten, Sir Gossuin de Meule and a number of others. From the land of Brabant came the lord of Duffle,[1] Sir Thierri de Walcourt, Sir Raes van Gavere, Sir Jehan de Chastebercke, Sir Jean Pyliser, Sir Gille de Coteberque, the three brothers of Harlebecque, Sir Gauthier de Huldenbergh and several more. From Hesbaye came Jean le Bel, canon of Liège,[2] accompanied by his brother Henry, Sir Godefroy de la Chappelle, Sir Huars d'Ohay and Sir Jehan de Libine, all four of whom were knighted there; also Sir Lambert d'Oupey and Sir Gillebert de Hercs. A number of knights came independently, too, from the Cambrésis and from Artois, so that Sir John of Hainault had in his company fully five hundred superbly mounted heavy cavalry.[3] Then, at the feast of Pentecost, Lord William of Jülich[4] arrived with his companion the lord of Wildeberg; Lord William was later to become Duke of Jülich, but at that time he was at odds with his father the Count of Jülich; and with him came Sir Thierry de Heinsberg who later became Count of Loon, together with the lord of Branquebierge who was likewise on bad terms with his father, the lord of Henselode. These three lords had come of their own free will to join Sir John of Hainault when they heard news of his mission, and brought with them at least fifty men-at-arms, knights and squires. When they arrived at York they were joyously received and lodged where available in and around the priory.[5]

Chapter VIII

How the Hainaulter pages came into conflict with the English archers.

Then the young king, by way of further welcoming these lords and all their company, held a great court on the Feast of the Holy Trinity at the house of the Friars Minor.[6] That's where he and my lady his mother were lodged, each with his or her retinue: that is to say, the King with his knights and the Queen with her ladies, of whom she had many. At this court the king had fully six hundred knights seated in the cloister – he'd newly knighted several that day; and my lady the Queen was holding court in one of the dormitories, where at least sixty ladies were seated at table to welcome Sir John and these other lords. It was a sight to behold, finely, lavishly served as they were with abundant dishes and side-dishes, so exotic that I couldn't name or describe them all! And I wish you could have seen the ladies, gorgeously dressed and adorned.

But just after dinner a big fight broke out over a game of dice between the Hainaulter pages and the English archers who were lodging among them. And it led to serious trouble, as you'll hear, for when the boys started fighting with this band of English, all the other archers in the city, and others who were billeted

---

[1]   Henri Berthout, lord of Duffle.
[2]   i.e. the author himself.
[3]   '*armeures de fer*': see footnote 4, above, p.25.
[4]   '*Juliers*' in French.
[5]   '*l'ostel des Prescheurs*': probably the Holy Trinity Priory near the southern wall.
[6]   The Franciscan Friary on the north bank of the Ouse.

among the Hainaulters, came rushing with their bows, roaring and bristling like boars, and wounded many of the boys and forced them to retreat to their lodgings. Most of the knights and their masters were still at court and wholly unaware; but as soon as they heard about the rumpus they made straight for their lodgings – at least, those who could: some were forced to stay outside, for the devil had got into the archers (of whom there were a good two thousand), and they were shooting wildly as if to slaughter and plunder everyone, lords and servants alike. I was there myself, and my companions and I couldn't get into our lodgings to arm: I found such a crowd of English at our door, poised to smash it down and go looting, and such a cloud of arrows flying at us, that we had to withdraw and trust to luck with the others.

When those who'd managed to get into their houses had armed they didn't dare leave by the front for fear of the arrows; they left by the rear, through the courtyards, breaking down the fences behind and waiting at a certain spot till a good hundred of them had gathered, not counting those of us who'd been unable to arm. As soon as those with arms had assembled they rushed to the aid of their fellows who were doing their best to defend their houses on the main street; they passed through the house of the lord of Enghien, which had wide doorways to the rear as well as to the front overlooking the main street, and launched a fierce attack upon the archers. Some of our men were mortally wounded by bowshots, but the archers at last were routed, with fully 316 killed there and in the fields beyond; they were all the Bishop of Lincoln's men. I don't believe God ever sent such good fortune to any men as he did then to Sir John of Hainault and his company; for those archers were intent on nothing less than murdering and robbing us, even though we'd come to help them! And I assure you our troubles weren't over: no men were ever left in more wretched, mortal danger, with no hope of returning home, than we were, day and night, for the whole time we were in that country until we sailed back to Wissant; for defending our lives as we had done had earned us the hatred of all in the land (except the great lords): indeed, they hated us more than the Scots who were burning their country! Every day warnings came to our lords from those knights who didn't hate us – and from the king's council, too – that we should be on our guard, for they knew of fully six thousand English gathered in a certain town who would come and slaughter us all by day or night, and neither the king nor his council would be able to save us. There's no need to ask if we were alarmed by the news! We didn't know what to think or how to react; there was no question of turning back – we didn't dare leave the king and his lords, even though there was no hope of aid or protection from them. All we could do was resolve to defend ourselves and sell our lives dear, and fight for each other like brothers. Our lords and their counsellors established a number of good, well-conceived plans for our greater safety, insisting that we slept armed at night and stayed in our lodgings by day with all our gear ready; and we had to have constables stationed day and night watching the fields and roads around the city, and sent scouts half a league beyond to learn of any men approaching: we were given reports each day by reliable men, knights and squires, who claimed to have sound information. If these scouts heard of any moves towards the city they were to report back to those of us guarding the fields, so that we could mount at once and rally to our banners at prearranged locations.

In this tense and fearful state we remained around the city for three weeks; for truly, every day we received such reports – and often worse! – and sometimes saw worrying, alarming signs that made us stay in our lodgings with our arms at the ready. None of us dared venture into the city, except the lords, who sometimes went to feast with the king and queen and seek their advice, asking how long we'd have to put up with this before we were put to the work for which we'd been summoned.

Mind you, if it hadn't been for our miserable anxiety it would have been a pleasant stay! The city and the surrounding country were so plentifully provisioned that throughout the six weeks and more that the king and all the princes and barons of the land and all their men-at-arms and all our lords and their companions were staying there, the price of food never rose; and although no vines are grown in England and never were, so much wine was imported to York from Gascony and the Rhine that despite all those lords and all the English troops that passed that way, the price of a gallon rose by no more than a penny.[1] It was the same with poultry: you could buy a fat capon for three pence and the very best for four, and two fat hens for three; and a penny would buy you a dozen fresh herrings. And hay, straw and oats were daily offered for sale outside our lodgings as cheaply as if it were peacetime and there were no army in the city, so there was no need to go foraging the whole time we were there. We never ceased to wonder how the city came by such abundant supplies, but we were very glad it did, for we had enough to worry and fret about, ever on watch and sleeping armed! But there was some consolation: we were promptly paid each week in good English coin, more than enough to cover all reasonable costs.

Chapter IX

How the king and all his army left the city of York to march against the Scots.

We'd stayed thus for three weeks when we were informed by the king and his council that, in the week following,[2] each man should prepare transport and provisions for sleeping in the field, and equip himself with cooking utensils and everything else we'd need in marching against the Scots, for the king meant to delay no longer.

So everyone began to arrange supplies, each according to his rank and responsibility, buying tents and carts and the little draught-horses they use in that country – there were plenty for sale at a fair price – and bowls and pans and cooking pots and everything else needed on campaign.

When all was ready the king and his barons rode from the city and made camp a full six leagues further on. Sir John of Hainault and his fellow lords and companions lodged as close to the king as possible, both for fear of reprisals by

---

[1]   Literally 'sterling': an English penny of much admired, high-quality silver.
[2]   It was now early July 1327.

the English and to pay more respect to his lords. They stayed there for two days, waiting for the last of his forces to arrive and to make sure everyone had all he needed. On the third day the whole army struck camp and advanced, marching day and night until we reached the city of Durham, which stands a long day's march from the edge of the region called Northumberland, a wild land of moors and high mountains poor in everything but cattle. Winding across it is a stony, rock-strewn river called the Tyne; at the head stands the castle and city which the Welsh call Cardueil[1] and which was formerly held by King Arthur,[2] and downriver stands another called Newcastle upon Tyne. The Marshal of England[3] was stationed there with a large force of men-at-arms to protect the land against the Scots who were in the field and preparing to invade, and at Carlisle[4] was a great body of Welshmen[5] ready to defend the river-crossing, for the Scots couldn't enter the kingdom of England without crossing the Tyne, which is as wide and deep as the Ourthe.[6]

Until the King of England and his army reached Northumberland they had no news of the Scots. But then we could clearly see the smoke of the hamlets and villages they were burning – for the Scots had slipped across the river unchallenged: the men at Carlisle and Newcastle had known nothing of it, they said; and indeed, there's a distance of some fourteen English leagues[7] between Carlisle and Newcastle. But to give a better idea of what the Scots are like I'll leave the English for a moment and describe the Scots and their skilful conduct of war.

Chapter X

The nature of the Scots and their methods in war.

The Scots are exceedingly bold and fearsome fighters and have much experience of waging war, and at that time they had very little fear of the English – I don't know whether that's still the case. And when they mean to invade England their army will cover twenty or thirty[8] leagues at a stretch, by day or night. Anyone who didn't know their ways might well be amazed. The fact is that when they invade they're all mounted, except for the rabble[9] who follow them on foot; their knights and squires ride good sturdy rounceys[10] and the others little hackneys. And because of the mountainous terrain in those parts they have no baggage

---

[1]   Carlisle.
[2]   Cardueil is a place name that appears in many Arthurian romances.
[3]   The Earl Marshal, Thomas of Brotherton, Earl of Norfolk.
[4]   Le Bel continues to refer to it as 'Cardueil'; I have translated it from now on.
[5]   Perhaps, but Le Bel may be confused because of his reading of Arthurian romances, in which Cardueil frequently has Welsh connections.
[6]   The river that joins the Meuse near Le Bel's home city of Liège.
[7]   See footnote 2, above, p.35.
[8]   To be precise, the text reads (rather eccentrically) '20 or 32'.
[9]   'ribaudaille'.
[10]   The rouncey ('roncin') was a tough, multi-purpose working horse, lacking the *cachet* of the true warhorse, the '*destrier*', and costing only a fraction as much. It was generally used by squires or poorer knights.

train and carry no supplies of bread or wine; when they go to war their custom is such – and their abstinence so great – that they make do for long periods with half-raw meat (and no bread), and plain river water (no wine). And they don't bother with pots or pans: they cook their meat in leather – even in a beast's own new-flayed hide. They know they'll find plenty of cattle where they're going, so they take no provisions, except that each man carries a big flat stone between the seat and panel of his saddle and bags of flour behind him; and when they've eaten so much of this ill-cooked meat that their bellies feel tight and bloated, they throw the flat stone on the fire, mix some of the flour with water, and make little pancakes rather like the communion wafers made by the Beguine nuns,[1] and eat these to ease their stomachs. So it's no wonder the Scots cover more ground each day than others do, when, as you've heard, they're all mounted (except for the rabble) and have no carts or baggage.

In just such a fashion they'd now invaded the country and were burning and laying waste the land, and finding more livestock than they knew what to do with. They numbered three thousand heavy cavalry, knights and squires, riding good strong rounceys and coursers,[2] and fully twenty thousand other men, fierce and bold, armed in the fashion of their country and riding the smaller hackneys; and they never tether or groom them – as soon as they dismount they just send them off to graze on field or heath. And I tell you, they had two very fine captains: King Robert of Scotland was old and suffering (so it's said) from the unclean sickness, and so had appointed as their captains a most noble and worthy prince, valiant in arms, namely the Earl of Moray,[3] who bore a silver shield blazoned with three red cushions, and James, Lord Douglas,[4] who was considered the boldest and most daring knight in either kingdom; he bore a blue shield with a silver chief[5] and three red stars emblazoned on the silver. These two were the greatest lords in the whole kingdom of Scotland.

Chapter XI

How the King of England pursued the Scots who were burning and laying waste his land.

Now I'll return to my story. As soon as the King of England and his army saw the smoke described above, they realised the Scots had invaded. They immediately called everyone to arms and ordered them to strike camp and follow their banners. This was duly done; three great battalions on foot were promptly formed, and each had two wings of five hundred armoured knights who were to remain mounted. It was reckoned, truly, that we had at least seven thousand

---

[1] '*à maniere d'une oulée de beguines*': an interesting description of the early Scottish oatcake! The name has survived in the present-day wafer-thin waffle-like *béguines*.

[2] The courser ('*coursier*') was a better class of horse, fast and strong, used both for warfare and hunting.

[3] Thomas Randolph, King Robert's nephew.

[4] Known as 'Black Douglas'; Le Bel mistakenly names him William.

[5] i.e. a horizontal band across the top quarter or third of the shield.

heavy cavalry, knights and squires, and thirty thousand other troops; half of these were mounted on little hackneys and the other half were foot soldiers selected and paid for by the towns, in numbers according to each town's due; and there were twenty-four thousand archers on foot, not counting the rabble of followers. As soon as the battalions had formed we advanced in good order after the Scots, following the trails of smoke, until well past vespers. Then the army camped in a wood beside a little river, resting and waiting for the wagons and provisions to arrive. And all the while the Scots were burning the land five leagues ahead, but we couldn't catch up with them or their army.

At dawn next day everyone armed and the banners were taken to the fields and each man rallied to his battalion and banner as arranged; then the battalions advanced once more in this tight and perfect order and crossed four mountains and valleys without once getting any nearer the Scots – still busy burning the land before us – because of all the woods, bogs, wild moors and craggy mountains and valleys; but no one, on pain of beheading, dared ride ahead of his banner except the marshals.

As afternoon passed and evening approached, men and horses and carts and especially those on foot were too exhausted to go on. And the lords realised that it was all wasted effort, for it seemed the Scots were waiting till they found a good position on a mountain or in a pass where we'd be fighting at a massive disadvantage. Orders were given to make camp till morning, when a decision would have been made about the next move. So that night the whole army camped in a wood beside a little river, and the king took lodging in a poor abbey nearby. There's no need to ask if men, horses, carters and animals were weary.

When everyone had found a patch of ground for his tent, the lords held a council of war, debating how to deal with the Scots in such terrain. It seemed they were heading back to their own country, burning as they went, but there was no way of doing battle in those mountains without risking disaster and there was no overtaking them. But they had to cross the Tyne again, and if we were to rise before midnight and make better speed next day, we could bar the river-crossing and force them to fight on our terms or they'd be trapped in England. This plan was agreed, and orders went out for everyone to go back to his tent and eat what he could, and word was spread that as soon as we heard the trumpets sound we were to saddle and harness our horses; at the second trump we were to arm and at the third we were to mount without delay and rally to our banners, carrying just a single loaf of bread strapped behind us like poachers and leaving behind all our carts and baggage and other supplies, for we'd be fighting next day come what may, and all would be won or lost. These orders were duly followed, and at the stroke of midnight we were all mounted and ready, though few had slept despite our labours of the previous day. But before the battalions were properly organised day was beginning to break.

Then the banners rode forward at a furious pace over heaths and craggy mountains and valleys, without a single stretch of level ground. And these mountains and valleys were so littered with bogs and marshes and other obstacles that it's a wonder we weren't all lost there, for everyone kept riding on without waiting for his lord or companions. I tell you, if anyone did get stuck he was lucky to find anyone to help him; indeed, a good few of the carters and their horses got stranded and many a packhorse was never seen again – and other horses, too. And there were many false alarms that day: word would go out that our leading riders had engaged the enemy, and all who believed it would go charging over marsh and rock and scree, through valley and over mountain, helm on head, shield round neck, lance or sword in hand, without waiting for his father, brother or companion. And after riding half a league or more and reaching the place where they'd heard the cry they'd find they were mistaken: it had been a herd of harts or hinds or other wild beasts – they abounded in those woods and heaths – fleeing in alarm from all the banners and horsemen.

Chapter XII

How the English searched for the Scots and didn't know where they were.

And so the young king and his whole army rode all day through this mountainous wilderness without direction, guided solely by the sun, finding no road or track or any town, walled or otherwise. Late in the evening we came upon the River Tyne, which the Scots had earlier crossed and would have to cross again – so the English said. When we got there, stressed and exhausted as you can imagine, we crossed at a ford – but with a good deal of difficulty, for the bed was strewn with rocks – and then everyone went to find a patch of ground along the bank to make camp. But before we'd found anywhere darkness was setting in, and hardly anyone had an axe or wedge or anything else for cutting wood to make a shelter. And some had lost most of their companions and didn't know what had become of them. No wonder spirits were low. The foot soldiers above all had been left behind, and no one knew where or whom to ask for word of them, which is hardly surprising: those who knew the region said we'd ridden fully twenty-eight English leagues that day, having charged on without stopping, as you've heard, except to piss or to tighten a saddle-strap.

Men and horses alike were worn out; but we had to lie all night in our armour beside the river, each of us holding his horse by the reins, for it was too dark to see where to tether them – and we hadn't been able to bring our carts across that terrain, as I've told you, so they had no hay or oats or any other fodder all night. For our own part we didn't have a bite to eat all day or night except the loaf we'd strapped behind us as you've heard – so it was soaked with our horses' sweat. And we had nothing to drink but water, drunk straight from the river (though some of the lords had bottles in their baggage), and you can well imagine our mighty thirst with the heat and exertions we'd endured that day. And we had no fire or light all night and no means of making them, except for a few of the lords who'd brought torches on their packhorses. So we spent a wretched night without unsaddling or disarming.

With the coming of longed-for day, when we hoped to find comfort for ourselves and our horses and either make camp or do battle with the Scots (we couldn't wait, eager as we were to see the back of these abject, miserable conditions), it started to rain. It rained all day. It rained like fury and incessantly: by mid-afternoon the river where we'd camped was so swollen that it was impassable. So neither we nor any of the army could reconnoitre our exact position or find fodder or bedding for our horses, or bread or wine or other sustenance for ourselves. It meant an entire day and night of fasting for us, while our horses ate leaves from the trees and mouldy heath-grass. With our swords we hacked stakes – in the pouring rain – to tether them, and cut brushwood to make shelters to huddle in.

In the middle of the afternoon we found some poor folk of those parts and asked them where we were, for no one in our army knew the region or could say exactly where we'd ended up. They told us we were fourteen English leagues from Newcastle and eleven from Carlisle, and that there was no town any nearer where we could go and find provisions. This was relayed to the king and the lords, who immediately sent messengers on ponies and packhorses to fetch bread (and wine for those who had bottles), and oats for their horses. And at Newcastle a decree was made in the king's name that all who cared to earn good money should take bread, wine, fodder and other supplies to his army: they'd be paid up front and be given safe conduct. And it was made plain that the king and his army wouldn't be leaving till they knew what had become of the Scots.

Next day, around mid-afternoon, the messengers returned with all they'd managed to find in the way of bread, wine, fodder and candles and other supplies for the lords and their retainers – but it wasn't much. And with them came people seeking to exploit the situation, bringing ponies and mules with baskets of badly baked bread, big barrels of dreadful wine and other goods to sell; but it brought a good deal of relief to many in the army that day and the next and for all the days we were camped there by the river. There in the wilds we stayed for eight days, constantly awaiting the arrival of the Scots – but they didn't know what had become of us, any more than we did of them.

For a day and two nights we'd stayed by the river without bread, wine, fodder or any other supplies; and now for the next four days we had to buy poorly baked bread at six or seven pence a loaf when it wasn't worth a *parisis*,[1] and a gallon of wine cost twenty-four or twenty-six pence when it wasn't worth four. But we were so beset by hunger that men were fighting to grab it from the merchants' hands, which led to a fair few quarrels. And throughout these trials it did nothing but rain all week, so that saddles, panels and girths were rotting and falling apart, and all our horses – or most of them – had sores on their backs;[2] we had no way of re-shoeing those that had lost shoes, or of covering them with anything but our tabards. And most of us had no protection from the rain and cold except our haquetons[3] and our armour, and nothing to make fire but green wood which was of little use in the driving rain.

We spent a whole week in this miserable, wretched state in those mountains by that river, without any news whatever of the Scots who we'd imagined would have to cross there or thereabouts to return to their country. This led to much

---

[1] The *denier parisis* was theoretically the French equivalent of the English penny, but didn't match its purity of silver; indeed its size, weight and purity fluctuated markedly.

[2] I am guessing that this is what Le Bel means by '*blessiez sur le dos*' ('hurt on the back').

[3] The padded jackets worn beneath armour.

murmuring among the English: some were starting to accuse those who'd led us there of deliberately seeking to betray the king and his army. So the lords commanded that we move on and cross back over the river seven leagues upstream where it was lower and easier to ford, and the call went up at once to prepare to decamp next morning and to follow our banners. And a proclamation came from the king that there'd be a great reward for anyone bold enough: the first man to bring him news of the Scots and their exact location would be knighted by the king himself and granted an hereditable pension of a hundred marks. There was great excitement at this news; some fifteen or sixteen English knights and squires left the army in their eagerness to win the prize, crossed the river despite the danger and rode back into the mountains we'd come through; then each set out on his own, this way and that, to see what Fortune would bring.

Next morning the whole army struck camp; but we took it easy as we rode that day, for our horses were weak and in poor shape, sagging and cold-backed,[1] our saddles were rotting and falling apart and our bellies empty. Eventually we crossed the river, though it was difficult and dangerous: it was swollen with the rain and had broken its banks. Quite a few fell in and some Englishmen drowned – not that we were too bothered about that.

Once we were across we made camp nearby. It was a little better thereabouts: we found a fair bit of fodder, and spent the night in a village that the Scots had burnt – it felt like Paradise!

We left in the morning and rode all day through the mountains and valleys, following our banners, until late afternoon when we found some burnt-out hamlets amid fields of corn and grass and other crops, so we camped there that night. The next day was an exact repeat; we had no idea where we were going and no news of the Scots.

On the fourth day we struck camp early and rode on as ever. Then, some time between prime and terce,[2] with the weather quite good and the sun shining, a squire came galloping towards our battalions and said to the king:

"I bring news, my lord! The Scots are encamped on a mountain four leagues from here. They're waiting for you, not daring to move – they've been there for eight days, with no more news of you than you've had of them! I can assure you this is true and certain, for I ran straight into them and was caught and led before their lords; I told them where you were and that you were seeking them and wanted to do battle. Their lords released me at once when I said you'd promised a hundred pounds to the first man to bring you definite news of them, on condition that I promised not to rest until I'd done so! They say they're as eager to fight as you are, and you'll find them there."

---

[1] Literally 'broken-backed'.
[2] The first and third canonical hours: i.e. between about six o'clock and nine.

Chapter XIII

How young King Edward laid siege to the Scots, who were burning and laying waste his land, on a mountain.

As soon as the king and his council heard this news he ordered the whole army to halt; and there beside an abbey of white friars, known in King Arthur's time as the Blanche Lande,[1] he bade us let our horses graze in the fields and then tighten our saddle-girths to make ready. There each man made confession and his last testament, knowing he would live or die that day, and the king ordered many masses to be said to give communion to those so inclined; and to the squire who'd brought the news he amply fulfilled his promise, granting him the pension of a hundred pounds and knighting him at his own mass in the presence of all.

Once we'd rested and eaten a little the trumpet sounded; then we mounted and our banners advanced, following this new knight's directions. After him the battalions rode steadily over mountains and valleys, keeping the best order we could, until around noon we were so close to the Scots that we had a clear sight of them, and they of us. As soon as they saw us they emerged from their shelters on foot and deployed in fine array, in three good battalions, on the slope of the mountain where they were encamped. Over this mountain tumbled a fast-flowing river, so full of stones and huge rocks that we couldn't cross it without great difficulty and danger; and even if we did, there was nowhere between their lines and the river where our battalions could deploy. Moreover, the Scots had formed their first two battalions on a pair of rocky crags where there was no real possibility of mounting an attack, while they could have pelted and bombarded us with stones if we'd crossed the river, and there would have been no easy means of retreat.

When our commanders saw the Scots' position they ordered us to dismount and take off our spurs and form our three battalions as before. A good number were newly knighted then. And when the battalions were duly formed, some of the English lords led the young king to ride along our lines, to hearten the troops; he graciously appealed to each man to strive to fight well and preserve his honour; and he gave orders that no one, on pain of death, should go ahead of the banners or make any move until the command was given. It wasn't long before it came: the battalions were to advance towards the enemy at a steady walk. And so we did, each battalion advancing a fair distance to the foot of the mountain slope: this was done to see how the enemy would respond and whether they would come down from the crags. But we saw no movement at all. Our lines were now so close that we could identify many of their arms, as they could ours. We were ordered to stop while the next move was considered.

Some companions were now sent forward on coursers to skirmish and to test the river-crossing and the enemy's resolve; and word was sent via their heralds that, if they cared to cross the river and fight on level ground, we would draw back and give them space to deploy – it could be at once or next morning;

---

[1]   This is Blanchland Abbey in Northumberland, founded in 1165.

and if that wasn't to their liking, they could propose an alternative. The Scots considered this, and replied that they would do nothing whatever; it should be plain to the king and his lords that they were in his kingdom and had burnt and ravaged it, and if he didn't like it he'd have to come and sort it out, for they'd be staying as long as they wished! When the king's counsellors saw they'd have no other reply they gave orders for us to make camp exactly where we were. So we spent the night in wretched discomfort, on the hard, rough, stony ground, fully armed; and our pages could find no stakes or sticks to tether our horses, no fodder or bedding for them or ourselves, and no firewood.

When the Scots saw us camping down, they left some of their men in their battle lines while the rest retired to their shelters and made an astonishing array of blazing fires; and in the dark that night they started howling and wailing all together and blasting away on their huge horns, making such a fearful din that we thought all the demons of hell were come to devour us.

That was how we spent that night – the feast of Saint Peter,[1] August 1327 – until the lords had heard mass next morning; then we were ordered to arm and form our battalions as on the previous day. When the enemy saw this they likewise resumed their position of the day before; and the two armies stayed there until it was past noon, the Scots showing no sign of advancing towards us and we unable to mount an attack without risking dreadful losses. Some of our companions who had horses ready crossed the river to skirmish with the enemy, as did some on foot; and some of the Scots charged back and forth to join in combat, and there were men on both sides killed and wounded and taken prisoner.

In the afternoon the lords sent word that we should all go back and rest: there was no point standing there. We were only too glad – it was obvious there was nothing more we could do.

We spent three days like that, and the Scots for their part stayed on the mountain, unmoving. At all hours of the day there would be men from both sides skirmishing, and there were a good few killed and captured; and through the middle of every night the Scots would light so many fires that it was a wonder to behold, and made such a racket, blasting their horns and wailing all together, that it seemed as if all the devils of hell were gathered there.

The English lords had resolved to keep the Scots besieged on the mountain, since there was no way of doing battle; they thought they'd starve them out, as no supplies could reach them and they certainly couldn't leave, and the English had learnt from the prisoners they'd taken that they had no bread or wine or salt. They did have plenty of cattle, however, plundered from the country, and they could eat these boiled or roast as they chose – it doesn't greatly bother them if it's without bread or salt, as long as they have a little flour which they use in the way I described earlier. Some of the English in our army were using it in the same fashion, and were happy to sell us some when we'd run out of bread.

When we woke on the fourth day and looked towards the mountain where our enemies were encamped, there was no one to be seen: the Scots had departed

---

[1]   In the pre-1960 Roman calendar the feast of St Peter in Chains was 1 August.

in the middle of the night. Our lords were baffled: they couldn't think what had become of them. They immediately sent men over the mountains, both on horseback and on foot, to find out where they'd gone; and around prime[1] they were found camped on another mountain just two leagues from the one they'd left. They were by the river as before but in an even stronger position, encamped in a wood to give them cover, so that they could come and go in secret when they wished. As soon as they'd been found we were told to strike camp and take ourselves and all our gear to another mountain directly facing them. Then we formed our battle line and made as if to advance, but as soon as they saw us coming they left their shelters and smartly planted themselves close to the opposite bank of the river; but they wouldn't cross to meet us, and attacking them was impossible: we would all have been miserably slaughtered or captured.

So there we encamped, confronting them on that second mountain, for eighteen days in all. Every day we'd draw up our lines to face them, and they to face us; but they wouldn't cross the river to meet us, or give ground on their side to allow us to deploy, or accept our offer of ground on our side where they could do the same. And all the while they had no bread, no wine, no salt, and no leather or material to make hose or shoes: instead they made shoes out of raw cowhide, the hair still attached. Not that we were much better off: we had nowhere to lodge or shelter, and nowhere to forage but moor and heath. I can't tell you how frustrated we were about our tents and tools and baggage-carts: we'd bought them to make our lives easier and then had left them in a wood, unguarded, with no way of recovering them – we didn't even know where the wood was!

We spent a month in this abject, miserable state, with all our supplies missing when we needed them most. It's true that provisions were daily brought for sale from all directions throughout the time we were besieging the Scots and were stuck there facing them – but at what a price! A badly baked loaf (of low-grade grain) cost three pence when it would have been worth just a *parisis* in the town, and a gallon of warm, poor-quality wine cost twelve when a barrelful would have been worth but three. We had to feed ourselves and our pages very sparingly, constantly fearing greater hunger still and that our money would run out if we had to stay much longer.

The first night that our lords were camped on this second mountain, Sir James[2] Douglas, who was most valiant, courageous and daring, set off at about midnight with two hundred cavalry, crossed the river well away from our army to keep the manoeuvre secret, and boldly burst into the English host crying:

"Douglas! Douglas! You're all going to die, my English masters!"

And indeed, he and his company killed more than three hundred, and galloped up to the king's own tent – still howling and bawling "Douglas! Douglas!" – and cut through two or three of the ropes.[3]

---

[1] The first canonical hour of the day, about 6 o'clock.
[2] As before, Le Bel mistakenly names him William (James Douglas had both a father and a son named William).
[3] This is a description of the action that took place at Stanhope, in the Pennines in Weardale, on the night of 4 August 1327. It is sometimes rather grandly referred to as the Battle of Stanhope Park.

We spent twenty-two days in all on those two mountains, confronting the Scots. There was constant skirmishing between those so inclined, and almost every day we'd draw up and face each other once or twice; and very often, the moment we retired and disarmed, there'd be a fresh cry of "To arms! The Scots are coming!" and we'd have to arm again and rush to wherever it was. And after the raid by Sir James Douglas described above, we had to have constables[1] patrolling each night on three sides of the army with two hundred of our cavalry in each watch; for every day the English lords were given to believe that the enemy were preparing a night attack upon our army, being unable to stay as they were and endure starvation. This news kept us well alert, adding strain and tension to the dearth we were suffering. And we foreigners had even more on our plate: we had to keep a double watch – one on patrol with the English lords against the Scots, and the other back in camp against the English archers! They hated us more than they did the Scots! They made that very clear, often cursing us for the battle we'd had with them at York, as you've heard, and calling us murderers. So we had plenty to worry about, both day and night: we were in permanent fear of the Scots, so close at hand, and of the archers, camped among us and full of threats. And then there was the fear of starving and even greater hardship because of the continuing deadlock.

On the eighteenth day a Scottish knight, captured in a skirmish, resisted telling our lords anything about the enemy's position; but he did reveal how, that morning, their commanders had agreed that all the Scots should arm that evening and follow the banner of Sir James Douglas wherever he led them, and with all possible secrecy, but none of the knights knew for certain what he was planning. The English lords discussed this, and said that the Scots might well be coming to attack us from two sides: perhaps they'd decided to do or die, being unable to endure their hunger any more. So our lords commanded that each of our battalions should take up a position in front of our encampment on three separate stretches of ground; and we were to light great fires in each place so that we could see one another more clearly, and were to sleep armed and in position to await whatever God had in store and to be ready all together; our pages were to stay where we'd camped to look after the horses. Such was the order, and so it was done: everyone lay all night armed and in position, in front of the fires and beneath the banners, with his head on his companion's legs or backside.

At break of day two Scottish trumpeters ran into one of our patrols; they were captured and led before the lords and the king's counsellors and said:

"What are you keeping watch for, sirs? You're wasting your time! We swear by our lives the Scots all left before midnight! They're already four or five leagues away! They took us with them for a league so that we wouldn't let you know too soon, and then gave us leave to come and tell you!"

Hearing this, the lords realised they'd guessed quite wrongly; and they said, too, that chasing after the Scots was pointless – we'd never overtake them. But in case of trickery, they placed the two trumpeters under close guard and ordered

---

[1] The constable ('*connestable*') was an important member of a medieval household, effectively a 'security officer', organising protection and maintaining order.

us to hold our positions till the first hour of the day. Then everyone retired to camp to rest while the lords met to consider the next move.

Meanwhile some of the companions, myself among them, mounted our rounceys and crossed the river and climbed the mountain, steep and rugged, to take a look at the Scots' encampment. There we found more than five hundred big, fine, fat cattle newly killed: the Scots had slaughtered them because they'd have been too slow to follow them and they didn't want to leave them alive for the English. We found more than four hundred cauldrons, too, made of raw, hairy hide, hanging over the fires and full of meat and water ready for boiling, and more than a thousand spits laden with meat to be roasted, and more than ten thousand old, worn out shoes made of the same raw leather, the hair still on it: all this they'd abandoned. And we found five poor prisoners left by the Scots in the wood, shamefully bound to the trees stark naked, and two of them had had their legs broken. We didn't know what to say to them; we just untied them and let them go and rode back to our quarters.

We arrived there to find everyone striking camp, preparing to return to England by the lords' command. It was a great relief, though we were aggrieved at leaving with so little done after enduring so much hardship. Be that as it may, we all decamped and followed the banners all that day until evening, when we made camp in a beautiful meadow where we found good foraging: we needed it, as did our horses, which were so miserably cold and hungry, and so bruised and chafed by the rotting tack, that we could barely make them move or even sit on them: we had no panels or girths, cruppers or bridles that weren't broken and perished – most of us had to make panels of old doublets or tunics if we could find them, to cushion our saddles and stop the chafing of the girths. On top of all that, most of our horses were unshod for want of iron and farriers:[1] more than once I saw a horseshoe nail being sold for six pence. It's fair to say that, given all the setbacks and troubles and trials of the first campaign and this second one, no prince as young as our king had undertaken two campaigns as tough, as testing and as dangerous as these had been, and both were started and completed in a single year, when he was only sixteen. Such was the view of all the worthiest and most experienced men in our army.

And so we camped that night in this beautiful meadow beside a handsome park, and made ourselves as comfortable as we could – God knows we needed a bit of comfort – and slept a little more soundly.

Next morning we decamped and rode at an easy pace all day to spare our horses, until at vespers we reached a great abbey two leagues from the city of Durham. The king lodged that night inside and we and all the army camped in the surrounding meadow, where we found plenty of grass and vetch and corn. The army stayed and rested there next day, while the king and the lords went to see the city and the church of Durham, where the king received the homage of the bishop and the citizens, which he hadn't yet done. And there in the city we found our carts and wagons and all the gear that we'd left, as you've heard, in

---

[1] 'mareschal'. The 'marshal' was a high-ranking servant responsible for the care and management of horses in a household, and he would often be a skilled farrier.

a wood at midnight three weeks earlier! The citizens of Durham had rescued them at their own expense and stored them in empty barns, with an identifying pennon on each cart. There's no need to ask if we were pleased! All our clothes and belongings were in those wagons, and we had nothing to wear but our doublets, stinking with sweat and rain, and filthy, threadbare hose.

Next morning we hitched our draught horses to the carts and set off after the king and the lords. Three days later we arrived at the fine city of York, where the Queen was awaiting her son's return, and we all went back to the lodgings we'd left earlier. But before we reached York all the English departed and set off to their homes and lands, except some of the knights, who remained behind to accompany the king. We stayed in the city for six days after our return, and the noble knight Sir John of Hainault and all his company were fêted and highly honoured by the king, his court, the Queen and everyone, especially by the ladies present. And each man drew up an account of his expenses, and of horses lost or spent; and the king promised to repay all debts to Sir John who then made undertakings to his companions, for the king could not immediately raise enough money to pay for the cost of all the horses. But we were given a fair amount to cover our return home, and we were all repaid in full for our horses within the year.

We traded in our horses and bought little hackneys to carry us home, and sent our pages with our heavy gear and tents and baggage for which we'd no further use and told them to load them aboard a vessel that the king made available to us, and they put to sea with it all and landed at Sluys.

Meanwhile our lords and all of us took leave of King Edward and the Queen and the other lords, and the king gave us an escort of twelve knights to see us to Dover, for fear of the English and the archers who hated us and hurled threats at us when we parted: that's why we were armed throughout our ride across the kingdom to Dover. There we found vessels and ships made ready at the king's command, and we crossed to Wissant with all the speed we could summon: we couldn't wait to be home after all the hostility we'd suffered from the English and all the hardship we'd endured.

And once we'd landed at Wissant we took leave of each other with the greatest respect and courtesy and went our separate ways.

Chapter XIV

How the noble King Edward was married to the daughter of the Count of Hainault.

Not long after this great and taxing campaign, the noble king, my lady the Queen his mother, his uncle the Earl of Kent, Henry Earl of Lancaster, Lord Roger Mortimer and the other barons of England who remained as his counsellors, discussed the question of his marriage. They sent a bishop, two bannerets and two able clerks to Sir John of Hainault to ask for his help and guidance in arranging the marriage of the noble king, that he might pave the way for his brother, my lord Count William of Hainault, Holland and Zeeland, to send the king one of his daughters, for the king would love her more dearly on his account than any other lady.

That noble knight Sir John of Hainault welcomed this embassy with all his customary warmth and generosity; then he escorted them to my lord his brother at Valenciennes, who received them with the utmost honour and entertained them so magnificently that it would take a fair while to record. After this grand reception they delivered their message as bidden, most eloquently and exactly. The worthy and noble count replied promptly and most courteously, with guidance from his brother Sir John and my lady the countess (mother of the damsel in question), expressing the deepest thanks to my lord the king and his mother the Queen and all the lords for paying them the honour of sending such an illustrious embassy, and agreeing most gladly to their request, if our holy father the Pope and holy church permitted. This reply was most satisfactory, and the two knights and two clerks were sent at once to the holy father at Avignon to seek approval for the marriage: it couldn't take place without papal dispensation because the king and the count's daughter were closely related, being connected in the third degree – their mothers were first cousins, being daughters of two brothers.

Soon after their arrival in Avignon their mission was accomplished, the holy father and the college of cardinals consenting most happily in view of the high nobility of both parties. As soon as the embassy returned to Valenciennes with the papal bulls[1] the marriage was confirmed, and the count's daughter was provided with all the noble apparel befitting a damsel who was about to be Queen of England. She was then betrothed by virtue of a procuration[2] brought to her from the King of England, and was duly sent on her way to London to meet her husband who was waiting there to crown her.[3] She was escorted to London by the noble knight Sir John of Hainault, her uncle, who was mightily honoured and fêted by the king, my lady the Queen mother and all the ladies and barons of England. There's no need to ask if London was filled with celebration; there was a great host of noble lords, dukes, earls, barons, knights, and high-born ladies and maidens, richly bedecked and attired, for whose sake there was much jousting and tourneying,[4] and dances and music and glorious banquets every day: anyone who knows what befits true nobility would expect no less. And these festivities continued for a full three weeks until Sir John departed.

At the end of these three weeks he set off with all his company, laden with fine gifts bestowed from all sides, leaving the young queen with few of her fellow countrymen except a young gentleman named Walter Mauny, who stayed behind to serve her and to wait on her at table,[5] and who later gained such favour

---

[1]   The bull granting papal consent for the marriage is dated 30 August 1327.

[2]   Letters from Edward III dated 8 October 1327 gave the Bishop of Coventry permission to confirm the betrothal to Philippa of Hainault in Edward's name.

[3]   Edward and Philippa were married at York on 25 or 26 January 1328; Philippa was in fact not crowned until February 1330.

[4]   'bouhourder': the 'behourd' was 'one of the most popular means of training [a squire] before he attained knighthood', but it was also 'often held in conjunction with knighting ceremonies, coronations, royal marriages...[and seems to have been] a small-scale informal tournament'. Juliet Barker, *The Tournament in England, 1100-1400* (Woodbridge, 1986), pp. 148-9.

[5]   Literally 'to cut her meat'.

with the king and all his barons that he was welcomed into the most privy and august council of the land; and in time he achieved countless feats of prowess in many places, and so many bold missions – some of which you'll hear recounted in this book – that he was deemed the worthiest knight known.[1] And he should indeed be considered the most valiant of all, after the noble King Edward and the worthy Duke of Lancaster, who surpass all others in deeds and renown.

But for a moment I shall leave this matter and turn my attention to another.

Chapter XV

How the good King Robert of Scotland entrusted Sir James[2] Douglas with carrying his heart to the Holy Sepulchre.

After the Scots, as you've heard, slipped away by night from the mountain where the king and the English lords were besieging them, they rode twenty-two leagues from that wild place without stopping, and crossed the Tyne near Carlisle and returned to their own land next day and all set off for home. Fairly soon after, a number of lords and worthy gentlemen negotiated on behalf of the King of England and his council and the Scottish king, and agreed a truce to last for a term of three years.

It was in this time of truce that King Robert of Scotland, who had been so valiant, grew ever older and weaker – afflicted with leprosy, it was said – and was clearly close to death. When he saw that his death was imminent he summoned all his most trusted barons to him and said he was about to die as they could see; and he earnestly implored them to fulfil their loyal duty and protect the kingdom during the minority of his son David, and obey him when he was come of age and crown him king and arrange a fitting marriage. Then he called to the noble knight James Douglas and said to him in the hearing of all:

"Sir James, my knight and friend, you know I've had much to deal with in my time, and have suffered much in upholding this kingdom's rights. When I was most hard-pressed of all I made a vow which I've not fulfilled, and that failure weighs upon me: I vowed that, if I could bring my wars to a successful end so that I could rule the kingdom in peace, I would go to the Holy Land and fight with fervent strength against the enemies of Our Lord and those opposed to the Christian faith. My heart was ever set on this, but it was not Our Lord's will: He gave me much to do in my time, and now, at the last, has afflicted me with weakness and such grave sickness that I'm dying as you see. Since my body cannot go and achieve what my heart so desired, I wish to send that heart in the body's place to accomplish my desire and pledge. I know of no one in my kingdom more valiant than you or more capable of fulfilling my vow, so I earnestly entreat you, knight most dearly loved, to undertake this journey for

[1] Walter Mauny (1310-72), whose name is often but incorrectly transcribed as Manny, was a Hainaulter who became a major figure on the English side in the opening decades of the Hundred Years War. He is also famous as a founder of the London Charterhouse.
[2] Throughout this chapter and the following Le Bel continues, as before, to refer to him mistakenly as William.

my sake, to absolve my soul from my debt to Our Lord. Such is my faith in your nobility and loyalty that, if you accept this task, I know you will never fail; so if you'll give me your word I shall die more at ease. It must be thus: as soon as I die, I want you to take my heart and have it well embalmed; then take as much from my treasury as you think is needed to complete your mission, allowing for all those you wish to accompany you, and carry my heart to the Holy Sepulchre where Our Lord was laid to rest, since my body cannot go there. Do this in the style and with the escort and all the requisites befitting your station; and everywhere you go, let it be known that you're carrying the King of Scotland's heart as his envoy, since his body is unable to make the journey."

All those present began to weep bitterly. When Sir James was able to speak he replied:

"My noble lord, a thousand thanks for paying me this great honour, for entrusting me with such an illustrious task and such a dear treasure. Have no fear: with all my heart I will gladly do all in my power to fulfil your command, unworthy though I am of such a mission."

"Ah, noble knight," said the king, "thanks indeed! But you must swear it."

"Willingly, my lord," said Sir James, and there and then he gave him his solemn word as a loyal knight.

Then the king said: "God be praised, for now I shall die in greater peace, knowing that the ablest and most valiant knight in my kingdom will achieve what I never could."

Not long after this the noble King of Scotland passed from this world and was buried with all due honour,[1] according to the customs of that land, and his heart was removed and embalmed as he had commanded. And that noble knight Sir James Douglas began to make provision and preparation to set out on his promised mission when the time and season came.

It was only a little later that the noble and valiant Earl of Moray also passed from this world; he was the greatest and most powerful lord in the kingdom of Scotland, and bore a silver shield blazoned with three gold cushions.

Chapter XVI

How Sir James Douglas set out on his journey from Scotland.

With the coming of spring and the right season for crossing the high seas, the noble knight Sir James Douglas, having made the necessary provision, set sail from Scotland as bidden and made his way straight to Sluys in Flanders, to see if any from this side of the water were preparing to journey to the holy land of Jerusalem so that he could go with a greater company. He stayed at Sluys for twelve days before he set out again, but in all that time he never set foot on land; he remained on board, sitting in state with music of trumpets and drums as if he'd been the King of Scotland himself. In his company he had a knight banneret and six more of the noblest lords of the kingdom, and fully twenty fine

---

[1] Robert Bruce died on 7 June 1329, and was buried at Dunfermline.

young squires, the ablest he could find in Scotland, not to mention the rest of his household; and he had a vast array of silver plate – bowls, basins, platters, cups – and bottles and barrels and so forth, and all who went to visit him, provided they were men of rank, were lavishly served with two kinds of wine and two kinds of spiced wine also.

A few days into his stay Douglas heard that the Spanish king[1] was at war with the King of Granada,[2] a Saracen, and he resolved to head that way to make his journey all the more worthwhile: once he was done with his business there he would cross the sea to fulfil his mission. So he set sail from Sluys and made his way to Spain. He landed first at the port of Valencia, and then rode to join the Spanish king who was already in the field against the King of Granada: the two armies were close to meeting on the border between their lands. Soon after Douglas's arrival, the day came when the Spanish king advanced towards his enemy; the King of Granada advanced likewise, until the two kings could clearly see each other's banners and began to form their battalions to confront one another. Sir James Douglas set himself on one flank to make a more telling contribution and a better show. Then, seeing the battalions deployed and the king's line begin to move, he thought they were about to engage. Always preferring to be in the vanguard rather than the rear, he spurred forward with his whole company and charged towards the King of Granada's battalion, imagining that the Spanish king and all his army were following. But he was sorely mistaken: they never stirred that day, and Sir James and all his company were surrounded by the enemy and slaughtered to a man – not a single one escaped – which was much to the shame and discredit of the Spanish.[3]

It was shortly after Sir James Douglas set sail from Scotland on his pilgrimage that a number of lords, wishing to nurture the peace between the English and the Scots, negotiated and secured the marriage of King David of Scotland and the King of England's sister, both of whom were very young.[4]

Chapter XVII

How King Charles of France died and Lord Philip of Valois, by common accord, was crowned King of France.

Now you have heard how a truce was soundly established between the kings of England and Scotland, and how the Scottish king passed from this world having commissioned and instructed the worthiest lord of his kingdom to carry his heart to the Holy Sepulchre because his body couldn't make the journey,

---

[1]   Alfonso XI of Castile.
[2]   Muhammed IV, Sultan of Granada.
[3]   Le Bel has here described the death of Douglas at the Battle of Teba in Andalucia, August 1330. It is here, according to legend, that 'the Black' Douglas flung Robert Bruce's heart into the enemy lines and cried: "Now pass thou onward before us, as thou wert wont, and I will follow thee or die!" It is interesting that Le Bel, despite his appetite for tales of chivalrous deeds, appears to have had no knowledge of this.
[4]   Le Bel's chronology is incorrect: the marriage of young David and Edward III's sister Joan took place in July 1328, almost a year before Robert Bruce's death.

and how Sir James Douglas set out on this pilgrimage and how he and all his company were killed. Now I shall turn to another story: that is, of King Charles of France, uncle of the young King Edward of England, for it is relevant to our main theme.

This King Charles was married three times but died without male issue, which was to prove a grave misfortune for the kingdom as you'll hear in due course. The first of his wives was one of the most beautiful ladies in the world and was the daughter of the Countess of Artois;[1] but she was unfaithful to her marriage vows and spent a long while wretchedly imprisoned at Château-Gaillard[2] before her husband became king. When he'd succeeded to the throne and been crowned, the twelve peers and the barons of France didn't wish the kingdom to remain without a male heir if they could avoid it. They sought a way of arranging King Charles's marriage to the daughter of the Emperor, Henry of Luxembourg, and sister of the noble King of Bohemia;[3] so they had his first marriage – to the lady still imprisoned – dissolved and annulled by papal decree. By this second wife from Luxembourg, a most modest and worthy lady, the king had a son who died in infancy, and the mother died soon after, at Issoudun-en-Berry; and they both died somewhat suspiciously: a number of people were secretly charged. King Charles was now married for a third time, to the daughter of his own uncle, the noble Count of Évreux, and sister of the King of Navarre.[4] In time this lady became pregnant, but the king fell sick and was on his death-bed. When he realised his death was imminent he ruled that, if the Queen gave birth to a son, then Lord Philip of Valois, his cousin german, should be regent of France until the boy came of age to be king; and if the child was a girl, then the twelve peers and the other barons of France should discuss the matter and give the kingdom to the one they deemed the most rightful claimant. King Charles subsequently died, in the year 1328, about the month of March.[5]

Not long after, the Queen gave birth to a daughter,[6] to the dismay and distress of most of the kingdom. The peers and the other lords assembled at Paris as soon as they could, and unanimously agreed to give the kingdom to Lord Philip of Valois; they rejected the claim of the Queen of England,[7] the surviving sister of the recently deceased King Charles, because they said the kingdom of France was of such high nobility that it should not pass in succession to a female, as you heard earlier at the beginning of this book. Lord Philip was crowned at Reims on Trinity Sunday in the year of grace 1328;[8] this led to mighty wars and upheavals in the kingdom of France, as you'll discover later in this book, if it comes to be completed.

---

[1] Charles's first wife was Blanche, second daughter of Count Eudes IV of Burgundy and Mahaut of Artois.
[2] Richard the Lionheart's famous stronghold overlooking the Seine.
[3] Marie, elder daughter of Henry VII, Holy Roman Emperor, and sister of King John of Bohemia.
[4] Jeanne, third daughter of Louis d'Évreux and sister of Philip III of Navarre.
[5] Charles IV died on 1 February 1328.
[6] Blanche, born on 1 April.
[7] i.e. Edward's mother Isabella.
[8] 29 May 1328.

Chapter XVIII

How King Philip of France defeated the Flemings at the hill of Cassel.

Soon after his coronation King Philip summoned his princes, barons and all his men-at-arms and marched in full strength to camp in the valley of Cassel to do battle with the Flemings, especially those of Bruges, Ypres and Franck,[1] who had rebelled against their lord the Count of Flanders[2] and driven him from his land: the only place he could stay was Ghent, and even there not all were on his side. In the battle that followed, King Philip defeated an army of sixteen thousand men, who had taken up a position on the hill of Cassel to defend the border thereabouts, on the orders (and in the pay) of their cities.

I'll tell you how these Flemings that day tried to overcome the king and his army. At supper time they slipped in silence from the hill, having formed three divisions; one went straight to the king's tents and almost caught him just as he was eating, along with all his household; the second body headed for the noble King of Bohemia and found him in much the same position; and the third attacked the noble Count of Hainault, taking him and his brother Sir John so by surprise that their men barely had time to arm. So sudden was their coming that all the lords would have been killed but for God's miraculous aid; but by the grace and will of God they crushed each of the enemy battalions, all at once, all at the same time, so utterly that of those sixteen thousand Flemings not a thousand remained, though our lords knew nothing of each other's position till the battle was over. But of the fifteen thousand Flemings who were left there dead not a single one had turned his back: all were struck down in three huge piles, on the very spots where each battle had been fought. This took place in the month of August in the year of grace 1328.[3]

Chapter XIX

How Lord Robert of Artois was forced into exile from France.

The man who helped more than anyone in the world to bring King Philip to the French throne was Lord Robert of Artois. He was one of the greatest barons of France, of the highest lineage and royal extraction. He was married to King Philip's sister, and had always been his special and privy companion – which had made him a feared figure before King Philip was crowned. For three years this Lord Robert remained his chief counsellor: he was behind everything that was done, and nothing was done without him. But then the king took against him, on account of a case brought before the king relating to succession to the county of Artois,[4] which Lord Robert planned to win by means of an allegedly forged

---

[1] Franck (or 'Le Franc') was the coastal region of Flanders to the east of Calais, encompassing Dunkirk, Bourbourg, Bergues and Veurne.
[2] Louis I, Count of Flanders, Nevers and Rethel.
[3] On the eve of St Bartholomew, 23 August.
[4] Robert was disputing the succession with his cousin Jeanne, Countess of Burgundy.

document. Had the king been able to arrest him he would undoubtedly have had him hanged, even though he was one of the most closely related of all the magnates of France and his own brother-in-law. Lord Robert had to flee France, taking refuge in Namur with the young Count John and his brother, who were his sister's children.

When the king realised he'd escaped and gone into exile, he had Robert's wife – his own sister – arrested, along with her children, and kept under close guard: indeed he held them so fast and so long that the lady died in prison.[1] And after their mother's death – and their father Lord Robert's – the king kept the children imprisoned until they were old enough to become knights, in fact almost till the time of his own death;[2] and no matter what anyone said, heedless of any argument and regardless of their close kinship, he wouldn't change his mind: he confiscated all their property and kept them in wretched imprisonment as if they'd been thieves or murderers.

Next he sent word to the young Count John and his brother, telling them that, if they valued his love, they shouldn't harbour their uncle Lord Robert or he would defy them and all their land. He then persuaded the Bishop of Liège, Adolph de la Marck,[3] to defy them on his behalf; so Count John and his brother dared no longer keep the company of their uncle Lord Robert or let him stay in their land. In great alarm he fled to Brabant, for the Duke of Brabant was very powerful and he was so close to his children that he would surely not fail him. The king learned of this and sent word to the duke that, if he harboured Lord Robert in his land or supported him in any way, he would consider him his enemy and wage war on him with all his might. The duke no longer dared protect Lord Robert for fear of the king, but sent him to secret quarters at Argenteau-sur-Meuse while he waited to see what the king would do. But the king got wind of this – he had spies everywhere – and was filled with rage; and with the help of gold and silver he soon ensured that the noble King of Bohemia (the duke's own cousin), the Bishop of Liège, the Archbishop of Cologne, the Duke of Guelders, the Margrave of Jülich, the Count of Loon, the lord of Valkenburg,[4] the Count of Bar (also cousin german of the duke by their mothers, both sisters of the King of England), Sir John of Hainault and the young Count of Namur and his brother were all allied against the said duke. At the king's prompting they defied him and immediately entered his land, burning at will, and marched through Hesbaye destroying all in their path. Twice they invaded, staying as long as they pleased. And the king sent with them his Constable the Count of Eu and a large force, to make it clear that the campaign was undertaken at his behest. With his land in flames the Duke of Brabant negotiated a truce, by the intercession of the noble Count of

---

[1]   Robert's wife Jeanne was imprisoned – either at Chinon or Château-Gaillard – in 1334. She died, not in prison, in July 1363. King Philip frequently changed the place of the sons' imprisonment and their guardians.

[2]   The sons – Jean, Charles and Louis – were finally released, along with their mother, by King John II shortly after his coronation in 1350.

[3]   'Aust de la Marche'.

[4]   Here and elsewhere Le Bel uses the French name 'Fauquemont'. Valkenburg is in the province of Limburg, Holland.

Hainault. The duke placed himself entirely at the command of the king and his council, promising to do whatever the king and the allied lords required.

In consequence Lord Robert dared remain in France or Germany no longer, either openly or in hiding; and he made his way, as covertly as possible, to the noble King of England, who welcomed him gladly into his household and council and assigned to him the earldom of Richmond in England, which had belonged to his forebears.[1] Then the noble King Edward discussed with Lord Robert the rightful claim he had to the French crown; and it was partly on Lord Robert's advice that the king undertook the war for the kingdom of France, which has led to so many ills.

But I shall say no more about King Philip of France and Lord Robert until due time; now I shall turn my attention once more to King Edward.

Chapter XX

How King Edward ordered the executions of his uncle the
Earl of Kent and Lord Mortimer.

You've heard how the noble King Edward was married to the Count of Hainault's daughter; now you need to know something of how he governed. Know, then, that after he'd won back his kingdom and destroyed the Despensers, under whose influence his father had ruled so badly and he and his mother had been forced to leave and go to France as if banished, he was guided for a long time by my lady his mother, the Earl of Kent and Lord Roger Mortimer: these three were his foremost counsellors (along with a number of other knights, clerks and laymen), because those two lords had been driven into exile with him.

But eventually a rivalry began to grow between the noble Earl of Kent, a most worthy and likeable gentleman, and Lord Mortimer, a strikingly strong and impressive knight who, rumour had it, was intimate with the king's mother both in secret and otherwise. This rivalry intensified to such a point that Lord Mortimer, encouraged by the Queen Mother, persuaded and convinced the king to beware of the Earl of Kent, for he meant to imprison him and put him to death in order to take the kingdom, for he was the next in line after him, the king's young brother John of Eltham having recently died.[2] The young king was easily swayed – as young lords often readily believe those who are inclined to give bad advice rather than good – and had his uncle the earl arrested and publicly beheaded:[3] no protest of innocence was of any avail. Everyone in the land, noble and non-noble alike, was greatly troubled and distressed by this, and turned

---

[1] This is incorrect: the earldom of Richmond had been, and remained, in the family of the dukes of Brittany. But letters dated 23 April 1337 gave Robert of Artois use of the castles of Guildford, Wallingford and Somerton and hunting rights in the park at Guildford, and on 5 May he was awarded an annual pension of twelve hundred marks.

[2] This is incorrect: John of Eltham didn't die until October 1334, campaigning with Edward in Scotland. The charge made against the Earl of Kent was that he had spread a rumour that Edward II was still alive, and was conspiring to restore him to the throne.

[3] He was arrested at Winchester on 13 March 1330 and executed six days later.

very much against Lord Mortimer, feeling sure that it was at his prompting and instigation that the noble earl, considered by all to be a good and loyal man, had suffered this fate.

Then, soon after, a dreadful rumour started – whether it was true I don't know – that the Queen Mother was pregnant, and Lord Mortimer more than anyone was suspected of being the father. The rumour spread like wildfire until the young king was made fully aware of it; and he was assured, too, that it was solely through the malicious envy of Lord Mortimer that he'd been led to order the execution of his uncle the Earl of Kent, whom the whole country considered a most worthy lord. There's no need to ask if the king was upset and angry. He had Mortimer arrested at once and taken to London before a great gathering of his kingdom's barons, and he told the whole assembly of the deeds and works of Lord Mortimer as they had been presented to him, many of which were manifestly true; and he asked them to decide what sentence should be passed on a man guilty of such behaviour. Judgement was clear and swift, for they'd all been aware of the scandalous rumours before the king had known anything; and the sentence passed was that Mortimer should die in the same way as the Lord Hugh Despenser. And so it was done:[1] he was dragged through the streets of London on a hurdle and tied to a ladder at the place of execution; they severed his penis and testicles, cut open his belly, pulled out his entrails and burnt them, cut off his head and strung him up by the legs. Then the young king gave orders for his mother to be confined in a handsome castle, with ladies and maids and a household and squires enough to guard and serve her and keep her company, and assigned to her an ample estate to provide for her needs for the rest of her life. But he wouldn't allow her to leave the castle or be seen in public, so I heard, and I believe she's still there to this day.[2]

Chapter XXI

How young King Edward resumed war against the young King David of Scotland, his brother-in-law.

After King Edward, still in his youth, had administered these two most notable executions and confined the Queen his mother as you've heard, he formed a new council of the wisest and most respected men in all his land and governed with great distinction, maintaining peace in the realm with their sound guidance. And he arranged frequent jousts and tournaments and assemblies of ladies, and won great respect throughout his kingdom and great renown in every land.

---

[1] On 29 November 1330.
[2] The story of her permanent incarceration (supposedly at Castle Rising in Norfolk) is a great exaggeration: Isabella was placed under house arrest at Berkhampstead in November, but celebrated Christmas with Edward at Windsor and subsequently 'was never imprisoned... She was a frequent visitor to the court ... joining in [Edward's] hunting parties, attending religious ceremonies with him, and watching his tournaments. By 1348 she was again considered sufficiently respectable to represent Edward in diplomatic negotiations with France.' Ian Mortimer, *The Perfect King* (London, 2006), pp.330-1.

He continued this noble rule during the period of truce between himself and the kingdom of Scotland. But when this truce expired, he was offended at hearing that the young King David had taken possession of the city of Berwick – which rightly belonged to his kingdom and which the good King Edward[1] had always held freely and in peace (as had his father[2] for a good while after) – and also that King David, his brother-in-law, had not yet recognised the Scottish kingdom as a fiefdom of the English crown and paid him due homage for it. He at once sent great delegations to young King David and his council to request that he relinquish the fine city of Berwick, for it was his rightful inheritance and had always belonged to the kings of England his predecessors, and that he should come and pay him homage for the kingdom of Scotland which he ought to hold as his vassal. Young King David deliberated for a long while with his barons and countrymen, and after taking their advice at length he responded thus to King Edward's embassy:

"Sirs, I and all my barons are very surprised that my brother-in-law the King of England should make such a request, for we find no precedent for the kingdom of Scotland owing homage or anything else to the King of England. My father King Robert never paid homage to any previous kings of England however hard they waged war on him – and they tried hard enough! So neither I nor my council see any reason why I should, and I've no intention of doing so. As for the city of Berwick, my father won it in fair fight from King Edward's father, and held it as his rightful possession throughout his life; I mean to do likewise – I'll do all in my power to keep it. So I pray you, tell my brother-in-law the King of England to let me enjoy the same liberties as my forebears and keep the prizes won by my father in open war which he held in peace all his life. And let him not be led astray by malicious advice – indeed, if anyone meant me harm or wrong he should lend me aid and support for the sake of my wife, his sister!"

"My lord," said the messengers, "your response to our request is clear; we shall faithfully report it to the king."

And they took their leave and returned to the king with full details of the Scottish response. It greatly displeased both king and council, and he summoned all the barons and knights and aldermen of all the cities and towns of his land to assemble in London on the day when Parliament was due to meet, to discuss and fully debate the matter.

It was at this time that Lord Robert of Artois, who had earned the hatred of the King of France and been driven from France, Flanders, Brabant, Germany and Liège as you've heard, arrived in England disguised as a merchant, and came straight to King Edward and made himself known to him, being closely related as he was; and he explained how he was so hated by the French king that he could find no land or lord or country that dared to harbour him, and so had fled to him as a kinsman whom he would gladly serve. The noble King Edward felt great sympathy when he heard of his troubles and plight, and said he wouldn't fail him even if the rest of the world did; he gave him the freedom of his land and his castles, granted him the earldom of Richmond for his maintenance – it had

---

[1]   i.e. Edward I.
[2]   i.e. young Edward's father, Edward II.

belonged to his forefathers[1] and was currently held by the king in the absence of a vassal lord – and made him a member of his council.

When the day of Parliament came and all the dignitaries he'd summoned had gathered in London, the king ordered that his request to his brother-in-law the King of Scotland – to yield the city of Berwick which he was wrongfully holding, and to come and pay due homage for the kingdom of Scotland – should be read to them, followed by the Scottish king's response. He asked them all how he should proceed for the preservation of his honour. The barons, knights and aldermen from all the cities of the land debated this and declared with one accord that he should not tolerate the King of Scotland's offences, but should raise an army strong enough to invade Scotland, recapture the good city of Berwick (which had always belonged to his ancestors) and make the Scottish king only too happy to pay him homage and give him satisfaction; and they said they were all ready to go with him and to do his bidding. The noble King Edward was delighted by their response and his people's willing support and he thanked them deeply; and he bade them all be ready, each man according to his station, to meet him on an appointed day at Newcastle-upon-Tyne to go and recover his kingdom's rights and possessions. They all obeyed his request and returned home to make their preparations, each according to his rank. The king prepared likewise, and sent a second delegation to his brother-in-law to repeat his demands in the strongest terms, and to declare war if he didn't reply more favourably.

Chapter XXII

How King Edward invaded Scotland and burned and laid waste the land and captured cities and castles.

The appointed day came and the noble King Edward rode into Newcastle, and waited there for two days while the rest of his army arrived. On the fourth day he set out and marched towards Scotland by way of Berwick, for the Scottish king's second reply had been no different to the first, despite the clear demand and challenge. The noble king advanced into Scotland and burned and laid waste all the lowland country as far as Aberdeen, capturing and garrisoning numerous castles and even the greatest cities defended by fine moats and fortifications; and in all this while young King David never confronted him openly.

It's true, however, that various barons, lords and other good knights, of whom there were many in Scotland, would often come and skirmish with the English army, and there were frequent bold and daring deeds of arms performed and great feats of prowess seen on both sides. In the course of these Walter Mauny won much praise and esteem from the king and everyone, and was knighted there by the king's command; of all the army he was one of those who exerted himself and risked the most, and it earned him the king's great favour and a place as one of his most trusted counsellors. These Scottish lords who so often came to skirmish with the English kept lurking in the wilds among dense marsh

---

[1]   See note 1, above, p.58.

and forest where it was impossible to follow them; but they tracked the English so closely that there was fighting almost every day, and Sir Walter Mauny earned the most renown, along with Sir William Montagu, a strong and imposing knight who lost an eye in one of these clashes[1] and earned such favour with the king that he made him Earl of Salisbury.

It was in these wilds and forests haunted by the Scots that King Robert had often taken refuge when the good King Edward, the young king's grandfather, had defeated him and put him to flight, for he was sometimes so hard pressed and hotly pursued that he could scarcely find a man in his kingdom who would dare to shelter him in any castle or fortress, such was the fear of King Edward who had conquered Scotland so decisively that every city, fort and castle had surrendered to him. Sometimes, it is said (and recorded in the history commissioned by King Robert himself), the good King Edward would set packs of eager dogs and bloodhounds after him, and have him chased through those great forests for three or four days at a time; but he could never be caught, and despite all the trials he suffered he would never surrender to the good King Edward; rather, as soon as King Edward had conquered Scotland and garrisoned cities and castles throughout the country and returned to England, King Robert rallied troops wherever he could find them and reconquered the whole land all the way to Berwick, some places by force and others willingly. When the good King Edward heard this he was enraged, and reassembled his army and didn't stop until he'd defeated the worthy King Robert and conquered Scotland all over again. So the struggle between those two kings continued, King Robert reconquering his land five times; so great was their contest that they were considered the two most valiant princes in the world, until the good King Edward died at Berwick[2] and his body was carried back to London.

Chapter XXIII

How the noble King Edward laid siege to the good city of Berwick.

When the noble King Edward – the young king, that is – had done as he pleased and laid waste the lowland tracts of Scotland, he returned to Berwick. The city was well provisioned and manned by a large and valiant garrison: it was not to be taken as quickly as he would have liked, and he and his army besieged it for a long while before they could take the city, the defenders resisting with might and courage so that many feats of prowess were performed by both sides. And just when the besieging army thought they could rest, whether by day or night, those valiant men-at-arms still at large in the forests and marshes would launch frequent attacks to harry them, engaging in fierce and mighty skirmishes, with gains and losses on both sides. Day and night there was a constant stream

---

[1]   Le Bel uses the word *'tournoys'*, which had come to mean 'combats' as well as 'tourna-
     ments' – an interesting insight, perhaps, into how such skirmishing was viewed and
     conducted.
[2]   On 7 July 1307.

of news of these doughty fighters, as they attacked reinforcements coming from England or plundered supply trains on their way to the king: it happened all the time. Foremost among them was the young Earl of Moray,[1] followed by William, Lord Douglas, nephew[2] of that valiant knight of whom you've heard who was killed in Granada while carrying King Robert of Scotland's heart to the Holy Sepulchre. I cannot give you the names of the others involved.

Chapter XXIV

How the young Count of Namur and his brother crossed the sea to England and were captured.

While King Edward was besieging Berwick his renown was spreading to France, and many young knights and squires eager to gain experience in arms and test themselves and win honour set out to serve the noble English king whose fame was increasing by the day. Among them were the young Count John of Namur and his two brothers Sir Guy and Sir Philip;[3] they were keen to go and see the young King of England and how things stood between him and the Scottish king, and above all to see their uncle Lord Robert of Artois, knowing as they did that he was now well placed in King Edward's company. They gathered a fine escort of men-at-arms befitting their station, and when all was in order and they were fully equipped and ready they set off and made their way to England and asked for directions to the king. They were shown the way to London and from London to York, from York to Durham and from Durham to Newcastle on the River Tyne.

They rested at Newcastle and obtained supplies that might well have been lacking when they reached the king's army. While they were resting and organising provisions, knights and squires from England arrived on their way to join the king; the young lords were delighted by this and rode on with them for greater safety, as did a large band of merchants who were taking supplies to the army and had been waiting for an armed escort.

On the first night these young lords of Namur and the English knights and squires and merchants all stayed together in an old city which had been known in the days of King Arthur's Round Table as the Castle of the Maidens.[4] It was

---

[1] John Randolph, son of Thomas.

[2] Le Bel is again confused about the Douglas family; James's nephew William was a very young child at this time: he is thinking here of William Douglas, Lord of Liddesdale (c. 1300-53).

[3] All three died young and childless: John II in 1335, Guy II in a tournament in 1336 and Philip III in Cyprus in 1337.

[4] In the roughly contemporary romance of *Perceforest* the Castle of the Maidens is indeed specifically referred to as being in Scotland: 'Next morning they took their leave of Perceforest and the Queen and set out for Scotland where they knew they'd find the Castle of the Maidens.' *Perceforest*, tr. N. Bryant (Woodbridge, 2011), p.275. The idea probably derived ultimately from Geoffrey of Monmouth's 12th-century *Historia regum Britannie*, in which King Ebraucus is said to have 'founded the city of Alclud [Dumbarton] over in Albany [Scotland], and the castle of Mount Agned, which is now called the Maidens' Castle'. Geoffrey of Monmouth, *The History of the Kings of Britain*, tr. L. Thorpe (Harmondsworth, 1966),

a night of poor lodging and much worry: they found only women and children all destitute; for the men of those parts had left with everything they possessed for fear of the English and Scottish armies. So these lords and their fellows spent the night in great unease and made sure they were guarded; and they sent out patrols to watch for approaching enemies, and had the breached and collapsing walls barricaded and refortified throughout the night.

And then, as day was about to break, the young Earl of Moray and Lord William Douglas approached with a host of other Scottish knights and squires: thanks to their spies they were well aware of the arrival of these lords and their position. When those on patrol heard the sound of hooves they rushed back into the city crying: "To arms! To arms! The enemy's coming!" Everyone was quickly armed, for they'd been expecting no less, and gathered all together where they were most vulnerable to attack. As the sun rose the Scots appeared, advancing up the hill in a thundering charge. The defenders resisted the first onslaught with great valour; but their efforts would finally have been in vain if the young Earl of Moray hadn't intervened to save the young lords of Namur, for the Scots' numbers were growing constantly and they were attacking from the front and rear and every side, and if their foot soldiers had arrived they would have shown no mercy. But when the Earl of Moray and Lord Douglas saw the young lords' perilous plight they leapt forward and begged them to surrender, for if they waited till the infantry arrived there'd be no escape. Hearing this appeal, and realising their resistance was ultimately doomed, the young lords took their advice and yielded to these two knights, who took great trouble to save their lives along with some of their fellows. But they could do little to save many of the English, for the foot soldiers were already upon them, filled with hatred, and all but a few were slaughtered.

And so the young lords couldn't achieve their mission and see the king and his army or their uncle: they were taken as captives into the Scottish wilds. And the Scottish lords carried off all the supplies that the English had been taking to the army besieging Berwick.[1] When the noble King Edward and his men heard what had happened they were incensed, but there was nothing they could do. I could never discover whether the lords of Namur were kept in captivity or for how long or if they were ever released; but I shall leave them now and turn my attention to King Edward.

The noble King Edward was encamped before the city of Berwick for a long time, refusing to leave; he launched numerous attacks, but it was defended by such fine men-at-arms that the assaults made little impression, and they would never have surrendered the city if they'd had enough victuals. But it's not possible

---

p.79. The name came to be associated for a long time with Edinburgh Castle, until in fact at least the 17th century, when William Camden in his Britannia (1607) wrote that 'the Britans called [Edinburgh] Castle Myned Agned, the Scots, the Maidens' Castle and the Virgins' Castle, on account of certaine young maidens of the Picts' roiall bloud who were kept there in old time'.

[1]   Le Bel has here described the action at Boroughmuir, just south of Edinburgh, on 30 July 1335. Clearly, a route from Newcastle to Berwick by way of Boroughmuir is less than likely, and the chronology of Le Bel's account is inaccurate.

to resist without food, and it's better to bend than to break. The noble king had no intention of leaving until he'd achieved his goal, and he maintained the siege so long that the city's food supplies were exhausted. They could devise no way of smuggling in fresh provisions, and they endured much suffering; but in the end, when they could bear no more, they surrendered to the noble king after lengthy negotiation which would take too long to recount. And the noble king took mercy on them all, sparing their lives and their possessions, and entered the city in triumph and celebration and took lodging where he wished.

After disbanding his army and sending home those he could do without, he posted strong, well provisioned garrisons in a number of the castles he'd captured from the King of Scotland, the better to ensure that he kept what he'd won. He established even stronger garrisons in and around the city of Berwick, which was to be the point of command for all the rest.

Then he departed and returned to England, where he held many great feasts and courts attended by all the barons and lords of the land; and these great feasts and tourneys and jousts and assemblies of ladies earned him such universal esteem that everyone said he was the second King Arthur.

The men-at-arms and garrisons left at Berwick and the other walled cities and castles and fortresses fulfilled his commands so ably that he suffered no losses in Scotland for a long while. But they often had to deal with the lords who held sway in the Scottish wilds and other castles, and there were often vigorous pursuits and fierce skirmishes.

But I'll say no more about this for now, for I wish to tell of King Edward's great mission in relation to the kingdom of France. He had suffered a great injustice (and one that continues) on this account: so it seemed to him from what he'd been told by Lord Robert of Artois and other members of his council.

Chapter XXV

How the noble King Edward sent the Bishop of Lincoln to the
Count of Hainault to discuss war with France.

Afteter the noble King Edward of England had won back the fine city of Berwick as you've heard, and laid waste all the lowlands of Scotland and posted guards and garrisons everywhere he pleased and joyfully returned to his kingdom, he was so loved and honoured by all his people, great and small alike, for the high nobility of his deeds and words and for his great heart and glorious festivities and assemblies of ladies and damsels, that everyone said he was King Arthur.

He now held frequent discussions with his closest advisers, deciding how to respond to the great wrong done to him in his youth in relation to the kingdom of France. As Lord Robert of Artois had informed him, the kingship should rightfully have passed to him as the closest in line of succession, but the twelve peers of France had chosen and decided to give it to Lord Philip of Valois without considering any rival claim. He didn't know what to think: he was reluctant to let the matter stand if he could amend it; he felt that, if his council concluded that he should demand his right and it was refused (as would probably be the case), and he then kept quiet and failed to exert himself and set matters to rights, it would be much to his shame. On the other hand, he was well aware that it wouldn't be easy for him, given his realm's resources, to overcome the kingdom of France unless he was able to draw on his treasury to win over powerful lords or reach an agreement with some of the twelve peers or other barons of France. He frequently sought the advice and views of his closest counsellors, not wanting to venture further without guidance.

His counsellors finally replied with one accord: "Dear lord, this is a matter of such weight and magnitude that we wouldn't dare take it upon ourselves to decide. But if it please you, dear lord, we recommend that you send able ambassadors, well briefed about your intentions, to the noble Count of Hainault, whose daughter you've married, and to his brother Sir John who has served you so valiantly, to ask their advice in the name of friendship; for they'll have better insights in this matter than we, and they've good cause to uphold your honour and rights for the sake of our lady your wife. And if they decide to support your plan, they'll be able to advise which lords you might best approach, and how best to secure their help."

"This seems to me," said the noble king, "to be good and sound advice. I heartily agree; just as you've said, it shall be done."

Then the king asked the worthy prelate the Bishop of Lincoln to undertake this embassy for him, and commissioned two bannerets who were present but whose names I've forgotten, along with two clerks learned in the law, to accompany the bishop.[1] They had no wish to refuse the request of such a noble king; they willingly agreed and prepared for their journey with all possible speed. They set off as soon as they were ready and made their way swiftly to Valenciennes in Hainault, where they found the noble count in his bed, so disabled by gout and stones that he couldn't move. But his brother Sir John of Hainault was with him, and it goes without saying that they were welcomed with all joy and honour.

After they had been duly fêted they explained their mission to the noble count and his brother and why they had been expressly sent to them, and told them of all the noble king's misgivings. When the worthy count heard why they'd been sent, and the proposals and doubts on which the king wished for his opinion, he was not in the least unsympathetic. After pondering a while he declared that the king was very wise, for before embarking on a mighty venture it's important to consider carefully how best to achieve one's goal and give full thought to how to succeed. And the noble count then said:

"So help me God, if the king succeeded in this I'd be overjoyed. As you may imagine, I feel better disposed towards him, my daughter's husband, than to the king who means nothing to me even though I've married his sister; for he secretly obstructed the marriage of the young Duke of Brabant to my other daughter so

---

[1] In January 1337 Henry Burghersh, Bishop of Lincoln, was sent to Holland, Guelders, Flanders, Hainault and Brabant with an embassy including William Fitzwarin and the earls of Northampton and Suffolk. In a busy series of diplomatic missions he returned more than once that year to forge alliances in the Low Countries, as did the earls of Salisbury and Huntingdon.

that he could marry one of his![1] So if he decides to proceed with this I shall never fail my dear and much loved son the King of England; I shall give him all the aid and guidance that I can, as will my brother Sir John who has served him in the past. But he'll need more support than ours alone, for Hainault is a small country compared to the kingdom of France, and England is too far away to come to our assistance!"

"Truly, sir," replied the worthy prelate the Bishop of Lincoln, speaking for all the others, "you have given us fine counsel and shown us great love and goodwill, for which we thank you on behalf of our lord the king." Then he said: "Now, dear sir, advise us which lords our king might best approach and most trust: we shall return to him with your thoughts."

"Upon my soul," the count replied, "I can think of no lords who could better support him in this venture than the Duke of Brabant (who is his cousin german), the Bishop of Liège, the Duke of Guelders, the Archbishop of Cologne, the Margrave of Jülich and the lord of Valkenburg;[2] they are very fine warriors, and more than any lords I know in all the world they'd be able to raise great numbers of men-at-arms with speed: if they wished they could raise eight to ten thousand heavy cavalry[3] – as long as they were paid in advance: lords and soldiers alike, they're keen to make money! If my son the king secured their support and crossed the sea, he'd be strong enough to march on Paris and do battle with King Philip of France."

This response was very pleasing to the king's ambassadors; and they took their leave of the worthy prince and his brother Sir John and returned to England with this news and information from the noble count.

They arrived back in London to a warm welcome from the king, and when they reported the response of the Count of Hainault and his brother Sir John, the king was overjoyed and much encouraged. He immediately bade ten bannerets and forty other young knights make ready and, with rich provision, sent them across the sea with the noble prelate the Bishop of Lincoln, straight to Valenciennes to open negotiations with the lords named by the Count of Hainault, and with instructions to follow the advice of the count and his brother Sir John in all matters.

When they arrived at Valenciennes everyone gazed in awe at their splendid appearance: it was as lavish a display as if the king had been there in person, and all who saw them were amazed. And some of the young knights had covered the sight of one eye with a cloth; it was rumoured that they'd made vows with ladies of their country to see out of only one eye until they'd performed some feats of prowess in France, but when they were asked about this they wouldn't admit it and it was the source of much fascination.

After they'd been fêted and honoured at Valenciennes by the worthy count and the other lords and ladies and citizens, the Bishop of Lincoln and most of

---

1   This is a reference to the marriage of John of Brabant, Duke of Limburg, to Philip of Valois's daughter Marie.
2   'Fauquemont': see footnote 4, above, p.57.
3   'armeures de fer': see note 4, above, p.25.

his party, at the count's advice, made their way to the Duke of Brabant. The duke likewise gave them a splendid welcome; and they negotiated so fruitfully that he promised to give the king and his men all possible support in his land (as he should, being his cousin german), and freedom to come and go, armed or disarmed just as King Edward pleased. He and his council further promised that – for a decent sum of florins – he would join him in defying the French king and invading the kingdom of France and would serve him with a thousand men-at-arms. This he promised them upon his honour, but he later broke and went against his word, as you'll hear in due course. The English lords were in very good heart, thinking their dealings with the duke had gone excellently; so they returned to Valenciennes and sent messages – along with gold and silver – to persuade the Duke of Guelders, the Margrave of Jülich (on his own behalf and representing the Archbishop of Cologne), his brother Valerant and the lord of Valkenburg to come to Valenciennes for discussions in the presence of the worthy Count of Hainault (who could neither ride nor walk) and his brother Sir John. In the end – by giving large sums of money required for them and their followers – the English secured promises from each of these lords that they would defy the King of France and serve King Edward with a certain number of men-at-arms with crested helms. At that time the great lords took no account of men-at-arms unless they had crested helms, whereas now we count any with lances, cuirasses, hauberks and iron caps. In my own time things have changed a lot, it seems to me: the splendid caparisoned horses and crested helms of old, and the shining plate and heraldic coats, are gone, replaced by cuirasses, gambisons and iron caps. These days a humble page is as well and as finely armed as a noble knight.

These lords promised furthermore to secure the help of other lords from beyond the Rhine, who'd be able to raise great numbers of troops if they were given the wherewithal. With that they took their leave and returned home. Many an embassy was sent to the Bishop of Liège, Lord Adolph de la Marck, along with many a fine gift, but nothing could persuade him to act against the King of France, for he had paid him homage and become his liege man. No attempt, however, was made to win over the noble King of Bohemia: he was known to be so strongly bound to the King of France through the marriage of their two children, who were heirs to the kingdom,[1] that he would never go against him.

Having secured the commitment of the German lords, now heading for home, the English ambassadors stayed at Valenciennes in great splendour and at great expense. But I shall say no more about them until due time; I shall turn to another matter which has a close bearing upon my story.

---

[1] The King of Bohemia's daughter Bonne had married the future John II of France in 1332.

Chapter XXVI

How a man named Jacob van Artevelde held sway in Flanders.

At this time there was much discord between Count Louis and the Flemings: they wouldn't obey him and it was only by their leave that he dared remain in Flanders. At Ghent there was a man, formerly a brewer of mead,[1] named Jacob van Artevelde, who had acquired such prestige and popular support that throughout all Flanders whatever he proposed or commanded was well and truly done; indeed no one, however great his status, dared oppose his orders. He would parade through the city with a permanent escort of sixty or eighty armed men, three or four of whom were his confidants; and whenever he met a man he disliked or suspected he'd be killed on the spot; he'd ordered his boys that:

"As soon as I meet a man and make this sign, kill him there and then without mercy, regardless of his rank: don't wait for another word."

This happened frequently: he had several men of great importance killed; and it made him so feared that no one dared utter – or even think – a word to displease him. And when his sixty cronies had seen him to his house, they'd all go home to eat and then come back and loiter in the street until he decided to roam the city again, whereupon they'd escort him until supper. And truly, each of his thugs was given four Flemish groats per day as wages and expenses, paid regularly week by week. He had men in his pay in every town and trade centre in Flanders to carry out his orders, spying and informing on any potential rebel or anyone who spoke or protested against his deeds and intentions; as soon as he had word of any such in any town he wouldn't rest till he'd had them banished or killed. In particular, all the powerful knights and squires and leading citizens who appeared to support the count in any way he would banish from Flanders and seize half their wealth, leaving the other half for the maintenance of their wives and children. And those thus banished, of whom there were many, took up residence at Saint-Omer where they became known as 'the robbed' or 'the ultra-robbed'! In short, there was never – in Flanders or anywhere else – a duke or count or prince with a land so completely under his thumb as this Jacob had all Flanders. He collected all the rents, wine duties, taxes and revenues which the count had previously raised and were rightfully his, along with all the maletolts,[2] and spent it all just as he pleased, splashing it about without keeping any account; and whenever he said he was short of money they believed him – but then they had to: no one dared contradict him. And if ever he wanted to borrow from a citizen they wouldn't dare refuse.

But now I'll return to my English lords.

---

[1] Mead was a surprisingly common and popular drink in the middle ages, often flavoured with hops to give it a bitter, beer-like taste.
[2] Taxes on wool sacks.

Chapter XXVII

*How these English lords went to Flanders to secure the aid of the
Flemings and especially of Jacob van Artevelde.*

These lords who'd been sent across the sea and, as you've heard, were residing
in state at Valenciennes, thought it would be a great help to the king in his
planned enterprise if he had the support and assistance of the Flemings, who
were then at odds with the King of France and their count. They consulted the
worthy Count of Hainault, who agreed that it would indeed be a great advantage
to the king, but he didn't see how they could secure Flemish support unless they
first gained the favour of Jacob van Artevelde. They said they would see to this
at once.

They were soon on their way from Valenciennes and heading for Flanders,
some to Bruges, some to Ypres and some to Ghent; and wherever they went
they spent money so liberally, and promised it to all and sundry, that you'd
have thought the clouds were raining silver. In any event, the Bishop of Lincoln
and his companions went to Ghent and, by fine words and other means, won
the friendship and support of Jacob van Artevelde and the goodwill of the city,
notably of a most worthy old knight named Siger de Courtrai:[1] he was a banneret,
and he lived in Ghent and was much respected there; he was considered the
most gallant knight and the worthiest man in Flanders, having always served
the lords of the land with outstanding valour. This splendid knight entertained
and honoured the English lords most highly, with all the respect for chivalry that
worthy men should show; but he was ill rewarded for it, for the honour he paid
the English earned him the enmity of the King of France, who gave the Count
of Flanders strict orders to get hold of this knight in whatever way he could and
have him beheaded. The count dared not disobey the king, and somehow or
other he arranged for the old knight to come to him, whereupon he was instantly
seized and beheaded,[2] much to the distress of many people: they hated the count
for what he'd done.

Meanwhile the English lords were making excellent progress with their
mission, and this Jacob arranged several meetings of the cities' aldermen to
discuss the matter. The lords offered them great privileges from King Edward,
without whose favour Flanders couldn't prosper;[3] and negotiations continued
until the Flemish delegates agreed[4] that the King of England could come and go
through Flanders, or stay there, with armed forces or otherwise, as often as he
wished. But for the moment they asked that that should suffice, for they were
worried about their relations with the King of France: if they actively inflicted
harm or made any move against him they would incur a heavy penalty and it
might well end in serious trouble.

---

[1]   Le Bel refers to him as '*messire Courtesin*'.
[2]   He was arrested in July 1337 and executed the following March.
[3]   The supply of English wool was crucial to the Flemish cloth industry.
[4]   In a treaty concluded in June 1338.

The English lords were satisfied with this, and returned to Valenciennes in high spirits. They sent a stream of messengers to King Edward, informing him of their progress – and asking him to send plenty of money to cover their expenses and to pay the first half of what they'd promised to the German lords and the Duke of Brabant so that they could prepare their armies. The money arrived, and those lords soon had the first half of what had been agreed; but they didn't distribute it to their men as quickly as they'd promised: they held on to it, and were slow to come to King Edward's support after they'd raised their first troops. This was to cause him grave trouble, as you'll hear in due course.

Chapter XXVIII

How the King of England crossed the sea and landed at Antwerp, trusting in the promises made to his ambassadors by a number of lords.

The Duke of Brabant, having made his various pledges to the English lords, began to worry that the King of France, who'd been against him in the past, had got word of his dealings with the English; and if the King of England's planned venture failed, he feared the French king would come and wage war upon him and inflict the kind of penalty that fellow conspirators would have suffered. So from his Council he sent Sir Louis of Kraainem, a very astute knight, with several others to the King of France to make his excuses and beg the king not to believe any false information about him: the King of England was his cousin and he couldn't very well forbid him or his people to come to his land if they paid their way, but he would do nothing more to displease the French king.

King Philip believed him for the time being and was appeased. All the same, the duke raised troops in Brabant, in the bishopric of Liège and elsewhere, to the number that he'd pledged to the English – but he didn't pass on to those troops the money he'd received, though he promised them plenty! He was double dealing. He wanted to convince the French king that he intended him no harm – and kept it up for a long time even though the opposite was clear to all – and to cover himself all the more he kept sending Louis of Kraainem to make his excuses, finally telling him to stay at court and not return till he summoned him back; but all the while he was assuring the English and their allies that nothing in the world would make him break his promise: they'd see what he'd do!

So matters stayed all that winter. Then the following summer the King of England decided he would cross the sea with a great company of earls, princes, barons and knights.[1] He sailed straight to Antwerp, eager to learn at first hand the true position and intentions of his cousin the duke.

When news came of his landing at Antwerp, people flocked to see him and his splendid entourage. After due welcome, he decided to speak with his cousin the duke and his brother-in-law the Duke of Guelders and the Margrave of Jülich and Sir John of Hainault and the lord of Valkenburg and the other lords whose promises he'd received, to discuss how and when they would begin their

---

[1] Edward sailed from Orwell on 16 July 1338.

enterprise. They all responded to his summons, arriving at Antwerp between Pentecost and the feast of Saint John in the year '38.[1] They were splendidly fêted in the English manner. Then the noble King Edward took them aside and eloquently set forth his mission, wishing to know from each lord his intention. He asked them for a swift response: he had come with all his forces prepared, and it would be very damaging if they didn't move fast. These lords debated long and hard: they felt very much under pressure and they didn't all agree; and all the while they had an eye on the Duke of Brabant, who didn't look happy but was giving little away. After lengthy discussion they gave their reply to the noble King Edward, saying:

"When we came here, sire, it was principally to see you; we weren't ready or expecting to give an answer to this request of yours. We shall each go back to our people and then return to you on a day you name and acquit ourselves with a full response."

The noble king reconciled himself to having no more joy for the present; and they agreed to meet again to give their considered reply three weeks after the feast of Saint John. But the king stressed the great expense and trouble their delay would be causing him by the day: when he arrived he'd been expecting them to be as fully prepared as he. He told them he'd never return to England until they gave a clear statement of their intentions – or let him down.

With that the lords departed while the king stayed put, residing at Saint Bernard's Abbey.[2] Some of the English knights and lords stayed at Antwerp to keep him company, but others gadded about the country, enjoying themselves at great expense, some at Brussels, some in Hainault and others in the Flemish cities, where they were richly welcomed and entertained. The Duke of Brabant meanwhile had gone home and was sending great sums of money and gifts to the King of France by way of excuse and to beg that he believe no untoward reports.

The day arrived when the king expected the lords' response; but instead came shrewd prevarication: messages saying they were completely ready, but that the king must first ensure that the Duke of Brabant was prepared to join them, for he was the most closely related to King Edward but seemed reluctant to commit himself; as soon as they knew he was ready to move they would do likewise, and would be as quick to engage as he. The king spoke to the duke at once, showing him the lords' response and begging him in the name of friendship and kinship to consider well and not let him down: unless he stopped his obvious wavering, he feared he was going to lose him the support and aid of all the other lords. The duke, desperately embarrassed, said he would discuss it with his counsellors. After long deliberation he told the king he'd be ready to join him when the time came, but before responding further he would first speak to the other lords. The king realised this was the best he was going to get, and that a display of anger would be pointless; so he agreed to send word to the lords asking whether, if they wouldn't come all the way to him, they would meet closer to home, at Halle, on

[1]   Edward stayed at Antwerp to confer with his allies until 15 August.
[2]   The Cistercian monastery of St Bernard at nearby Hemiksem.

Our Lady's day in the middle of August, to confirm and agree their plans. He begged the duke to be there, and to show such clear commitment that day that the lords couldn't excuse themselves on his account. So it was agreed.

The day came, and the lords arrived – but not that noble prince the Count of Hainault: I've forgotten to mention that he had passed from this world the previous winter after knighting his son, the young Count William, by his own hand. This young count attended the meeting on behalf of his noble father, along with his uncle Sir John. When the lords were all assembled they debated long and hard, wrestling with themselves: they were reluctant to keep their promises but equally reluctant, for their honour's sake, to break them.

After lengthy deliberation they returned to the king and his council with their decision, saying: "Dear sire, we've considered this for a long while, for your proposed mission causes us much concern. We don't see we have any cause to defy the King of France on your account, unless you gain the support of the Emperor and he bids us defy the king on his behalf: he certainly has grounds and reason enough, as we'll explain. If he does so, we'll have no more qualms about placing ourselves at your command as we promised. The Emperor's grounds for defying him are these: there is a long-standing pact, sealed and sworn on oath, between the Emperor of Germany and the King of France that the latter – whoever he may be – cannot and must not take possession of anything belonging to the Empire. But King Philip has broken this pledge: he has taken the castle of Crèvecoeur, the castle of Labbel near Cambrai and several other estates in the region, all of it Imperial land, and he is holding them still; so the Emperor has good cause to challenge him and to bid others do likewise on behalf of him and his subjects. So we pray you seek his approval for your mission; it will reassure us that we're acting honourably, and then we shall strive to support you."

The noble King Edward was appalled by this reply: he was sure it was a delaying tactic and that the words came from his cousin the Duke of Brabant. But he could see there was nothing to be done, and that flying into a rage would do no good; so he looked as cheerful as he could and said:

"Indeed, sirs, I knew nothing of this; if you'd told me sooner I'd have considered it already! But I shall act upon it as you advise, so tell me how to proceed, for I'm a stranger on this side of the sea – though I've been here long enough, doing nothing at great expense! So give me good guidance now, for your honour's sake as well as for mine – for truly, if my mission is in any way wrong you'll gain no honour from it."

Chapter XXIX

How the Margrave of Jülich went to the Emperor to seek aid and guidance for King Edward against the French.

It would take a long time to recount all the discussions that followed. But it was finally agreed that the Margrave of Jülich would go and speak to the Emperor with clerks from the king and knights and men from the Duke of Guelders, and that they would carry out their mission as faithfully as possible. The Duke of

Brabant was unwilling to send a representative; but he did lend the king the castle of Leuven[1] to be his residence until the summer if he wished, for the noble king had told them he'd no intention of returning to England, as it would be shameful to go back having achieved no part of his much publicised purpose. And now that the duke had offered him the castle of Leuven, he said he would send for the young queen his wife.

With that the meeting broke up, and all the lords vowed in each other's presence that they would seek no delay or excuse but would declare their enmity to King Philip of France beginning at the feast of Saint John in the year of grace 1339, and would be ready to act as they'd promised. Then they set off for their respective lands, while the Margrave of Jülich and his company made their way to the Emperor and found him at Nuremberg.

Why should I recount at length all they said and requested? I couldn't in any case, as I wasn't there; but the margrave spoke so graciously to the Emperor that they achieved all they'd hoped and more: it was there that Jülich, thitherto a count, was made a margrave, and Guelders, formerly a count likewise, secured the title of duke. And the Emperor commissioned four knights and two worthy clerks of the law to make King Edward his Vicar throughout the Empire, with power to mint gold and silver coin in his name, and with a decree that all his subjects should obey King Edward as if he were the Emperor himself. With their mission fully accomplished, the margrave and his companions prepared to return.

Meanwhile the young King David of Scotland was unable to regain the lost part of his kingdom, such was the strength of his brother-in-law the King of England, and he left Scotland in secret with his wife the Queen and a small escort of retainers and sailed to France, where he met with King Philip and explained all his troubles and needs. The French king, well aware that the King of England was preparing to make war upon him and seize his kingdom if he could, was delighted to have the King of Scotland take refuge there with his wife and so small an escort: he listened with all sympathy and welcomed him most warmly, making his castles available for his residence and providing him with money for his keep, on condition that he made no pact or truce with the King of England without his permission. The young king accepted all this very gratefully and promised him what he'd asked. It seemed to King Philip that it would be much to his advantage – and a great problem for King Edward – if he could arrange for the barons and lords still in Scotland to keep the English so well occupied that few of them would be free to cross the sea to fight him; indeed, their king might have to sail back to protect and save his realm!

It was with this in mind that King Philip kept the young king and queen of Scotland at his side and entertained them for a long while, providing for their every need, and sent great delegations to the Scottish lords and barons at war with the English king's garrisons, offering them generous aid and support from France as long as they didn't stop fighting or propose a truce without the approval

---

[1] 'Louvain' in French.

and bidding of himself and their king, who was with him and had agreed to this. The Scots met together to discuss the matter, and were overjoyed to hear news of their lord King David and this promise of support from the King of France; they were in full accord, and now waged war upon the English with more intensity than ever. When the King of England heard this he sent orders for his garrisons to be reinforced and great numbers of troops to be sent to the borders. But now I shall leave this matter and return to the former.

Chapter XXX

How the Emperor, through the Margrave of Jülich, commissioned
King Edward to be his Vicar and lieutenant.

When the discussions between the noble King Edward and the other lords broke up, as you've heard, the king withdrew to Leuven and had the castle prepared as his residence, and sent word to his wife the Queen that he would be very pleased if she would cross the sea to join him, for he couldn't sail home all that year. He also sent back a great many of his knights to guard his land, especially on the Scottish borders. The other English, who stayed on this side of the sea, were spread right across Flanders, Brabant and Hainault.

The Margrave of Jülich and his companions returned from the Emperor around All Saints; and he sent word to the noble King Edward that their mission, he felt, had been a great success, and that he should summon the other lords to meet him on Saint Martin's Day at Mechelen[1] or at Leuven or at Diest[2] to hear his report. The noble king was overjoyed at this news, and discussed it with his cousin the Duke of Brabant, who agreed the date well enough but didn't want the assembly to take place in his land, being anxious to carry on hiding his intentions from the King of France; nor did he wish to go to Maastricht,[3] which would have been a good place for the meeting, but wanted it to be held at Arques, fairly close to his land but in the county of Loon. So eager was the noble king to press on with his mission that he felt obliged to yield to all the duke's wishes now that things had gone this far, and agreed to hold the meeting at Arques. Word was sent to all his allies, and they came at his bidding on Saint Martin's Day as planned.

When they all arrived the town was filled with lords, knights, squires and a great host of other people, and the market hall, where bread and meat and other goods were sold, was decked with fine drapes as if it had been the king's own chamber. The king himself was seated, crowned, a foot higher than everyone else, on a block where a butcher cut and sold his meat: never was a market hall graced with such honour. And there, before all the lords and people, the Emperor's letters were read appointing the noble King Edward of England his Vicar and lieutenant, with powers to pass judgement on his behalf and to mint gold and silver coin in his name, and commanding all his princes and subjects

[1]   'Malignes' ('Malines' in modern French).
[2]   In Brabant.
[3]   'Tricht'.

to obey him as his deputy as they would himself, and pay him homage as Vicar of the Empire.[1] When these letters had been read, each of the lords paid him homage and vowed to obey him as Vicar of the Empire, and certain cases were brought and heard before him, right there and then, as if before the Emperor himself. And an imperial statute was renewed and confirmed, decreeing that any man who wished to make war upon another or to exact compensation for a past wrong should send a clear declaration of defiance three days in advance. All agreed that this judgement was reasonable, but I don't know that it's always been observed.

When all this had been done the lords departed, having sworn and promised that they would all be ready, three weeks after Saint John's Day, to lay siege to Cambrai, which rightly belonged to the Empire but had turned to the French king. Meanwhile the noble King Edward, Vicar of the Empire, went to meet my lady the Queen, who had lately arrived at Leuven most nobly attended – in pursuing my theme I'd forgotten to mention this. They kept their court in great state at Leuven all that winter, and ordered the minting of great sums of gold and silver coin at Antwerp along with écus stamped with an imperial eagle, similar to the écus minted by the King of France. This was a much respected currency, as it is still.

All the while the Duke of Brabant continued to play his double game, which earned him widespread disrespect, as he kept sending messengers to the King of France declaring intentions contrary to those he held; it was so glaringly obvious that everyone was amazed, but no one dared say anything. And he finally ordered one of his closest counsellors, Sir Louis of Kraainem, to go yet again to the King of France and stay there with his court and keep assuring him of the duke's innocence and deny all contrary information. Sir Louis didn't dare refuse, and diligently carried out the duke's command; but he was poorly rewarded in the end, for he died in France of grief: when it became clear to the French that all his claims on the duke's behalf were false, he was so overcome with shame that he wouldn't return to Brabant but stayed in France in an attempt to avert suspicion; and the duke, seeing him refuse to return to Brabant as commanded, had all his lands confiscated and issued an order for his arrest; Sir Louis brought this to the attention of the King of France who pardoned him and granted him a pension for the rest of his life – but sadly that wasn't long.

Winter passed and the feast of Saint John[2] drew near. Then the German lords began to prepare for their expedition. The King of France made counter-preparations, knowing a good deal of their intent. The noble King Edward had supplies made ready in England and troops sent over as soon as Saint John's Day came, and he went himself to Vilvoorde[3] to take lodging with his army. Once all billets in the town were taken he bade the others pitch tents and pavilions in the fields and meadows outside; and there they stayed from the feast of the

[1]   Edward was not in fact proclaimed Vicar at Arques but at Koblenz, on 5 September 1338.
[2]   Saint John the Baptist, 24 June.
[3]   In Brabant, just north of Brussels.

Magdalene until after the feast of Our Lady in September,[1] waiting week after week for the arrival of the other lords – and for an end to the Duke of Brabant's vacillation.

When the noble King Edward realised that the Duke of Brabant and the other lords weren't coming, he sent new messages to them, summoning them, by their oath and pledge, to meet him at Mechelen on Saint Giles's Day[2] to explain their delay. And so the noble king had to stay at Vilvoorde – at vast expense, obviously – wasting time: it annoyed him deeply but there was nothing he could do. He was daily supporting at his own cost fully six hundred élite men-at-arms, brought across the sea from England, and a good five thousand archers, not to mention all the army followers. It must have been a heavy expense – and infuriating while they were all inactive. On top of this were the vast sums he'd given to the lords who were spinning him along with fine promises. There was also the cost of the huge force he was keeping at sea to oppose the fleet of Genoese, Normans, Spaniards and Bayonnais who were sailing the seas in King Philip's pay to inflict damage on the English: with Sir Hugues Quiéret as their admiral and commander, along with 'Barbevair',[3] a most redoubtable pirate, these ships caused the English frequent trouble, harm and disruption both then and later, as you'll hear.

The German lords, the Duke of Brabant and Sir John of Hainault answered the king's summons and came to Mechelen; and after much discussion they all agreed that the king could march in a fortnight, for they would do so then or after, in time to meet him at Cambrai on a specified day. And there and then they sent messages of defiance to the King of France on behalf of them all – except the Duke of Brabant, who was still unwilling to defy him yet. With that they all left Mechelen and hurried to make their preparations, while King Edward returned to his army in better heart than before, and told them to be ready to march within the fortnight. The Duke of Brabant now realised that he, too, could vacillate no longer, and ordered his forces to prepare.

Chapter XXXI

How King Edward and his allies marched into the Cambrésis because
Cambrai had turned to the King of France.

After the feast of Saint Lambert,[4] in the month of September in the year of grace 1339, King Edward set out from Vilvoorde in Brabant to burn and lay waste the land of France and to do battle with King Philip of Valois who was forcibly and wrongfully holding the kingdom. With him King Edward had sixteen hundred heavy cavalry, the noblest knights in all England, among them the Bishop of Lincoln, bold and valiant, who'd worked long and hard in the cause

---

[1]   i.e. from 22 July until after 8 September.
[2]   1 September.
[3]   A corsair from the Mediterranean named Pietro Barbavera. 'Barbevair' would imply a
      striking mottled beard of grey, black and white.
[4]   17 September.

of this mission, and the young Earl of Derby, son of the Earl of Lancaster, Henry 'Wryneck'.[1] This young man was to perform so many feats of prowess in so many places that he deserved to be deemed exceedingly valiant – and accounted so he was indeed; and after his father's death, a most worthy man himself, the noble King Edward created him Duke of Lancaster, a title he holds still. The most splendidly valiant to be seen or found anywhere in the world was the Earl of Northampton,[2] and the Earl of Gloucester, too;[3] and the Earl of Warwick[4] was there, and the Earl of Salisbury,[5] who was marshal of the army; and the Earl of Suffolk[6] and Baron Stafford[7] and Sir John, viscount of Beaumont,[8] and a good number of other princes and barons, bannerets and of higher rank still, and many more whose names I don't know. But not to be forgotten is Sir Reginald Cobham, who should rightly be considered the worthiest in his land at that time, as he is still; nor should we forget Sir Walter Mauny, whose many feats of arms and prowess in Scotland and elsewhere had earned him such favour with the king and all the English, great and small, that the noble king had taken him into his innermost council and granted him such great estates in England that he was now a banneret, of higher status indeed than any other there.

And let me tell you, there were a great many lords, knights and barons who so loved the king that they were willing to serve him at their own expense, and refused to accept any pay or provisions from him until they'd completed the year – if the campaign were to last that long. And know this, too: when the noble King Edward first secured the kingdom in his youth, the English generally were held in little regard: no one spoke of their prowess or courage – or indeed of that first campaign against the Scots; and they knew nothing of plate armour and bascinets and intricate refinements, just great hauberks and doublets blazoned with their arms and padded with scraps of old cloth, and on the head a hefty cap of iron or boiled leather. But now, in the noble King Edward's time, they've learned so much about arms – since he's had them so often engaged – that they're the finest and most superbly presented fighters known.

But to return to my theme: the day came when the noble king was due to march on France, as agreed among the lords at Mechelen. He set out from Vilvoorde with his whole army, and advanced into Hainault by way of Nivelles, making a series of short marches as he waited for his allies who were all following behind.

[1]   The Earl of Derby is Henry of Grosmont, son of Henry 'Wryneck' ('*Tort Col*') 3rd Earl of Lancaster. As Le Bel says in the following sentence, he is later to become the 1st Duke of Lancaster: see also above, p.28.
[2]   William de Bohun, 1st Earl of Northampton.
[3]   Hugh de Audley, 1st Earl of Gloucester. Le Bel mistakenly refers to 'the Earl of Northampton and Gloucester', as if they were one and the same person.
[4]   Thomas de Beauchamp, 11th Earl of Warwick.
[5]   William Montagu, 1st Earl of Salisbury.
[6]   Robert de Ufford, 1st Earl of Suffolk.
[7]   Ralph de Stafford, 1st Earl of Stafford, 2nd Baron Stafford.
[8]   There were no English viscounts at this time. This could be another reference to Sir John of Hainault, whose title was lord of Beaumont, but in view of later references (and since Le Bel is here listing English lords) it is more probably John, 2nd Baron Beaumont. See also below, p.88, where the 'viscount of Beaumont' and Sir John of Hainault appear in separate lists.

At last they were all together, and marching straight from Hainault into the Cambrésis – except the Duke of Brabant, who arrived six or seven days after the rest.

When the lords were all assembled they decided that, while waiting for the Duke of Brabant to appear, they would continue their joint advance on Cambrai and lay waste the surrounding country, because the city of Cambrai was opposed to them, refusing them lodging and sustenance. This decision was duly carried out, and the Cambrésis was ravaged terribly.

The young Count of Hainault, Lord William, was one of their company; but some of his wise counsellors advised him not to take part in this ravaging of the King of France's land, because when all the other lords were gone, his own land of Hainault, which bordered the kingdom, would pay for it: it would be inevitable, and he'd be helpless to prevent it. He took their advice and sent high-ranking envoys to the King of France, his uncle, who was now at Péronne in the Vermandois with the greatest army he could possibly raise, to beg his forgiveness that those hostile forces had passed through his land, and to offer his service with a company of five hundred men-at-arms in the defence and protection of his kingdom. The King of France received these envoys with apparent goodwill, but he was convinced that it was all a sham and that his nephew was more inclined towards his enemies than him. But he showed no sign of this, and told the messengers that he would accept his nephew's service, and bade them say that when battle was clearly imminent he was to come and join him, for he would welcome him with pleasure and gratitude.

Chapter XXXII

How King Edward first entered France and ravaged a large part of the Thiérache before the eyes of the French king.

While King Edward and the allies were burning and ravaging the land around the city of Cambrai,[1] and the King of France had come with all his forces to Péronne in the Vermandois to protect and defend the kingdom – supported by the noble King of Bohemia with a thousand élite men-at-arms, knights and squires, and the Bishop of Liège with six hundred heavy cavalry from his land – the Duke of Brabant arrived in the Cambrésis to join the noble King Edward in fulfilment of his pledge, bringing with him twelve hundred superbly equipped knights, much to the delight of the noble king and all the other lords. The king bade them stay for another two days while the last of their forces arrived, and to let the duke rest before he finally sent his message of defiance to King Philip at Péronne – to the dismay and confusion of Sir Louis of Kraainem who'd been giving the king constant assurances to the contrary: it led to him dying of grief as you've heard.

As soon as the Duke of Brabant had defied the French king, the King of England and his allies left the Cambrésis and marched into the kingdom of France, burning

---

[1]   The devastation of the Cambrésis lasted from 20 to 27 September 1339.

and ravaging the land as they passed. On the first night they camped around an abbey of white friars – which was completely destroyed – called Mont-Saint-Jean.[1] This was right near the King of France's position at Péronne, but he had his whole army before him, not to mention a great river that would be a challenge to cross. The noble King Edward and the other lords stayed there throughout the following day, thinking that the King of France, seeing his kingdom burnt and ravaged (something never witnessed before), would surely cross the river to do battle – but he decided against it. When they realised he wouldn't cross they sent him word that, if he wouldn't come and fight on their side of the river, they'd no intention of risking such a dangerous crossing, so he'd have to see what they did next, and it would be like nothing he'd seen before! And they struck camp first thing next morning and, following the line of the river as closely as they could, they burned and laid waste the whole country till they found themselves at Origny[2] on the banks of the Oise. They took towns and castles without any resistance, and vast quantities of loot at will: it was a rewarding area to plunder, the people having hidden, removed and locked away nothing. It was here at Origny that a Benedictine convent was ruined and set ablaze, and many of the nuns were raped by the English, which was a grievous shame.

They struck camp next day; and the Earl of Salisbury, the army's marshal, along with the Earl of Suffolk and Sir John of Hainault, rode with five hundred men-at-arms to Marle and then fired the suburbs and township of Crécy-sur-Serre[3] and all the surrounding country; they found it richly abundant and looted exactly as they pleased, before returning that afternoon to the abbey at Vadencourt-et-Bohéries, where the noble King Edward and all the other lords had taken lodging.

They left there next morning and passed through the Thiérache, burning and wasting everywhere, and finding such an abundance of cattle and all manner of things that they didn't know what to do with it all. Anyone who fancied buying could have a fully grown ox or cow for a groat or a couple of sheep for a penny.

The King of France now left Péronne and came to lodge at the abbey of Vadencourt just vacated by King Edward: he was following the English with the intention of bringing them to battle – so he said. That night the King of England camped in the area around La Capelle and La Flamengrie in the Thiérache, where news reached him that the French king, the right noble King of Bohemia and the Bishop of Liège were pursuing him, seeking battle. So all the English lords met and agreed to hold their ground until next day, to see what the King of France and his allies would do, for they would willingly do battle if they could, and await the will[4] of God.

Next morning the King of France and all his army advanced and made camp two short leagues from their enemy, in a town called Buironfosse and the surrounding villages; they all expected to engage the following day. Meanwhile

---

[1]   It was in fact the abbey of Mont-Saint-Martin.
[2]   Origny-Sainte-Benoîte.
[3]   'Cressy en Lannoys'.
[4]   Le Bel interestingly uses the word 'aventure', implying chance and the workings of Fortune.

the young Count William of Hainault, having sent his envoys to speak to the King of France as you've heard, had left the allied lords and withdrawn to Le Quesnoy in Hainault while he waited to see if his uncle the king meant to do battle. When he heard that King Philip had left Péronne and gone after the allies and intended to fight, the count set out from Le Quesnoy with four hundred cavalry and rode to join his uncle at Buironfosse, where he was discussing with his men whether or not to do battle with the enemy who were burning and ravaging his land. He greeted his uncle with all due courtesy, but the king didn't welcome him as warmly as he'd expected; the count was most put out that he seemed to have grave doubts about his integrity, and returned at once to Le Quesnoy, from where he'd set off in the middle of the night, and left his uncle to do whatever he decided.

Next day, when the noble King Edward and the lords encamped at La Capelle and La Flamengrie learned that the King of France was so near, they rose at first light and heard mass most devoutly. Then they went into the field and formed three battalions, all on foot, fairly close together and all prepared to meet the King of France's army; they sent their horses and gear to be kept behind a nearby wood. All the lords and their men stayed standing there till past midday, waiting for the King of France and his mighty army to appear. But King Philip was still at Buironfosse, discussing with his princes and barons how to proceed. There was much debate and quarrelling over this: some of the French lords said it would be a great disgrace and dishonour if the king didn't fight when he knew that his enemies, who'd been burning and ravaging his kingdom before his very eyes, were now so near and still in his own land; but others declared that on the contrary it would be a great folly to do battle, for there was no way of knowing what everyone was thinking and if there was any danger of betrayal – or of being sure, in any case, that he wasn't on a hiding to nothing: for if Fortune turned against him and he was defeated, he'd lose both his kingdom and his life, and even if he beat his enemies it wouldn't mean he'd won the kingdom of England or the lands or possessions of the other English lords.

They quarrelled and wrangled long into the afternoon and still could reach no agreement. For their part, King Edward and the other lords, who'd been standing in the fields in battle array since early morning without a bite to eat or a drop to drink, realised that the King of France and his men were not inclined to fight. They met together to discuss the next move. Opinions differed and many words were exchanged, but there was finally unanimous agreement that no one who heard what had happened could reasonably blame or reproach them if they left: they had, after all, offered battle to the king when they first entered his kingdom, before they'd started ravaging the land; they'd then spent seven days burning and destroying everything in full view of the king and his whole army – no man had ever seen the like; and they'd waited there all day, ready for battle, when the king was just two short leagues away, in open country, with no river or fortification to impede him, and still he didn't come to meet them – or even show himself or make the slightest stir. In the meantime they were short of victuals and wine and bread and didn't know how to arrange supplies, and so, all things considered, they unanimously agreed to leave; and they set off and came, late that night, to make camp around Avesnes[1] with all their baggage and booty.

When King Philip and the French realised the English had gone they left, too, all going their own way and returning home, but claiming that honour was on their side, having chased the enemy away. They might have burnt and ravaged a large part of the kingdom, but they hadn't won it, for the king had plenty left undamaged, and if the King of England wanted to conquer the kingdom of France he'd have to make many more such expeditions.[2] Such was the reasoning of the French, wishing to claim that honour was with them as the two sides parted, but the English made a counter-claim for the reasons given above, so that both sides awarded themselves honour in the affair. Everyone who hears these claims can judge for himself where the honour lay, according to reason and chivalry.

Chapter XXXIII

How and why the King of England took the name and the arms of France and called himself King of France and England.

And so the great campaign ended with both sides thinking honour was theirs. The Duke of Brabant and the German lords went their separate ways, while the noble King Edward led his English back through Flanders. He was warmly received there by Jacob van Artevelde and all the Flemings; and he promised them that if they would help him in the continuance of his war he would help them to recover Lille, Douai and other major towns that the King of France had taken from them and was very wrongfully withholding. The Flemings discussed this long and intently, because they'd made a pledge to the papal camera that they wouldn't go to war with the French king or act in any way against him; if they did so, they would forfeit a great sum of money. But they finally agreed that if the King of England called himself King of France in his letters, they would accept him as such and obey him as their sovereign lord – since the county of Flanders owed homage to the French king – and help him secure his kingdom; in this way, they felt, he being king would absolve them of their pledge and their money wouldn't be forfeit.

When the noble King of England heard this response he had serious need of good counsel and guidance, for it was a weighty matter and a very great step to take the arms and title of a kingdom of which he'd won no part – and didn't know if he ever would. On the other hand he was reluctant to refuse the support of the Flemings, who could be of greater help in his mission than anyone else in the world. At last, after all the pros and cons had been considered and pondered and weighed, he took the arms of France and quartered them with those of England, and called himself thenceforth King of France and England. And he did all that the Flemings had requested, absolving them as King of France of all obligations

---

[1]   Avesnes-sur-Helpe, a well fortified town further north.
[2]   '*chevachies*': the word 'chevauchées' was to assume a particular significance as the wars in France progressed, as systematic devastation became a feature of English campaigns.

to the French king. In return the Flemings gave him assistance, as you'll hear, throughout the time that Jacob van Artevelde held sway.

Then the king left the earls of Salisbury and Suffolk on this side of the sea with a hundred men-at-arms, to wage war on the garrisons at Lille and Douai while he sailed back to England to see how his forces were coping against the Scots. The earls of Salisbury and Suffolk, supported by some Flemings, mounted several campaigns on the king's behalf against the Lille garrison; but on the final occasion they ventured too far and found themselves trapped amid earthworks: they suffered heavy losses, and the earls themselves were captured and imprisoned at the Châtelet in Paris, where they stayed for more than two years. But I don't know enough about the other campaigns and adventures, so I'll say no more.

Chapter XXXIV

How the King of France sent an army into the land of Hainault around Chimay.

The King of France greatly strengthened his naval forces, of which Sir Hugues Quiéret was marshal and commander along with a seaman called 'Barbevair',[1] and they launched repeated raids and attacks upon the English, with both losses and gains. Among their gains were some fine ships built in magnificent style by the King of England, including one called the *Christopher*, and several others loaded with wool and other merchandise exported by the king; the French were jubilant, and celebrated and bragged about these gains, which added to the English anger.

The King of France also launched a mighty campaign all that winter – the year of grace 1339 – against Sir John of Hainault, because of all his enemies he was the nearest to hand. He ordered a number of attacks to be made against him and his lands of Chimay and Beaumont by Sir Jehan de la Bove, Sir Jehan de Moret and several other knights and squires with four or five hundred cavalry; they burned the country in repeated raids around Chimay, Baileux, Robechies, Salles, Villers-la-Tour, Froidchapelle and all the other villages, right up to the place where Chimay's gibbet stood. Count William of Hainault, Sir John's nephew, was incensed; both as his nephew and as his lord – his uncle held the lands of Chimay and Beaumont as his vassal – he sent a message of defiance to the King of France (who was also his uncle) and sided firmly with the other allies of the King of England. Indeed, he came to be King Philip's most bitter and intractable adversary in the whole war. And after he'd defied the king he raised a great army and went and seized Aubenton, a major city in the Thiérache, the finest in the region, and burned it to the ground.[2]

The whole winter was spent this way, burning the land and fighting the French; Hainaulters attacked Frenchmen, Frenchmen attacked Hainaulters, and at sea the French attacked the English and the English attacked the French. Then, when Lent came, the King of France assembled mighty forces at Le Cateau-

---

[1] See footnote 3, above, p.77.
[2] The exact date is uncertain, but it was some time in March 1340.

Cambrésis, and they went early one morning and burned the town of Bavay[1] in Hainault along with several of the surrounding villages; but in the course of their retreat Lord Boucicaut, one of the foremost of all the French knights, was taken prisoner.

When Easter was past King Philip of France summoned all his forces and sent his eldest son Lord John, with his Marshal and his Constable, to burn and utterly destroy the county of Hainault. They marched through the Vermandois and besieged the castle of Escaudoeuvres near Cambrai, which belonged to Sir John of Hainault. It was amply provisioned with everything needed to withstand a siege and defend it for a year, and there were two captains in the castle who were considered very brave and loyal: one was Sir Gérard de Saissignies and the other Robert Marmyon, and they had plenty of good companions. I don't know what went on, but various negotiations took place and, either because their courage deserted them or through treachery, the castle was surrendered and fell to the French on the sixth day.[2] What I do know is that Lord William, Count of Hainault, and his uncle Sir John had them dragged through Mons and broken on the wheel.

After the castle of Escaudoeuvres had fallen, Lord John of France, then called the Duke of Normandy, simply left, much to everyone's astonishment: no one could think or understand why such a huge army should leave with so little achieved; they could have wasted and destroyed the whole of Hainault if they'd wished, and most of Brabant with it – indeed, everyone had been expecting it.[3] But they did leave strong garrisons at Le Cateau-Cambrésis and Douai, who launched frequent attacks upon Valenciennes and other parts of Hainault; and the Count of Hainault sent Sir Thierry, lord of Valkenburg, with a hundred men-at-arms to hold Le Quesnoy against the French garrison at Le Cateau-Cambrésis, and sent another company to the castle of Bouchain, who launched attacks against the French at Douai; there were frequent adventures in both places.

Chapter XXXV

How the Duke of Normandy took a great army to besiege, capture and burn the mighty castle of Thun in the Cambrésis.

During the eight days after Pentecost the King of France issued another great command, sending the Duke of Normandy, his eldest son, with his Constable and his marshals to lay siege to the castle of Thun,[4] which Sir Walter Mauny and his men had won from the Bishop of Cambrai while the King of England and his allies were in the Cambrésis.[5] The Count of Hainault thought this huge force

---

[1] The attack on Bavay took place in July.
[2] The siege began in the second half of May and the castle surrendered on 3 June.
[3] This sudden retreat is doubtful. The French appear not to have withdrawn at all, but to have moved straight on to lay siege to Thun-l'Évêque, as described in the following chapter, just a few days later, on 14 June.
[4] Thun-l'Évêque.
[5] The castle had been captured by Mauny on 21 September 1339.

must be coming to lay waste his land and to complete what they'd left undone before; so the young count made such preparations as he could, and persuaded the Duke of Brabant, whose daughter he'd married, to send all his forces to help him protect his land of Hainault. The Duke of Guelders, too, and the Margrave of Jülich and several others answered the Duke of Brabant's appeal for aid, while the Count of Hainault went to the chapter at Liège cathedral to raise the support of the whole of Bishop Adolph's land; he swore fealty to the bishop and paid him the homage that he owed, and then asked him to come and defend his fief as by right he should. The bishop considered this and replied that he would gladly do what he could and should, but before taking any action he would first make a strong appeal to the King of France and bid him do nothing against his fiefdom; once he'd done that he would willingly fulfil his obligation. The count and his counsellors were satisfied with this, and he left Liège and rode as fast as he could to confront the French army on the River Scheldt.

The French were encamped before the castle of Thun, with the river between the two armies. The Duke of Brabant was there with a large force, as were the Duke of Guelders, the Margrave of Jülich, the Count of Loon, the lord of Valkenburg and Sir John of Hainault; they had at least five thousand men-at-arms, and were expecting the Flemings to join them but they didn't arrive in time. The Count of Hainault would gladly have crossed the river if he could, to raise the siege and do battle with the French king's army; but it wasn't possible, and he stayed encamped there in the fields for three days.

At the end of those three days, when the count realised there was no way of crossing the river to engage the French or raise the siege and that he was stuck there doing nothing with supplies running out, he made a very good and shrewd decision: he sent a secret message to the men in the castle, telling them that, as they could plainly see, he was unable to come to their aid, for which he was very sorry, and that they should escape from a tower under cover of darkness, set fire to the castle and save their lives by crossing the river. They took his advice and did as he bade, diving into the dangerous river and being helped from the water by some of the troops on the other bank. Then the Count of Hainault's allies departed and headed home to their own lands – as did the French, not realising what had happened, and imagining that all the Hainaulters had been lost in the fire.

Chapter XXXVI

How King Edward of England, on his way to help the Count of Hainault, defeated the King of France's admiral.

It was on the eve of Saint John the Baptist,[1] in the year of grace 1340, that the two great armies parted, as you've heard, and the castle of Thun was burnt. That very night God sent a mighty blessing upon the noble King Edward, who had put to sea to come and aid his brother-in-law the Count of Hainault. Sir

---

[1] 23 June.

Hugues Quiéret, informed of his approach, had assembled his whole great fleet to engage the king at sea. He was prowling the waves, stalking him, convinced that he couldn't escape, given the vast number of mighty ships at his command. He tracked him down right between Sluys and the isle of Cadzand, so that the onslaught and fighting that followed could be clearly seen from the dykes and harbour at Sluys. So great a battle at sea had never been witnessed before, and it lasted all day, from prime to vespers.

The French had at least twice as many ships as their adversaries, including the great ship called the *Christopher* which could destroy many smaller vessels; it did indeed inflict much damage on the English, and if God hadn't come to their aid they would have had no hope of resisting the French. But King Edward displayed such valour and performed such personal feats of prowess that he cheered and gave heart to all the rest; and through his prowess, and that of the Earl of Derby and of Sir Walter Mauny who fought magnificently (as did many others whose names I don't know), and principally by the grace of God, the French, Normans, Gascons, Bretons and Genoese were finally killed, drowned and utterly defeated: very few escaped. The English, too, suffered many losses, but they won back the mighty ship called the *Christopher* and a great number of other vessels. Sir Hugues Quiéret and a good number of his kinsmen were killed in this battle, along with fully thirty thousand men either slain or drowned, so it was said; a great many of their bodies were washed up by the sea on the beaches of Sluys and Cadzand, some of them fully armed, just as they had fought.

After God had granted King Edward this noble victory, he stayed on board his ship all that night and docked next morning at Sluys. The following day he set out on a pilgrimage to the church of Our Lady at Aardenburg,[1] and then came to Ghent[2] where he was welcomed with great joy and honour, and the Flemings, men and women alike, worshipped him as if he were God. The news of the great battle spread at once through every land. The King of France and all the French were downcast and dismayed, but all their enemies rejoiced. The King of France has never again had such domination of the sea: the noble King Edward has ever since been its sovereign prince.

When the noble Count of Hainault heard that King Edward had arrived in Ghent after his wondrous good fortune he was overjoyed, and set off at once to hail him and celebrate his triumph. They spoke together for a long while about their recent deeds, and decided to summon the Duke of Brabant and all the other lords to meet and discuss how they could mount a more effective campaign than the last against the King of France now that they had the support of the Flemings. It would be held, they decided, at Vilvoorde, and they asked Jacob van Artevelde to come, and to bring representatives of the principal cities of Flanders and those he knew would have the most telling influence in this matter; he returned word that he would gladly do so.

[1] This was renowned throughout Flanders as a place of pilgrimage in the Middle Ages.
[2] Edward was at Ghent from 10 to 18 July.

Chapter XXXVII

How the King of England and other great lords of his alliance
besieged the city of Tournai.

The day came when the allied lords and the Flemings were due to confer. The lords duly arrived – namely the noble King Edward, the Duke of Brabant and his council, the Count of Hainault and his uncle Sir John, the Duke of Guelders, the Margrave of Jülich and the lord of Valkenburg – and Jacob van Artevelde came with a great many aldermen from the cities of Flanders. It was agreed that day by all the lords and delegates present that their best possible move would be to lay siege to the city of Tournai; for if they had Tournai under their control they would have an open road through France as far as Compiègne and even Choisy, and the Flemings could easily mount sieges of Lille and Douai with an uninterrupted supply line from Tournai. With this resolved they departed to make their various preparations, having agreed a date when they would gather before Tournai to begin the siege.

The King of France soon had word of this and ordered the townspeople to stock the city with ample provisions to avoid any shortage, and sent his Constable with a huge force of men-at-arms to take control of the city and ensure its citizens mounted a proper defence.

On the day agreed by the lords and the Flemings they all arrived outside Tournai and laid siege to the city on every side.[1] The noble king took up a position on one side with Jacob van Artevelde and the Flemings close at hand; the Duke of Brabant was on another side with all his forces; and the Count of Hainault and all the other lords formed a third army on another so that the city was completely besieged; and they later built several bridges of boats across the Scheldt, which is wide and deep at that point, so that the armies could easily and safely cross to each other.

As soon as the siege had been established, the Count of Hainault, who was young and had undertaken the mission with zeal, mounted a series of ruinous raids into the kingdom of France: he burned all the land around Lille, setting fire to the town and abbey of Saint-Amand,[2] the town and abbey of Marchiennes and the whole of the country between Tournai and Douai. I would never be able to name all the towns and villages that were burned and wasted then, for the siege lasted a long time, the city being filled with good people most unwilling to give in. Chief among them was Lord Raoul, Constable of France and Count of Eu, with his son the Count of Guînes, Viscount Aimery of Narbonne, Sir Aymard of Poitiers, Sir Geoffroi de Charny, Sir Girard de Montfaucon, the governor of the city of Tournai Sir Godemar du Fay, the King of France's marshal Sir Robert Bertrand, the seneschal of Poitou[3] and the lord of Cayeu. These were all noble men, counts and bannerets, and in their company were the flower of the squires of

---

[1]   The siege of Tournai began on 1 August 1340.
[2]   Saint-Amand-les-Eaux.
[3]   Jourdain de Loubert.

France, of Poitou, of Gascony and all the other lands, who conducted themselves most honourably, despite all the troubles and shortages they encountered in the city; and they fought many fine skirmishes with men of the besieging armies when they saw an opportunity.

Now I shall name the besiegers: first among them were the noble King Edward and the noble prelate the Bishop of Lincoln, the Earl of Derby who is now Duke of Lancaster and the worthiest knight in the world, the earls[1] of Northampton and Gloucester, the Earl of Warwick, and Lord John, viscount of Beaumont.[2] Lord Robert of Artois arrived later, along with forces from Ypres and Poperinghe and a great host of Flemings who weren't present at the start of the siege – though Jacob van Artevelde was there at the outset with men of Ghent and Bruges, as you've heard.

Besieging the city on other sides were the Duke of Brabant with the knights and squires and commoners of his fine towns and land, and the Duke of Guelders, the Count of Hainault and his uncle Sir John, the Margrave of Jülich, the Count of the Marck, the lord of Valkenburg and the flower of chivalry to be found in their lands and elsewhere. A huge number of Flemings were involved, too – indeed, almost the whole population! – for with the agreement of Jacob van Artevelde and the allied lords, the men of Ypres and Poperinghe and Vans and Cassel, fully forty thousand in all, were encamped outside the city of Cassel to oppose the French king's garrisons at Saint-Omer and Aire[3] and stop them entering Flanders from that side.

And indeed, a notable adventure befell this Flemish army, of whom King Edward had appointed Robert of Artois captain. One day some of these Flemings went to attack Saint-Omer, breaking into many houses in the suburbs and being so hungry for booty that they looted whatever they could find. Some of the French knights stationed in Saint-Omer sallied through another gate – some sixty in full armour and three hundred more in brigandines[4] – and rode around the town until they found these Flemings robbing and pillaging, without a captain or any order, and charged through them in their herds just as they found them and slaughtered a huge number. Others seeing this took to flight – it was every man for himself – and kept going till they reached their camp at Cassel, while the knights of Saint-Omer rode back into the town rejoicing over their great success. And then something quite extraordinary happened – I've never heard of anything so strange. That very night, just after their rout, these Flemings, lying asleep in their tents outside Cassel, were seized around midnight by such a terrible fear and dread, all of them together, that they leapt up in terror, struck their tents and pavilions, loaded their carts in panic-stricken haste and, without waiting for each other, went rushing off in all directions. Their captain Lord Robert of Artois and his fellows couldn't make them stop even long enough to

[1] As before (above, p.78), Le Bel uses the singular, thinking they were one and the same person.
[2] As noted previously (footnote 8, above, p.78), there were no English viscounts at this time. This is presumably John, 2nd baron Beaumont.
[3] Aire-sur-la-Lys.
[4] 'lx armeures de fer et ccc brigans' : see footnote 4, above, p.25, and below, p 222.

explain what was wrong. Those who were slower than the others abandoned their tents and pavilions and went rushing off after the rest, and before day broke they'd already gone two leagues: no plea or entreaty would make them stay with Lord Robert. Seeing there was nothing he could do, Lord Robert didn't want to linger among his enemies – especially in a place where he was so hated – so he set off smartly with the rest and made his way to King Edward outside Tournai to report this strange affair, which was a mystery to all. The Flemings who'd fled turned up in gaggles to rejoin their fellows at Tournai; they recounted their wild adventure, but could no more explain how or why it had happened than if they'd been enchanted.

Around prime, when the men of Saint-Omer heard that the Flemings had disappeared, they went to their camp and found a vast array of carts, horses, tents and all kinds of gear, and bread and wine and other provisions, and took the whole lot back to Saint-Omer: it was a mighty horde they'd won, and it brought them much joy and comfort.

Chapter XXXVIII

How the King of France came within two leagues of Tournai to raise
the siege, but a settlement was made and agreement reached.

This siege of Tournai lasted a good while. It was hard enough on the besiegers, despite the fact that all necessary supplies arrived in great plenty up the Scheldt from Flanders and Brabant and elsewhere, and a fair amount by wagon; but as for the people inside the city, they would have been in serious trouble if they hadn't taken action, for nothing at all could reach them and the King of France was slow to come to their aid. They discussed what to do, and sent out of the city, right through the enemy lines, all manner of people – men, women and children – who were of no use to them and didn't have the wherewithal to support themselves; and if the lords and men-at-arms in the city hadn't taken these decisive measures, the citizens wouldn't have been able to hold out so long, for they could see their supplies were rapidly dwindling and, much to their dismay, they had no news of definite help from the king.

King Philip of France, very unhappy to have his people suffering so in Tournai and to see the shame and disgrace that were being inflicted upon him, sent a strict and urgent command throughout his kingdom, near and far, that all men without fail, young and old alike, except those he'd stationed in his fortresses, should come at his bidding to Arras where he was awaiting them. Day by day they streamed in, and as they arrived he saw them billeted in the country towns and villages between Arras and Douai. The king also sent the most earnest appeal possible to the noble King of Bohemia and to Adolph de la Marck, Bishop of Liège, and to the Bishop of Metz and the Duke of Lorraine and the counts of Bar, Savoy, Geneva, Saarbrücken and Montbéliard, and to the lord of Montfaucon and Sir Jean de Chalon – all from the Empire, not from his kingdom – asking them to come to Arras with all the troops at their disposal. When they joined the French lords at Arras you may be sure they made a formidable army and a mighty host of fine warriors, namely the lords of France, the king, his eldest son John who was at that time Duke of Normandy, the young King David of Scotland, the King of Navarre, Sir Louis de Clermont, the Duke of Burgundy, Lord Charles the Count of Alençon, the dukes of Brittany and Athens, the counts of Blois, Flanders, Armagnac and Harcourt, the viscounts of Thouars and Ventadour, the worthy prelate the Bishop of Beauvais, the lord of Noyers and a great many more noble knights, barons and bannerets whose names I don't know.

When all the above-named lords had gathered at Arras, the king decided to advance upon his enemies besieging Tournai. He set out, followed by everyone in due order, and they rode on until they came to a little river some two short leagues from Tournai.[1] It was narrow but very deep, and surrounded by mires and marshes; the only way to the further bank was by a little bridge[2] so narrow that a single man on horseback would have been hard pressed to cross. So the whole army camped in the fields, the river being impassable, and stayed there all the following day while the lords closest to the king discussed how they could cross the river and the marsh in greater safety.

That evening, some Hainaulters and men of Brabant and Hesbaye, realising that the King of France's army was so near, conferred and agreed to go next day and reconnoitre their position, and if they saw an opportunity they'd venture an attack. They did as planned: next morning they rode up close to the enemy; but they didn't cross the river and couldn't see any French troops they could engage. Not wanting to return without leaving their mark, they set fire to two poor dwellings that remained unburnt and then rode back to their quarters.

Other young companions from Hainault and Hesbaye and Brabant who were in Sir John of Hainault's company, hearing what these others had done, thought they'd do a better job. They rose before daybreak; Sir Waflard[3] was to guide them, as he knew the surrounding area well having waged a long campaign against the people of Lille (and inflicted a good deal of harm), and he promised to lead them to a useful spot if they cared to follow him.

Now, that same morning, some fellows from the Bishop of Liège's force, encamped closer to the river than the rest, had risen along with troops from Hesbaye,[4] from the lands of Monthalt and the Condroz and Bouillon, to go and forage in the fields beyond the river, thinking there'd be better foraging on the Tournai side. Before dawn they crossed the bridge, one by one, and went off in separate bands to start cutting sheaves where they found the best corn. There was such a thick mist that morning that they couldn't see each other half the length of a lance away. Riding through this mist, unable to see a thing, were the Hainaulters and men of Hesbaye from the Count of Hainault's company; and just as the sun came up they ran into troops under the Bishop of Liège's banner who

---

[1]   The Marque, which flows into the Deûle at Marquette near Lille after running through an area of marshland.
[2]   This is probably the bridge at Tressin.
[3]   Waflard (or Vauflart) de la Croix.
[4]   There are men from Hesbaye (the country around Liège) fighting on both sides.

were guarding his foragers, scattered about the fields, gathering their sheaves of corn. The company with the bishop's banner numbered no more than twenty, while there were fully seventy Hainaulters and men of Hesbaye from the Count of Hainault's army, all top men, being knights and squires of the highest quality. They rode so close to the foragers that, before they realised what had happened, they were right on top of each other and there was no withdrawing. They launched themselves at one another and a fine contest followed. When Connars de Lonchiens – who was subsequently knighted and made master of the bishop's banner (though another was its bearer at the time, and unaware of the clash that had taken place) – realised there was no force to oppose these Hainaulters and men of Hesbaye and Brabant and that things were looking bad, he dismounted to make a stand, preferring to die than flee. So did Henry d'Asse, a canon of Saint John at Liège, whose prowess had often been witnessed; and Thierry de Mohalt, canon of Huy, dismounted likewise, as did the squire Colart le Panetier. These four mounted such a valiant defence that they earned great honour; they bore the full brunt of the fighting from first to last, without any of the foragers coming to their aid when they heard the sounds of combat – but they didn't know what was going on because of the thick mist. But some of the Bishop of Liège's men did join the fighting and conducted themselves well alongside the four; among them were Sir Henry de Fexhe and his brother Sir Ogier, Sir Baldwin of Saint-Servais and his brother Sir John, Sir Colin Freypont, Sir Robert de Tuwegnies, Liebert d'Almonses, master Conrard who was the bishop's cook and performed as well as any, and Jehan de Walhain; and also a worthy clerk, the rector of Winchekus, who acquitted himself splendidly and received a cut across the nose and face; a number of fellows from Bouillon fought well, too. Of the party from Hainault Sir Jehan de Wargny was killed, as were Sir Gautier de Pourelach from the county of Namur and Sir Willaume Pypempoys from Brussels, all three of them knights, along with some others whose names I don't know; and taken captive were Sir Jehan de Sorre, Sir Daynals de Blise and Sir Race de Moncheaulx, most worthy men, and Sir Loys de Jupeleu and a number of other squires and fine companions whose names I cannot at the moment give. The Hainaulters and men of Hesbaye, realising the tide was turning against them, retreated in good order as soon as they saw a chance.

When the King of France heard the news that the Bishop of Liège's men had performed so well and held the field against the enemy he was overjoyed. But it was a day of fortune and honour for the men of Hesbaye who'd fought on both sides: those of the bishop's party had defended themselves valiantly when attacked, but those on the Count of Hainault's side had withdrawn in good order when they saw things were going amiss, so there's no reason – other than animosity – to reproach them for it.

But now I shall return to the story and tell how the two armies parted.

Chapter XXXIX

How a truce was made between the two kings at the siege of Tournai,
through the mediation of my lady of Hainault, sister of the French
king and mother of the Queen of England.

At this time that sovereign of good ladies, my lady of Hainault, was the abbess
of Fontenelle.[1] She had been the wife of the worthy Count of Hainault,
father of the living count who was waging war alongside the others, and was
mother of the young queen of England; she was also the sister of King Philip
of France, and so was very unhappy to see this conflict last so long. She had
frequently ridden on horse or wagon after her brother King Philip to see if she
could intervene; but she could never make any headway, even though she often
threw herself in tears at her brother's feet. Nonetheless she continued to follow
him earnestly; and when the king and his army were encamped very close to their
enemies, as you've heard, the good lady, with the help of the most noble King of
Bohemia, obtained leave to go and speak to her son the Count of Hainault and
his fellow lords to see if there was any way of reaching agreement – either a truce
or permanent peace. At her request the noble King of Bohemia sent Sir Louis
d'Aigimont with her, because he was well liked by all the lords on both sides.

With Sir Louis's help the good lady, after much effort, managed to secure a
meeting on the following day to which each party would send four eminent men
to explore all paths to reconciliation, if it pleased God; and it was agreed that
all hostilities would be suspended for three days: neither side was to harm the
other. The meeting was to take place at a chapel that stood in the fields at a place
called Esplechin. The good lady and Sir Louis returned to the King of France
and his council and told them how they'd fared with the opposing lords; and
after much discussion the King of France, knowing from reliable reports that his
people inside Tournai were short of food and couldn't hold out much longer,
and realising he couldn't easily come to their aid because of the risky crossing
of the river and the marsh, agreed to the meeting on the proposed day and to
the suspension of hostilities. And he and the other lords, when they heard his
decision, spread word of this to all his forces.

Next morning, after mass and refreshment, the delegates met in the said
chapel, the good lady with them. From the King of France's side came the King
of Bohemia, the Bishop of Liège, the Count of Alençon (the king's brother), the
Count of Flanders and the Count of Armagnac; from the King of England's
side came the Bishop of Lincoln, the Duke of Brabant, the Duke of Guelders,
the Margrave of Jülich and Sir John of Hainault. Once they'd all arrived they
greeted each other with great respect and cordiality, and then began to discuss a
settlement.

All that first day they debated how they could come to terms; and all the
while that good lady was trying to mediate, humbly beseeching both parties to

---

[1]   Jeanne de Valois, wife of Count William I of Hainault, had retired to the abbey of Fontenelle
      when he died in 1337.

compromise. But the day passed without any clear agreement, and they went their separate ways with a promise to return to the chapel next morning. The following day they duly returned to continue negotiations, and finally found ways of coming to terms; but it was too late in the day to set it all down in writing, so the meeting broke up with renewed promises to come back in the morning to complete the business. On the third day the lords reconvened and a truce was agreed. It was to last a full year, and the year was to begin at once for all the lords there present; but for those fighting in Scotland, Gascony, Poitou and Saintonge it was to begin in forty days: during that time both parties were to inform their supporters in those lands – without any deviousness – that the truce had been made but that in those parts they would be free to observe it or to carry on fighting as they wished. This truce was made on condition that each party, in the period of the truce, would hold in peace the territory they currently possessed.

With the truce agreed and sealed by both sides – much to the joy of the Brabançons, who desired only an end, honourable or otherwise – at first light next day tents were struck and wagons loaded and everyone rushed to pack barrels and chests. Anyone who'd seen this would have said: "I'm witnessing the dawn of a new age!"

And so, as you've heard, the two armies separated thanks to the efforts and intervention of that noble lady (God have mercy on her soul); and the fine city of Tournai was left free and unharmed having been on the brink of disaster – all its supplies had been running out: they hadn't enough to last even three or four more days.

The Brabançons were quick to leave: they couldn't wait to be gone. The noble King Edward wouldn't have left at all if he'd had any choice, but he had to accept the advice of the other lords and accede to their wishes in part. The Count of Hainault and his uncle Sir John would have been equally reluctant to agree if they'd known as much as the King of France about the plight of the men inside the city, and if the Duke of Brabant hadn't privately told them that he was struggling to keep his Brabançons there, and that in any event he wouldn't be able to stop them leaving that day or the next if no agreement was reached.

The King of France and his army were happy enough to go: they couldn't put up much longer with the stench of the cattle slaughtered so close to their quarters, or with the heat; and they thought honour in the affair rested with them, reasoning that they'd rescued and saved the good city of Tournai and seen off the great force besieging it, who'd achieved nothing for all their effort and expense. But the lords on the other side likewise claimed the honour: they'd stayed so long in the kingdom of France and laid siege to one of its finest cities and burnt and laid waste the King of France's land before his very eyes, and he'd done nothing to send aid in the time he should and had finally agreed to a truce when his enemies were encamped before his city and burning and ravaging his land, so he was carrying home, to his chambers in Paris, the unredeemed shame inflicted upon him.

And so both sides wanted to claim the honour, which has led to many debates and arguments – in taverns and noble chambers and elsewhere – between companions in arms and people who think themselves judges of such matters, whenever there's been a clash of allegiances. Some may be surprised and wonder how it was that the allied lords should have upped and left without further action, when they'd committed so much effort and expense to besieging Tournai, and had been there so long that the city's supplies were bound to be running low, and could plainly see that the French king could neither cross the river unless they let him nor raise the siege without breaking through their lines, and had achieved no part of their intention in coming there. To anyone who puzzles so, the answer that might be given is this: it was because of the men of Brussels, who had worked on the other Brabançons and completely undermined their will to stay. The Flemings were close to going as well, which would have left the lords bereft of men and made their leaving a hundred times more shameful. All this was the work of subversive, meddling misinformers; but their treachery was soon laid bare as I'll explain.

It was not long after all the lords had departed and returned to their own lands that the Duke of Brabant was informed that he and all the allies had been betrayed by the devious work of certain citizens of Brussels, who in their haughty pride have always wanted to be the greatest in Brabant, though Leuven is the duchy's principal city. These men of Brussels had received a great deal of money from the King of France to enable them to bribe those of their city and of Leuven and Antwerp and all the other towns to leave the army and return home, so that the lords would be unable to sustain the siege and would have to abandon it in shame. The King of France had given them liberty to distribute gold and silver wherever they thought it would be best used, to the people who would have the most subversive influence. The duke felt deeply betrayed – and thought the King of France's money had been well spent, for those Brussels folk had done their work most effectively! He was very angry, and feared he himself might be suspected by the allied lords in view of the long delay he'd caused the other campaign. He decided to discuss this with Sir John of Hainault, whom he wholly trusted, and to keep quiet about it until he'd decided what to do. So as soon as he could he asked Sir John to come to him, and told him everything that had happened and how he felt about it and how he'd come to learn of it. Sir John was appalled when he heard about the plot, and demanded the names of all those involved; they were given to him in writing, secretly. Among them was the king's most secret agent, who went back and forth to Paris frequently, always taking a furtive route by way of Chimay and the Thiérache. Knowing this, Sir John had him watched until he and his son were arrested one morning between Anor and Mondrepuis and taken to Beaumont, shocked and very scared. As soon as Sir John heard of their arrival he went to speak to the man and grilled him about his business. He was sharp and chose his words cleverly, but he didn't hide his name, revealing that he was Evrard Hyerclais. Sir John was overjoyed, knowing he'd found one of the chief culprits.

When news of his capture reached Brussels, all the man's companions were horrified and fled from the city at once: Watyer Engloye and his son Renier and two others went to Tournai, while Sir Clays Zuaure, a knight of Brussels, fled to Namur; and as soon as the duke knew this he sent men in pursuit to see if they could catch him. When Sir Clays Zuaure spotted them he didn't feel too comfortable: he slipped across the bridge over the Meuse and headed for Dinant. But the duke's men got wind of this and swiftly caught up and captured him and took him right through Namur to Wavre.[1] That's where the duke was; he was overjoyed, and had him beheaded before all the people of his land and aldermen of cities elsewhere.

The Count of Hainault was delighted to hear how matters had progressed, and he sent word to his uncle Sir John to have Evrard Hyerclais sent to Mons in Hainault; there the count had him dragged through the streets to the gibbet, but after desperate pleading he had him beheaded without being broken on the wheel.

The other men who'd fled from Brussels stayed a long while in exile, helpless with shame; and although they finally made their peace with money and returned absolved to their homes and possessions, the infamy stayed with them forever. Just as you've heard, so it was that the treachery was uncovered.

Of the adventures that occurred meanwhile in Gascony, Poitou and the other regions I'm not well informed and shall make no mention; nor shall I speak of events in Scotland between the English and the Scots, for I might well stray from the truth. It's better that I say nothing until I have more time and am better informed, for I'm reluctant to say anything that isn't true. And certainly, what I've written so far I've kept as accurate as possible, according to what I've witnessed myself and can remember, or have heard reliably reported by those who've been present when I have not; and if I've made mistakes at any point, I ask pardon.

Chapter XL

How the kings of Spain and Portugal defeated three heathen kings who had entered Spain and were besieging a great city.

As it would be wrong to forget the adventures that took place in distant lands while these wars were being waged, I don't want to overlook the great adventure and good fortune that befell the King of Spain[2] in his battle in Castile against the Saracens, and all Christendom should forever thank Our Lord for the wondrous power He manifested then. Know, then, that in the year of grace 1340, in the month of September, three Saracen kings were besieging a fine and mighty city in the kingdom of Castile named Tarifa, which stood beside the sea or very near. These three kings were the King of Granada,[3] the great king of the Benimerines[4] and his son King Abu Umar; they had an immense army, estimated at sixty thousand mounted men-at-arms and three hundred thousand men on foot, armed with pikes, bows, crossbows and weapons of their own kind – not

[1] A possible interpretation of 'Vuive'.
[2] Alfonso XI, King of Castile.
[3] Yusuf I.
[4] Abu al-Hasan, sultan of the Benimerines – the house of Banu Marin (hence the name 'King Benmarin' which is shortly to be used by Le Bel) – a powerful Berber dynasty in North Africa. He ruled from 1331-51.

counting their commanders, and not to mention their queens and wives which they always take to war with them. They'd been encamped before the city for a long while, much to the fury of the King of Spain.

At last, unable to endure this affront any longer, he summoned all the great lords of his land and all the men and elders of his cities and his other chief towns to meet on a certain day to discuss how they could defend and purge their country of these people bent on ruining and destroying them in their thirst for conquest. They concluded that they would rather put their lives and possessions in the hands of Our Lord in defending their land and the Law of Christ against the infidels and die in honour, than suffer such wrong and live in shame, even though they could raise small numbers to oppose such a mighty host. They fixed a date to gather, all prepared to live or die, at a place just two short leagues from the Saracens.

When the day came and they were all assembled, they found they had no more than thirteen thousand foot soldiers, which hardly matched the vast number of men on horse and foot mentioned above; nonetheless, they trusted so much in the justice of their cause and in the grace of Our Lord, for whose faith they were fighting, that they agreed with one accord to advance against the enemy. They sent messengers to the Saracen lords bidding them withdraw and make amends for the harm they'd done or be prepared to do battle on the third day.

On the first day after their council of war, the King of Spain and the King of Portugal[1] advanced towards their enemies with their whole army, all resolved to live or die and to await the will of Our Lord. They did likewise on the second day and the third, and camped just two short leagues from the waiting foe. When the Saracen hosts saw them approaching, they left their camp and formed three immense battalions, each one hundred and twenty thousand strong, fairly close to the river that the Christians had to cross. Of these three battalions King Benmarin[2] had the greatest and was positioned in the centre; the King of Granada's was stationed to the left of the great King Benmarin's, closer to the river and the crossing the Christians had to make; and King Abu Umar, king of Tlemcen,[3] son of the great King Benmarin, commanded the third battalion on his father's right hand. As soon as the King of Spain and the King of Portugal saw these three battalions thus arrayed they decided to make confession and receive the body of Our Lord as true Christians; then they would place themselves at the will[4] and pleasure of God. So they both heard mass most devoutly, especially the King of Spain, who allegedly had never made confession before in all his life, and who had never been faithful or chaste towards the Queen his wife who had borne him two fine sons; he had kept another lover, whom he called 'the ravishing Donerde';[5] he'd had several children by her, and kept this extraordinary beauty

---

[1]   Afonso IV ('the Brave').
[2]   See footnote 4, above, p.95.
[3]   'Tramente'. The kingdom of Tlemcen (roughly the western part of modern Algeria) had been annexed by Abu al-Hasan in 1337.
[4]   Again Le Bel uses the word 'aventure': see footnote 4, above, p.80.
[5]   'la riche Donerde'. The scribe of the extant manuscript seems to have struggled here: per-haps it should read 'Done Eléonore' or the like, as Alfonso's famous mistress, by whom he

in such great state and luxury – with ten times as fine a household and attire as the Queen his proper wife – that everyone was amazed. But now he made confession and received the holy sacrament with all devotion; and he prostrated himself, fully armed, with a deeply contrite and repentant heart, before all his people, noble and non-noble alike. They were all moved to pity and fired with a will to do well, and the king vowed then that he would thenceforth be a good Christian and a true son of Holy Church and behave chastely, if God would grant him victory that day against his enemies. Then he stood and made the sign of the true cross and mounted his charger at once, and commanded the banners to advance to the river.

He had just six thousand mounted troops in his battalion; he'd sent all his foot soldiers to join the King of Portugal, who'd deployed his battalion to the King of Spain's left, confronting the King of Granada. The third of the Christian battalions, commanded by the marshal of the army, numbered about four thousand mounted men, and faced the battalion of King Abu Umar, king of Tlemcen.

Having sworn his oath the King of Spain spurred forward, a man without fear, and rode with his banners and his men and, by the grace of God and with the utmost difficulty and the utmost fortune, forded the river and engaged King Benmarin's battalion so mightily that, by the grace of Our Lord, most of the Saracens took to flight. The great King Benmarin hesitated, but when his men saw each other fleeing they all turned and fled. Their spirits soaring, the King of Spain and his men charged among the Saracens like ravening wolves among a flock of sheep, killing as many as they could and pursuing them all day long, from terce[1] to nightfall without respite. And the other battalions did likewise, killing and slaying so many that no certain count was ever made; but it was said that there was never such a slaughter in any battle, and some numbered the dead at more than one hundred thousand men, though the Christians lost no more than forty, some good men, some not. The mighty King Benmarin and the King of Granada somehow managed to escape, but the King of Tlemcen was captured along with many other great lords whose names I don't know.[2]

When it had grown so dark that the Christians could no longer see or recognise each other they gave orders to return to camp – or to the Saracens' camp, to take whatever they found. They rode all night, almost till dawn, without anything to eat or drink. And when they reached the Saracen camp they found that the people of the surrounding country had plundered everything and killed women and children, noble and lesser alike, including the Queen, the wife of King Benmarin and daughter of the King of Tunis,[3] and a vast number of other ladies of high degree: they were beyond all counting – as were the riches and the treasures found there. Next day the king and all the Christians had three most solemn masses sung, thanking Our Lord for the great grace He had sent them, before they all set off homeward, each to his own land.

---

had ten children between 1330 and '45, was Eleanor of Guzman.
[1]   The third canonical hour, about 9 a.m.
[2]   Le Bel has here described the Battle of Río Salado, fought on 30 October 1340.
[3]   '*Thumes*'.

When summer came, the King of Spain, with a keen desire to win back those cities and castles that the Saracens had conquered, summoned all his people and led them to a mighty castle held by the Saracens: they had a huge garrison there, waging constant war on the surrounding country. The castle was called Alcalá; the king besieged it for a long while before he could take it, and great lords and valiant men from all parts of Christendom flocked to this siege, as pilgrims, to test themselves and enhance their honour, and stayed there with the king until the castle was surrendered and recovered.[1]

Shortly after, the King of Spain, not content to stop at that, laid siege by land and sea to the fine and noble city called Algeciras, right at the very tip of his kingdom. He stayed there for two years before he could take it, indeed longer; and in a place outside its walls many fine displays of arms were seen between the pilgrims from foreign lands and the Saracens. The Christians lost more often than the Saracens in these clashes and skirmishes, for they were too reckless in their attempts to enhance their honour against the mighty, eminent lords who had come there from every land – there were pilgrims on both sides. Those lost there included the young knight Sir Godefroy de Loon, son of Count Thierry of Heinsberg and Blankenberg, which was a grievous pity. And to this siege came, as pilgrims, the noble King of Navarre and the Count of Foix, both of whom died natural deaths there; also the Duke of Lancaster, whose title then was Earl of Derby, and the Earl of Salisbury and a host of other lords – counts and dukes and great barons of France and England and Germany and other countries I can't name. Many of them died there, either a natural death or in combat.

Chapter XLI

How Lord Charles of Bohemia was crowned King of Germany.

During the period of war and peace between the kingdoms of France and England, many notable events, as I'll explain in due course, took place in Gascony, Poitou, Limousin and Brittany and in the Scottish marches, for the truce agreed at the lifting of the siege of Tournai was not well observed in all parts, as you'll hear.

In the year of grace 1344, on Saint Hubert's day,[2] Adolph de la Marck, Bishop of Liège, died at the castle of Clermont; he had been faced by many and frequent challenges in his life, sometimes in his own lands and sometimes against his neighbours, and had been bishop for fully thirty years. The Roman curia appointed to the bishopric after him his brother's son, Engelbert, Count of la Marck, who had previously been provost of Liège; and within three years of his arrival he was to have a testing time with the municipalities of Liège and Huy and Hesbaye and the Condroz and all his other lands.

In the year of grace 1345 the Emperor Louis of Bavaria died; and that most noble king, the King of Bohemia, set to work at once, and ensured that his eldest

---

[1]   On 15 August 1341.
[2]   3 November.

son Lord Charles was elected by the majority of the electors of the King of Germany, and had the consent of Pope Clement VI and all the Roman curia. But Lord Charles was later to face many trials and misfortunes after the death of his father the King of Bohemia, who died at the battle at Blanchetaque near Crécy-en-Ponthieu,[1] where the noble King Edward, with only a small force, defeated King Philip of France and his mighty army: there the worthy King of Bohemia was killed, along with the Count of Alençon (the King of France's brother), the Count of Blois (his sister's son), the Count of Flanders, the Duke of Lorraine and many other great lords and barons of whom you'll hear in this history, if it comes to be completed.

After his noble father's death Lord Charles, elected King of the Romans as I say, couldn't be crowned at Aachen as soon as he would have liked. He had to be crowned instead at the city of Bonn which stands on the Rhine, because there were two electors opposed to him who had elected another at Frankfurt: that was where according to ancient custom, they said, kings of Germany were to be chosen, whereas Lord Charles had been elected at Koblenz on the Rhine. And so it was that Lord Charles couldn't be crowned in peace at Aachen but had a long battle on his hands, because these two electors – the Duke of Bavaria and the Marquis of Brandenburg – were fiercely opposed to him. He finally had to make peace with them, and married the young Duke of Bavaria's sister; and then, by common consent, he was crowned again at Aachen, with his wife the young queen and all the high lords of Germany in glorious array. This was in the year of grace 1349, in the month of August.[2]

It was at this time that the whole world was afflicted by an all-encompassing mortality from a disease called 'the swelling'[3] or 'the epidemic'. It affected some people under the left arm and others in the groin, and they died within three days; and when it had struck a particular street or house one person caught it from another, so that few people dared help or visit the sick and it was barely possible to make confession because it was hard to find a priest willing to minister; nor did anyone dare wear or even touch the clothes of the stricken. No one knew what to think or how to cure it; rather, many thought it was a miracle, God's vengeance for the sins of the world, which is why some then, out of deep devotion, began a harsh and extraordinary form of penance. In Germany, and elsewhere, people began to roam the land in great bands and companies, carrying crucifixes, flags and big silk banners, processing through the streets, two by two, loudly singing songs in rhyming verse to God and Our Lady; and twice a day they'd stop and strip down to their underclothes and flog themselves with all their might – singing all the while – with spiked scourges so that blood poured from their shoulders and all over them, and then threw themselves on the ground three

---

[1]   This is a surprising confusion. As Le Bel later seems perfectly aware, the engagement at Blanchetaque was a separate action that took place two days before the battle at nearby Crécy where the blind King John of Bohemia was killed.

[2]   Charles IV was crowned Holy Roman Emperor at Bonn in November 1346 and at Aachen in July 1349.

[3]   'la boche': I take this to be 'la bosse' – 'the hump' or 'lump' – a reference to the swellings associated with bubonic plague.

times as a mark of devotion. They endured it all with great humility, and after these various rites they would take charitable lodging wherever it was offered. They said they had to continue their penance for thirty two and a half days, and that they knew this from divine example, remembering Our Lord who walked the Earth for about thirty two and a half years.

When some of these penitents came to Liège people flocked to witness their sufferings and watched in awe, and gave them money with sincere devotion; and those who couldn't offer them lodging were ashamed, for all felt they were holy people sent by God to give an example to everyone to do penance for the remission of sins. Some men of Liège learned from them and translated their songs into the vernacular, and gathered a great number of their fellows and went through the lands of Liège and Brabant and Hainault and many other parts, performing the rites described above and calling themselves brothers. So many followed their example that it seemed that everyone was inspired with devotion, wanting to copy them; and eventually this craze spread to such a degree that every town was filled with these people, who bound themselves with the names of flagellants and brothers, and they urged each other on until their mortification turned to pride and presumption. If the Pope hadn't restricted their behaviour by imposing severe sentences they could have brought down Holy Church; indeed, they'd already begun to disrupt the Church's services and offices, some of them claiming in their madness that their songs and rites were of more worth than those of the Church, so that there were fears that this hysteria might spread until it brought the Church down, and that they would start killing priests and clerks, coveting their property and benefices.

While these flagellants were at large, an extraordinary thing happened that should certainly not be forgotten. When people saw this mortality and pestilence wasn't going to stop despite their penance, a rumour arose and spread that it was caused by the Jews: that the Jews had thrown venoms and toxins in wells and springs throughout the world to poison the whole of Christendom and gain mastery and possession of all the Earth. This fired everyone, great and small, with such loathing towards them that, everywhere the flagellants went, the Jews were all burnt and put to death by the local lords and justices. But they all went to their deaths dancing and singing as if they were going to a wedding, and refused to be converted to Christ, mothers and fathers alike, and no amount of pleading would persuade them to let their children be baptised: they insisted they'd found in their books of prophets that when this sect of flagellants appeared in the world all Jewry would be destroyed by fire, and that the souls of those who died happily, in steadfast faith, would go to Paradise. So when they saw the fires, women and men alike leapt in, singing, carrying their children in their arms for fear they might be taken away to be baptised.

Chapter XLII

How a great conflict arose between Duke Wenceslaus[1] and
the Count of Flanders over the duchy of Brabant.

Now I shall return to Charles, King of Germany and the Romans, who was well occupied after the aforementioned solemnities at Aachen and the coronation of his young wife – but then, it's not often that the German king can live in peace if he wishes to correct and solve all the problems in Germany. All the same, King Charles did his work well until the time came when he crossed the mountains – whereupon he managed what no King of Germany had managed before him, and it was so remarkable that I shall record it here.

It should be known that he handled matters so astutely, despite the divisions and factions that existed in Tuscany and Lombardy, that he spent the year 1354 in Lombardy and had himself crowned at Milan with the agreement and consent of the Milanese lords; then he was led by the Marquis of Montferrat with a mighty escort to Rome, where, without trouble or contest, he was crowned Emperor for the third time. He then made his way back, quite peacefully, through Tuscany and Lombardy, and in 1355 returned to his kingdom of Bohemia as rightful Emperor.

It was in that same year of '55, after the feast of Saint Nicholas, that Duke John of Brabant died.[2] He had three married daughters; the eldest had first married Count William of Hainault who had died in Frisia,[3] and was then married a second time to Lord Wenceslaus, Duke of Luxembourg, brother of the Emperor Charles; the second daughter was married to Count Louis of Flanders and the third to Duke Reginald of Guelders. After Duke John's death Duke Wenceslaus of Luxembourg went with his wife lady Jehanne to all the cities and all parts of Brabant and claimed lordship of the whole duchy as the eldest heir by virtue of being married to the eldest daughter. But the Duke of Guelders also claimed part of the duchy on behalf of the lady his wife.

The Brabançons met to discuss this and would not allow the duchy to be divided. They made Duke Wenceslaus many promises, among them being that they would accept him as Duke of Brabant, as regent during his wife's lifetime, and that, after her death, the duchy would go to the rightful heir; and to the Count of Flanders and the Duke of Guelders, as their wives' share, they offered great sums of money. This wasn't enough for the Count of Flanders; he said he was rich enough already and that he wouldn't sell his wife's inheritance: he would claim his right when he could. And he demanded of the duke and the country that they relinquish possession of Mechelen which was his rightful inheritance,

---

[1]   Duke Wenceslaus of Luxembourg (from 1355), the son of King John of Bohemia by his second wife.
[2]   To be precise, he died on the eve of Saint Nicholas, 5 December.
[3]   Count William II of Hainault had been killed in 1345 at the Battle of Staveren while suppressing a revolt in Frisia.

his father having acquired it from the bishopric of Liège,[1] though the late Duke of Brabant had wrongfully held and kept it for a long while.

   Duke Wenceslaus and the Brabançons were shocked by this demand and were not inclined to agree, and this promptly led to a mighty war between the two lands of Brabant and Flanders. Their armies confronted each other in great numbers around the abbey of Affligem[2] between the feast of Saint John and August in the year of '56. There a treaty was made through good and wise discussion; it was to the satisfactory honour of both parties, but when the men of Brussels returned to their city it seemed to them, in their pride, that they had been betrayed by their negotiators and they threw all those they could find in prison, so that the peace did not proceed as agreed. The Count of Flanders and all the Flemings felt deceived, and some reassembled and marched back to a place between Affligem and Brussels. The Duke of Brabant, Lord Wenceslaus, was still in Brabant then, with a great force of men-at-arms at Brussels; with him were Count Thierry of Loon and the Count of Mons, son of the Margrave of Jülich, with a great number of bannerets and other knights. They advanced from Brussels and camped in the fields confronting the Flemings – who had no cavalry except some from Ghent and a few others from their land who were with their lord the count. All the men from Leuven and Brussels and the rest of the Brabançons went and camped there in the fields with their lord the duke.

   Next day they resolved to do battle with the Flemings, and left camp and formed their battalions with great determination.[3] The Flemings did likewise; but they had a good deal fewer foot soldiers than the Brabançons and not a quarter the number of cavalry, and when the battalions were formed on both sides and the Brabançons were arrayed against the Flemings they felt sure they would rout them. But when the point of engagement came, the commoners of Leuven and Brussels took to their heels without striking a blow; the lords, seeing this, were utterly dismayed and turned and fled likewise, not stopping till they reached Brussels. Duke Wenceslaus fled to Leuven and the Count of Loon back to his land, each as best he could.

   When the Flemings saw their enemies fly they marched onward in fine order, right to the gates of Brussels, and could easily have entered if they'd wanted, for there was no one to oppose them. They lodged in the suburbs all that day and most of the night, while the Count of Flanders and a number of others camped in the pavilions that the lords had left abandoned in the fields. Anyone keen to plunder found rich pickings there, for the Brabançon lords had taken only what they wore on their backs: they'd left tents, equipment, provisions and all their baggage. As for the duchess, who'd been at Coudenberg,[4] she fled alone, with just a single chambermaid and a single page, and didn't stop riding until she reached Binche.

---

[1]   The bishop and chapter of Liège had sold Mechelen to the Count of Flanders in 1333.
[2]   In Brabant, a few miles north-west of Brussels.
[3]   Le Bel is about to describe the Battle of Scheut near Anderlecht, 17 August 1356.
[4]   The ducal palace at Brussels.

The citizens of Brussels, terrified that the Flemings would enter the city, plunder their houses, rape their daughters and their wives and kill them, decided next day to surrender. They yielded the city to the Count of Flanders, and promised to acknowledge him as their lord and to give him written assurances and eminent hostages, and wished him to take the title of Duke of Brabant.

When the people of Leuven heard this they decided to tell Duke Wenceslaus and the Count of Mons to get out and go; they could no longer take refuge there because they meant to surrender the city to the Count of Flanders and accept him as their lord as the men of Brussels had done. So the duke left with a small escort and headed for Diest, and next day made his way as best he could to his friends in Germany and his brother the Emperor, who'd just returned from Rome as you've heard, to tell him of his plight and to seek his advice and support and aid against the Flemings.

Meanwhile the Count of Flanders came to terms with the men of Brussels and received their oath of fealty and homage – with forty eminent citizens as hostages to make it binding – and then entered Brussels amid great celebration. The people of Leuven did likewise, followed by those of Antwerp, Nivelles and Tillemont and all the other major cities except Bois-le-Duc which was opposed to the move.

Once the Count of Flanders had received all these oaths of fealty, with hostages as security, he placed garrisons of his men in every city. Then he summoned all the knights and squires of the land to Coudenberg on a certain day, and all the commons too, and before the aldermen of the cities of Flanders and Brabant he asked each knight and squire to swear him fealty, and the commons likewise, as the cities' aldermen had done. Having considered this and realised that all the cities' councils were in favour, they all agreed to pay homage, some reluctantly, some happily.

When it was all over the Count of Flanders kept the relevant documents and released the hostages. This was a very bad move, because as soon as the cities had their hostages back they started to reconsider and regret that they'd so lightly surrendered the land to the count and rejected their lord Duke Wenceslaus. And so it was that the day came when the Count of Flanders was less than safe in the city of Leuven, because some of the commons were unhappy with their council's action.

Chapter XLIII

How Leuven and the other cities, with one accord, took Duke Wenceslaus as their lord in opposition to the Count of Flanders.

Meanwhile in Poitou, near Poitiers, the Prince of Wales, son of the noble King Edward of England, defeated and captured King John of France – at the very heart of his kingdom with all his mighty army – and took and imprisoned him in Bordeaux along with one of his children and many of his most illustrious barons, as you'll hear in due course.

When the Duke of Normandy and Dauphin of Viennois[1] – the eldest son of King John of France and his queen lady Bonne, daughter of the King of Bohemia – returned to Paris after this battle, the Count of Flanders, thinking his position in Brabant was secure, rode to Paris to see him and the other royal children to voice his sympathy and share their grief at the misfortune that had befallen them. But when the Brabançons realised he'd left the country they sent secret word to Duke Wenceslaus and his duchess that, if he could return to Leuven with plenty of troops, they would open the gates to him and receive him as their lord, despite all their promises and sealed agreements with the Count of Flanders. The duchess and Lord Wenceslaus were overjoyed, and they prevailed to such effect upon the Count of Loon and the Count of Mons and a host of other knights that they mustered a good thousand or twelve hundred men-at-arms on a certain day and advanced into Brabant with all speed, heading first for Leuven where this had all been instigated. Meanwhile the people of Leuven had very shrewdly made a pact with Bishop Engelbert of Liège – an ally of the counts of Flanders and Namur – to help him reclaim the city of Mechelen which Bishop Adolph and the chapter of Liège had sold to the previous Count of Flanders.[2] They intended thereby to make up for the various blows and injuries dealt by Brabant and its duke, in the past and in the present, to the bishopric of Liège, in return for which the bishop had ordered the burning of many towns in Brabant – Hannut, Landen and several more (and at the gates of Landen the bishop's men had routed and captured a great number of Brabançons) – and the Count of Namur had burned a wide area around Nivelles, Gembloux and Jodoigne. Now the men of Leuven and the other Brabant cities lying in the diocese of Liège, with the helpful mediation of the Count of Loon, came fully to terms with the bishop; they promised to help him and his successors to enjoy free and peaceful possession [of Mechelen], and in return the bishop agreed to cease all hostilities against the Brabançons and to let his loyalty to the Count of Flanders lie dormant.

And so it was that Duke Wenceslaus and all his army passed untroubled through the county of Loon and rode to Leuven to be received as lord. He installed his officers and justiciaries in Leuven and all the other cities without opposition, removing those installed by the Count of Flanders – except at Mechelen, where the Count of Flanders still had a great many troops who would have strongly resisted any move against him. But I shall leave this now and return to the first matter.

---

[1] 'dauphin de Vienne': this was the title given to the heir to the French crown after 1350.
[2] See note 1, above, p.102. The text reads 'sold to his father' – i.e. '[the count of Flanders's] father'.

Chapter XLIV

How the Count of Hainault made peace between the Count of Flanders and the people of Brabant, and how the Emperor came to hold a great court at Metz.

When the Count of Flanders returned from France and realised he'd been deceived by the Brabançons, he was, needless to say, enraged. He went straight to Mechelen and reinforced his garrison, and declared war on the men of Brussels and all the people of Brabant. But the Flemings couldn't hope to mount sieges or organise supply trains from their territory because of the onset of winter, so the count mounted attacks and blockades by boat and ship, playing for time until summer came and the Flemings could venture forth on campaign. The Brabançons meanwhile hired hordes of foreign troops and stationed them in great numbers at Leuven, Brussels and Vilvoorde. They were voracious and foraged far and wide in Brabant, but they could do little damage to the Flemings and their land because of the difficult roads and river crossings. The Brabançons were resting their hopes on the support and aid of the Emperor, brother of Lord Wenceslaus whom they'd once more accepted as duke; they said he would surely bring such a huge army that they would easily have revenge upon the Flemings. And all the while the Count of Namur was hard at work, burning the country of Brabant day by day.

The Bishop of Liège was keeping quiet, however, because of the promises he'd made to the Brabant cities; and when the Count of Namur and the Count of Flanders called upon him to honour his alliance to them, he courteously replied that he would always do his duty but that his land was not completely under his control; he sent his Marshal, though, with a body of troops to support the Count of Namur.

And it was now that a memorable adventure befell the Marshal and his men and the Count of Namur. Some of the Brabançons left their garrisons, some on foot and some on horseback, intending to burn and ravage land of the count's people, their strength in numbers filling them with confidence. The Marshal, along with Sir Bureau de Jupleu and the companions in arms who were with him in the garrison at Boneffe, ventured out and heard the commotion; they were few in numbers compared with the Brabançons, but they rode forward until they saw the enemy, and although it was very late in the day they launched a vigorous attack and routed them, and the spoils were such that the Count of Namur was well reimbursed for the costs he'd incurred and all the companions involved made a handsome profit.

Meanwhile the Emperor Charles had come with a mighty escort to the city of Metz, and summoned all the barons and lords and prelates of Germany to join him there. They came in such numbers that they could barely be lodged in the city and the suburbs. And on Christmas Day in the year of grace 1357 he held a court more magnificent than any King of Germany before him. Each of the German prelates and lords performed his service and office with all the solemnity befitting the high court of an Emperor, according to ancient rule and custom, and the Emperor ordered the feast to be served upon plate and in goblets of fine gold.

The Duke of Normandy – eldest son of the King of France and nephew of the Emperor – was in noble attendance there with a great and illustrious company of Frenchmen, as was the Cardinal of Périgord, legate of the Pope and the Roman curia.

It was the general view that the Emperor had held this great feast to rally more forces and support for his brother Lord Wenceslaus, and that with the addition of those who'd come he would reconquer all Brabant and destroy the land of Liège and the whole of the county of Flanders and win their unconditional surrender.

But before coming to Metz the Emperor had sent distinguished embassies to the Bishop of Liège and the Count of Namur and to his brother, to broker a truce between them and to summon them to Metz, for he wished to secure a peace and settlement. At that point Duke Wenceslaus, the Count of Loon and the Count of Mons had invaded the county of Namur with large numbers of troops, so the Count of Namur was not inclined to make a truce while they were burning his land (despite the fact that he had earlier laid waste a larger area of Brabant); so at the request of the Emperor's envoys Duke Wenceslaus withdrew to his own country. Then they agreed to cease hostilities, though fighting between the Flemings and the Brabançons continued elsewhere.

When the great feast at Metz was over most of the lords returned to their own lands, and the Emperor went and stayed for a long spell at Maastricht,[1] continuing all the while his attempts to secure peace between his brother the Duke of Brabant, the Bishop of Liège and the Count of Namur. Agreement was finally reached – though not between his brother the duke and the bishop, for the bishop insisted that the duke must cede free possession of the city of Mechelen to the Count of Flanders who held it in fief from the bishopric. The duke and the cities of Brabant would not agree to this and the matter remained unresolved; and the Emperor departed without having settled his brother's affairs, much to the dismay of the Brabançons who lost all hope of the Emperor's support.

So they sought an alliance with William, Count of Hainault, Holland and Zeeland,[2] who had taken the title Count of Hainault because he was the son of the Emperor Louis of Bavaria and of the eldest sister of Count William who was killed in Frisia.[3] They promised him a huge sum of florins and gave him free possession of the mighty castle of Heusden and the full extent of its castlery, and in return he joined forces with them against the Count of Flanders, swearing on the holy sacrament to do all in his power to help them until the war was brought to an end. This enraged his whole country; it was clear to the Hainaulters that they would pay for this alliance, for there would be no way of stopping the Flemings burning and ravaging all the land whenever they liked. They reproached their lord severely for making such a promise and oath to the Brabançons without consulting them, and pressed him to do all he could to make

[1] 'Tret'.
[2] The second son of the Emperor Louis IV by his second wife, Margaret of Holland and Hainault, his titles were Count William III of Hainault, Count William V of Holland and Count William IV of Zeeland.
[3] Count William II, killed at Staveren: see note 3, above, p.101.

peace between Flanders and Brabant before he started defying the Flemings and waging war. And so by their advice and prompting he worked at brokering peace, and negotiated with each party in turn until the two lords and the two lands of Flanders and Brabant placed the matter entirely in his hands and made a sealed undertaking to do just as he decreed. A truce was agreed between them pending his pronouncement, though it was said that both parties had a good idea what he was going to say. And when the day came when he was due to give his verdict, he called both sides and the two lords together between the two lands[1] and delivered his decision in writing, which was as follows:

The Count of Flanders would be lord of Mechelen and its dependent lands, freely and legitimately, as his rightful inheritance, and would hold it in fief from the bishopric of Liège, along with Grandmont and Bornem. He would also be legitimate lord of the city of Antwerp through his wife the countess who had inherited it from her late father.

Further, the Count of Flanders and his successors would be dukes of Brabant after the death of lady Jehanne – the then duchess – if she died without heir; in the meantime the Count of Flanders could if he wished call and sign himself Duke of Brabant as well as Count of Flanders.

Further, all prisoners of both sides were to be released and restored to their possessions, and all bad blood was to be forgiven.

Those most responsible for the conflict had lost the most. The Brabançons had certainly paid dearly – the destruction of their lands and grievous damage to their persons and their honour – through the pride of the cities who'd shown no respect for their lord or any other. The first peace hadn't been enough for them, but how much more honourable and beneficial it would have been both for them and for their lord, that's obvious! As it turned out they'd now lost the city of Antwerp, and all because, in their overweening pride, they'd tried to lay wrongful claim to the city of Mechelen and to rob the Count of Flanders and the bishopric of Liège of their hereditary rights. But I'll leave this now and return, if I'm granted the time, to the noble history of the King of England.

Chapter XLV

How Count William of Hainault went insane, losing his wits and his reason.

First, however, I wish to tell what happened to Duke William of Bavaria, Count of Hainault, Holland and Zeeland. He was, truly, young and tall, strong and swarthy and agile, more fleet and dexterous than any man in his land, and he had married the daughter of the worthy and valiant Duke of Lancaster; but he was curiously distant and inscrutable: he wouldn't welcome or acknowledge people in the manner of a great prince, and took no pleasure in the company of ladies or damsels, at feasts or otherwise; nor did he have any close confidants (except just one, called master Thierry); and you could never be quite sure whether you

---

[1] At the town of Ath (actually in Hainault, but close to the Flemish border), where a treaty was concluded on 4 June 1357.

were in favour with him or not. And in the end, not long after he'd arranged the peace between the Count of Flanders and the Duke of Brabant, he lost his wits entirely, and most of the time he had to be bound hand and foot. From that point on, the two lands of Hainault and Holland were governed by the lady his wife, and subsequently, since she never had a child by him, by his younger brother Duke Albert.

Chapter XLVI

How the Count of Montfort seized the land of Brittany after the death of his maternal half brother and found great wealth at Limoges.

I've taken a little break from my main theme; now I'll return to the noble history of the worthy King Edward of England and continue where I left off, at the raising of the siege of Tournai in the month of August[1] in the year of grace 1340. The siege was ended thanks to a truce agreed between the two kings; but it wasn't well observed, especially by those in distant parts such as Gascony and Saintonge and the Toulousain, where supporters of the King of France and the King of England kept fighting and winning cities and strongholds from each other, and there were often great feats of arms and prowess performed, as you'll hear in due course.

What happened next was this. After the truce was signed and sealed before Tournai, all the lords and all the ranks on both sides struck camp and headed for home. King Philip of France and his barons and lords went to Paris before going their separate ways to their own lands. Among them was the Duke of Brittany, who'd brought a greater contingent to the French army than any of the other princes, and he was heading back to his country when he fell so seriously ill that he passed from this world before he was half way home. This was a grievous pity, for his death led to great conflict and destruction of cities, castles and people, as you'll hear. To explain more clearly why this happened I'll tell a little of what I know and have learned from those who were present when I was not.

This duke, whose name I don't know, had never had children by his duchess or any hope of doing so;[2] but he had a half brother (his mother's son from her second marriage) named the Count of Montfort[3] who was still alive and married to the sister of Count Louis of Flanders. The duke had also had a full brother, sharing both father and mother, who had died but had left a daughter; the duke, as her uncle, had married her to Lord Charles of Blois,[4] youngest son of the Count of Blois by the sister of King Philip of France, and had promised her the duchy of Brittany after his death, fearing that the Count of Montfort would claim it as next

---

[1]   To be precise, Edward left Tournai at the end of September.
[2]   Duke John III, who died at Caen on 30 April 1341, had no children by any of his three wives.
[3]   This is incorrect; John of Montfort was his half brother by their father, Duke Arthur II.
[4]   This other, full-blood brother was Guy of Brittany, Count of Penthièvre, who had died in 1331; his daughter Jeanne was married to Charles of Blois in 1337.

in line, even though he wasn't his full brother.[1] He felt that the daughter of his brother by both parents had a better claim to succeed him after his death than his half brother the Count of Montfort, who was not of Breton stock.[2] It was because of this long-standing fear – that the Count of Montfort would use his power to deny his young niece her rights – that he had married her to Lord Charles of Blois, so that King Philip, being Lord Charles's uncle, would give her better and more committed help to defend her inheritance against the Count of Montfort if he made any move to take it.

And indeed, what the duke had always feared happened: as soon as the count heard the duke had died on his way back to Brittany he made straight for Nantes, the duchy's chief and key city, and persuaded the citizens and the people of the surrounding land to accept him as their lord, as closest successor of his brother the late duke, and they all paid him due homage and fealty.

Having received the homage of the citizens of Nantes and the lords and people of the country thereabouts, he and his wife – a lady with the heart of a man and indeed of a lion – decided to hold a great court and a solemn feast at Nantes, and to summon the barons and elders of all the duchy's lands and cities to come there and do homage and swear fealty; they sent eminent envoys to every town and city in the country. Meanwhile the count left Nantes with a great body of men-at-arms and headed for the city of Limoges, for he knew that the vast wealth his brother had amassed was housed there. He was welcomed to the city with all honour and made a magnificent entry, and all the people paid him homage and fealty as their lord; and the late duke's great store of wealth was delivered to him with their consent, in return for substantial gifts and promises. After staying as long as he pleased he left with this great treasure and returned to Nantes, where his wife was overjoyed by the news; and they stayed there, celebrating lavishly, until the day when the great court was to be held.

The due day came, but the Count of Montfort and his wife were dismayed and enraged when Sir Hervé de Léon (noble and powerful though he was) was the only knight who responded to their summons. They spent three days feasting with the citizens of Nantes and the good people round about, but they felt great resentment towards those who hadn't deigned to come as bidden. They decided to recruit and pay all knights and foot soldiers who would join them, and to use their great wealth to achieve their ambition and force all rebels to surrender. Everyone present – knights, clerks, citizens and the rest – concurred, and soldiers were enlisted from every side on generous pay, until they had great numbers of horse and foot, noble and non-noble alike.

When the Count of Montfort saw the numbers he'd mustered he resolved to go and take control of the whole country, either by force or willingly, and to crush all the rebels that he could. So he left Nantes and made first for a mighty castle standing by the sea, called Brest. Its guardian and castellan was a valiant knight named Sir Garnier de Clisson; he was a kinsman of the late duke and

---

[1]   Duke John III had always been determined to deny his half brother the duchy; in 1334 he
     had even considered ceding Brittany to the King of France when he died.
[2]   i.e. because he wasn't the son of his father the duke; but this, as noted above, is incorrect.

of Sir Olivier de Clisson, a noble knight and one of the most eminent barons of Brittany whom King Philip of France later had basely beheaded in Paris on suspicion of treason, for which he was much reviled: everyone thought the knight was innocent, and that the king had ordered his execution principally to seize his possessions. Before reaching Brest, the count had pressed the intervening country into following him, on foot or horseback, so much so that he now had a truly massive army. As soon as he arrived outside the walls with all his forces he sent Sir Hervé de Léon to appeal to the aforementioned knight Sir Garnier de Clisson and bid him show obedience and surrender the fortress as to the Duke of Brittany. The knight replied that he was not inclined to do this and would not do so, nor would he recognise the count as his lord unless instructed to do so by the one who was the castle's rightful lord. So the count withdrew a short distance and then sent a formal challenge to the knight and the men of the castle.

Next morning, after mass, he gave orders for everyone to arm and lay siege to the castle. The knight, Sir Garnier de Clisson, was just as brisk in preparing for its defence; he had three hundred well armed troops, and he took forty of the boldest and came out to the barriers[1] to try to prevent the enemy battalions gaining a foothold there. There was a tremendous clash at this first attack, both sides fighting fearsomely and suffering casualties, dead and wounded; Sir Garnier performed many fine feats of arms and should be deemed most valiant. But the assault was so strong and determined, and the count pressed so insistently, that he won the barriers at last and forced the defenders back towards the castle in disarray. That valiant knight Sir Garnier did all he could to defend his men and get them safely back inside the gate, but when the men on the gate saw the rout they feared the castle was about to be lost, and they dropped the portcullis, shutting out Sir Garnier and his companions and leaving them embroiled with the enemy. That valiant knight was sorely wounded, as were all his fellows, but they refused to yield despite their foes' appeals. The men in the castle, seeing the knight's plight and gallant struggle to defend himself, rained huge stones on the enemy and forced them to retreat; then they raised the portcullis a little, allowing the knight and some of his companions, gravely hurt and wounded, back into the castle, while the attackers withdrew to their quarters, wounded themselves and exhausted.

The Count of Montfort, mightily frustrated that the knight had escaped him, gave orders next day for engines and machines to be made to bombard and storm the fortress, declaring that nothing would make him leave until it was his.

Then, on the third day, a spy brought word that the good knight Sir Garnier de Clisson was dead. The count commanded everyone to arm and renew the assault. They returned to the attack with all their might, and the count called up some contraptions that had been devised to throw across the ditches and reach the castle walls. But the men of the castle mounted a fierce defence, hurling stones and blazing brands and pots of boiling lime, and the fight continued until about noon. Then the count sent an appeal to them to surrender and accept him

---

[1]   The 'barrières' were outlying palisades or barricades, beyond a castle's walls and gates, to
     slow and impede besieging forces.

as their lord, promising to take no retribution, and called a halt to the attack. At last, after long discussion, they all agreed to yield to the count, with a guarantee of safety for their lives and limbs and property. Then the count entered the castle of Brest with a small escort and received the homage of all the people of the castlery, and installed a trusted knight as castellan before returning to camp.

Having returned to his men and garrisoned the castle of Brest, the count decided to move on to the nearby city of Rennes.[1] Everywhere along the way he made people of all ranks submit and swear fealty to him, and took with him all the able-bodied to strengthen his army still further: no one dared refuse for fear of reprisal. When he arrived at Rennes he had his men surround it with their tents and lodges, and the people of the city, seeing this vast host, made a fine show of preparing their defence.

Among them was a noble knight of those parts, valiant and bold, whom they'd appointed their captain and governor: his name was Sir Henry de Spinefort. One day he decided he'd go and rattle the besieging army if he could raise a company; so he rallied two hundred willing men and slipped from the city at the crack of dawn and attacked one side of the enemy host, smashing down tents and lodges and killing a good number. A great cry went up and the besiegers leapt to arms and began to defend themselves. A knight and his companions on guard patrol heard the cries and commotion, and as they spurred that way they met Sir Henry heading back to the city; they launched a vigorous attack and a mighty fight ensued. Other besiegers came running after, and when the men from Rennes saw so many coming they retreated to the city – at least, those who could, for a fair number were killed and captured. The most notable captive was Sir Henry de Spinefort; he was taken to the Count of Montfort, who was very pleased to see him.

The battle over, the count decided to lead the captive knight below the city walls and to declare that unless the citizens surrendered and paid him homage as their lord he would have Sir Henry hanged outside the gate: he'd heard the knight was much loved by the townsfolk. The announcement was duly made, and the people of the city were most distressed to see the knight's wretched plight. They debated how to respond to the count's demand and were strongly divided: the common folk felt great love and compassion for the knight – and hadn't the provisions to endure a long siege; but the high-ranking citizens, who had ample supplies, were unwilling to yield. The division grew so strong that the great burghers drew aside and called upon all who agreed with them to come and join them; fully two thousand did so, and the common folk, seeing this, began to rise against them, howling abuse and foul threats, and finally killed a great many. The burghers, horrified, cried for mercy and promised to accede to the commoners' will. This brought an end to the rioting; and they opened the gates and surrendered the city to the Count of Montfort, and all ranks paid him homage and swore fealty, as did the knight Sir Henry de Spinefort, who was

---

[1] Rennes is hardly 'near' Brest: it's at the opposite end of the duchy. Le Bel's haziness about Breton geography raises uncertainty about the identification of some place-names later on. See in particular footnote 1, below, p.132.

rewarded with a place in his council and household. Then the count entered the city amid great celebration, commanding his army to stay encamped in the fields; and he reconciled the burghers and the commons and appointed bailiffs, provosts, sheriffs and sergeants.

He and his army stayed at Rennes for three days while he considered his next move. On the fourth day he struck camp and ordered his army to make for one of the strongest castles in the land, named Hennebont: it stands at a sea port, with water filling its moats on every side. When Sir Henry de Spinefort realised the count was heading for Hennebont, he was afraid some terrible misfortune would befall his brother Sir Olivier, who had long been the castle's governor and still was. So he drew the count aside and said to him privately:

"My lord, I'm a member of your council and owe you fealty. I see you're heading for Hennebont; I promise you, the castle and the town are so strongly fortified that there's no way of taking them as you plan. You could lay siege and waste a year of your time before you'd force its surrender. But I'll tell you how you can take it. Stratagem is needed where force is of no avail; so place, if you will, about six hundred men-at-arms at my command, and I'll lead them four leagues ahead of your army with the banner of Brittany before me. I have a brother in Hennebont, the city's castellan, and as soon as he sees the Breton banner and recognises me he'll open the gates; I'll take him and bring him to you as a captive unless he agrees to come to terms with you – but you must promise not to harm him."

Sir Henry's idea delighted the count, and his plan was carried out. And so it was that the Count of Montfort became lord of the castle of Hennebont and installed his garrison there.

He headed next for the city of Vannes, where he negotiated with the citizens until he secured their surrender and they swore fealty and paid him homage as their lord. He appointed all manner of officials in the city and stayed there for three days.

He moved on then to besiege a very strong castle standing on a hill overlooking the sea called La Roche-Périou.[1] Its commander was a most noble knight named Olivier de Clisson, cousin german of the Olivier who was later to be hanged in Paris, as you'll hear in due course. The count laid siege to the castle for eight days but could find no way of winning it or of making the noble knight submit, either by promises or by threats. He decided to postpone the siege till a later date, and moved on once more to besiege another strong castle ten leagues away called Auray.[2] The castellan there was a noble knight named Sir Geoffroi de Malestroit, who was accompanied by another knight named Sir Yves de Trésiguidi. The count launched two assaults to see if anything could be achieved, but when he saw there was little chance of success he agreed to a truce and parley, as advised by Sir Hervé de Léon, who was with him as he had been ever since the feast held at Nantes. The two knights – Sir Geoffroi de Malestroit and Sir Yves de Trésiguidi

---

[1] It is in fact some way inland, near Le Faouët.
[2] 'Chastel de Roy'.

– came to the barriers[1] and held long discussions with the Count of Montfort and Sir Hervé. They finally came to terms, so much so that they became firm friends; and the two knights swore fealty and paid homage to the count, and remained castellans and guardians of the castle and governors of the surrounding land on his behalf.

The count departed then and marched on to another nearby castle called La Forest.[2] Its castellan, seeing the count's huge army, realised that resistance might well prove disastrous; and advised and urged by Sir Hervé de Léon, who was a friend and had been his companion in arms in Granada and other lands, he agreed terms with the count and swore fealty and paid him homage and remained castellan on his behalf.

The count left at once and headed for Carhaix, an important city with a fine castle. Its lord was a bishop who was an uncle of Sir Hervé, and at his prompting and out of affection for him he agreed terms with the count, and acknowledged him as lord until such time as another should come who could prove a better claim to the duchy of Brittany.

Why should I lengthen the story? In this way the Count of Montfort conquered the whole country and secured obedience and recognition as Duke of Brittany. He made his way then to a sea port called Redon,[3] where he divided his forces and sent them to garrison his strongholds. Then he put to sea and sailed with an escort of twenty knights to the noble King Edward, who gave him a joyful welcome. The count had decided to hold the duchy of Brittany as a dependency of the King of England; the king was delighted, and promised to be his guardian and protector and to help him defend his land, and at the count's departure he gave him and his companions generous gifts and handsome presents. Then the count put to sea once more and sailed back to the city of Nantes, where he found his wife the countess who received him joyfully.

But now I shall leave them for a little and tell of Lord Charles of Blois who, as you've heard, had a claim to the duchy of Brittany through his wife.

Chapter XLVII

How Lord Charles of Blois went to Brittany and won back a large part of the country by force of arms and captured the Count of Montfort.

Lord Charles of Blois, who believed his wife to be the true heir to Brittany, heard how the Count of Montfort was conquering the land, and went to Paris to complain to his uncle King Philip. The king consulted the twelve peers of France,[4] and they declared in conclusion that the count should be summoned to appear on a certain day to hear their verdict on the matter. This was duly

---

[1] See footnote 1, above, p.110.
[2] This has been variously indentified as La Forêt-Landerneau in Finisterre, Goy-la-Forest (in Froissart's Chronicle) and, most convincingly, the 'château de la Forêt' at Lanvaux, a little way north of Auray.
[3] 'Grendo'.
[4] See footnote 10, above, p.23.

done: an imposing embassy was sent to give the count a forceful summons. They found him at the city of Nantes, still in the thick of celebration; he appeared to welcome them warmly enough, but he thought more than once before agreeing to go to Paris according to the king's bidding. At last, however, he replied that he would obey the king and respond to his summons, and he arrived at Paris on the required day.

There sat the king in an illustrious company, including the twelve peers and Lord Charles of Blois. When the Count of Montfort knew that the king and all his barons were assembled in the palace, he made his way there and was greeted with much respect by all the lords; and he stepped forward and bowed most humbly to the king, saying:

"I have come, sire, at your bidding and your pleasure."

The king replied: "Count of Montfort, sir, I am grateful to you. But I am most surprised that you have dared to take it upon yourself to invade the duchy of Brittany. You have no right to the dukedom; there is one closer in line than you whom you are trying to disinherit. And to strengthen your position, I'm told, you have gone to my enemy the King of England and sworn him fealty and paid him homage for the duchy as its overlord!"

"Ah, never believe it, sire! You've been woefully misinformed! I wouldn't dream of such a thing! But as for the inheritance, sire, I don't believe anyone has a better claim to the duchy than I, for the late last duke was my brother. But if it were judged and proclaimed that another was closer in line, I would feel no shame in withdrawing my claim."

The king, hearing this, replied: "That is well said, sir; but I command you, by all that you hold as my liegeman, not to leave the city of Paris for a fortnight, until the barons and peers have judged who is closest in line of succession: then you'll know whether you have a rightful claim. If you do otherwise you will incur my wrath."

"Sire," replied the count, "your will be done."

And with that he left and returned to dine at his lodgings. Back in his chamber he turned the matter over in his mind, and began to think that if he waited for the barons' decision there was every chance it would go against him, for he was convinced that the king would favour the claim of Lord Charles of Blois – his nephew – above his own; and it was clear to him that, if the judgement was indeed adverse, the king would have him arrested until he'd surrendered everything: cities and castles and the vast wealth he'd found at Limoges (and spent). He fancied it would be better to incur the king's wrath and slip quietly back to Brittany than risk staying in Paris. He did just that, and was back in Brittany before the king realised he'd gone: everyone thought he was lying ill at his lodgings.

When he returned to his wife at Nantes he told her the whole sorry tale; and at her prompting – lion-hearted lady that she was – he went to all the cities, towns and castles and strengthened his garrisons and their provisions. Once this was done he returned to Nantes, to the lady his wife and the citizens, who seemed to love him dearly for all the favours he showed them. But I'll leave him for a moment and return to the King of France and Lord Charles of Blois.

You may be sure that King Philip and Lord Charles were enraged when they realised the Count of Montfort had escaped them. Nonetheless, they waited till the end of the fortnight when the barons and twelve peers of France were to deliver their verdict on the dukedom. They decided entirely in favour of Lord Charles of Blois and rejected the Count of Montfort's claim on two grounds: one, that Lord Charles's wife was daughter of the late duke's full-blood brother, and was therefore closer in blood than the Count of Montfort, who had a different father[1] who'd never been Duke of Brittany; the other reason was that the count had disobeyed the king's command – so that even if he'd had a rightful claim he would have forfeited it – in contravening the king's demand that he remain in Paris and departing without leave.

When this unanimous verdict was delivered by all the barons, the king summoned his nephew and said:

"My dear nephew of Blois, a fine and great inheritance is bequeathed to you. Make haste now, and strive to win it back from the one who wrongfully withholds it. Call upon your friends to help you in your cause; I for one will never fail you: I shall lend you gold and silver and will instruct my son the Duke of Normandy to share command with you. But I implore and bid you to hurry, for if our enemy the King of England, to whom the Count of Montfort has paid homage for the duchy, were to come to Brittany he would inflict grave harm upon us: he could have no better point of entry to our kingdom, especially if he had the land and strongholds of Brittany on his side."

Then Lord Charles of Blois bowed to the king, thanking him most humbly; and there and then he requested the aid of his cousin the Duke of Normandy, his uncle the Count of Alençon, the Duke of Burgundy, his brother the Count of Blois, Lord Louis of Spain,[2] the Duke of Bourbon and his brother Lord James, the Viscount of Rohan, the Count of Eu and his son the Count of Guînes, and all the other princes and barons present; and they all promised to follow him and their lord the Duke of Normandy most willingly, each with all the forces he could muster. With that the princes and barons went their separate ways, sending messengers ahead to prepare everything necessary for war and for a campaign to such a distant land: they knew they would have a lot to do if they were to achieve their goal.

When all these lords were prepared and ready to march with Lord Charles of Blois to reconquer Brittany, they gathered at the city of Angers[3] and then advanced to Ancenis, at the edge of that corner of the kingdom of France. They stayed there for three days, putting their battalions and baggage train fully in order. Then they took to the field, reckoning their forces at five thousand men-at-arms – not counting the Genoese, who numbered fully three thousand, so I've heard, led by

---

[1]   As noted previously (footnote 3, p.108), this is incorrect.
[2]   Louis de La Cerda, great-grandson of Louis IX of France. Philip VI appointed him Admiral of France in 1341.
[3]   The forces met at Angers at the end of September 1341, though the Duke of Normandy did not arrive until the middle of October.

two knights from Genoa named Sir Ayton Doria and Carlo Grimaldi[1] – and there was a great body of crossbowmen led by Sir Galoys de La Baume.

On leaving Ancenis the army headed for a mighty castle that stood on a lofty eminence above a river; it's called Champtoceaux[2] and is the key and gateway to Brittany, and it was strongly provisioned and garrisoned with men-at-arms commanded by two most valiant knights from Lorraine named Sir Mille and Sir Valeran. When the Duke of Normandy and the other lords named above saw the castle's strength they decided to besiege it, for if they marched on and left such a garrison at their backs it could be a great threat and danger. So they encircled it and launched several mighty assaults – especially the Genoese, who threw themselves forward with wild abandon, wanting to make a fine show from the outset; in consequence they suffered heavy losses, for the men of the castle mounted a stout and well-marshalled defence. The lords spent a long while there without success. Finally, however, they had their men drag huge piles of timber and faggots to the moats, and while they continued a fierce bombardment they filled in the ditches so that they could cross right up to the walls. No one could have defended themselves better than the men of the castle, loosing volleys of arrows and a storm of stone and lime and firebrands; but their attackers had built contraptions to keep them covered as they worked at the walls with their picks.

Why should I lengthen the story? The men of the castle realised they couldn't hold out much longer, for the walls were being breached, and they knew that if they were taken by force they could expect no help or pity; so they decided to surrender on terms that guaranteed their safety, and appealed to the besieging lords for mercy. And so it was that this first castle was captured by the lords of France,[3] and they were jubilant, thinking it a fine start to their campaign.

When the Duke of Normandy and his fellow lords had thus taken Champtoceaux, the duke, who was commander-in-chief, delivered it straight to Lord Charles of Blois as his own; and they installed an able castellan and a strong garrison there, to guard the entrance to the land and to direct any troops who might follow them on their campaign. Then they struck camp and headed for Nantes where they assumed their enemy the Count of Montfort to be.

It so happened that, on the way, the marshal of the army and the advanced guard came upon a good-sized town, well protected by ditches and palisades. They attacked it fiercely, and the defenders, poorly armed men of little account, couldn't hold out against their onslaught, especially against the Genoese crossbowmen, and the town was swiftly taken and looted, and half of it was burned and all its people put to the sword, which was a grievous pity. The town is called Carquefou, and lies three leagues from Nantes.

The lords camped thereabouts that night, and next morning struck camp and marched upon the city of Nantes and laid siege to it on every side, pitching tents

---

[1] 'Otto Darue et... Charle Germain'. Doria (from Genoa) and Grimaldi (from Monaco) had signed contracts with Philip of France to provide galleys and crews in support of his fleet, and launched a number of raids on the English coast. They are also named by the Italian chronicler Villani as two of the Genoese captains at Crécy.
[2] Formerly 'Châteauceaux', a major castle on the Loire.
[3] In late October 1341.

and pavilions as splendidly as you know the French can. A mighty garrison of men-at-arms was ready to defend the city, and they immediately armed and took up their appointed stations and stayed smartly on the alert all day. The besiegers spent that day making camp and foraging. But some of the Genoese and others went to skirmish at the barriers; a band of troops and townsmen came out to meet them, and in the exchange of missiles there were men killed and wounded on both sides, as there often are in such actions.

As long as the siege lasted there were attacks and skirmishes two or three times a day. And a pretty wild adventure finally occurred, I've heard, when some of the soldiers and townsmen sallied forth one morning to try their luck, and found about fifteen food-laden carts being taken to the army by an escort some forty strong. They attacked at once, killing some and wounding and capturing others, and were soon on their way back to the city with the carts. When word of this reached the besiegers a band of them took up arms and set off and caught up with them near the barriers. The fight now turned really fierce, as men from the army came in such numbers that the city men were hard pressed indeed; but they managed to unhitch the horses so that, if the besiegers recovered the carts, they'd have a tougher job hauling back the supplies. Then other soldiers in the city, seeing the fighting, realised their companions were up against it and came out to their aid; the combat lasted a long time, as fresh and rested men arrived from all directions, and there were dead and wounded on both sides.

At last Sir Hervé de Léon, who was one of the foremost counsellors to the Count of Montfort and the city, saw they had more to lose than to gain in the skirmish and ordered his men to retreat. But they were so closely pursued that there was a huge pile of dead at the gate, the best part of two hundred – most of them townsmen, much to the distress of their fathers and mothers and brothers. The Count of Montfort was upset, too, and berated Sir Hervé for having ordered the retreat so soon. Sir Hervé took this so much to heart that from that day forth he would rarely attend the count's council, to the astonishment of all the city.

Then, as I've heard, some of the burghers, seeing their property in the city and outside being destroyed and their children killed or captured, and fearing that worse would surely befall them, met together and decided to treat with these lords of France in secret, to try and negotiate a peace and the release of their captive friends and children. And agreement was reached: the prisoners would be set free if they would leave one of the city gates open to let the French knights enter. This was duly done: early one morning the French lords slipped into the city with a select band of men and went straight to the Count of Montfort's hall and broke in; and they grabbed the count and whisked him out of the city without the slightest disturbance. Some claimed that it was done with the consent and connivance of Sir Hervé de Léon because the Count of Montfort had reproached and abused him, as you've heard. I don't know if that was true or not but it certainly seemed so, for thereafter he was always to be seen in the council of Lord Charles of Blois.

Thus it was that the Count of Montfort was captured in the city of Nantes in the year of grace 1341, about the feast of All Saints. And as soon as he'd been taken to the besiegers' camp, the lords entered the city unarmed, and all the citizens of Nantes swore fealty and paid homage to Lord Charles of Blois as their rightful lord amid much rejoicing.

The lords stayed there for three days in great celebration, resting and discussing their next move. They considered they'd achieved a great deal, and thought it best to return to France and to the king, and to deliver the Count of Montfort as his prisoner. And because winter was now upon them and it wasn't the time to be on campaign, they advised Lord Charles of Blois to stay in the city of Nantes and thereabouts till Christmas and to do the best he could for his soldiers. Then the lords departed and returned to Paris, where they delivered the Count of Montfort to the king. He was delighted; and he had him imprisoned at the Louvre in Paris, where I'm told he died: if that's wrong I ask pardon.[1]

Now I'll return to that lion-hearted lady the Countess of Montfort. She was at Rennes when she heard that her husband the count had been captured. If she was distressed it's not to be wondered at, for she was sure they would put him to death rather than keep him imprisoned. But despite her grief she behaved not as a woman but as a man of high courage; stirring the hearts of her friends and her soldiers, she showed them her young son and said:

"Ah, sirs! Don't despair for our loss of my lord – he was but one man; here is my little son who'll restore all our fortunes if it please God! And I have riches enough, and will seek out a captain who'll give strength to your hearts and fine leadership."

After these rousing words to her friends and her troops the good lady went to all the towns and cities and castles, taking her son with her, to strengthen all the garrisons and their supplies. She came then to Hennebont, a very strong castle by the sea, and spent the whole winter there, sending frequent deputations to inspect the garrisons and keep up their morale, and to pay them with astonishing generosity.

But I shall leave this matter for now and return to King Edward of England, to tell what became of him after he left the siege of Tournai.

Chapter XLVIII

Here the book returns to its proper story and recounts the great feats of arms and high prowess performed by the Scots against the English.

Now I shall return to the noble history of the valiant King Edward of England, to tell what befell him after the siege of Tournai, for I've said nothing about him for a long while. You earlier heard, if you remember, how he conquered all Scotland as far as the great forest called Jedburgh,[2] the refuge of the wild Scots because the forest is so bewildering and full of vast bogs that no one dares venture in unless he knows the ways and tracks. Then, before beginning his

---

[1] It is wrong. The count escaped from the Louvre after some three years in prison and made his way to England. He then returned with English forces to Brittany, and died in 1345 shortly after leading an attack on Quimper.

[2] '*Gendours*'.

war with King Philip of France, he continued his conquest, leaving no castle or stronghold untaken, right to the city known in Scotland as Saint John,[1] because King David (even though he'd married King Edward's wife) refused to pay him homage for the land: the Scots wouldn't countenance it. You've also heard how young King David and his wife travelled to France with their poor, modest escort and how King Philip gave them shelter and support for a long while in exchange for certain pledges.

Now you should know that Sir William Douglas (son of the sister of the other Sir William[2] who died in Spain), the young Earl of Moray,[3] the Earl Patrick,[4] Simon Fraser and Alexander Ramsay[5] had stayed as captains of the remaining bands of wild Scots, holding out in those wild forests for seven years and more, winter and summer, like the valiant warriors they were. They waged constant war upon the fortresses held by King Edward, meeting with many stirring adventures which would take too long to recount.

And while King Edward was on this side of the sea campaigning in France, King Philip sent men to Scotland, to the city of Saint John, to appeal to the above mentioned lords to mount a major attack on the kingdom of England, so that King Edward would be forced to return and abandon his war over here; he promised to supply them with troops and money. And so it was that, while King Edward was besieging Tournai, these Scottish lords answered King Philip's request and raised a great army to attack the English. As soon as they'd mustered sufficient men they left the forest of Jedburgh and advanced through Scotland, retaking such strongholds as they could, past the city of Berwick and over the Tyne and into Northumberland, which had once been a kingdom of its own and where they found huge herds of fat cattle. They burned and laid waste the whole country as far as the city of Durham and beyond, and then took a different course, burning and ravaging all the way, until they'd devastated all of the king's land within a four days' ride. Then they returned to Scotland and won back their fortresses, except the city of Berwick and three other strong castles, one called Roxburgh, one Stirling and the other Edinburgh. Edinburgh was the strongest of them all, standing on a rock so high that it surveys the whole country round about: the climb is so hard that it's almost impossible to ride up without stopping to rest two or three times, and your horse will be half dead! It was this castle of Edinburgh that had given the Scots the most trouble; its governor was a valiant knight named Sir Walter de Limousin. But it was soon to be captured with great daring and ingenuity and all its defenders slain, as you'll hear in a moment.

When King Edward heard that these Scottish lords had invaded his kingdom he was enraged. He left France and returned to London at once and considered what to do; he resolved to send a general summons throughout his land for all

---

[1] Perth. The original name of Perth was 'Saint John's toun' (preserved in the name of the city's football club).
[2] As noted previously (above, pp.40 and 63), this should read James (the 'Black' Douglas), and Le Bel is not thinking of James's nephew but of William Douglas, Lord of Liddesdale.
[3] John Randolph, the 3rd Earl.
[4] 'Patris': Patrick of Dunbar, 9th Earl of March.
[5] 'Symon Frisel et Alixandre de Ramesay'.

men to be ready to meet him at York in a month's time, to go and destroy the rest of the kingdom of Scotland. This was around All Saints in the year of grace 1340.[1]

While this gathering at York was waiting to take place, the good knight Sir William Douglas decided to attempt a feat of great peril and ingenuity. He revealed his plan to some of his companions – Earl Patrick and Alexander Ramsay and Simon Fraser, who had raised and been guardian of the young King David – and they all joined him in this daring enterprise, taking two hundred of the wild Scots to carry out an ambush, as you'll hear. These four lords, who were all captains of the Scots and knew each other's minds, put to sea with their company, taking aboard supplies of oatmeal, white flour and coal. They landed at a harbour four leagues from the mighty castle of Edinburgh, a greater thorn in their side than any other. They slipped ashore by night and took some fifteen or eighteen of their most trusted companions and dressed themselves in old tattered coats, disguising themselves as poor traders; and they loaded twelve little ponies with a dozen sacks of oatmeal, flour and coal. Then they stationed the other Scots in a ruined abbey at the foot of the castle rock.

As soon as it was light these 'traders', secretly armed, set off up the hill, and when they were half way up Sir William Douglas and Simon Fraser went ahead, telling the others to follow slowly. Then they went up to the gatekeeper and told him they'd braved the journey with grain, flour, oats and coal, and if they were in want of such things in the castle they would sell them at a good price. The gatekeeper said they were running short indeed, but it was much too early to wake the governor; but if they cared to bring in their goods he would open the first of the barrier gates. This was music to their ears. They called their companions forward and they all passed through the first gate. Now, Sir William Douglas had spotted that the gatekeeper had the keys to the castle's main gate – he had even asked him which unlocked the gate and which the wicket! So they unloaded their sacks at the first gate, right on the threshold so that it couldn't be shut again, and then seized the gatekeeper and killed him so cleanly that he didn't make a sound. They took his keys and unlocked the castle gate; then Sir William blew a blast on his horn, and he and his companions threw off their tattered coats and tipped the sacks full of coal in the middle of the gateway so that it couldn't be closed; and when the others in the band, lying in wait below the castle, heard the horn they ran up the castle hill as fast as they could. The watchman, who'd been fast asleep, heard it, too, and awoke to see soldiers running up; he sounded his own horn and started yelling: "Treachery! Treachery!" At this the castellan and the others woke and armed and ran to shut the gate – but they couldn't: Sir William and his thirteen companions barred the way. There was a ferocious combat then, for the men of the castle were fighting for their lives and the Scots were battling to accomplish their daring plan. Seeing the ambush party appear, the men of the castle were aghast; they fought with all their might to defend it,

---

[1]   This date and the order of events given by Le Bel in the following pages are incorrect. Edward's campaign began in the autumn of 1341, some months after the capture of Edinburgh Castle (in April) and the return of King David (in May) which are about to be described.

but in the end, although they killed and wounded some of the attackers, their efforts couldn't prevent Sir William Douglas winning the castle. He killed the entire garrison without mercy.

They stayed there all that day, appointing a castellan and all manner of officers to guard the castle, and installed a strong garrison. Then they returned in the highest spirits to their companions in the Jedburgh forest. And so it was that the mighty castle of Edinburgh was taken by force and cunning.

When Sir William and his companions rejoined their men in the forest, news reached them that the noble King Edward had returned to England and gathered forces in such numbers that they couldn't hope to resist them. They discussed what they should do: they were few and poorly clad, they'd been waging war for seven years and in all that time had slept and drunk and eaten badly, and they had no news of their lord the king. They'd all had enough, and agreed to send a bishop and an abbot to King Edward to ask for a truce.

The bishop and abbot found the king at the city of York with fully six thousand cavalry, knights and squires, and sixty thousand infantry, ready to destroy the rest of Scotland. Seeing this, they spoke most graciously; and they successfully secured a one-month truce on condition that word was sent to King David of Scotland that if he didn't come within two months to confront the might of England, his knights would surrender to King Edward. Such was the agreement, and messengers were sent to France while the Scottish delegation returned to Scotland.

When the news reached King David in France, he reflected on how he'd been away from his country for seven years and sensed it was suffering greatly, and decided to take leave of King Philip of France and return to his land and his people. This he did, setting out with his wife the Queen and putting to sea under the captaincy of a mariner named Sir Richard the Fleming,[1] and landed at the port of Moray[2] in Scotland before any of the Scottish lords knew of his coming. They were overjoyed when they heard the news, and gave him the grandest of welcomes and led him to the city of Saint John,[3] noted for the fine salmon caught there. When the young King David and his wife the Queen arrived in the city you may be sure there was mighty rejoicing, for in his absence all the people had suffered such misery, poverty, fear and distress.

When the celebrations were over he was given heartfelt accounts – both general and particular – of the damage inflicted on the land, and was made to realise how the King of England had treated them since his departure. The young king was most upset to hear his people's complaints, as was his wife who wept a good deal. And when he'd heard of their various sufferings he did all he could to restore their spirits, vowing to take full revenge or die in the attempt and lose all. He resolved to send messengers to all his friends, near and far, humbly

[1] This is probably a reference to Malcolm Fleming, who played an important part in arranging the young David's safe exile in France, and was created Earl of Wigtown on the king's return to Scotland in 1341.

[2] According to the Annals of Scotland he landed at Inverbervie, Kincardineshire, on 4 May 1341.

[3] Perth: see footnote 1, above, p.119.

beseeching them to be armed and ready to do their duty before the two months of the truce had elapsed, for otherwise he would lose his land. The Earl of Orkney, a great and powerful lord (and husband to King David's sister), responded to this summons, bringing with him a great company of knights and squires from Sweden and Norway and other neighbouring lands. So many came from every side that when they were all assembled around the city of Saint John they found they numbered sixty thousand on foot and hackneys and three thousand heavy cavalry, knights and squires, along with the lords of Scotland. As soon as they were ready they set out to lay waste and ravage all they could of the kingdom of England and to do battle with King Edward, who'd done so much harm in Scotland.

They came first to the castle of Roxburgh which the English had won and occupied, their garrison making frequent sallies and harrying attacks. The Scots launched an assault, but their losses outweighed their achievements; so King David decided to waste no more time there, and to besiege no other stronghold but to march straight into England. He ordered his army onward, and they advanced by way of the city of Berwick into the kingdom of Northumberland, wasting and burning the whole country along the Tyne until they came to Newcastle. King David and his army camped outside that night to see what could be done.

As morning approached some fellows in the city, about a hundred of the most daring, slipped out through a gate in secret to give the besiegers a surprise. Their attack struck the quarters of the Earl of Moray, who bears a silver shield emblazoned with three red cushions, and they found him in his bed. They seized him and killed a great number of his men, and before the rest of the army was awake they'd claimed a handsome store of booty and returned and delivered the Earl of Moray to the castellan, who was jubilant. When the besiegers realised what had happened they ran to the barriers[1] and launched a long assault; but they achieved next to nothing, for there was a large garrison in the city who mounted a spirited defence and forced them to retreat.

King David and his council, seeing there was clearly no point in staying there, left Newcastle and moved on. The Scots now marched into the Bishop of Durham's land where they burned and ravaged, and then advanced on Durham itself and laid siege to the city. They launched numerous assaults like men gone wild, both at their loss of the Earl of Moray and because they knew there was great wealth amassed in the city, all the people of the region having taken refuge there. They mounted their attacks with all their might, and the king had engines and contraptions made to enable them to get to the walls in safety.

Meanwhile, as soon as the Scots had left Newcastle, the castellan had put to sea at once and sailed to London to tell the king how his land was being ravaged and to present the Earl of Moray to him. The noble king was delighted to receive the prisoner, but was enraged to hear of the destruction of his land and of the siege of the city of Durham. He immediately summoned his whole kingdom to make swift preparations and to follow him to Durham, for he was determined

---

[1]   See footnote 1, above, p.110.

to raise the siege and drive his enemies out of the country. Everyone responded with all possible speed, for never was a king more loved or more feared.

While this noble king was heading for the city of York with all his people following, King David of Scotland attacked Durham with such might that the defenders couldn't prevent him taking it by force. The whole city was plundered and put to the torch, and women, children, priests and clerics who had fled to the cathedral were all burnt inside. In all the city no woman or child, no house or church, escaped utter destruction. It was a grievous pity: God grant mercy to the souls of the dead and absolution to those perpetrators who truly repent.

When all was done, King David decided to withdraw towards the Tyne and make for the city of Carlisle[1] at the entrance to Wales. On the way he lodged one night near a strong castle called Wark[2] which belonged to the Earl of Salisbury, who'd been captured along with the Earl of Suffolk outside Lille in Flanders: they were still imprisoned in the Châtelet at Paris. The noble Countess of Salisbury,[3] one of the worthiest and most beautiful ladies in England, was staying at the castle, which was well garrisoned with able men-at-arms, the castellan being a worthy squire who was the son of the Earl of Salisbury's sister: he was named Sir William Montagu after his uncle.[4] When morning came the king and his army struck camp and continued their march towards Carlisle, laden with the booty they'd won at Durham, and as they did so they passed before Wark.[5] When Sir William Montagu saw they'd marched past and weren't going to stop and attack the castle he rode out with sixty armed companions and secretly followed the train; and he overtook the hindmost so laden with baggage that they were stuck at the edge of a wood. He and his companions killed more than two hundred, and led a good six score of their laden hackneys and horses back towards Wark Castle.

The clashes and cries of the fighting had reached Sir William Douglas with the rearguard, and word soon spread to the whole army. What a terrifying sight it would then have been, as the Scots charged back over mountain and valley, Sir William at their head, right to the foot of the castle hill and up; but before they reached the barriers the men of the castle had already shut the gates with all the captured booty safe inside. The Scots were in torment and began a mighty assault; the men inside responded in kind and there was a tremendous barrage from both sides. The attack continued until the whole Scottish army had arrived, including the king; but when he and his council saw his men lying dead in the fields and others being wounded in the fruitless assault, he commanded all his forces to withdraw and make camp, for they weren't going to leave or march on

---

1   'Cardueil': see footnotes p.39. Le Bel's confusion about its location ('at the entrance to Wales') may well be due to his reading of Arthurian romances, in which Cardueil often has Welsh connections.
2   The scribe (or Le Bel himself) confuses the name of the castle with that of its owner and writes 'Salbry' ('Salisbury'). This is Wark Castle, which had passed to the Earl of Salisbury in 1329.
3   Catherine Montagu (c.1304-49).
4   See footnote 1, below, p.146.
5   The MS continues, here and throughout, to refer to the castle as 'Salbri'.

until he'd found a way to avenge their losses. What a mess it was then, as the Scots swarmed around, trying to find places to camp or hauling and dragging back their dead while the wounded staggered back in a pitiful state. And so the Scottish army lay that night below the castle while, inside, the valiant lady of Salisbury celebrated with the companions, keeping their spirits high.

Next morning the enraged King David commanded his whole army to prepare to attack: he was going to bring up his siege engines to see what damage they could inflict. Then the assault began, dangerous and terrible, and both sides acquitted themselves well. The valiant lady gave constant encouragement to her men, and truly, the exhortations and the sight of such a lady should give any man the strength of two. The assault raged on for a long while, and there were great numbers killed and wounded, especially among the Scots, as they strove with all their might to drag trees and piles of wood to fill the ditches and heave their engines to the wall. But the men of the castle mounted such a valiant defence that the Scots achieved little that day. So they withdrew again, though the king commanded that the siege engines be kept ready for another assault next day, and the day after and the day after that: he was determined to win the castle whatever it took, such was his rage at the losses suffered by his men. And so the attackers retreated, some mourning the dead, others trying to comfort the wounded.

Chapter XLIX

How the Countess of Salisbury sent Sir William Montagu to King Edward for help against the King of Scotland who was besieging her.

The men of the castle, very tired and with many wounded, realised that if King David kept his resolve they'd be in trouble. They decided to send word to the King of England, but none of them was willing to go and leave the defence of the castle and the fair lady: it led to a fierce argument. Sir William Montagu saw his companions' commitment but also the disaster that could befall them if they didn't get help, and he said:

"Sirs, your courage and your loyalty are clear. For my lady's sake and yours I shall go as messenger; I have such faith in you that I know you'll hold the castle safely till I return, and I have such trust in the King of England that I'll bring you good and speedy help."

When darkness fell Sir William prepared to leave as quietly as he could, making sure he wasn't seen by the besiegers. Luckily for him it rained so heavily all night that none of the Scots dared stir from their shelters, so he left the castle at midnight and slipped right through the enemy lines without being spotted. Once he was through and dawn broke he rode carefully on until, some half a league beyond, he met two Scots who'd found a pair of oxen and a cow in a wood and were taking them back to the army. Sir William realised they were Scots and wounded them both and killed the cattle, not wanting their army to enjoy them, and said:

"Go and tell your king that I, William Montagu, have wounded you out of hatred for him; and you can tell him that I'm going to find the noble King Edward, who'll soon send him packing!"

The pair promised to take his message if he'd let them go. So he set off then and made his way to the noble King Edward at York, where he'd already assembled a fine company and was daily expecting still more. He bowed to the king most humbly and gave his message on behalf of the noble Countess of Salisbury, explaining the plight faced by her and her men. The noble king replied that nothing would stop him helping the lady, and gave orders for everyone to make ready to leave next day. And in the morning the noble king set out in high spirits from the city of York to respond to Sir William's appeal; right behind him were fully six thousand men-at-arms, ten thousand archers and eighty thousand foot, and more were joining constantly.

When the Scottish barons and King David's chief counsellors learned that Sir William Montagu had slipped through their lines and was going to seek help from the King of England, who they knew was at York with a huge army and was of such great courage that nothing would stop him riding to the aid of the lady and the castle, they came together to discuss their position. It was clear to them that their king was sacrificing his men for nothing and that the King of England would be upon them before the castle could be taken. With one voice they told the king that staying there would bring him neither profit nor honour. Their campaign, they said, had been a notable success: they'd inflicted great harm upon the English, who'd seen them burn, destroy and ravage their land for twelve days and storm and sack the city of Durham; but they advised him to return to Scotland now, to the forest of Jedburgh, for they knew for certain that the King of England was coming with a massive army and they wouldn't be able to face him in open battle, and delay might be disastrous. The young king would gladly have awaited battle and the will of God, but his men put forward so many arguments – too many to recount – that the army decamped and made for the forest of Jedburgh, to wait and see what the King of England would do.

Chapter L

How King Edward came to Wark Castle, expecting to find the Scots, but they had already gone; and how he fell in love with the beautiful Countess of Salisbury.

King David of Scotland left the castle in the morning; on the very same day, at noon, the noble King Edward arrived. He was enraged to find that the Scots had gone: he would have gladly done battle. He'd come with such speed that his men and their horses were very tired, and he gave orders for everyone to make camp there, for he wanted to go and see the castle and the noble lady: he hadn't seen her since her wedding day. As soon as he was disarmed he took ten or twelve knights and rode to the castle to visit the noble lady and to see how the Scots had mounted their attacks and how the defences had been managed.

The moment the noble countess knew of the king's arrival she commanded that all the gates be opened; then she came out to meet him, so gloriously attired that everyone was stunned: no one could have his fill of gazing upon the lady's stately splendour and gracious bearing. When she reached the king she bowed down to the ground before him, thanking him for the great favour he had shown her; then she led him into the castle to entertain and honour him like the fine hostess she was.

Everyone was gazing at the countess in admiration, and the king in particular couldn't take his eyes off her: he was sure he'd never seen a more beautiful lady. As he gazed, a spark of love[1] was struck in his heart, and it stayed burning there: he was convinced there was no lady in the world more worthy of being loved. They entered the hall hand in hand, and her chamber likewise – which was so gorgeously bedecked that it was a wonder to behold. And all the while the noble king's gaze seemed so impassioned that the lady felt embarrassed and unsettled. Eventually he went and leaned, distracted, at a window, while the lady, thinking no more of it, went to entertain and welcome the knights and lords in her eminently gracious way, and gave orders for all necessary arrangements to be made and for dinner to be prepared.

Once she had given the requisite instructions she returned smiling to the king, still deep in thought, and said: "Dear lord, why are you so preoccupied? You've no reason to be troubled; saving your grace, I'd say you've every cause to celebrate – you've driven off your enemies who didn't dare await you. Let someone else worry about the rest!"

"Ah, my dear lady!" the noble king replied. "I tell you, since I arrived here an unexpected trouble has appeared! I can't stop thinking about it: I don't know where it's going to lead me but it's taken hold of my heart!"

"Ah, dear lord," said the countess, "you need to stay cheerful to keep your followers in good heart. Leave all this worrying and fretting. God has been so kind to you in all you've undertaken hitherto that you're the most feared and respected prince in Christendom, and if the King of Scotland has done you offence and harm you'll be able to avenge it whenever you please. So stop all this brooding, I pray you, and come and join your knights in the hall: dinner will soon be ready."

"Ah, my dear lady, the weight on my heart is not what you imagine! I tell you truly: the elegant bearing, perfect wit, high nobility, grace and wondrous, peerless beauty of your sweet self have taken such a hold of me that I have to be your lover! And I pray you, if you are willing, grant me your love – though truly, no refusal will quench my desire!"

The noble lady was aghast, and said: "Dearest lord, don't test or mock me! I don't believe you mean this, or that a prince as noble as you would dare make such an unworthy proposition, especially when you know my husband has served you so loyally, and is still suffering imprisonment for your sake. Such an act would earn you little respect! And truly, dearest lord, such a thought has never entered my heart and never will, if it please God, for any man born; and if

---

[1]   Le Bel uses the term *'fin amour'* – the courtly love of medieval literature.

I were guilty of the deed you should revile me – no, not revile, but cut me limb from limb!"

With that the spirited lady turned and left the king crestfallen, and went back to the hall to see that dinner was ready. Then she returned to the king with some of his knights and said: "Come and dine when you wish, my lord; the knights are waiting for you so that they can begin: they have fasted long enough."

The king went into the hall and sat down to dine, as did the lady. But the king ate and drank little, for his heart craved something else; all he could do was gaze, brooding, at the lady. His men were astonished: they weren't used to seeing him like this; some said it was because the Scots had escaped him, but that wasn't the problem! Love of the lady had taken such a grip upon his heart that no argument or refusal could shake it free; and finally Love's dart was to spur him to a deed that earned him bitter reproach and blame, for when he couldn't have what he wished of the noble lady through love or entreaty he took it by force, as you'll hear later on.

Chapter LI

How King Edward left Wark Castle with all his army and
pursued the Scots to the forest of Jedburgh.

In any event, the king spent the whole day at the castle in a deeply troubled state, not knowing what to do. At times he reconsidered, as Honour and Loyalty reproved him for these shameful thoughts which would dishonour such a worthy lady and such a noble knight; but then back would come Love, so insistently that She overwhelmed and vanquished Honour. The noble king wrestled with his thoughts all day and all night.

Next morning he ordered his army to strike camp and head after the Scots to drive them from his land. And he took his leave of the countess, saying:

"Dear lady, I commend you to God till my return; and I pray that you'll decide to change your mind."

"Dear lord," she replied, "may the King of Heaven guide you and wash away all base thoughts; I shall always be ready to serve you to your honour and my own."

With that the king departed, and went after the Scots and followed them beyond the city of Berwick[1] and camped four short leagues from the forest of Jedburgh: that's where King David and his men had gone, because of the great fortresses in those parts.

The King of England stayed there for three days to see if the Scots would venture out to do battle. And throughout those three days, you may be sure, there were so many skirmishes between the two armies that people wearied of watching them, and there were a good many killed and captured. Most often seen, and most impressive, was Sir William Douglas, who bore a blue shield

---

[1]   The text reads '*Euurwic*' ('York'), which makes little geographical sense; it is presumably a misreading of 'Berwick'.

blazoned with three red stars, and he inflicted many a blow upon the English. And all the while a number of gentlemen were holding talks to try to secure a truce and accord between the two kings. A truce was finally agreed, to last for two years if ratified by King Philip of France – for the King of Scotland's alliance with him was now so close that he could do nothing without his approval; and if King Philip would not agree, the truce was to last until Saint John's Day, on condition that King Edward gave no support or aid to the English who'd taken the strongholds of Roxburgh and Stirling, and that the Earl of Moray was released from captivity if King David could secure the release of the Earl of Salisbury by the King of France before the feast of Saint John.

King Edward agreed to this truce quite readily; for anyone who has three or four wars to conduct is wise to settle one or two or three of them – or indeed all – if he can, and no one has ever heard of a king engaged in so many wars at once as King Edward. He was at war with King Philip in France, Brittany, Gascony, Poitou, the Toulousain and Saintonge and was also at war with the King of Scotland, and had committed great numbers of troops to all parts.

And so the truce was agreed as you've heard. The King of Scotland departed with his army, who all dispersed to their own lands, and sent messengers to King Philip of France to secure his approval for what had been done. It wasn't long before King Philip released the Earl of Salisbury at the King of Scotland's request, and King Edward received him joyously and immediately released the Earl of Moray and sent him back to Scotland.

But now I shall leave the wars between England and Scotland for a while, and return to the war in Brittany and the story of Lord Charles of Blois.

Chapter LII

Here the book returns to the adventures in Brittany, to tell how
Lord Charles of Blois laid siege to the city of Rennes.

A s you've heard, the Duke of Normandy, the Duke of Bourbon, the Duke of Burgundy, the Count of Blois, Lord Louis of Spain, the Constable of France[1] and the other French lords had left Brittany after they'd taken the mighty castle of Champtoceaux and then the city of Nantes and captured the Count of Montfort and delivered him to King Philip of France, who had imprisoned him in the Louvre at Paris; and Lord Charles of Blois had stayed quietly at Nantes and in the surrounding country which was now obedient to him, waiting for the summer, a better season than winter for campaigning and waging war. Now you should know that, with the return of that sweet season, all the above-named lords of France and many others made their way back to Brittany in great strength to help Lord Charles of Blois to reconquer the rest of the duchy. Many remarkable adventures followed, as you'll now be able to hear.

When they reached Nantes they found Lord Charles of Blois and decided to lay siege to the city of Rennes, and there they went. The valiant Countess of Montfort

---

[1]   Raoul, Count of Eu.

had provisioned and garrisoned the city so well that it wanted for nothing, and had appointed as its governor and captain a worthy knight named Sir Guillaume de Cadoudal, a Breton gentleman of high standing. The valiant lady had placed great, strong garrisons in all the other cities, too, captained by fine nobles of the land who were loyal to her, having secured their support with fair words and gifts and promises; one such was the Bishop of Léon; also Sir Amaury de Clisson, Sir Yves de Trésiguidi, the lord of Landreman, the castellan of Guingant,[1] Sir Olivier de Spinefort brother of [Sir Henry,] Sir Geoffroi de Malestroit, Sir Guillaume de Cadoudal, the two de Quarick brothers and many other knights and squires whose names I don't know. But there were many Bretons, too, who sided with Lord Charles of Blois as Sir Hervé de Léon had done; Sir Hervé, as you've heard, had first supported the Count of Montfort (and been his chief adviser) until the city of Nantes fell, for which he was greatly reproached, people claiming that it was through his doing that the Count of Montfort had been captured. And indeed, Sir Hervé now strove harder than anyone against the valiant countess in the cause of Lord Charles of Blois.

Chapter LIII

How the Countess of Montfort sent to England, pleading for help from the king, who sent her Sir Walter Mauny.

Lord Charles of Blois and the other lords were encamped for a long while before the city of Rennes, inflicting much damage and launching mighty attacks by the Spaniards and the Genoese. But the city's defence, led by Sir Guillaume de Cadoudal, was so well marshalled that the attackers often lost more than they gained.

Meanwhile the valiant countess, as soon as she heard that these lords had come to Brittany in such strength, sent Sir Amaury de Clisson to England to speak to the noble King Edward and plead for his aid and support, on the understanding that the Count of Montfort's young son would marry one of the King of England's daughters and would be given the whole of the county of Montfort and the duchy of Brittany.

King Edward was then at London, celebrating the Earl of Salisbury's release from prison. He greeted Sir Amaury with great warmth and honour and granted his request with alacrity, for he saw two great benefits in doing so: firstly, the duchy of Brittany was a mighty prize if he could win it; secondly, it was the best possible entry point for conquering the kingdom of France as he intended.[2]

---

1   This is not modern Guingamp, but Guémené-sur-Scorff, which in the 14th century was called Kémené-Guingant. This becomes an important distinction later: see below, pp.133 and 140.

2   In a letter from London dated 22 February 1342 ('the third year of our reign in France and the sixteenth in England'), Edward informed 'all those to whom these letters come' that it had been agreed between himself and 'Sir Amaury de Clisson, tutor and guardian of John of Brittany, son and heir of the noble John, Duke of Brittany and Count of Montfort, that the towns, boroughs, castles, fortresses, seaports and points of entry in the duchy of Brittany should be made ready and entrusted to us and ours, for the reception and security of

He commanded Sir Walter Mauny, a knight he dearly loved for his outstanding service in a number of perilous missions, to take as many men-at-arms as Sir Amaury should propose, along with two or three thousand of the finest archers, and prepare at once to go to the countess's aid.

Sir Walter responded with a will to the king's command, and put to sea with the forces requested by Sir Amaury.[1] With him went the two Lande-Halle[2] brothers, Sir Louis and Sir Jehan La Haze from Brabant, Sir Hubert de Fresnay, Sir Alain de Sirehoude and many more whose names I don't know, along with six thousand archers. But a mighty storm struck them at sea and kept them there for fully forty[3] days before they could land at Hennebont. There the valiant countess was daily awaiting them, deeply distressed at knowing what they must be suffering.

Chapter LIV

How the citizens of Rennes surrendered the city to the
lord of Blois in defiance of their captain.

Now, Lord Charles of Blois and the other French lords besieged Rennes for so long that they inflicted a great deal of damage. The time came when the suffering citizens would have happily surrendered if they'd dared; but the worthy knight Sir Guillaume de Cadoudal absolutely refused. When the commons and the burgesses had had their fill and saw no sign of help arriving from anywhere they were desperate to yield, but Sir Guillaume wouldn't countenance surrender; finally they seized him and threw him in prison, and promised Lord Charles of Blois that they would yield next day if he let them leave with all their possessions and go where they chose.

And so the city was surrendered to Lord Charles at the beginning of May in the year of grace 1342. But the worthy knight Sir Guillaume de Cadoudal wouldn't take Lord Charles's side and went to Hennebont to join the countess, who was still very worried about Sir Amaury de Clisson and his company.

When the city of Rennes had surrendered and the citizens had sworn fealty to Lord Charles, the French lords debated where best to go next to achieve their

---

ourselves and our men for the duration of this war, and for the greater protection of that country; though it is not our intention that every town, borough, castle, fortress and seaport should be delivered to us: only such and as many as are now or in the future necessary to receive us and our men for the safety of the country, in the view of those we shall send to join the supporters of my lady Jeanne of Flanders, Duchess of Brittany and Countess of Montfort'. [The National Archives, C 76/17/m.47; printed in Viard and Déprez's edition of Le Bel, Appendix I].

[1] In early May 1342.

[2] The name is given here and later as '*Layndale*' or '*Lendale*', but since this is a list of knights from the Continent it is likely that these are the 'Lande-Halle' brothers referred to in Froissart, perhaps from Halle near Brussels.

[3] The text says 'LX' but later changes this to the less extravagant (but still daunting!) 'XL', below, p.134. Le Bel presumably means us to understand that the ships were forced to shelter and remain at anchor for a long while rather than being blown hither and yon for weeks on end. One redaction of Froissart gives the period as fifteen days rather than forty, and Knighton's Chronicle suggests that Mauny undertook operations around Brest before arriving at Hennebont.

goal. The decision was taken to go to Hennebont, where the countess had been since the count's capture, for if they could take the castle and the countess the war would be over. This was duly done, and they laid siege to the town and castle of Hennebont. The valiant countess was so well supplied with provisions and men-at-arms that she was well equipped to hold out; but she was still waiting anxiously for aid from England, and no news came and she was fearful of the outcome of the storm at sea. With her at Hennebont was the Bishop of Léon in Brittany, uncle[1] of Sir Hervé de Léon who was now on the other side; also Sir Yves de Trésiguidi, the lord of Landreman, the castellan of Guingant[2] and many others whose names I don't know.

When the valiant lady and her supporters heard that Lord Charles was coming to besiege them, they gave orders for all their troops to arm and for the great bell to be rung to summon everyone to the city's defence. This was done without demur. And when Lord Charles and the French lords drew near and saw the city's strength they ordered their men to make camp in positions for a siege. Some of the young Genoese and Spanish fellows – French, too – went to skirmish at the barriers, and some of the defenders came out to meet them, as always happens; and there were a number of fierce clashes in which the Genoese, through their recklessness, lost more than they gained. When evening drew in everyone returned to quarters.

The lords decided to launch a full assault upon the barriers to see how the defenders would respond and if they could make any headway. This they duly did on the third day; the assault lasted from morning to mid-afternoon, but the defenders fought so valiantly that the attackers were driven back leaving dead piled high in their wake.

The French lords were furious at seeing their men retreat and ordered them back to the attack. The defenders fought with renewed vigour, and the valiant countess, armed and riding a great charger from street to street, was cheering and summoning everyone to the city's defence, and commanding the women of the town, ladies and all, to take stones to the walls and fling them at the attackers, along with pots of quicklime.

And now you shall hear of the boldest and most remarkable feat ever performed by a woman. Know this: the valiant countess, who kept climbing the towers to see how the defence was progressing, saw that all the besiegers had left their quarters and gone forward to watch the assault. She conceived a fine plan. She remounted her charger, fully armed as she was, and called upon some three hundred men-at-arms who were guarding a gate that wasn't under attack to mount with her; then she rode out with this company and charged boldly into the enemy camp, which was devoid of anyone but a few boys and servants. They killed them all and set fire to everything: soon the whole encampment was ablaze.

When the French lords saw their camp on fire and heard the shouting and commotion, the assault was abandoned as they rushed back in alarm, crying:

[1] The text implies here that he was his nephew, but this is contradicted later, below, p.134.
[2] See note 1, above, p.129.

"Treachery! Treachery!" The valiant countess, seeing them alerted and the besiegers streaming back from all sides, rallied her men and, realising there was no way back to the town without grave loss, rode off in another direction, straight to the castle of Brayt,[1] some four leagues away. When Lord Louis of Spain reached the burning camp and saw the countess and her men riding away he set out in pursuit, determined to catch them if he could, and managed to overtake and kill some of the less well mounted; but the valiant countess and most of her men rode so well that they reached the castle of Brayt in safety, and were warmly and joyously received there. When Lord Louis learned from some captured men that it was the countess who had carried out the raid and had now escaped, he was distraught; he rode back to the army and told his fellow lords the whole story.

Meanwhile the gentlemen still inside Hennebont, having seen off the assault, couldn't have imagined the valiant lady would conceive such a plan, and worried all night that neither she nor any of her company had returned to the town.

Next morning the French lords, having lost their tents and all their provisions, decided to build lodges of trees and branches closer to the city, and to keep a better watch. So they went to great lengths to make this new camp nearer the walls, and called out to the defenders: "Go on! Go and find your countess! She's lost for sure: it'll be years before you see her again!" When the people in the town, men-at-arms and everyone else, heard this they were horrified, and feared some disaster had befallen their lady. They didn't know what to think: she hadn't come back and they had no news of her.

Their worry continued for five days. Then the valiant countess, guessing her people would be alarmed and fearing for her, raised about five hundred troops, well armed and clad and mounted, and rode from Brayt at midnight and came at the crack of dawn to one of the gates of Hennebont's castle and entered to a triumphant blast of trumpets and drums and other instruments. This brought the French leaping to the alert; they armed and went rushing to the walls, while the defenders ran to the battlements. A mighty assault began which raged till the ninth hour;[2] but then the French lords called off the attack, for their men were letting themselves be killed and wounded to no purpose. They retired to their lodges and decided that Lord Charles of Blois would go and lay siege to Auray,[3] built and fortified by King Arthur; with him would go the Duke of Bourbon,

---

[1]   This is problematic. 'Brayt' is the same spelling used earlier in the MS for Brest (above, p.109). If this, too, is a reference to Brest then Le Bel's statement that it was 'some four leagues' from Hennebont (and his later assertion that the countess's return journey took her from midnight to dawn), is clearly inaccurate. If, however, his information was reliable, 'Brayt' might possibly be Brech (north of Auray, on the road between Hennebont and Vannes); but although this would be in the right location to make sense of Le Bel's account, there is no evidence that Brech was fortified in the middle ages, and the fact that, as we're about to be told, the countess took 'five days' before she actually made her return may well be significant. It's worth remembering, too, Le Bel's shaky grasp of Breton distances in relation to Brest and Rennes (above, p.111). In a later chapter Le Bel makes another reference to 'Brayt' which causes similar uncertainty: see below, p.151.

[2]   The ninth canonical hour, about 3 in the afternoon.

[3]   'Chastel de Roy'.

the Count of Blois his brother, and the army's Marshal [Sir Robert] Bertrand. Meanwhile Sir Hervé de Léon and some of the Genoese, along with Lord Louis of Spain and the Viscount of Rohan and most of the Spaniards, were to stay and continue the siege of Hennebont, and they sent for twelve great engines that they'd left at Rennes so that they could bombard the town and the castle, for they realised they'd gain nothing by assault. So the French formed two armies, one remaining at Hennebont while the other went to besiege Auray which was quite close by. It's of that siege that we'll tell now, and leave the other for a moment.

Chapter LV

How Lord Charles of Blois held two castles under siege.

Lord Charles of Blois advanced to Auray with all his men and encamped before it, besieging it on all sides. Assaults and skirmishes followed, as the castle was well provisioned and garrisoned with men-at-arms to withstand such a siege. They had no wish to surrender, or to leave the service of the valiant countess who'd shown them many favours, to join Lord Charles of Blois, no matter what promises he made – for Frenchmen have always promised well and paid poorly. There were a good two hundred companions in the castle, all committed to supporting each other, captained by two valiant brothers, Sir Henry and Sir Olivier de Spinefort.

Four leagues away was the city of Vannes, fiercely loyal to the countess, where the captain was Sir Geoffroi de Malestroit, a worthy and valiant gentleman. In the other direction lay the town of Guémené-sur-Scorff,[1] enclosed only by ditches and a palisade; its captain, appointed by the count, was a valiant man called the castellan of Guingant, but he was currently besieged inside Hennebont with the countess, while his wife and daughter were left at Guémené with his son Sir Regnault as captain in his place. Between these two towns stood a very strong castle that was held for Lord Charles, who had garrisoned it well with men-at-arms, all of them Burgundians. The governor and master was a worthy squire named Gérard de Malain, and with him was a bold knight named Sir Pierre

---

[1] *'Dynant'*. The place-names in the following passage are again problematic. To assume that *'Dynant'* was the modern Dinan would make no geographical sense. Froissart in his chronicle reverses the names of relevant people and places in such a way that he makes the town, rather than the castellan, 'Guingamp'; if this were right, it would certainly place the castle of La Roche-Périou, mentioned below, roughly midway between Vannes and Guingamp, but it must be said that the distances involved would be extraordinary for the 'daily sorties' described in a moment – though 'daily' may of course be an exaggeration. It is most likely (not least because of the name of its governor, the castellan of Guingant) that it is neither Dinan nor Guingamp but Guémené-sur-Scorff, which (as noted above, p.129) was known in the middle ages as Kémené-Guingant. This would certainly make distances more feasible and fit with movements of armies described later (especially in Chapter LVIII below). Guémené-sur-Scorff did have a motte and bailey castle, but only a stone gateway and modest walls survive, so the later description of the rudimentary defences ('enclosed only by ditches and a palisade') raises slight doubts but may well be accurate, referring to the town rather than the castle (and certainly does not describe Dinan). Despite the small measure of uncertainty, I have translated *'Dynant'* as Guémené-sur-Scorff throughout the following pages.

Porteboeuf; these two, with their companions, pillaged and laid waste the whole country, so harassing the city of Vannes that it was impossible for any supplies or goods to be taken in or out. They made daily sorties, one day towards Vannes, the next towards Guémené; but on one of their expeditions Gérard de Malain and his band of some twenty-five companions were caught in an ambush by Sir Regnault de Guingant. In the process Sir Regnault rescued fourteen or fifteen merchants with all their goods, who were being abducted to a castle called La Roche-Périou; but the young knight Sir Regnault took them all and led them back to Guémené, which earned him much honour.

But I'll leave this for a moment and return to the valiant countess at Hennebont, where Lord Louis was maintaining the siege. His engines had so battered and smashed the town and its surrounding walls that the defenders' courage was beginning to fail and they were thinking of making terms, for they could see no sign of help arriving and had heard no word of its approach. And so it was that Sir Guy, Bishop of Léon – uncle of Sir Hervé de Léon who'd been complicit, as you've heard, in the Count of Montfort's capture – held a parley with his nephew one day and finally agreed, after much debate, that the bishop would persuade his companions to surrender Hennebont to Lord Louis of Spain on behalf of Lord Charles of Blois, while for his part Sir Hervé would secure those companions a pardon and free passage from Lord Charles with no loss of any of their possessions. That was how the parley ended, and the bishop went to speak with his fellow lords. The countess immediately feared the worst, and begged them, on Our Lady's honour, not to do anything rash, for she was confident that aid would arrive within three days. But the bishop was insistent and persuasive, filling the lords that night with alarm and dread. He carried on next morning, until they were all but convinced that they should yield; and Sir Hervé was just on his way to the town to accept their surrender when the valiant countess, looking out to sea from a castle window, began to shout in jubilation, crying with all the strength she could summon:

"I see the aid I've desired so long!"

All the people in the city ran to the walls to see what she had seen; and there, as plain as could be, they beheld a vast fleet of vessels, great and small, heading for Hennebont. They were mightily cheered, all certain that it was Sir Amaury de Clisson bringing aid from England, as you've heard, after battling against the winds for forty days.

Chapter LVI

How Sir Walter Mauny came with a mighty company to Hennebont,
where the Countess of Montfort was besieged.

Then, when the valiant castellan of Guingant and Sir Yves de Trésiguidi and Sir Galeran de Landreman saw help approaching, they told the bishop to take back what he'd said for they'd no intention of doing as he'd urged. The bishop was furious, and said:

"Then we'll be parting company! You stay here and I'll go to the one I'd say has the rightful claim!"

And with that the bishop left Hennebont, defying the lady and all the inhabitants, and went to join Sir Hervé. He explained what had happened and Sir Hervé was enraged; he called up the biggest engine they had and ordered a constant bombardment by day and night. Then he took his uncle to Lord Louis of Spain, who welcomed him with joy and honour.

Meanwhile the countess was happily arranging chambers, halls and houses for the comfortable lodging of the approaching English lords, and sent a splendid reception party to meet them. As soon as they landed she went down and – little wonder! – welcomed them with the greatest celebration and gratitude imaginable. Then she led all the knights and squires to lodge in the castle, and presented them with a magnificent feast next day. And all the while, both night and day, the enemy bombardment pounded on.

After the lords had dined and been gloriously fêted by the countess, Sir Walter Mauny, commander-in-chief of all the English, took Sir Yves de Trésiguidi aside and asked him about the position of the town and its attackers; and he looked out and said that, if any were willing to follow him, he felt a fierce desire to go and destroy the great engine that was placed so close and inflicting so much damage. Sir Yves replied that he'd be right behind him from the start, as did the lord of Landreman.

So Sir Walter and all his company went and armed at once, and slipped quietly through a gate, taking with them a body of three hundred archers who loosed such fine, dense volleys that they drove back the men who were guarding the engine. The men-at-arms then advanced and killed a good number, and toppled the great engine and smashed it to pieces before charging into the enemy camp and setting it ablaze, killing plenty before the besiegers were awake and could respond. Then they calmly headed back towards the town. But the army, now thoroughly aroused, came running after them like men deranged; and the valiant knight Sir Walter Mauny, seeing this, cried aloud:

"May my dear love never embrace me more if I return to the castle before I've unhorsed and grounded one of these attackers – or he topples me."

And so the worthy knight turned back, lance in hand, shield hung from neck, to face the enemy. So did the Lande-Halle[1] brothers La Haze from Brabant, Sir Yves de Trésiguidi, the lord of Landreman and all the other companions and Brabançons; and they sent many of the first arrivals tumbling with their legs in the air, though some of their own side were also unhorsed. Then a mighty fight began as the besieging army kept coming, and in the end the English and Bretons had to retreat to their fortress. There were many fine charges and captures and rescues made by both sides; and praise and honour were won above all by Sir Walter Mauny, and by his companions such as Sir Yves de Trésiguidi and the lord of Landreman, who were thoroughly mindful of their duty and performed such feats of prowess that they should be deemed worthy indeed.

[1]   See footnote 2, above, p.130.

When they saw it was time to retreat they withdrew in good order to the ditches, where they carried on fighting till their men were safe inside. And the other archers, who hadn't been involved in attacking the siege-engines, had now come out and were shooting so well that they sent the French host reeling back with a great many killed and wounded. When their commanders saw their men on the receiving end and suffering such losses to no avail they ordered them back to camp. The town's defenders withdrew likewise; and anyone who saw the valiant countess then come down from the castle and kiss Sir Walter Mauny and his companions two or three times in turn, would have said she was a lady of noble spirit indeed.

Chapter LVII

How Lord Louis of Spain left Hennebont and went to besiege and capture two towns, Guémené-sur-Scorff[1] and Guérande.[2]

Next morning Lord Louis of Spain summoned the Viscount of Rohan, the Bishop of Léon, Sir Hervé and the captain of the Genoese to discuss what they should do, for they could see that the city of Hennebont was now so strong thanks to the reinforcements – especially the archers, who were slaughtering them – that they were merely wasting time: there was clearly nothing to be gained. They agreed to strike camp next day and head for Auray, which Lord Charles of Blois was besieging. So they set out next morning, and when the people of the town saw them striking camp they jeered and hooted in their wake; some made a sortie and struck at their tail, but they were vigorously repulsed and a few were killed before they could make it back to town.

When Lord Louis of Spain arrived with his men to join Lord Charles of Blois's forces, and told him exactly why he'd abandoned the siege of Hennebont, he was commanded to take his army and lay siege to Guémené-sur-Scorff, which was enclosed only by water and a palisade. So Hennebont was left for a while in peace, and repaired and greatly strengthened its defences, while Lord Louis left Lord Charles's army and headed for Guémené.

On the way he passed close to an old castle called Conquest.[3] Its captain was a valiant knight from Lombardy who was holding it for the countess: his name was Sir Martin, and he was a fine, courageous fighter, and had a good number of soldiers with him. When Lord Louis heard that the castle supported the countess he led his army before it and launched a fierce assault which lasted all day until nightfall. They camped there that night and resumed the attack next

---

[1] 'Dynant': see footnote 1, above, p.133.

[2] 'Garlande'.

[3] The difficulty with identifying places continues. If 'Dynant' were (very improbably) Dinan, 'Conquest' might possibly be the castle near Concoret, which would have been more or less on the way. If 'Dynant' is Guémené-sur-Scorff, there is a fair distance between there and Auray in which this 'old castle' (with less than impressive defences) may have once stood and since disappeared. If Le Bel's following account is accurate, 'Conquest' needs to be within a morning's ride of Hennebont.

day, advancing so close to the walls (the ditches being of no great depth) that the defenders couldn't stop them making a great breach; they poured through and slaughtered everyone. Then Lord Louis appointed an able castellan and sixty Spaniards to guard it, before moving on to besiege the town of Guémené-sur-Scorff.

The valiant countess and Sir Walter Mauny received word that Lord Louis and his army had stopped before the castle of Conquest, and Sir Walter summoned all his companions and soldiers and said:

"Sirs, it would be a fine adventure if we could drive the army from Conquest and defeat Lord Louis!"

They all agreed, and rode next day from Hennebont; they arrived at Conquest between noon and the ninth hour,[1] only to find that the castle had been taken the day before and the garrison put to the sword and replaced by other men. The valiant knight Sir Walter was distressed when he saw this and realised there was no chance of battle with Lord Louis; he vowed he wouldn't leave until he found out who the occupants were and how the castle had been captured. His men made ready to attack and advanced upon the castle in a fury. Seeing this, the Spaniards mounted a vigorous defence, raining stones on their attackers; but the assault was just as mighty, the archers using their bows to such awesome effect that the defenders didn't dare show their heads above the battlements. The attackers pressed on and reached the walls and found the breach where Lord Louis's men had broken into the castle; and through the very same place the English entered and killed all but ten, who were spared by the lords. Then the English and Bretons returned in triumph to Hennebont, abandoning the castle of Conquest which had been taken on one day and retaken the next, a feat of great prowess indeed.

Now I shall return to Lord Louis of Spain. He ordered his men to pitch camp around the town of Guémené, and to build little craft so that they could attack by land and water.[2] When the townsfolk saw this – knowing as they did how poorly their town was fortified against such an army – all of them, of every degree, were terrified. They unanimously decided to surrender if their lives and possessions would be spared, and this they did on the fourth day in defiance of their captain Sir Regnault de Guingant: they killed him in the middle of the market place when he refused to agree.

After Lord Louis had been in the town for two days and received the citizens' oaths of fealty, he appointed as their captain the squire Gérard de Malain, whom he found imprisoned there with Sir Porteboeuf. He set off then towards a mighty city on the coast called Guérande,[3] and laid siege to it by land. Quite close by[4] he found a great number of ships and boats laden with wine brought there by merchants; it didn't take them long to sell it now, but they weren't exactly well paid. And next day Lord Louis requisitioned all these vessels and sent men-at-

---

[1]   The ninth canonical hour, about 3 p.m.
[2]   If 'Dynant' is indeed Guémené-sur-Scorff, this would imply attacks from the river.
[3]   'Garlande'.
[4]   Almost certainly at the nearby port of Le Croisic.

arms aboard, Spaniards and Genoese, so that the city could be besieged by land and sea. It didn't hold out for long: it was soon taken by storm and looted and destroyed, and all, great and small, women and children, were put to the sword, and five churches were burnt and desecrated, at which Lord Louis was enraged and had fourteen hanged for the deed. A mass of booty was taken there, for it was a prosperous city of abundant riches.

Having captured this wealthy town and not knowing where to go next, Lord Louis decided to set sail in the company of Sir Ayton Doria[1] and some of the Genoese and Spaniards to try his fortune at sea, while the Bishop of Léon, the Viscount of Rohan, Sir Hervé de Léon and all the rest rejoined Lord Charles of Blois's army, still encamped before Auray. There they found a great number of lords and barons of France newly arrived, such as Count Louis of Valence and the Count of Auxerre and many more.

The people inside Auray were so beset by hunger that for the past eight days they'd been eating their horses; but they wouldn't be granted mercy: unconditional surrender was demanded. Realising their desperate plight they put themselves in God's hands and tried to slip through the enemy lines on one side of the city. Some of them were spotted and killed, but Sir Henry de Spinefort and his brother and others whose names I don't know escaped through a wood and made their way straight to Hennebont and a warm welcome there.

And so, by starving it out in a ten-week siege, Lord Charles of Blois won back the stronghold of Auray. He gave orders for the town to be restored and freshly provisioned and its defences all repaired, and then set off with his whole army to besiege the city of Vannes, where the captain was Sir Geoffroi de Malestroit. Next day some Breton companions left the city and made their base at a town called Ploërmel; when they saw the chance they rode out and engaged the French in a fierce skirmish, but they were reckless: they got themselves surrounded, which cost them many of their number. Those that could escape fled back to Ploërmel, pursued by the enemy all the way.

The French now launched a mighty attack upon Vannes, taking the barriers at the gates by storm. The assault then was ferocious, with many killed and wounded, and it raged on till midnight. Then a truce was agreed, to last all the following day, to allow the citizens to discuss whether to surrender.

Next day they decided to do so in defiance of their captain Sir Geoffroi de Malestroit. Seeing the way things were going, he left the city without being recognised while they continued their negotiations, and made his way to Hennebont.

And so it was that Lord Charles of Blois won the city of Vannes, and entered and received the citizens' oaths of fealty. He stayed for five days before moving on to besiege a town called Carhaix. But I shall leave him for a little and tell of Lord Louis of Spain.

---

[1]   See footnote 1, above, p.116.

Chapter LVIII

How Sir Walter Mauny and his companions pursued
Lord Louis of Spain across the sea and defeated him.

The truth is that Lord Louis, having taken ship at the port of Guérande, roamed the sea with his companions until, in the Breton-speaking part of Brittany, they came to the port of Quimperlé, not far from Quimper and Saint-Mathieu in Finisterre.[1] There they went ashore and burned and pillaged all the surrounding country, finding amazing wealth and riches; then they set off elsewhere and did the same and found no one to oppose them.

When the valiant knight Sir Walter Mauny and Sir Amaury de Clisson heard of this they resolved to head after them and do battle with Lord Louis of Spain. They shared their plan with Sir Yves de Trésiguidi, the lords of Guingant, Landreman and Cadoudal, Sir Geoffroi de Malestroit, Sir Henry de Spinefort, the two Lande-Halle brothers La Haze, Sir Hugue de Milhy, Sir Jehan le Boutillier, Sir Hubert de Fresnay, Sir Alain de Sirehoude[2] (captain of the archers), and all the knights and squires at Hennebont. They all agreed to go with them.

They boarded vessels and kept sailing till they came to where Lord Louis's ships were anchored. They seized them and killed all the guards, and were astounded by the mass of booty they found aboard; then they went ashore and found towns burnt and land laid waste on every side. They shrewdly divided into three battalions to find the enemy more quickly, and left three hundred archers to guard their own ships and those they'd captured; then they set off along their separate paths, following the trails of smoke.

When Lord Louis heard that the English had come he was very alarmed; he gathered his men together and headed back towards his ships. All the people of the country were following him, men and women alike, for he was carrying off all their plundered belongings. He ran into one of the three divisions and realised he had no choice but to fight. He ventured to attack, so fiercely that this first division would have been defeated if the other two hadn't responded to the cries and commotion. The fighting now intensified, and the archers were so effective that the Genoese and Spaniards were routed and almost all were slain, for the country people themselves attacked with pitchforks and mattocks and slaughtered them like pigs, and recovered all they could of their stolen goods. Only narrowly did Lord Louis escape the battle; wounded in several places he fled to his ships, and of a good six thousand men barely three hundred made it with him. Among the dead he left a nephew: his name was Sir Alfonso of Spain; he'd knighted him there that very day. But when Lord Louis reached the ships he found them so well guarded that he couldn't board; so he struggled on to a

---

[1] '*Campecornetin*' and '*Saint Molos de Fine Poterne*'. As noted above (p.111), Le Bel's notions of distances in Brittany are not very precise.
[2] His name is given this time as '*Surhonde*'.

boat called a lugger[1] with such men as he had left, and put to sea as swiftly as he could.

The English and Breton lords had defeated their enemies but realised Lord Louis of Spain had escaped; they went after him with all possible speed, leaving the country folk to deal with those who were left. When they reached their ships they saw Lord Louis sailing away and out to sea as fast as he could; they boarded and sailed straight after him, feeling they'd have achieved nothing if he got away. They had the best wind they could have wished for, but it helped Lord Louis escape them: his crew managed to sail him to a port called Redon.[2] There they disembarked, but they hadn't been there long before they heard the English had arrived. Lord Louis instantly borrowed whatever horses he could get in the town and made for Rennes, which was fairly near, followed by as many of his company as could find a mount. The English and Bretons, hearing this, chased after them and killed every one they caught; but they couldn't overtake Lord Louis, and returned to Redon and stayed there that night to rest.

They put to sea again next day, intending to return to the valiant countess at Hennebont, but the wind was against them and they were forced to land some three leagues from Guémené;[3] and they set off across country, burning the land around Guémené and taking whatever horses they could find – some without saddle, some without bridle – and found themselves at nightfall close to La Roche-Périou. Arriving there Sir Walter Mauny said:

"Truly, if anyone'll join me I'd gladly go and attack this castle, weary though I am."

"Go ahead, sir, and boldly!" said the others. "We'll follow willingly!"

So they all advanced up the hill to attack the castle. At this point its castellan was the squire named Gérard de Malain who'd been imprisoned at Guémené as you've heard,[4] and he ordered all his men to arm and prepare to defend the castle. A fearsome assault now followed, and many knights and squires were wounded there; among them were Sir Jehan le Boutillier and Sir Hubert de Fresnay, whose wounds were so severe that they had to be carried down the hill to lie with the other casualties in a meadow.

This Gérard de Malain had a brother named Renier de Malain, a courageous squire who was castellan of another little castle called Le Faouët,[5] less than a league from La Roche-Périou. When he heard that Bretons and English were

---

[1]   This is an attempt to translate 'ling'. This may be a transcription of an old Breton word, or conceivably a misreading of *lougre*, though the latter may be a little anachronistic. The implication in any event is that it is a local vessel, inadequate for the number of men and of a kind unworthy of Lord Louis.

[2]   'Gredo'. Although it is not on the coast, Redon enjoyed a thriving maritime trade in the middle ages thanks to its position on a major river, the Vilaine.

[3]   'Dynant' again. This is final confirmation that 'Dynant' is not Dinan, which is on the wrong coast. Guémené-sur-Scorff is certainly more than three leagues from the sea, and it's hard to see where they would have landed after leaving Redon that would have brought them to Guémené rather than Hennebont, so some of Le Bel's details may not be accurate, but Guémené's proximity to both La Roche-Périou and Le Faouët makes perfect sense of the story that follows.

[4]   Above, p.137.

[5]   'Fauete'.

attacking his brother, he summoned about forty companions to arm and headed for La Roche-Périou to see if there was any way to help him. He luckily stumbled upon the meadow where Sir Jehan and Sir Hubert were lying with the other wounded, and he took them captive and led them back to his castle of Le Faouët. Some of their household ran to tell Sir Walter what had happened; when he and his fellow knights heard the news they were dismayed and called a halt to the attack, and went galloping off, each as fast as he could, towards Le Faouët to rescue them; but they weren't quick enough: Renier de Malain was already back inside his castle with his prisoners. When Sir Walter Mauny's men had all arrived, one after the other, they launched an attack upon the castle, tired though they were; but they achieved little, for Renier and his companions mounted a valiant defence. It was late by this time, and the attackers decided to camp for the night around the castle, to be in better shape for a renewed assault in the morning.

Gérard de Malain soon learned that these lords had gone from La Roche-Périou, and was thrilled when he heard of his brother's fine deed in bringing him aid; and knowing that they'd gone to attack Le Faouët, he decided to go to his brother's aid as his brother had done for him. So he mounted and rode through the night and arrived at Guémené just before dawn; there he spoke to his good companion Sir Pierre Porteboeuf , now the commander at Guémené, and told him what had happened and why he'd come. They decided that as soon as day broke they'd gather the people of the town together, explain the position, and bid them arm and go and raise the siege of Le Faouët. Once it was fully light the townspeople were assembled, and it was agreed that they would indeed go and raise the siege; a good six thousand men set off, of one kind and another.

Sir Walter Mauny and his companions were informed of this by a spy; they decided that, all things considered, it would be safest and best to leave and withdraw to Hennebont: if they dallied there they might well suffer. So they departed, leaving their two companions imprisoned until another chance should arise to rescue them.

On their way back to Hennebont they passed a castle called Glay la Forest,[1] which a fortnight earlier had surrendered to Lord Charles of Blois; he'd left it in the hands of Sir Hervé de Léon and Sir Guy de Glay (who had held it previously), but they weren't there at present, for they were with Lord Charles at the siege of Carhaix. When the valiant knight Sir Walter Mauny saw the castle of Glay la Forest, which was very strong, he told the Breton lords that he wouldn't leave, weary though he was, until he'd delivered an attack and tested the defenders' mettle. He ordered everyone to arm and the archers to prepare, and he took up arms and rode up the hill to the barriers and ditches before the castle. All his companions followed him, English and Bretons alike, and they mounted a vigorous attack; but the defenders didn't fail to respond, even though they had no captain, and there was a fine contest which lasted till well past vespers, every man acquitting himself valiantly. Sir Walter urged his men on with a passion,

---

[1]   This is probably Coët Colay ('coet' being Breton for 'wood'), north of Hennebont near Languidic.

and he himself was always at the forefront, in the greatest peril; and the archers' volleys were so incessant that the defenders didn't dare show their heads above the battlements. Then Sir Walter and his companions ordered the ditches to be filled with wood and straw so that they could reach the walls, which they hacked and battered with iron mallets until they'd made a breach six feet wide. And so it was that they took the mighty castle by storm, and put everyone they found there to the sword.

They lodged there for the night and set off next morning for Hennebont. When the valiant countess heard of their arrival she went to welcome them joyously with kisses and embraces in her eminently gracious way. She had the castle prepared most nobly to receive them; and at the feast she gave for the knights and squires she asked them all about their fine adventures and wondrous deeds – even though she knew a good deal already. Many daring feats of prowess were recounted then, as each man told of his bold and perilous exploits and deeds of arms. They deserved – as they do still – to be reputed worthy indeed, especially Sir Walter Mauny, who never feared to undertake the most dangerous and daring feats. Anyone who considers the deeds of arms he performed in defeating Lord Louis of Spain, in slaying the Genoese and Spaniards, in chasing Lord Louis over land and sea, in attacking the castle of La Roche-Périou followed by the castle of Le Faouët, and then taking the strong castle of Glay la Forest by storm before returning to where he'd started – Hennebont – safe and sound, must surely deem his campaign most notable and worthy of high honour, and all who were with him courageous and valiant men.

Chapter LIX

How the French lords took the town of Carhaix and then laid siege to Hennebont.

While these English and Breton lords were returning to Hennebont, Lord Charles of Blois had won the city of Vannes and laid such close siege to the town of Carhaix that it couldn't hold out for long. So the valiant countess and Sir Walter Mauny sent high-ranking messengers to King Edward, to make clear that Lord Charles of Blois had taken the cities of Rennes and Vannes and other towns and castles in Brittany and would conquer all the rest if he didn't bring speedy help. These messengers sailed across the sea to England and delivered their message as eloquently as they could.

But I'll stay with affairs in Brittany for the moment, and tell you that the people of Carhaix couldn't hold out long enough for help to arrive, and surrendered to Lord Charles of Blois with their lives and possessions spared. And when Lord Charles and his fellow lords had received the citizens' oaths of fealty and had rested there for six days, they decided to go and lay siege to Hennebont, and resolved not to leave, come what may, until they took it and were avenged upon the English who'd defeated Lord Louis of Spain. So they marched to Hennebont, which was now greatly strengthened and well provisioned. Lord Louis was lying wounded at Rennes and had not yet fully recovered, but when he heard this news he made himself ready and travelled to join Lord Charles's army outside

Hennebont. Lord Charles and the others were overjoyed to see him and gave him a grand welcome, for they hadn't seen him since the aforementioned battle.

The French army was growing mightily by the day, for great numbers of French lords and knights, passing through Poitou as they returned from the King of Spain's war in Granada against the Saracens, rode to join them when they heard of the war in Brittany. And Lord Louis had deployed fifteen or sixteen huge siege engines which pounded the walls of Hennebont with a constant barrage of massive stones. But it did little to daunt the defenders; indeed, they came to the battlements and bobbed up and down, baiting their attackers with cries of: "Go and find those mates of yours lying in Quimperlé!" This riled Lord Louis of Spain no end.

Chapter LX

How Lord Louis wanted to behead two knights who were
valiantly rescued by Sir Walter Mauny.

One day Lord Louis came to Lord Charles of Blois and asked a favour, in the presence of all the lords, in return for his services to him. Lord Charles didn't know what favour this would be, but readily agreed; whereupon Lord Louis said:

"Many thanks. I ask that you have the two knights imprisoned in the castle at Le Faouët – Sir Jehan le Boutillier and Sir Hubert de Fresnay – brought here to me to do with as I choose. That's the favour I crave. They've pursued, defeated and wounded me, and killed my nephew Sir Alfonso whom I dearly loved, and I want no other vengeance than to behead them in front of their companions behind those walls!"

Lord Charles was taken aback, and replied in courteous fashion, saying: "Truly, sir, I'll give you the prisoners, but it would be little honour to you – and a great shame and mark of cruelty for all of us – if you treated these knights as you say. We would be eternally reproached, and our enemies would feel justified in treating our men likewise when they take them prisoner – which can happen every day. I beg you to reconsider."

But Lord Louis replied at once that no one in the world could change his mind. "And if you won't keep your promise to me, I'll leave forthwith and will neither serve nor love you any more!"

Lord Charles could clearly see he was in earnest and didn't dare annoy him further; so he sent a party to the castle of Le Faouët to fetch the two valiant knights. This was duly done, and the two knights were brought early one morning to Lord Charles's tent. When Lord Louis of Spain heard they'd arrived he went to see them with a number of the other lords; and he said to them:

"Sir knights, you've wounded me and taken the life of my dearly beloved nephew, so you must die, too: no man alive can save you. So make confession if you wish, and pray to Our Lord for mercy, for your final day has come."

The knights were deeply shocked, and said they couldn't believe that worthy men of true prowess would commit or allow such a barbarous act as to put to death knights who'd been captured in combat, in warfare between lords; if it were done, many others might suffer the same fate. The other lords present felt great sympathy for their words, but no pleading or argument would change Lord Louis's mind: the two knights were to be beheaded after dinner.

The words that had passed between Lord Louis and Lord Charles about these knights were quickly relayed to Sir Walter Mauny and Sir Amaury de Clisson by spies, who were constantly moving in secret between the two armies. Sir Walter and Sir Amaury told their companions of the knights' piteous plight, and they all started pondering one plan and another. At last the worthy and valiant knight Sir Walter Mauny spoke up, saying:

"Sirs, it would be a great honour for us if we could rescue those two knights. And if we were to try but fail, we would earn the gratitude at least of good King Edward, and of all worthy men who heard we'd done everything we could. I'll tell you my thoughts, if you're willing to join me: I believe it's only right to risk one's life to save two valiant knights, and I propose, if you will, that we arm and form two divisions. The first will leave at once, while everyone's at dinner, and go through the gate here and deploy along these ditches and make as if to skirmish with the enemy – I'm sure they'll come running to engage at once. You, Sir Amaury, will be captain, if you please, and take good archers with you to stop the attackers and drive them back. I meanwhile will take a hundred of my companions and five hundred archers, and we'll leave in secret through a postern and strike their empty encampment from the rear. I have men who know the way to Lord Charles of Blois's tents where the two knights are being held, and I promise you we'll do our best to rescue them and bring them back to safety, if it please God."

This plan was pleasing to all, and what the noble knight had proposed was done: the two knights who were about to be beheaded after dinner were rescued and brought back to Hennebont, and all their guards were killed. For his part Sir Amaury, having kept the enemy host engaged, returned to the city with his company in the highest spirits – all, that is, except the lord of Landreman and the castellan of Guingant who'd been captured by the other side; but it was strongly believed that they'd let themselves be taken, for they were immediately released and joined Lord Charles of Blois's side, turning against the valiant countess who'd shown them so much kindness. That night, inside Hennebont, the English and Bretons celebrated joyously for the success of their bold mission and the rescue of the two knights, while outside, Lord Louis of Spain was deeply vexed at having lost them.

Three days after this adventure, all the French lords besieging Hennebont met in Lord Charles of Blois's pavilion to discuss how to proceed, for they could see that the town and castle were immensely strong and garrisoned with fine men-at-arms who had little fear of them. Moreover, fresh supplies were constantly reaching the town by sea, while the surrounding land had been so ravaged that there was nowhere for the besiegers to go and forage, and with winter fast approaching they couldn't stay much longer. All these points considered, they unanimously agreed that they should leave, and advised Lord Charles to place good garrisons and men he could safely trust in all the cities, towns and fortresses, and if he could arrange a truce till Pentecost he should readily accept it.

All those present agreed to this, for it was now between the feasts of Saint Rémy and All Saints[1] in the year of grace 1342. So the entire army, lords and all ranks, departed and headed home to their own lands, while Lord Charles of Blois made his way to Carhaix with those Breton lords and barons who had taken his side, and also retained a number of French lords to help and counsel him.

He had arrived at Carhaix and begun to organise his affairs and garrison when a wealthy merchant and citizen of the town of Guingamp[2] was stopped by his marshal, Sir Robert de Beaumanoir, and arrested and brought before Lord Charles. This merchant was responsible for all the countess's supplies and was much in her favour; and he was much respected, too, in the town of Guingamp, which was well situated and splendidly fortified, with a fine castle which was held for the countess, its castellan being a valiant knight named Sir Gérard de Rochefort. This captured merchant was terrified that he'd be put to death, and begged to be released for a ransom. In short, Lord Charles had him interrogated on a range of matters, until he finally promised to betray the town of Guingamp by leaving one of the gates unlocked on a certain day: he was held in such trust in the town that he was the keeper of the keys. To secure the deal he left his son as a hostage, and Lord Charles promised him hereditable land worth five hundred pounds in rent.

On the appointed day the gate was opened at midnight and Lord Charles entered the town with a mighty force. The castle watchman spotted them and began to sound his horn and cried: "To arms! Treachery! Treachery!" At this the unsuspecting townsfolk arose and fled to the castle – not least the merchant who'd betrayed them who, to maintain his cover, went fleeing with them and took refuge in the castle with the others. As soon as it was light Lord Charles and his men broke into the people's houses and took everything they found; and Lord Charles, seeing the castle's strength, declared he wouldn't leave till it was his. The castellan and the townsfolk soon discovered that the merchant had betrayed them, and hanged him at once from the castle battlements: quite right, too, in my opinion.

Realising that Lord Charles wouldn't leave till the castle was in his hands, and that they hadn't the provisions to support so many people, they agreed to surrender if their lives and remaining possessions would be spared. Lord Charles agreed to this and received their vows of fealty. And so it was that he won the town and castle of Guingamp.

While all this had been going on, a number of worthy men had negotiated a truce between Lord Charles and the valiant countess, to last until the first day of May in the following year, 1343. The countess readily agreed, as did all her allies,

---

[1] Between 1 October and 1 November.
[2] 'Gigan'. In their edition Viard and Déprez surprisingly assume this to be the town of Jugon. It is surely – in view of location, the description of its fine fortifications and the later spelling 'Gingan' – to be identified as Guingamp, the next substantial town north-east of Carhaix.

for the noble King Edward had sent a message urging this; and as soon as the truce had been concluded the valiant countess put to sea and went in person to speak to the King of England.

But I shall leave her and Breton affairs for a little and tell now of King Edward.

Chapter LXI

How the King of England held a great feast in London, and the
Countess of Montfort came to ask him for help.

You have earlier heard how King Edward had had to conduct a series of mighty wars in many lands and marches, at vast cost and expense: in Picardy, Normandy, Gascony, Saintonge, Poitou, Brittany and Scotland. And you've also heard of his passionate love for the valiant lady of Salisbury, named Alice;[1] he couldn't help himself, even though the Earl of Salisbury was one of his closest counsellors and most loyal servants. And so it was that, for love of that lady and in his longing to see her (and also to alert his people to the harm that the King of Scotland was doing, retaking the castle of Roxburgh and all of Scotland as far as Berwick, and to seek their advice on this), he had announced throughout the land a great festival of jousting in the city of London in the middle of August in the year of grace 1342: it was to last for fifteen days. He summoned every lord, baron, knight and squire and all ladies and damsels to attend without excuse, if they truly loved him; and he commanded the Earl of Salisbury to ensure that his wife was there, and that she should bring with her all the ladies and damsels she could find. The earl willingly consented, not suspecting what was going on; but the worthy countess came most reluctantly, fearing as she did the king's motives, though she didn't dare reveal this to her husband.

It was a magnificent feast; none so great had ever been seen in England, for there were twelve earls and fully eight hundred knights in attendance, and five hundred ladies of high lineage, and the jousting and dancing continued for fifteen days.[2] The only shadow cast on the proceedings was the unfortunate death in a

---

[1] The Countess of Salisbury's name was Catherine, not Alice. There is a slight possibility that the mistake could be explained by the fact that there was an Alice, Countess of Salisbury, in the 15th century, at a time coinciding with the production of the surviving manuscript of Le Bel's Chronicle; there may, too, have been some belated confusion with Edward's famous mistress Alice Perrers. More interesting, however, especially given the doubts that have been expressed about the accuracy of this story, is the fact that the Earl of Salisbury's brother, Edward Montagu, had a wife named Alice. Edward Montagu, indeed, may well have been the castellan of Wark, in which case he may have been the figure understood by Le Bel to have been the 'the son of the Earl of Salisbury's sister: he was named Sir William Montagu after his uncle' (above, p.123), as the Earl had in fact no nephew named William. These issues are discussed at length by Ian Mortimer in his biography of Edward III, *The Perfect King* (London, 2006), pp.191-8.
[2] The king was in London for the whole of August until the 27th, and a feast was held on the 26th.

joust of Sir John, eldest son of the viscount of Beaumont,[1] a most worthy squire who bore a blue shield scattered with gold fleurs-de-lis and blazoned with a lion rampant and a red baton. All the ladies and damsels in attendance were dressed in their best finery, each according to her station – except the Countess of Salisbury, who didn't want to give the king cause to start gazing at her or speaking to her, for she had no wish to obey the king in any unworthy act which might bring dishonour to her or to her husband.

The princes present were the following: Lord Henry 'Wryneck', Earl of Lancaster; his son the Earl of Derby; the Count of Hainault, brother of the Queen of England; Lord Robert of Artois, Earl of Richmond;[2] the earls[3] of Northampton and Gloucester; the Earl of Warwick, the Earl of Salisbury, the Earl of Suffolk, the Earl of Pembroke, the Earl of Arundel, the Duke of Cornwall,[4] the Earl of Oxford[5] and the Earl of Stafford.

Before the end of this noble feast the king received several unwelcome embassies. One came from Brittany, on behalf of the Countess of Montfort and Sir Walter Mauny, asking for relief and aid and explaining how Lord Charles of Blois had already reconquered a large part of Brittany and would win back the rest unless the valiant countess had speedy help. Another came on behalf of Sir Gérard de La Bret and the people of Bordeaux on the Gironde, informing the noble king that the supporters of the King of France were daily harrying them and waging war with increasing intensity, and that he would lose part of Gascony unless he sent urgent help. The valiant king responded to these messages by telling the envoys to urge their parties to maintain their commitment and defend their towns and lands and fortresses with due resolve, for as soon as the new campaigning season came he would bring them all the aid that they required; if until then they could secure a truce and suspension of hostilities they should do so. It was in response to this that the valiant countess, as you've heard, agreed a truce with Lord Charles of Blois until the first day of May.

No sooner had he dealt with these messages than another came from Lord Robert Balliol,[6] captain of the city of Berwick, informing the king that the Scots had won back the country's strongholds and the mighty castle of Roxburgh. The princes present advised the king to respond to Lord Robert as he had to the others, but at the same time to send his brother-in-law, the worthy prelate the Bishop of Lincoln, to the King of Scotland to negotiate a truce to last, if possible, for two or three years. The king was reluctant to agree, feeling it a weak and feeble move in the light of what the Scots had lately done. The lords replied that, saving his grace, it should be taken into account that he had previously ravaged the whole kingdom of Scotland, and that he was now engaged in several wars

---

[1]   As noted above (footnote 8, p.78), there were no English viscounts at this time. This is John, 2nd Baron Beaumont, son of Henry the 1st Baron.

[2]   See footnote 1, above, p.58.

[3]   See footnote 3, above, p.78.

[4]   i.e. Prince Edward.

[5]   My interpretation of 'Abenfort' (on the basis of the most plausible scribal misreading, for 'Oxenford').

[6]   'Robert de Bailheu'.

in different countries, and any lord was considered wise who, when involved in several wars at once, took the opportunity to settle one, either permanently or at least for a period of truce. This argument was so well made that he agreed that such a truce should be sought, and the worthy prelate the Bishop of Lincoln set out and headed for Scotland. But it was a wasted journey: he achieved nothing, and returned to the king with the news that King David of Scotland was not inclined to agree a truce or cessation of hostilities. King Edward was furious, and declared that he would soon reduce the realm of Scotland to a state from which it would never recover; and he summoned all the men of his kingdom to be at York on Easter Day, ready to follow where he led them.

Easter Day came, and all the lords and commons of England's cities were gathered at York. Many issues were debated there; I don't know exactly how or when the discussions ended, for the one who told me of it wasn't a member of the king's privy council, but I do know that the King of England didn't carry on to Scotland this time. I don't know why he decided not to, but it was at this point that the valiant Countess of Montfort arrived to ask for help, laying before the king the dire plight of her husband, imprisoned for having paid him homage for the duchy of Brittany; and she told him how Lord Charles of Blois had won back most of the cities and strongholds in Brittany, and that she feared he would conquer the rest with his mighty army.

The noble king and all the other lords welcomed her with great celebration and much honour, respecting her highly for her valiant defence and upholding of her husband's cause. And the noble king, at the prompting of Sir Robert of Artois, promised her that, before the truce she'd made had expired, he would send her enough help to see her gain supreme revenge upon her enemies, even if, indeed, it meant he abandoned all other missions. And he immediately asked Lord Robert of Artois, the Earl of Salisbury, the Earl of Suffolk, the Earl of Pembroke, the Earl of Oxford,[1] the Earl of Stafford and many other lords to gather an army of fully four thousand cavalry, ten thousand foot soldiers and as many archers and prepare to set sail, and to spare no efforts until the valiant countess was restored to her inheritance in defiance of all her enemies; and if necessary he, too, would join them with all his forces. The valiant countess thanked him fulsomely, and was about to fall at his feet in humble gratitude, but the king would not permit it.

When the lords were ready they put to sea with all necessary provisions and sailed with the countess back to Brittany.[2] I can't recount all the adventures they encountered, as I wasn't present, and those who've told me of this expedition have given so many different accounts that I'm not sure which to believe. I've found in one book in verse, composed by some minstrel or other, so many wild tales and fictions that I wouldn't dare repeat them here. So I'll say nothing, so

---

[1]   'Kenfort': this is almost certainly a transcription of 'Oxenford'; see footnotes above, p.147 and below, pp.157 and 159.

[2]   Robert of Artois is known to have been at Southampton, preparing to sail, on 13 August 1342.

that no one can accuse me of falsehood, and if I say too little or too much at any point I ask pardon, but I wasn't present at every event that occurred.

But I do know that Lord Robert of Artois and his company had much to do in Brittany – and indeed before they arrived there, for Lord Louis of Spain, Sir Carlo Grimaldi and Sir Ayton Doria[1] had learned of their coming and assembled a great fleet of Spaniards and Genoese. They attacked them by night and captured three or four of their vessels laden with supplies and killed a great number of their men, though they, too, suffered losses. I'm not sure how the English got away, but I do know that they landed in Brittany quite near the city of Vannes and split into two divisions and besieged it from two sides, for the truce had now expired. But they found the city well provisioned and garrisoned with able men-at-arms. The city's bishop was there, along with Sir Olivier de Clisson and many others of his family, for he was lord of one part of the city; Sir Hervé de Léon was with them, too, appointed captain by Lord Charles of Blois. They mounted a stout defence, and there were fine exploits and great feats of prowess performed by both sides – but I couldn't describe them with certainty so it's better that I say nothing. What I do know is that the English lords besieged the city for a long time before they could take it, and all the while they pillaged and laid waste the whole country and returned to their quarters laden with loot. And finally, though I don't know the details, I understand the city was taken by storm – following a secret agreement, so it was rumoured, between Lord Robert of Artois and Sir Olivier de Clisson – and the whole place was sacked, pillaged and destroyed and its people driven out. But straight after, Sir Hervé de Léon and Sir Olivier de Clisson (despite the accusations laid against him) rallied the people of the surrounding country and the ousted citizens, and they won the city back from the English, killing and capturing a great number. Lord Robert of Artois himself was gravely wounded there, so much so that he had to be taken back to England where he died soon after, which was a grievous pity; and the King of England was most distressed, and said he would attend to nothing else until he'd avenged Lord Robert's death and crushed the land of Brittany so totally that it wouldn't have recovered in forty years.[2] He sent letters throughout his kingdom, summoning all, nobles and non-nobles alike, to be ready to go with him at the end of the month[3] to ravage and lay waste the land of Brittany. He ordered vessels and all provisions to be prepared.

Chapter LXII

How King Edward came to Brittany and laid siege to three cities in a single day.

At the end of the month King Edward and all his company put to sea, and came ashore near the city of Vannes, exactly where Lord Robert of Artois

[1] 'Germain Charles' and 'Otton Doriie': see footnote 1, above, p.116.
[2] Robert of Artois died in Brittany some time between 6 October and 20 November 1342, and was buried in London at the end of January 1343. His death was not the motive for Edward's setting out for Brittany: his expedition had been announced in August.
[3] Edward sailed from Portsmouth on 23 October 1342.

and his forces had landed previously. They disembarked and laid closer siege to the city than before, for their army was far greater. But the city, too, was now massively strengthened and provisioned with both supplies and men-at-arms, and the surrounding country had been so thoroughly ravaged that such a great army couldn't be supported for long; the situation needed serious thought. The noble King Edward, seeing the city's strength and the country's dearth, realised that Vannes couldn't be quickly taken; and he'd heard that the earls of Salisbury and Suffolk and the other lords who'd come earlier with Lord Robert of Artois had laid siege to the city of Rennes since Lord Robert had left them, and had mounted many assaults and lost a fair number of their men – it's inevitable that some men are lost in any assault – and they'd also mounted expeditions into the surrounding country and encountered some fine adventures. So the noble king decided to leave a large body of his men before Vannes to maintain the siege and to guard his fleet nearby, while he would go with the rest of his army and join the other lords outside Rennes, which had already been besieged for forty days or more.

So he set off, burning and laying waste all the land where his forces had not yet been, and came to Rennes to bring new heart and spirit to his men; the sight of him gave them as much joy as the sight of the body of Jesus Christ, if not more, for no king was ever so loved by his men as he.

He stayed there for two days. But then he heard that Lord Charles of Blois and Lord Louis of Spain were at Nantes with a great army, and he resolved to bring them to battle or besiege them there. So he set out[1] and burned and ravaged the land around Nantes[2] and deployed his battalions in splendid array, in full view of the enemy; but no one came out to do battle, though there was a good deal of skirmishing in the suburbs. And so the king pitched his tents and pavilions and laid siege to the city on one side; and then, after several days, he mounted an assault which achieved very little at the cost of a good number of his men. In view of this, seeing little progress made and that the surrounding land had been laid waste and couldn't long support so large a force, he left some of his men there to await reinforcements and set out elsewhere in search of adventures. So the noble king, finding no one to fight, left the siege of Nantes and went through the country burning and destroying everything, until he came to the town of Guémené-sur-Scorff.[3]

And so it was that, amid this burning and destruction of the land of Brittany, the noble King Edward had three armies besieging three cities and one town. And after he'd been outside Guémené for three days, and seen that it was enclosed only by a palisade and ditches, he ordered an assault. The attack lasted a long while, for the defenders resisted vigorously; but in the end it was taken by storm, pillaged, destroyed and burnt so utterly that no house, great or small, survived the engulfing fire. Not even a church remained: all was razed to the ground; and men, women and children were slaughtered, much to the king's dismay. The

---

[1]   Edward sent a large force there but did not go to Nantes in person.
[2]   The text accidentally repeats 'Rennes'.
[3]   Still given as 'Dynant'.

booty won was beyond all counting, for it was a town of great wealth and plenty. After all was done, the king left there and went to stay at Brayt,[1] which was fairly close to his fleet and to the port through which all his supplies arrived. This was at the beginning of winter in the year of grace 1343.[2]

King Philip knew that the King of England had lately arrived in Brittany and was burning and ravaging the country far and wide, for Lord Charles of Blois had sent word informing him that he would lose the whole land unless he received help. King Philip was not so much concerned that his nephew Lord Charles might lose his land, the duchy of Brittany, as he was afraid that the English king would advance from there into France. So he commanded his son the Duke of Normandy to head for the duchy, partly to aid the Duke of Brittany, but also to prevent any incursion into France. He promised to supply him with all the troops he needed, and sent an immediate summons throughout his land calling upon all, nobles and commons alike, to make ready to follow his son to Brittany; the response from both nobles and commons was so great that the roads and fields were filled with men. The Duke of Normandy and the other lords stopped at Angers to await them all, and sent to Lord Charles at Nantes for information about the state of the country and the movements of the enemy.

I daren't venture further details about how these two great forces proceeded or the adventures that took place, because I wasn't present; and although I find many things recorded in those verse romances I've mentioned, I wouldn't dare repeat them because they contain more lies than truth. But I understand that these two great armies were parted by a truce,[3] and I know for certain that King Edward left Brittany, taking with him as a prisoner Sir Hervé de Léon, and that the three long-standing sieges of the aforementioned cities were lifted. And the Duke of Normandy and all the lords who'd come with him departed, each returning to his own land and the duke going to see his father the king in Paris.

It was shortly after this that Sir Olivier de Clisson was arrested on a charge of treason. I don't know if the charge was true, but I find it hard to believe that a knight as noble and valiant and truly illustrious as he would have been willing or able to contemplate treachery. Be that as it may, on such a base charge he was arrested, and he was dragged through the streets and beheaded in Paris and hanged by the arms at Montfaucon,[4] and his heirs were disinherited. It was a great shame and a pity indeed if he was innocent.

---

[1]   See footnote 1, above, p.132. If Le Bel's account is correct and Edward's fleet was still near Vannes, then Brech (just north of Auray) would indeed be 'fairly close'. But the strength of Brest and its known importance as 'the port through which all his supplies arrived' in Brittany makes it a more likely interpretation of the name.

[2]   i.e. the winter of 1342-3.

[3]   The Treaty of Malestroit was agreed on 19 January 1343.

[4]   Olivier de Clisson was executed at Les Halles on 2 August 1343; he had indeed switched sides and joined the Montfort faction. The royal gallows at Montfaucon, just north of the city, were used for public hangings until the seventeenth century.

Chapter LXIII

You have heard how Sir Olivier de Clisson was beheaded in Paris;
here are details of others who suffered the same fate.

Following this, several great lords of Brittany and some from Normandy were similarly charged, and executed at Paris like Sir Olivier:[1] namely the lord of Malestroit and his son, the lord of Nagor, Sir Thibault de Morillon and several other Breton lords, ten knights and squires in all. And not long after,[2] four more knights suffered the same fate: namely Sir Henry de Malestroit, Sir Guillaume Bacon, a most noble Norman knight, the lord of La Roche-Tesson and Sir Richard de Percy, all of them knights of might and valour.

All that year Lord Charles of Blois held without much trouble the French-speaking region of Brittany that he'd conquered; but he didn't have control of the Breton-speaking part, which held out for the Countess of Montfort.

But I'll leave the land of Brittany now and the adventures and fine feats of arms and prowess that took place there – well worthy of record though they are, and there were a good deal more of them than I've said – and tell of the wars in Gascony and Saintonge and Poitou, according to reliable reports I've heard from those who were there. God grant that I arrive at the truth, and that the deeds of arms which I mean to relate may be pleasing to all those who hear or read them; no man alive could record them all, or even a tenth of them.

But first I'd like to explain how the suspicions arose about Sir Olivier de Clisson, as I've recently heard tell. You've heard how the King of England's men had laid siege to three cities in Brittany – Nantes, Rennes and Vannes – all at the same time, and you can be sure that there were many skirmishes, flights and pursuits by one side and the other which I haven't detailed. Among these was a fierce clash outside Vannes, which brought the lords and all the men in the city out to engage the English; a mighty battle followed, with many killed and wounded. Sir Olivier de Clisson and Sir Hervé de Léon were at the forefront of the action, so much so that they were seized and led as prisoners to King Edward – who was quite nearby as you've heard – and he received them joyously. The men of Vannes, seeing their lords and captains taken, retreated to the city as best they could, and a valiant knight named the Earl of Stafford pressed forward so eagerly in pursuit that he was wounded and captured and led back to the city. Negotiations took place in the light of this and it was agreed that the captive Earl of Stafford would be released in exchange for one of the lords, Sir Olivier or Sir Hervé, whichever the king chose. The king preferred to release Sir Olivier rather than Sir Hervé; he had always treated him with more honour than Sir Hervé, simply because, as it happened, Sir Hervé had been a more troublesome opponent to him and the Countess of Montfort than anyone else. And it was because the king favoured Sir Olivier de Clisson above Sir Hervé that the envious assumed something other than the truth, and a suspicion arose which became

[1] Executions of the Breton lords took place on 29 November 1343.
[2] On 3 April 1344.

so strong that it led Sir Olivier to his foul death. He would have been better remaining – or dying – in prison.

Chapter LXIV

How King Edward had Windsor Castle restored and announced a great feast to be held there.

Now I shall relate, if I can, the adventures and deeds of arms that took place in Gascony, Saintonge and Poitou, for they are no less admirable than those I've recounted thus far. But first I shall speak of the great King Edward, who was filled with all noble qualities: I never heard a base thing said of him – except one, of which I shall speak now, to which he was driven by the power of Love.

You have earlier heard how he left Brittany and returned to England after agreeing a truce – it was to last for two years or three, I'm not sure which – and he took with him Sir Hervé de Léon, who'd been such a fierce adversary to him and his men. Once he was back in England his noble heart inspired him not only to restore and improve the castle at Windsor, which King Arthur had built and where the Round Table was first established in honour of the worthy knights of that time, but also to create a counterpart to that Round Table for the greater honour of his own knights; for they'd served him so well and he considered them most worthy: their like were not to be found in any kingdom, and he loved them so dearly that he felt he couldn't honour them too much. So he announced a great feast and a plenary court for the founding of this Round Table, summoning ladies and damsels, knights and squires from all parts of his kingdom, insisting that no one on any account should fail to attend this great feast at Windsor, at Pentecost[1] in the year of grace 1344.

In the meantime he received word that King Philip of France had ordered the executions of Sir Olivier de Clisson and the others mentioned above on suspicion of treason, as I've said. King Edward was bitterly aggrieved; he was convinced that the French king had done it as a deliberate affront, and considered that the truce agreed in Brittany was therefore broken and void. He thought of treating his prisoner Sir Hervé de Léon in like fashion, and his anger was such that he would have done so had he not been dissuaded by his cousin the Earl of Derby. The earl, who was the flower of chivalry, disapproved strongly, and in the presence of the king's council gave a host of eloquent reasons why the king should accept what had happened, begging him above all to deal with Sir Hervé as he would surely wish his own men should be treated, by ransoming him for a fitting sum. The king – who wanted only to do the honourable thing – decided that his cousin the Earl of Derby's advice was sound, and he tempered his anger and called Sir Hervé before him. The knight came in dire terror, thinking he was about to suffer the same foul death as Sir Olivier; and when the king saw him he said:

"Ah, Sir Hervé, Sir Hervé! King Philip of Valois has given a dreadful demonstration of his cruelty, ordering the death – as an affront to me – of such a

---

[1]   This planned meeting of the Round Table at Pentecost 1344 did not finally take place.

valiant knight on mere suspicion of treason, along with many other Breton and Norman knights. If I were inclined to match his cruelty I would do the same to you, for you've been my most active foe in Brittany. But I'll leave cruelty to him and keep my honour intact, and out of love for my cousin the Earl of Derby I shall hold you to the fair and respectable ransom that your status demands, on condition that you do what I say."

The knight was overjoyed when he heard he wasn't in danger of death, and told the king he would willingly do whatever he commanded. Then the king said to him:

"Sir Hervé, I'm well aware you're one of the wealthiest knights in Brittany, and if I were to press you, you'd give me more than thirty thousand écus for your ransom! But I'll tell you what you're to do: you're to promise me you'll never take up arms against me or any of my allies, and never seek to cause me harm or trouble; and as soon as you leave here you're to go to King Philip of Valois and tell him of the courtesy I've shown you, and inform him that, since he has baselessly, and as an affront to me, put to death such valiant knights, I defy him and all who support him, and renounce the truce because in my view he has broken and infringed it. And although I know you can afford to pay me more, I release you on condition that you either send ten thousand old écus[1] to me in London within three months or promise to return to me at the end of that time and yield yourself as my prisoner once more; if you fail in this, I promise you'll not escape again for twice the price! But you're to tell the knights over there in France that my challenge to King Philip shouldn't deter them from attending my feast at Windsor: we'll be glad to see them and will show them all possible honour and guarantee their safe conduct."

The knight thanked the king most humbly, and his heart was filled with admiration for the great courtesy he'd shown him; and he promised, as a faithful knight, to do all that the king had bidden. Then he took his leave and put to sea, and made his way to King Philip in Paris and delivered his message in full. But he did so with grave difficulty, for in crossing the sea he was stricken by an incurable illness and died before the three months' term was out. So he was released from captivity indeed – and I don't know if the noble King Edward ever received the ten thousand.

Chapter LXV

How King Edward committed a great wrong when
he raped the Countess of Salisbury.

I wish to tell you now about the unworthy act committed by King Edward: it is much to his discredit, for it was no small matter from what I've heard.

---

[1]   The écu had been worth about four shillings sterling, but repeated debasement of French coinage had led to its value falling to below three, so that people began to discriminate and stipulate that they required the old, higher-quality coins.

I've already made plain that he was in love with the beautiful Countess of Salisbury, so much so that he couldn't restrain or suppress his feelings despite all her rebuffs, rejections, humble prayers and harsh words. And then, after he'd sent the good lady's husband, the worthy Earl of Salisbury, to Brittany with Lord Robert of Artois, he couldn't resist going to see the noble lady under the pretence of touring his country to inspect his fortresses; when he came to the borderland where the lady lived in the castle of Wark[1] he went to see her, wondering if he would find her more amenable than before.

The good lady received him with all the respect and good cheer she could summon, understanding what was expected of a lady to her lord; but she would rather he'd gone elsewhere, fearing greatly for her honour. Be that as it may, the king stayed there all that day and all that night, but for all his humble entreaties he couldn't gain the response he craved. He was mightily vexed and frustrated; and that night, as he lay in the splendid bed provided for him, a bed befitting his station, and knew that the noble lady was in her chamber and the whole household and all his retainers except his privy chamberlains were asleep, he rose and ordered his chamberlains not to get in his way, no matter what he did, or they'd find themselves at the end of a noose. And he entered the lady's chamber, locked the door of the adjoining room[2] so that her maids couldn't help her, and seized her and stopped her mouth – so hard that she uttered only two or three cries – and then forced himself upon her, so painfully, so punishingly, that no woman ever was so brutally abused. And he left her lying there, unconscious, bleeding from her nose and mouth and elsewhere: it was a distressing and a grievous wrong. Then he left next morning without saying a word, and returned to London, deeply disturbed about what he'd done. From that day forth the good lady was never happy again; her heart was so troubled that she never again shared in festivities or mixed with worthy people.

Immediately after this, the noble king went to Brittany to help the men he'd sent there, as you've heard; and then he returned to England – and the Earl of Salisbury with him. When the earl arrived home, the good lady did all she could to celebrate his return all day, giving no hint of anything having happened. But that night, when the earl retired to bed, she didn't come to lie with him as was her custom, and he called for her and said:

"What's the matter, lady? Why aren't you of good cheer and coming to bed?"

The good lady sat down on the bed beside him, weeping bitterly, and said, when she was able to speak: "Truly, sir, I'm not fit to share the bed of such a worthy man as you."

The good knight was taken aback by her words and anxious to know what she meant. "Holy Mary!" he said. "Why do you say that, lady? I must know the reason, truly."

---

[1] Le Bel again refers to it as *'le chastel de Salbry'*: see footnote 2, above, p.123.
[2] *'la garde robe'*.

The good lady, as happy to tell him then as later, revealed the whole story from start to finish. There's no need to ask if it pained the worthy knight's heart; if ever grief and anguish might have given him cause to despair it was then, as he recalled the great friendship and honour the king had always shown him, not to mention the great service and the testing, perilous deeds he'd performed in return; and now the king had betrayed him and disgraced him and dishonoured the worthiest lady alive. It's no wonder he was heartsick: the wonder is that he didn't give way to despair. As I understand it, he never felt joy in his heart again.

When he and the good lady had finished grieving he said: "Truly, lady, what's done cannot be undone. I can't remain, disgraced, where I've enjoyed so much honour. I shall go and live out the rest of my days in another country. You can stay here, as the noble lady that I believe you still to be, and have half my land to support you and my child your son. You will have to raise and nurture him, for I'm sure you'll never see me again. I shall keep the other half to support me through what remains of my life, wherever I may be – though I don't think it'll be for long: God grant that my death comes soon, as I wish, and may He in His pity grant me mercy."

Anyone who'd seen them then plunge deeper into grief and not felt pity and compassion would have had a heart of stone.

Then the valiant earl, lamenting bitterly, left his wife and took his young son – he was only twelve years old – with him to London. He came into the hall and stepped before the king and said:

"My lord, you have shown me many favours and honours in times past – may God reward you for it. And God knows I have always served and loved you as faithfully as I could. But now you've dumped me right in the shit and foully dishonoured me! No lord of your nobility should ever have contemplated such a thing! You should be utterly ashamed: it will stay as a black mark against you forever, and all your fine deeds will be stained and tarnished by this base act. I take my leave of you, and all I hold in fief from you I bestow upon my young son here, for neither you nor anyone else will ever see me in this land again!"

With that the noble knight left King Edward's court, bitterly distressed and leaving his son behind, and set sail and crossed to this side of the sea. All the lords of England were deeply upset and angry, and the king was reproached by everyone.

After crossing the sea the earl went to join the King of Spain, who was at war with the King of Granada and the Saracens and was besieging a mighty city called Algeciras. It was at this siege that the valiant knight died,[1] as did many other lords before the city was taken. And I understand that the countess, that good lady, didn't long survive him, for no good lady could live long in such distress. But I'll say no more. May God have mercy on them.

---

[1]   See above, p.98. In fact the Earl of Salisbury attended the tournament at Windsor in January 1344, competed poorly because of ill health and died a few days later.

Chapter LXVI

How a feast was held at Windsor in the year 1344;
and of the men-at-arms sent by King Edward to Gascony and Brittany.

Now I'll return to the great feast at Windsor. It was a magnificent affair with splendid jousting, attended by a vast host of ladies and damsels and lords and knights and squires. And it witnessed the creation and establishment of a noble company of knights deemed truly worthy;[1] it was modelled upon the Round Table, but I can't describe it in detail so I'll leave it at that.

To this feast at Windsor came new embassies to the king from the city of Bordeaux and the lords of Gascony, requesting help and reinforcements. So before the feast was done he arranged which of his men should go to Gascony and which should go to Brittany to aid the valiant Countess of Montfort, and how many troops he would send to each place. And he proposed that for his own part he would go to Flanders to see if he could have the county for his son the Prince of Wales, as previously suggested by Jacob van Artevelde, who planned to use his influence upon the Flemish towns in such a way that, when King Edward arrived in strength in the land, they would reject their lord and make the prince the Count of Flanders. The king had such faith in Jacob van Artevelde, who had long held sway in Flanders, that he made ready to sail to Sluys.

Meanwhile he commanded his cousin the Earl of Derby, by this time one of the most illustrious men in the kingdom,[2] to go to Gascony with as much gold and silver and as many supplies and troops as he required. He likewise commanded a worthy knight named Sir Thomas Dagworth[3] to go to Brittany to aid the Countess of Montfort, who was still at the castle of Hennebont.

The noble Earl of Derby, whose prowess was already renowned in every land, made the best possible preparations, assembling six thousand picked archers and six hundred men-at-arms, among them the Earl of Pembroke, the Earl of Oxford,[4] the Earl of Stafford, that noble knight Sir Walter Mauny (by then counted worthy indeed), and also Sir Frank van Hale, who was to win much praise and great esteem before he returned. The two Lande-Halle[5] brothers were with them, too, as were many other knights and squires from England whose names I don't know.

When all was ready they put to sea[6] in most noble array, and sailed to a fine city called Bayonne where they were welcomed with great honour and celebration; and the citizens promised the worthy Earl of Derby that whenever he needed they would provide him, either on land or sea, with five thousand strong and valiant men.

---

[1]   i.e. the Order of the Garter, proclaimed at Windsor but not founded until 1348.
[2]   His father's death in 1345 was to make Henry of Grosmont the new Earl of Lancaster. Le Bel continues to refer to him as the Earl of Derby.
[3]   'Thomas d'Argourne'.
[4]   'Akenfort'; see above, p.148.
[5]   'Leynendale'; see footnote 2, above, p.130.
[6]   The expedition to Brittany set sail in June 1345; the Earl of Derby sailed for Gascony in July.

For his part the noble King Edward prepared a mighty force and came to Flanders, trusting in the support of Jacob van Artevelde. All was arranged[1] when he received certain news that a mob in Ghent had killed Jacob in his own house[2] and appointed another master and governor, a weaver named Gérard Denis. This news dismayed the king: he realised his plans were foiled, for he'd lost a valuable ally who could have been a great help to him. He decided to disband his force, and remained a long while in the land.[3]

Chapter LXVII

*How the worthy Earl of Derby arrived in Gascony and
won many towns and castles there.*

After the worthy Earl of Derby and his company had been in the city of Bayonne for six days and thanked the citizens for their warm welcome and generous offer, he sailed to the city of Bordeaux. They'd been eagerly awaiting him and were overjoyed at his arrival: he was given a glorious reception. He gave orders for the horses and equipment to be brought ashore, and then his men set out into the country upriver from the Gironde, burning towns and villages and laying waste the land; they discovered the region to be so wealthy that they didn't know what to do with all they found.

They carried on until they came to the strongly fortified town and castle of Bergerac, where King Philip of France had placed a large garrison of men-at-arms. They stayed before the castle all that night, and in the morning the worthy earl prepared for an assault. When the citizens saw this they feared they were surely lost, and they spoke to their captain and, by common agreement, surrendered on condition that their lives and goods were spared.[4] The worthy earl granted them mercy on behalf of the King of England, and installed an able captain and a sufficient garrison of men-at-arms and archers to defend the town and castle; then he set off upriver,[5] burning and destroying all, until he reached a town called Sainte-Bazeille and besieged it as he had Bergerac. The citizens, seeing the strength of his army and hearing that the people of Bergerac – with a much stronger city and castle – had surrendered, made similar terms, and the worthy earl accepted them in the King of England's name and installed a good and ample garrison.

The Earl of Derby continued his advance, burning and wasting the country far and wide, until he came to the castle of Aiguillon, which was immensely

---

[1] Edward had landed at Sluys around 5 July and held talks with van Artevelde, but Le Bel says simply: 'When he [Edward] was completely ready he received...'
[2] The date of van Artevelde's death is uncertain, but it was around 17 July.
[3] It's not surprising that Le Bel is somewhat vague here. After holding negotiations with leading merchants in Bruges, Ghent and Ypres, Edward set sail for an apparently secret destination (in France?) later in July, but the fleet was caught in a storm and driven back to England, putting in at Sandwich on the 26th.
[4] Bergerac was taken on 24 August 1345.
[5] This is not strictly accurate. The Earl of Derby has evidently left Bergerac (on the Dordogne) and made his way across country to the Garonne.

strong; but before he reached there he had taken Meilhan-sur-Garonne[1] and the mighty castle and substantial town of Monségur, which stands on a great river called the Lot.[2] Then he came before Aiguillon, one of the strongest castles in the world and one of the best situated, standing as it does between two mighty rivers, one flowing to its right and the other to its left and meeting just beyond it: one is called the Lot and the other the Garonne, which runs down from the city of Toulouse. As soon as the castellan of Aiguillon saw the Earl of Derby advancing with such a mighty army, and heard that all the other towns and strongholds had yielded to him, he immediately surrendered the castle. The earl was more delighted than if the King of England had elsewhere won a hundred thousand pounds; and he established it as his own refuge and residence if the need arose: he thought he'd never seen such a fine and well-positioned castle. As its captain he appointed a most worthy knight named Sir John Montgomery.[3] Then the worthy earl took by storm the stronghold called Castelsagrat,[4] and then the very strong town and castle of La Réole, which had once endured a lengthy siege by King Philip's father Charles of Valois.[5] After taking this town and garrisoning it as he wished he went and took Montpezat, one of the strongest castles in the world, and garrisoned that likewise.

Straight from there he went and launched a mighty assault upon the town and castle of Castelmoron-sur-Lot.[6] The attack was unsuccessful, but the castle was captured next day thanks to an ingenious plan devised by a Gascon noble named Alixandre, lord of Chaumont. It was thus: the Earl of Derby struck camp and gave the impression of heading elsewhere, but left a small body of men outside the town with the Earl of Oxford.[7] When the people and troops in the town saw such a small band, they thought they could overcome them with ease and sallied forth to do battle. The English, seeing them approach, fell back and pretended to flee; the enemy pursued them far from the town, whereupon the Earl of Derby sprang from his hiding-place and cut the enemy off from the town and forced his way in. Thus was the stronghold of Castelmoron taken, castle and town alike, and the citizens held to ransom. It was by similar craft and trickery that the strong town of Villefranche[8] was taken and sacked and pillaged, and freshly garrisoned and provisioned; and a valiant knight named Sir Thomas Coke[9] was appointed castellan.

No greater or finer campaign[10] was ever heard of, truly, than that conducted by the worthy Earl of Derby, capturing so many well fortified towns and impregnable castles. It involved some great and notable feats of prowess and remarkable

---

[1] 'Roche-Millon'.
[2] There is more than one Monségur in the region, and it is far more likely, given the other places mentioned, that this is the Monségur on the river Dropt.
[3] 'Jehan de Gombry'.
[4] 'Segrat'.
[5] In 1324.
[6] 'Mouron'.
[7] 'Akenfort': see above, pp.148 and 157.
[8] This is probably Villefranche-du-Queyran, between Aiguillon and Casteljaloux.
[9] 'Cok'.
[10] 'chevauchée'.

adventures – it would be tiresome to recount them all: there'd be no end to it! – and no man alive could count the vast wealth and incalculable riches that were won either from looting or by ransoming towns and captives.

After arranging affairs as he wished at Villefranche the worthy earl made his way to Miramont, another very strong castle, which he gave to a valiant squire named Jehan de Brusto,[1] and then he took the castles of Tonneins and Damazan. From there he went and laid siege to the city of Angoulême; it surrendered fairly quickly and he installed his own garrison and guards there. And after winning the city of Angoulême the worthy earl – he wasn't one to rest – headed for one of the strongest towns and castles in the world, by the name of Blaye. The Gironde river is very wide there, and although the earl besieged it as closely as he could he achieved little, for it was enormously strong and very well garrisoned with able men-at-arms. So he left there and went to take the stronghold at Bourg, further upriver.

Having conquered all these castles, as you've heard, and all the surrounding land of Gascony – which stretches for fully fifty leagues – the earl retired with all his men to the city of Bordeaux. They took with them a vast treasure: they were now so rich, lords and commoners alike, that they didn't know what to do with all their wealth, and valued gold and silver no more than straw. At Bordeaux he dispersed his forces, sending them to the towns and castles he'd won. It was now the beginning of winter in the year of grace 1345.[2]

But I'll leave him for a little and tell of the French, of whom I've said nothing for some while.

Chapter LXVIII

How the Duke of Normandy went to Gascony with a very great army and won back several places there.

I wish to tell now of the French as well as of the English, as I must if I'm to proceed correctly. Know, then, that when King Philip of France learned that the Earl of Derby and the other English lords had invaded his land of Gascony and were burning, wasting and looting and taking towns and castles he was enraged; and he immediately ordered his eldest son, the Duke of Normandy, to prepare with all possible speed to go to Gascony and oppose these English who were ravaging it so: he would provide him with all the gold, silver, lords, knights, squires and troops, mounted and on foot, that he required. Then he sent word throughout the kingdom of France that all should meet on a certain day at Orléans, to go with his son the Duke of Normandy to confront the English in Gascony, where they were destroying everything.

The Duke of Normandy was at Orléans on the appointed day and waited for everyone to arrive. Many great lords joined him there, each bringing as many men as he could; namely: the Duke of Burgundy and his son, the Duke of Bourbon,

---

[1]   John Briscoe?
[2]   The text mistakenly reads 1344.

the Count of Blois, Lord Louis of Spain, the Bishop of Beauvais, the Count of Auxerre and many other lords and bannerets, each with his own troops. A huge number of men arrived from all directions, and they set off through Poitou, Berry and Limousin; and day by day their numbers grew as new forces joined them from every region along the way. They marched on until they reached Gascony, and headed first for the castle of Miramont. On the way they laid siege to a large town called Villefranche;[1] they attacked it for two days and finally took it by storm and slaughtered all the English within, and looted everything and broke open a thousand barrels of wine they found in the cellars, and then set fire to the town and razed it to the ground, though they left the castle intact. They moved on then to besiege the castle of Miramont and took it by storm. From there they made for the city of Angoulême which they besieged from all sides, having sufficient numbers to do so: it was said they had fully forty thousand horse and foot, not counting an innumerable mass of followers.

When the Earl of Derby, at Bordeaux, learned that the Duke of Normandy and all the other French lords had come to win back the land of Gascony which he'd conquered as you've heard, and had already taken Villefranche and burned and pillaged it except for the castle, he was furious but not in the least bit daunted. He immediately sent four worthy knights in whom he trusted – namely Sir Stephen Tombey,[2] Sir Richard Hebden,[3] Sir Ralph Hastings[4] and Sir Norman Swinford[5] – with orders to take sixty or eighty companions and go to Villefranche and take possession of the castle, which had been left intact and empty, and put it back in order – the gates of the town, too – and to arrange fresh provisions and a new garrison of men-at-arms and local people; and if the French returned to attack it again they were to defend it with all their might, for he'd come to their aid at once, no matter what the risk. The knights followed his orders willingly.

Then he asked the Earl of Pembroke, Sir Walter Mauny, Sir Frank van Hale, Sir Thomas Coke, Sir John de Lisle[6] and many other knights and squires – two hundred men-at-arms in all – to go to Aiguillon and defend the town and the mighty castle there, and he sent with them five hundred good archers. They were later to be well occupied, and were involved in some fine exploits and feats of great prowess as you'll hear in due course.

When the aforementioned knights were ready to go to Villefranche, they rode through the country taking cattle, sheep, pigs, wine, corn and flour and whatever other provisions they found and took the whole lot to Villefranche, which they put back in good shape, ready to mount a strong defence. They soon had a

[1] This is probably not the same place, Villefranche-du-Queyran, suggested above (p.159). It is more possibly Villefranche-de-Lonchat, a well fortified town further north and 'on the way' to Miramont. The fact that Le Bel introduces it as 'a large town' certainly implies that it is not the same as the earlier Villefranche.
[2] 'Estienne de Thomby'.
[3] 'Richart de Hebedon'.
[4] 'Raoul de Hayestinges'.
[5] 'Normand de Sinefroide'.
[6] 'Jehan de Lile'.

garrison of three thousand – both troops and local men – and supplies enough to
last three whole months.

The Duke of Normandy had now taken the mighty castle of Miramont and
was camped before the city of Angoulême; and he was bitterly regretting having
abandoned the castle and town of Villefranche when he heard that the English
had restored it to order: it was later to cause him a good deal of trouble. But he
sustained the siege of Angoulême and launched several fierce assaults, though
he made little headway – it cost him instead a good number of men – for the
city had a very fine garrison commanded by a worthy captain named Sir John
of Norwich.[1] Realising they couldn't take Angoulême by storm but rather were
steadily losing men, the duke and his council called off all attacks but ordered
their men to move their encampment as close to the city as they could; this was
done.

Then one day the seneschal of Beaucaire, a valiant knight, came to the duke
and said: "My lord, I know this region well. If you give me six or eight hundred
cavalry I'll venture out in search of cattle and provisions, for we'll soon be
running out."

This suggestion was welcomed by the duke and his council, and next day
the seneschal took the Bishop of Beauvais, the Duke of Bourbon, the young
Duke of Burgundy, Count of Boulogne,[2] the lord of Montmorency, Marshal of
France, and many other knights and squires, fully eight hundred cavalry in all,
and rode all night till daybreak when they came within half a league of a large
town that had surrendered to the English, by the name of Antenis.[3] A spy came
to the seneschal[4] and told him that the English had six score men-at-arms and
three hundred archers in the town who would defend it well if it was attacked.
"But I've seen," said the spy, "some quarry outside the town: that is, six or eight
hundred fat cattle grazing in the meadows!"

When the seneschal heard this he said to the lords: "I suggest, sirs, that you
stay and wait for me in this valley here; I'll take three or four score companions
to round up the cattle, and if the English sally forth as I expect them to I'll make
sure they chase me back this way, to you!"

They all agreed; and the valiant seneschal, as planned, went and took the
quarry and started leading it back from outside the town, whereupon Gascons
and English promptly came riding out to rescue them, fully armed. Seeing this,
the seneschal kept driving the cattle onward and rode swiftly after, pretending
to flee, and the English and Gascons, anxious not to lose their cattle, went in
hot pursuit. In his apparent flight he led them straight into the ambush; the
lords came charging out and a mighty combat ensued: the Gascons and English,
realising there was no way back to the fortress, rallied together and defended

---

[1]   'Jehan de Norwick'.
[2]   i.e. Philip of Burgundy (1323-46), who was Count of Boulogne (and Auvergne) and the only
      son and heir of Eudes IV, Duke of Burgundy.
[3]   It is not easy to identify this place-name with any certainty, especially in view of the later
      reference to it, below, p.164.
[4]   The text says 'mareschal', but it should probably be a reference to the seneschal of Beaucaire,
      commanding the expedition.

themselves with all their might, and there were fine deeds of arms performed by both sides. In the end, however, the English and Gascons were defeated and most of them killed, for they were greatly outnumbered. Then the French lords headed for the town and took possession of it, and stayed there all that day and the following night, for they'd fought hard and hadn't slept at all the night before. Next morning they left men-at-arms and crossbowmen to guard the town, and returned with their booty to the army outside Angoulême: they were greeted there with praise and jubilation.

John of Norwich, master and captain of Angoulême, seeing that the duke had no intention of leaving until the city was in his hands, and hearing that he'd taken a good number of places such as Villefranche, Miramont and Antenis, and knowing that the town's supplies were running out and that its burghers and common folk alike would be more inclined to side with the French than with the English if they dared, devised the following artful plan.

On the eve of Our Lady's Purification at the beginning of February, he went up to the battlements all alone, without revealing his intentions to anyone, and signalled with his cap that he wished to speak with the duke or his marshal. The duke responded at once, assuming that he meant to surrender, and asked him if he wished to yield. Sir John replied that he hadn't yet discussed it with his companions, but he'd come because the following day was due to be a great and solemn feast, and he felt that, out of respect for Our Lady, they ought to suspend hostilities that day; and if the duke would agree to a three-day respite he would speak to his companions and discuss whether or not to surrender.

The duke promptly accepted the three-day truce and announced it to all his army. Meanwhile Sir John went next day to his companions and told them of his plan – which you'll hear in a moment – and they were so impressed that they all agreed to follow it. This next day was the feast of Candlemas; and as both sides, town and besieging army, sat at dinner, Sir John told his fellow men-at-arms to pack all their equipment and belongings – without letting the townsfolk know – and then called for the gate to be opened and rode out with all his company. When the besiegers saw them coming they stirred and began to arm, of course; but Sir John told them they'd no cause or need to arm, for a respite had been agreed and was still current and he meant them no harm. So the besiegers relaxed and Sir John and his company rode past them and carried on to Aiguillon, where he was given a joyous reception when he told of his adventure and why he'd left Angoulême. The Duke of Normandy realised he'd been duped by agreeing to the truce: he'd let Sir John pass through his army in peace and forbidden any of his troops to follow him. It was through this ruse that the English saved their lives – and their honour, too, for they hadn't surrendered the town. It couldn't hold out much longer: once they'd gone the duke and the French lords advanced upon the town and the citizens immediately surrendered with their lives and possessions guaranteed. Then the French lords entered the town amid great celebration, and stayed there all winter until April – though some went home, promising to return when April came.

As soon as it did – the year was 1346 – all these lords, knights and squires returned to the Duke of Normandy, and all agreed to make for Aiguillon, the main refuge and base of the English in that region. They advanced up the River Garonne,[1] which flowed down from Aiguillon, and passed through the town of Antenis[2] and came to a castle called Monségur which they attacked and took by storm; they found abundant booty and provisions in the town. Then they marched on towards Aiguillon. Close by they found a small fortified town occupied by the English called Port-Sainte-Marie; they took it, killing at least two hundred English, before advancing on Aiguillon,[3] where their marshals arranged a fine encampment in the beautiful meadows along the banks of the river, which is navigable there by big ships.

Chapter LXIX

Of the outstanding deeds of arms and feats of high prowess reported at the siege of Aiguillon.

Before the mighty castle of Aiguillon was seen the greatest besieging army to be heard of in the kingdom of France – or anywhere else – for a long while; and the siege lasted all that summer till the end of harvest. There were at least one hundred thousand troops involved, on horse and foot, and in no history have you ever heard tell of so many great exploits and fine deeds of arms as were performed by both sides during this siege: no men-at-arms besieged in a fortress ever suffered or endured so much, or mounted such a gallant defence or performed so many bold exploits, as the lords, knights and squires in Aiguillon. They had been worthy and valiant before, but now they should be reputed doubly so, and it's only right that I should name those I remember, though I don't know the names of them all.

Foremost among them was the Earl of Pembroke – after, that is, the valiant knight Sir Walter Mauny who should be remembered before all others; and certainly, he should wear the laurels here, for he bore the burden and responsibility, giving heart and spirit to all the defenders, and was always the first to arm, the first to go, the first into battle and the last to return, and nothing he saw or heard discouraged him – rather, he drove his companions on to ever finer deeds. Next to be mentioned is Sir Frank van Hale, a most able knight who earned great credit here; then Sir Robert d'Arteine, John of Norwich, Sir John de Lisle, Sir Alixandre de Chaumont from Gascony, the lord de la Lande and John Montgomery,[4] and many more, fully three hundred knights and squires in all, and a good six hundred fine archers with them. And truly, no men besieged were ever kept as busy – not even at Lucerne during the long siege by Charlemagne, nor at Tyre when it was besieged by Alexander, nor at Nicaea or Antioch or Jerusalem in the days of Godfrey of Bouillon – as those knights and squires and their companions at Aiguillon; for every day, as long as the siege lasted, every one of them had to

---

[1]   'Geronde'.
[2]   See footnote 3, above, p.162.
[3]   The Duke of Normandy began the siege of Aiguillon between 10 and 15 April 1346.
[4]   'Jehan de Maugombry'.

fight two or three times, most often from morning till evening without respite, as fresh forces – Genoese and others – constantly attacked them and never let them rest.

The duke had ordered the construction of a wooden bridge over the wide River Garonne, big enough for the whole army to cross. The building of this bridge prompted many a fine battle and many great and bold exploits with many casualties, dead and wounded; and it cost a vast sum of money, for every day there were fully three hundred carpenters working on it. But as soon as it had reached mid-river, the defenders of Aiguillon set off in three boats and drove the workmen and their guards away and destroyed the half-bridge they'd built so far, much to the fury of the French lords. The following day the lords prepared vessels to oppose them, with men-at-arms aboard to protect the workmen. They'd been working till mid-afternoon when Sir Walter Mauny and some of his companions boarded their craft and attacked the workmen and their guards and there was a great, ferocious fight; in the end the workers and guards were driven off, and all their work was destroyed again and some of their number were killed or drowned. This went on for several days, until the whole besieging army had to be armed and deployed each day to protect the workmen. There was fierce fighting daily, and the besiegers suffered heavy casualties as the defenders of Aiguillon did all they could to stop the building of the bridge.

But finally, after the contest had lasted for fifteen days, the bridge was finished; and when it was complete and the army was ready, they launched a massive assault and lost many men, while the men of the castle mounted such a splendid defence that they lost none. When evening came the besiegers withdrew to their quarters, battered and exhausted, while the defenders repaired their damaged walls.

Next day the lords met to discuss how they might have more success, for it seemed all their attacks were fruitless and costly. They decided nonetheless that, to put the defenders under more intense pressure, they would divide their army into four: the first division would attack from dawn till prime[1] and then withdraw; the second from prime till noon, the third from noon till vespers and the fourth from vespers till midnight. They felt sure the defenders wouldn't be able to endure such a trial, and they all agreed to this. But the defenders resisted so valiantly that their attacks made little impression: they fought with such vigour, despite their weariness, that the besiegers couldn't gain the bridge at the gate to the town and castle; instead they lost more than four hundred men in four days – good men and bad alike – not to mention countless wounded.

Realising the plan wasn't working, the lords debated how else they might break their defence, for the Duke of Normandy had vowed not to end the siege until he'd taken the town and castle. He sent for siege engines from Toulouse, and eight colossal ones were brought and four even bigger were built. They began a constant bombardment then, both day and night; but they did the defenders little harm for they were well sheltered, though a few houses suffered damage.

---

[1]   The first canonical hour: around 6 a.m.

And indeed, the defenders had two good machines themselves and smashed and battered those outside, wrecking six or seven. Yet more attacks and ferocious skirmishes followed, as Sir Walter Mauny and many of his companions sallied from the castle and down to the river, causing the duke and the French lords no end of trouble.

Why should I make such a long tale of this? Never did men under siege resist and respond with such valour; never, as long as the siege lasted, did they show any cowardice or weariness; rather did Sir Walter and his companions make frequent sorties, his banner and pennon before and behind, to forage and bring back all manner of livestock from beyond the river.

And one day, around Ascension, they ran into the Marshal of the French army driving a great herd of cattle back across; Sir Walter and his companions launched a bold attack, despite being few in numbers – though he sent to the castle for help, which soon arrived. A mighty battle ensued and there were many wounded on both sides; but the men of Aiguillon were finally victorious and led the captured cattle back to the castle along with a good number of prisoners. They should be credited with great honour for this deed.

The besiegers were enraged, but had to admit that they'd never heard of such bold and valiant fighters as those in Aiguillon, each and every one of them. Above all others they praised Sir Walter Mauny and John of Norwich and Sir Frank van Hale.

The French lords gave orders for the men of Toulouse and Carcassonne and their castleries to arm and attack the castle till midday, and for those of Cahors and Agen to do likewise after; and the first man to take the bridge at the castle gate would be given a hundred écus. Then the duke assembled a great number of boats and bigger vessels, and while some boarded these to cross the river, others advanced across the bridge. The castle's defenders were at the ready. There now began a fiercer assault than any so far; anyone then who had seen the attackers racing ahead of each other in their eagerness to win the bridge and the promised hundred écus, and the men of the castle standing firm and ready to defend it valiantly, and the besiegers fearlessly risking life and limb to win, would have witnessed great prowess in the defenders and great madness in their foe. In any event, with the battle at its height some men steered a boat beneath the bridge and used iron hooks to heave on the drawbridge till they broke the chain and forced the bridge down. If you'd seen the attackers then surging on to the bridge, tumbling over each other in a wild stampede, and the defenders flinging down tubs of quicklime and massive beams and huge stones, you'd have seen a vast pile of men falling maimed and dying, never to rise again. Nonetheless, the bridge was finally taken and they reached the main gate, though it cost the attackers far more men than they'd have wished: there were so many dead and wounded that it would be painful to relate. But even with the bridge taken they were no better off: they could see no way of taking the gate and withdrew to their quarters, for it was now so late that it was almost dark, and they'd fought long and hard and it was time to rest. And as soon as they'd gone the men of the castle came out and repaired the bridge, making it stronger than before.

Next morning two master carpenters came to the duke and the lords and said that if they were given enough timber they would build three great, tall towers on three big ships that could be sailed up to the castle walls: they'd be high enough to top the battlements, so that men on the towers would be able to engage the defenders on the walls in hand to hand combat. The duke was delighted by the idea and gave orders for four such towers to be built, and for all the carpenters in the region to be engaged – and paid generously, so that they went at it all the more keenly and rapidly. So the four towers were built to the two masters' design. They cost a fortune. And it was all for nothing, for when they were finished and filled with men-at-arms and had sailed to the middle of the river, the men of the castle loosed four catapults[1] that they'd built to smash and batter the towers; these four catapults bombarded them with so many massive stones that they were soon wrecked and shattered: the men-at-arms were left unprotected and had to retreat before they were even half way across. One of the towers was sent plunging to the river bed, which was a grievous pity, for there were a great many knights and squires inside, all of them eager to enhance their honour and prowess, and all of them drowned.

The duke and the lords, seeing this disaster and their plan come to nothing, were beside themselves with fury; they realised they were wasting their time and spending vast sums fruitlessly. But no matter what anyone said, the duke still wouldn't raise the siege until his father the king commanded him to, for it was his first ever siege and that's what he'd vowed. The French lords, at a loss for any other way of taking the castle, decided to send the Count of Guînes, Constable of France, and the Chamberlain de Tancarville[2] to tell the king how matters had progressed and to ask what he wished to be done. They left the army and set off on their mission, as did several others with the duke's leave.

But now I'll leave the siege of Aiguillon and return to King Edward, to tell how he prepared to come to Aiguillon's aid or to invade France as he'd said. No man alive could recount all the fine feats of prowess performed by both sides at Aiguillon, so I'll leave it at that.

Chapter LXX

How King Edward left England and sailed to Normandy and laid waste the land.

Some people, when they hear this story read, may wonder why I call the King of England 'the noble King Edward' but the French king simply 'King Philip of France'; they might well imagine I'm biased or partisan. Saving the grace of all listeners, it's not a question of taking sides; I do this to honour the one who behaved most nobly in this story, and that's King Edward, who cannot be honoured too highly, for in all his deeds he always followed sound advice, and loved his men and knights and squires, and honoured each man according to his degree, and defended his land well against his enemies (and won a good deal

---

[1] 'martinès'.
[2] Jean, vicomte de Melun, seigneur de Tancarville, Chamberlain of Normandy.

from them), and bravely put his life at stake alongside his men both at home and abroad, and paid his troops and allies well and gave generously of his own wealth; for these reasons all should be glad to serve him and he deserves to be called 'noble king'. None of this can be said of King Philip of France, who allowed his land in many parts to be ravaged and laid waste, and stayed ensconced around Paris in comfort and safety, and always followed the poor advice of clerics and prelates, especially those who said:

"Dear sire, don't fret, and don't go putting yourself at risk; you could easily be betrayed – you just don't know who to trust. Let this young King of England waste his time and money: for all his bluster he'll never take your inheritance, and when he's spent all his money he'll have to go home! He hasn't yet taken Boulogne or Amiens or Saint-Omer, and as soon as he's gone you can easily recover what you've lost."

King Philip listened to such counsellors and ignored the lords and barons of his land – indeed, he had some of them foully executed on suspicion of treason and their children disinherited, and for that he should be less esteemed and respected by all. What's more, he squeezed his people hard with taxes and the church with tithes; and he was constantly minting poor coin in many places, and then melting it down before producing more to create inflation, and then devaluing it when he pleased, so that no one could agree on prices; and his troops were never well paid: they often had to spend their own money for want of pay, and even sold their horses and armour as they chased the paymasters in vain. Any prince who governs like this should be less well loved by his people; and it's a great pity and shame that the kingdom of France, which had surpassed all others in honour, wisdom, learning, chivalry, trade and prosperity, should have been brought by poor governance into its present troubled state, in which its enemies and its own shortcomings have led to the one who should be its lord being now a captive[1] and almost all the lords and knights of the land being killed or imprisoned. It's a wonder that God allows it! But I mustn't keep on – I've said enough; I'll return to my main theme and tell of the noble King Edward, who has well deserved the love, esteem and respect of all: God be thanked and praised.

The noble King Edward was well aware that his men besieged at Aiguillon were very hard pressed; and he was mindful of having declared that he would soon invade the kingdom of France and inflict more damage than ever before. So all that winter and summer[2] he prepared a great fleet of ships and boats and all necessary supplies, and sent a general summons throughout the land to be ready to embark at the feast of Saint John[3] and to accompany him on his intended expedition. Saint John's Day came and all were duly ready; and when everyone had boarded the boats and ships the mariners set sail with all speed.[4]

---

[1]   i.e. at the time of writing. John II had been captured by the English at Poitiers in 1356.
[2]   i.e. the months leading into the summer of 1346.
[3]   John the Baptist, 24 June.
[4]   It wasn't quite that straightforward: in a letter of 7 July Edward told his Chancellor and Treasurer that 'our passage has been much delayed by lack of ships, which grieves us much, but now we are embarked and have been aboard ship for the last ten days near Yarmouth on the Isle of Wight; and thank God, all our men and horses are catered for. All

King Philip of France had learnt of these preparations quite early, and sent great numbers of troops to his kingdom's borders to guard the points of entry, not knowing where King Edward meant to land; and he sent his Constable the Count of Guînes, who had returned from the siege of Aiguillon, to the city of Caen in Normandy with a great force of men-at-arms to defend the land – while he stayed in Paris with his money men, relaxing and keeping safe.

King Edward meanwhile had been sailing swiftly across the sea: he gives no thought to rest and amassing wealth, for wealth is worthless unless it's put to good use and spent and given generously. He sailed on until, at the beginning of August in the year of grace 1346, he arrived at the isle called Guernsey. With him was a most noble knight named Sir Godfrey de Harcourt, brother of the Count of Harcourt at that time; this Godfrey was in exile from the kingdom of France because he was suspected of treason, and if King Philip had got hold of him he'd have dealt with him as he had Sir Olivier de Clisson. In his army King Edward had four thousand heavy cavalry, knights and squires – no more, whatever anyone may say – and ten thousand archers and ten thousand foot soldiers. After landing on Guernsey – a broad, expansive island – he stayed there for four or five days, burning and ravaging it all, and captured its mighty castle[1] where very rich booty was found. Then the king held council and resolved to make for Normandy, and to head first for the fine land called the Cotentin; this was on the advice and at the prompting of Sir Godfrey de Harcourt, who knew the whole region well. He would send a third of his troops by sea to ravage and destroy the land along the coast – it was a rich and abundant region indeed, with a large number of important towns – while the noble king and his young son the Prince of Wales, who had not yet received his arms,[2] would go over land and destroy and lay waste Normandy and advance upon Paris to greet King Philip. The noble King Edward appointed Sir Godfrey de Harcourt marshal of his army – he accepted most gladly – and appointed another, namely the Earl of Suffolk.

When King Philip – in Paris with the exchequer – heard the news, he sent letters to the lords and barons of all his lands bidding them make ready; but it was very late: he'd have done better to heed the advice of men other than his treasurers and accountants. A great number of lords answered his summons and came to Paris: namely that noble and valiant-hearted man the King of Bohemia and his son Lord Charles (elected King of Germany through the efforts of his worthy father, and soon to be crowned Emperor at Milan and Rome without dispute); also the

---

the lords are of one accord and go with us very willingly; and with their agreement we have resolved to cross on the next tide (with the aid of God) and to take our course and land where God grants us grace and according to the wind...' Edward adds that 'because we have heard there are numerous spies in London sending word back to France from day to day, we bid you guard the roads between London and Sandwich and wherever else is necessary, and grant passage to no man of any degree until eight days after our crossing...' [The National Archives, C 81/452, no. 31617; printed in Viard and Déprez's edition of Le Bel, Appendix XII].

[1] Castle Cornet.
[2] It was shortly after landing at Saint-Vaast-la-Hougue that Edward knighted his 16-year-old son along with several other young nobles.

Duke of Lorraine, the Count of Salm,[1] the Count of Saarbrücken,[2] the Count of Flanders, the Count of Namur and Sir John, lord of Beaumont.[3] These lords, all from the Empire, came with all the forces they could muster. Of the lords of France there came King Philip's brother the Count of Alençon, Count Louis of Blois, the Count of Auxerre, the Count of Harcourt, the Count of Sancerre, the Count of Roucy, the Count of Saint-Pol and the Count of Porcien; their army numbered twenty thousand men-at-arms and fully sixty thousand foot soldiers, Genoese and others.

Now I shall return to the noble King Edward, and describe how the land of the Cotentin and the fair country of Normandy were ravaged and laid waste. He had divided his army into two. The earls of Warwick and Stafford went by sea along the coast, taking all the vessels they could find, large and small; archers and foot soldiers went with them, and they burned, destroyed and pillaged everything. They made their way to a fine port called Barfleur, which they took,[4] the people surrendering in fear of death; but their surrender didn't prevent the whole town being plundered, and such a hoard of gold and silver and jewels was found that even the lowest ranks[5] didn't bother with fur-lined gowns and cloaks and the like. And they forced all the men of the town to leave and board their ships and go with them, not wanting them to rally together and cause trouble.

After the thriving town of Barfleur had been taken and pillaged, they carried on up the coast doing exactly as they pleased, meeting no opposition from any troops or soldiers of King Philip. On they went till they came to another rich and prosperous city with a fine port by the name of Cherbourg,[6] which they took and plundered just as they had Barfleur; and they did the same at Montebourg, Valognes[7] and all the other major towns, finding and taking riches beyond counting. Then they came to a well fortified town with a strong castle called Carentan, manned by a large contingent of King Philip's soldiers and men-at-arms. The English lords and men-at-arms left their ships and made ready to attack the town; and when the townsfolk saw this they feared for their lives and possessions and, ignoring the garrison, surrendered on condition that they and their wives and children would be spared – but they didn't try to save the booty: they already knew it was lost. The English lords didn't want to let the castle be, and launched such a mighty two-day assault that the defenders, anticipating no help, surrendered with their lives and possessions spared. The English did as they pleased with the town and drove the men aboard their ships and took them away with the others.

---

[1]   'Sames en Samur'.
[2]   'Salebruges'.
[3]   i.e. John of Hainault, who despite his long association with Edward (his niece being Philip-pa, Edward's queen) had now sworn allegiance to France, angry at Edward's non-payment of money promised to his nephew the Count of Hainault.
[4]   On 14 July.
[5]   'garchons'.
[6]   'Tyrebourch'.
[7]   'Avalaigne'.

Why should I lengthen the story? The above-named English lords and their company conquered, burned and ravaged all the land along the coast, from the Cotentin to the far end of Normandy, doing whatever they wished, unopposed and unhindered. They sent all their booty back to England with a host of prisoners; the loot and the ransoms yielded a great treasure from which King Edward paid his troops generously. But I shall leave those lords for now and return to the noble King Edward.

Chapter LXXI

How King Edward conquered numerous towns and castles in Normandy, namely the isle of Guernsey, Saint-Lô, etc.

After the noble King Edward had sent his men to destroy and ravage the Norman coast, as you've heard, he left the isle of Guernsey and landed in the Cotentin at Saint Vaast-la-Hougue.[1] He gave orders for the horses to be disembarked, ready for an advance over land to ravage and destroy the Cotentin and then the country of Normandy. Once they were all ashore Sir Godfrey de Harcourt, who knew Normandy and the Cotentin like the back of his hand, took five hundred men-at-arms and two thousand archers and left the king and his army and went fully six or seven leagues ahead, burning and destroying the land. They found it a thriving country indeed, abounding in all things: its granaries were full of corn, its houses full of riches, its people possessed of carts and horses and wagons and sheep and ewes and pigs and calves and cows and oxen; and they seized the lot and took it back to the king's army. But they didn't hand over the vast hoard of gold and silver they'd found – they kept that for themselves. Sir Godfrey, as marshal, set off on such an expedition each day, to the right of the king's army, returning with his company to where he knew the king intended to lodge – though when he found the land rich in booty he would sometimes be gone for two days. The other marshal[2] set off likewise, to the left of the king's army, with a similar force of five hundred men-at-arms and two thousand archers, burning and ravaging the country, and like Sir Godfrey he returned each evening to the king's intended stopping-place. Meanwhile the noble king and his son, the Prince of Wales, advanced with the rest of the army in short daily marches, regularly making camp between terce[3] and noon because they found the land so plentiful that they didn't need to go looking for supplies – except for wine, and they found enough of that, too, for the people, taken unawares, had hidden nothing away. It's no wonder they were in a state of shock: they'd never experienced war or ever seen a man-at-arms, and now they were seeing people slaughtered without mercy, houses set ablaze and pillaged, and the land laid waste and burnt.

---

[1]   'Hogues'.
[2]   i.e. the Earl of Suffolk: see above, p.169.
[3]   The third canonical hour, around 9 a.m.

The noble King Edward had a force of fifteen hundred men-at-arms, six thousand archers and eight thousand troops on foot, not counting those[1] who were with the marshals; and on he pressed like this, burning and laying waste the land; and when he found the town of Coutances[2] not worth the detour he headed on to the wondrously rich commercial city of Saint-Lô, three times wealthier than Coutances. It had a thriving trade in cloth and all manner of merchandise, and many prosperous citizens: fully eight thousand men plied their trades there, both wealthy burghers and artisans. When the noble king drew near he made camp outside – he didn't want to take lodging in the town for fear of fire. But this great town was taken with little effort and sacked and pillaged from top to bottom. No man alive would ever believe the wealth of booty plundered there, or the vast quantity of cloth they found – you'd have got a good price if you'd fancied buying: it was there for the taking! But few were interested in that: they were more intent on the piles of gold and silver they found – so keenly intent, indeed, that the city was spared the flame. But a great many of the wealthy burghers were taken prisoner and sent to England to be ransomed, and a lot of the common folk were killed when the town was first entered – and a good number of fair townswomen and their daughters were raped, which was a dreadful pity.

When King Edward had done as he pleased with the town of Saint-Lô in the Cotentin, he left there[3] and made for Caen, the wealthiest city (other than Rouen) in Normandy, a city filled with great riches and prosperous burghers and noble ladies, with two splendid abbeys and all manner of merchandise. He'd heard that the Count of Eu and Guînes, who was Constable of France, had been sent there by King Philip, along with the Chamberlain de Tancarville and Sir Robert Bertrand, Marshal of France, and a large body of knights and squires and other men-at-arms, and also that a great many of the knights of Normandy had gathered in the city. So the English headed there all the more eagerly. They set out in the order you've heard had been established by the king; they were spread over a wide area even though he had only fifteen hundred mounted men-at-arms (whatever anyone else may say), and in this way they advanced, ravaging and laying waste the land for six or seven leagues on either side, burning and destroying every unfortified town and village, abbey and priory in their path.

The noble king continued his advance until he drew near to Caen and made camp two leagues away. The Constable of France and his fellow lords posted the best possible watch all night, and in the morning[4] commanded all their forces to arm, knights and squires and everyone, ready to defend the city. They marched out and deployed before the gate to face the English line of approach, giving every sign of being ready to put their lives on the line and mount a valiant defence.

The English were up very early that morning and raring to go – their appetite for loot and gain was insatiable. The king was up, too, and organising his troops,

---

[1]   The MS reads 'sans chevaulx [without horses] qui s'en aloient avecques les mareschaulx' rather than the more logical 'sans ceulx [without those] qui...'
[2]   'Costentin'.
[3]   On 23 July.
[4]   It was 26 July.

for he was anticipating action. With battalions deployed he advanced in good order, his marshals riding at the forefront with his banners, right up to the suburbs close to where the French lords had deployed. When the men of the city saw the King of England's banner, and a finer array of men-at-arms than they'd ever beheld, they were so terrified that no one in the world could have stopped them fleeing to the town whether the Constable and marshals liked it or not. Suddenly men were a-quiver and a-tremble, incapable of resisting, panicking to reach the town and safety. Many knights, too, turned and rode back to the castle where they were safe. The Constable, the Chamberlain de Tancarville and numerous other knights and squires took refuge in the city's gatehouse, and as they looked down from the windows they saw archers slaughtering defenceless people without mercy. They were very afraid they'd do the same to them; and as they stood in terror, watching the killing, they spotted a worthy knight named Sir Thomas Holland who had only one eye, and five or six fine young knights with him whom they'd often met and accompanied during campaigns in Prussia, Granada and elsewhere. They called down to them imploringly, saying:

"Ah! In God's name, sir knights, come up here and save us from those pitiless men who'll kill us like all the others if they catch us!"

When Sir Thomas heard this and recognised them he was overjoyed, as were their other former companions; they climbed up to join them in the gatehouse, and the Constable and the Chamberlain who'd taken refuge there surrendered as their prisoners. Sir Thomas and his fellows accepted them most gladly and strove to protect them, and placed able guards about them to stop anyone doing them harm. Then they set off through the town to prevent and restrain the great slaughter that was under way and to save the women and girls of the town from rape and abuse. Riches beyond counting were discovered and looted there; and it was pitiful to see the townsmen and their women, daughters, children: they didn't know which way to turn, and had to watch their mothers or their sisters murdered before their eyes, or their wives or daughters raped, their houses smashed open and all their belongings plundered. Truly, anyone who was in a position to protect them and failed to do so was not a good Christian. At opposite ends of this fair city stood two great and splendid abbeys, one of black monks[1] and the other of black nuns.[2] The latter, of course, are required to be most worthy women; they were 120 in number along with 40 half-prebendary lay sisters, and they were all raped; and both abbeys were virtually razed to the ground along with a large part of the town.

A great deal of booty was taken in this city that never came to light, I promise you, and a vast amount of pointless damage was done. But these things happen in war and they have to be accepted. And a good number of citizens and a host of knights were spared and taken captive with the Constable and in other parts of the town where they were found. They were all sent back to England to be ransomed – and truly, their ransoms equalled what the king had spent in mounting this campaign and in gifts to his men.

[1] The Benedictine abbey of Saint Étienne (the 'Abbaye aux Hommes').
[2] La Trinité (the 'Abbaye aux Dames').

When the noble king had sent all his prisoners to England he set out[1] on the road to Paris where he believed King Philip to be. Advancing at an easy pace – for the benefit of his men who had so much booty that their carts and wagons could barely move – he arrived in the county of Évreux, burning and laying waste the land as they'd done before, and made his way to a thriving town called Louviers, which produced more cloth than anywhere in France and was almost as grand as the city of Évreux or Saint-Lô in the Cotentin. It was taken quickly and with little effort, for it was unfortified; and it was as thoroughly sacked and pillaged as Saint-Lô, and as much booty or even more was found; and when all was done it was set ablaze.

I'm mentioning only those towns that were particularly big and wealthy; I couldn't give you the names of all the middling or small towns and ordinary villages – the list would never end. But I tell you this: between the city of Paris and the port of Saint Vaast-la-Hougue in the Cotentin where the king landed, the most direct route would be a journey of five or six days; and over all that distance, along a front at least a day's ride wide, that whole rich land was laid waste.

Having done as he pleased with the town of Louviers, and Saint-Lô, and the county of Évreux, the noble king avoided the fortresses and frontier towns, not wishing to be detained by any strongholds and preferring to continue his advance on Paris where he assumed King Philip to be. From Louviers he headed for the River Seine and ravaged all the country around Mantes. Next he came to the prosperous town of Vernon and left it a burning ruin, and then to Poissy,[2] another fine town. There he found the bridge destroyed, as he had at Vernon, and was very frustrated to see that he couldn't cross the river. He stayed there for five whole days while he had the bridge repaired as well as possible, and in the meantime sent his marshal Sir Godfrey on an expedition to Saint-Cloud, just two short leagues from Paris, to set it ablaze so that King Philip could see the smoke.

Once the bridge at Poissy had been repaired well enough to take carts and wagons, the king and all his army crossed untroubled, finding no one to oppose them. This is astonishing in more than one respect. The first wonder is that the English could rebuild the bridge at Poissy in such a short time – just four or five days – when they had no one lined up to do it, no vessel of any kind to support them in midstream, and no timber to hand of the required length: yet it was done in four or five days! The second wonder is that, when the bridge was repaired, King Philip, who was at Paris just seven leagues away, with the full might of all his lords and men-at-arms, having summoned all his forces to his kingdom's defence, made no attempt to attack his enemies who were sending flames and smoke billowing over his head. He might at least have come to defend the crossing! The third wonder is that, knowing they were so near at hand, he didn't go and attack them on the other side of the river; for he knew that all the bridges over the Seine had been destroyed so that they couldn't retreat or cross the Seine without rebuilding a bridge somewhere. I just don't understand it. To put it

[1]   On 31 July.
[2]   On 13 August.

bluntly, he never had the stomach or the courage to fight, for his advisers had
bewitched him into believing he'd be betrayed and lost if he did battle: they'd put
it into his head that his betrayers would be some of the most noble and powerful
men in the land. These suspicions had already led some of them to a foul death,
as you've heard. And it was thanks to such promptings that King Philip didn't
dare risk battle – for no prince who distrusts his men will ever undertake fine
deeds. It's more likely that those who advised him so were the ones bent upon
betraying him – not the noble knights, falsely suspected, who risked their bodies
and their lives for him. But I'll say no more – I've possibly said too much! I'll
return now to our story.

After repairing the bridge at Poissy and crossing the Seine with all his army
as you've heard, the noble King Edward realised that King Philip had no desire
to come and do battle, despite his signals to the contrary,[1] so he turned back and
headed for the city of Beauvais and the country thereabouts.[2] On the way, his
marshal Sir Godfrey de Harcourt, riding apart with the advance guard, met a great
body of men from Amiens, both horse and foot, on their way to Paris in response
to King Philip's call. He attacked and routed them, killing and capturing many.
King Edward was jubilant; and he went steadily on, day by day, burning and
laying waste the whole land far and wide, just as he had in Normandy.

I couldn't name all the cities, towns and villages that they destroyed or describe
each daily ride in detail, but King Edward's journey brought him one night to an
abbey called Saint Messien[3] near the city of Beauvais. Next morning, as he left
and set out on his way, the next thing he knew the abbey was all ablaze; he was
deeply upset by this.

The king now passed by the city of Beauvais, not wanting to stop to waste
that area: his sole aim, since he couldn't bring King Philip to battle as he wished,
was to lay siege to the mighty city of Calais. So he marched on past and lodged
at a town in the Beauvaisis called Milly.[4] But his two marshals passed so close to
Beauvais that they couldn't resist going to attack the barriers and the suburbs on
three sides of the city, and they burned, pillaged and destroyed two fine abbeys
outside the city walls, along with several nearby villages and the three suburbs,
right up to the city's walls and gates; they took an unimaginable amount of
loot. Then they set off and went in separate directions, pillaging, burning and

---

[1] In a letter to 'Philip of Valois' (as opposed to 'Philip, King of France') sent from Auteuil on
     15 August, Edward refers to 'the letters by which you have indicated that you wish to do
     battle with us and our army between Saint-Germain-des-Prés and Vaugirard near Paris
     or between Franconville and Pontoise this Thursday, Saturday, Sunday or next Tuesday...'
     [French original printed in *Calendar of Patent Rolls, 1345-8*, 516-7].

[2] In the same letter Edward formally challenged Philip to battle and rebuked him for failing
     to come and meet him earlier. 'We waited at Poissy,' he wrote, 'for three days waiting
     for you and the army you've assembled. You could have come from whichever direction
     you wished. But since we couldn't do battle with you we decided to carry on across our
     kingdom to punish those who rebel against us and to support our loyal friends whom you
     wrongly claim to be your subjects... If you truly wish to do battle with us as your letters
     purport, and to save those you claim to be your subjects, whenever you care to come you'll
     find us ready to meet you in the field...'

[3] In fact Saint-Lucien.

[4] Milly-sur-Thérain, north-west of Beauvais.

ravaging the country on all sides, until evening came and they went to lodge at Milly where the noble king was staying that night.

The king left Milly next morning and continued his advance across the country, ravaging and destroying with all his might, and came to lodge at a fine town called Grandvilliers. He left next day and passed Dargies, where they found no one defending the castle, so they burnt it and all the surrounding land until they reached the town of Poix. There were two castles there, and a good, substantial town, but none of its lords had stayed: they'd abandoned the town and both castles, but had left behind two fair damsels, daughters of local lords, who would have been promptly raped had it not been for two knights who took them under their protection and led them before the king; he received them warmly and treated them with great honour and had them safely escorted to where they wished to go. That night the whole army was quartered in the town and surrounding villages, and the king took lodging in the finer of the castles; and the good people of the town negotiated with the army's captains and marshals and agreed to pay a certain sum of florins in the morning to spare the town from burning.

When morning came the king and his army departed, leaving a few men to collect the promised money from the people of Poix. But when the townsfolk gathered to pay the florins, and saw that the army had been gone a fair while and left only a handful behind, they rose up and began to kill them. But a few escaped and ran after the king's army; he made a speedy return, and all the people of the town were slaughtered without mercy and the town was set ablaze, with justification.

The king and his army went next to Airaines, where he decreed that no one, on pain of hanging, should do any damage or arson, for he wanted to stay and discover where would be the easiest place to cross the River Somme.

Now I wish to return to King Philip of France, who'd been at Paris with a great host of lords and all manner of men while the English had been at Poissy and burning Saint-Germain and the castle of Montjoye and all the surrounding country. When he heard that King Edward had crossed the bridge at Poissy and was marching across the Beauvaisis straight towards the county of Ponthieu, he decided at once to leave Paris with all his lords and to overtake him around Amiens if they could, and to engage him in battle, come what may. So in great trepidation he set out, followed by all his lords and men on horse and foot, and after a series of long marches he lodged with all his forces about him at a town called Copegueule,[1] three leagues from the city of Amiens and only five leagues from the English army. There's no need to list all the great princes who were with him, as I've named them above.

Meanwhile the king of the English had spent two days at Airaines, and sent his marshals to ravage and destroy the land along the River Somme and to find the best crossing place. They carried out his orders, rising early in the morning and

---

[1]   In a footnote to their edition Viard and Déprez identify this (without explanation) as Nampty. Froissart gives the name Coppigny les Guises. Is it perhaps a strange scribal misreading of Picquigny?

setting off with a large body of men-at-arms and archers. They passed through Longpré and came to the bridge of Pont-Rémy. Here they found a great number of knights and men of the region gathered, along with a huge band of crossbowmen and others, ready to defend the bridge. The English attacked at once, launching a mighty hail of arrows in an attempt to capture the bridge, but without success. When they saw the French standing firm, not giving way to their volleys, they withdrew and made their way, burning and pillaging everything they found, to a large town called Fontaine-sur-Somme. They continued their burning and pillaging here; then they came to another town called Long-en-Ponthieu,[1] and this they burned, too, but they couldn't take the bridge. From there they went to Longpré-les-Corps-Saints,[2] a fair town with fine church foundations,[3] and it was razed to the ground and an incredible wealth of booty was taken. But the bridge had been destroyed, making the river impassable, so they made their way back to Airaines, burning and ravaging everywhere.

When they came before the king they told him all they'd done, and that they'd found every bridge either destroyed or so well defended that there'd been no chance of crossing. The noble king was less than pleased, and began to ponder; then he gave orders for everyone to make ready, for he was determined to find a way forward next day. First thing next morning he set off with his whole army, and advanced through Vimeu,[4] making straight for Oisemont and the city of Abbeville in Ponthieu, burning and ravaging all the way as ever.

That very same day the King of France struck camp at Copegueule and commanded Sir Godemar du Fay to ride through Amiens with a great body of men-at-arms and defend all the crossing places along the Somme, so that the English couldn't cross without obstruction and a fight. Sir Godemar set out to fulfil the king's command, while the king rode on and at noon arrived at Airaines, which the King of England had left that very morning. He lodged there all that day and all the next, waiting for his men who were following slowly; he was very frustrated at having missed his foe.

The noble King Edward and his marshals meanwhile went sweeping on, burning and laying waste all the country in their path, until they came to Mareuil.[5] There they burned the town, the castle, the abbey and all the villages round about – I don't know the names; so great was the blaze that the flames could be seen from Abbeville. They advanced then to the town of Oisemont, where all the men of Vimeu had assembled. When they saw the English approaching across the fields they came out of the town, intending to put up a fight, but as soon as they felt the English arrows they fell back sharpish and took to their heels. A great number were killed and wounded and captured, and the town was taken and pillaged.

---

[1] 'Lon sur Somme'.
[2] 'Lompré sur Somme'.
[3] One of its churches housed a notable collection of holy relics – hence the town's name.
[4] The area on the west side of Picardy, between the Bresle and the Somme.
[5] Mareuil-Caubert.

The noble king lodged that night in the finest mansion, pondering upon how to proceed; and next morning he had all the prisoners brought before him, and told them that if anyone could tell him how and where to cross the river he would release him and three or four companions and give him a hundred gold écus. One fellow couldn't wait to accept the offer and replied:

"Yes, sire, in God's name! If you promise to keep your word I'll show you a place tomorrow morning where your whole army'll be across the river by terce,[1] or you can have my head! I know a ford where, twice a day, a dozen men abreast can cross with the water only up to their knees: when the tide comes in it's too deep to get across, but when it ebbs the water's so shallow and calm that it's easy! It's the only place. And carts can cross there safely, too, because there's a bed of good, firm chalk, which is why it's called Blanchetaque."[2]

The noble king wouldn't have been more pleased if he'd been given twenty thousand écus! He told the fellow that if he found it was as he said he'd release all his companions for his sake. He sent out orders for his whole army to be ready to move as soon as the trumpet sounded. He didn't sleep at all that night, and was up at midnight and calling for the trumpet to sound; and as soon as all was ready, the baggage packed and riders mounted, he set off, the local man and his companions showing the way. On through the land of Vimeu they rode until, around dawn,[3] they came to the ford called Blanchetaque; but the tide was so high that they couldn't cross and had to stop awhile – and he had to wait for his men to catch up in any case. So the king stayed there till after prime[4] when the tide began to ebb. But before it was fully out, Sir Godemar du Fay appeared on the further bank with a great body of troops and men of the region who drew up in line of battle, ready to defend the ford.

But the noble king would not abandon the crossing. He sent his marshals forward into the river and commanded his archers to set to work. A mighty battle began, for the French fought like fury to stop anyone reaching the further bank; the first wave had a hard time getting across, and a good few were killed and wounded in the river. Nonetheless the English made the crossing and the French were routed and put to flight, leaving a great many dead in the fields. Then the rest of the army crossed the ford untroubled, along with the carts and wagons and packhorses. That the noble king was given such timely guidance was a great blessing from God: some consider it an outright miracle; for if he hadn't crossed the river that very day King Philip would have had him cornered and the English at his mercy.

With the baggage train safely across the English were in high spirits, and wanted to take lodging in a fine town called Noyelles; and when they learned that it belonged to the Countess of Aumale, Lord Robert of Artois's sister,[5] they

---

[1]   The third canonical hour, 9 a.m.
[2]   'Blanche Tache': literally 'white stain'.
[3]   On the morning of 24 August.
[4]   The first canonical hour, around 6 a.m.
[5]   Catherine, widow of Jean II de Ponthieu de Aumale.

guaranteed the safety of the town and the lady's land for his sake, for which she humbly thanked the king and his marshals.

Next morning the marshals rode ahead to a thriving town called Le Crotoy, rich in wines and all manner of wealth thanks to its position as a sea port. They took it with ease, and plundered and wasted all the surrounding country, and returned with a herd of livestock, large and small, to rejoin the army heading for Crécy.

The noble King Edward swore then that if the King of France were to come he would wait for him, even if he had ten times more men than he, because the ground on which he stood was his rightful inheritance, given to his mother at her marriage but usurped by King Philip.[1]

But I shall leave the English now and tell of the King of France.

Chapter LXXII

In which you may hear of the astonishing battle of Crécy,
where the greatest lords of France were defeated and captured.

You've heard how King Philip arrived at Airaines just after the King of England had left, and stayed there waiting for the rest of his forces to catch up. Next day he set off in pursuit of the English, and found his land burnt and devastated on all sides. He hadn't gone far before he heard that the English had crossed the river at Blanchetaque with much slaughter: there's no need to ask if he was shaken. He stopped and asked if there was anywhere for his own army to make the crossing, and was told that the only way was by the bridge at Abbeville. So to Abbeville he went and waited there for his army, and sent them on over as they arrived so that they'd be ready to advance first thing next day.

In the morning he set out from Abbeville with standard unfurled. It was a fine sight, with the lords magnificently armed and mounted, their banners fluttering in the wind; and truly, that army was estimated at twenty thousand heavy cavalry and more than one hundred thousand men on foot including twelve thousand Genoese and auxiliaries, while the King of England had no more than four thousand cavalry, ten thousand archers and ten thousand Welshmen and other troops on foot.

King Philip ordered his army to press on and catch up with the English, and sent a party of knights and squires ahead to find out where they were: he was sure they weren't far away. He'd gone about three leagues when these scouts returned and reported that the English were less than four leagues ahead. Then the king commanded a most able and experienced knight and four others to ride on after the English and observe their position and demeanour. These worthy knights did so willingly, and when they returned they found the French banners only a

---

[1]   Edward is referring to the county of Ponthieu. The kings of England had acquired the county through Edward I's marriage to Eleanor of Castile, who was Countess of Ponthieu in her own right. Edward II had given it to Isabella in 1308 as part of her dower; Philip had confiscated it at the outbreak of war in 1337.

league from the English and told them to stop and wait for the rest of the army; then they came to the king and reported that they'd seen the English less than a league away, and observed them deploying in three battalions ready to meet them. The king needed to decide what to do, and he asked the aforementioned knight – being a most skilled and knowledgeable fighter – for his advice. This fine knight, le Moyne de Basle,[1] was reluctant to voice his opinion before all the other lords, but he had no choice, and said:

"Sire, your army is trailing a long way back across the fields and it'll be very late by the time they're all assembled – it's already past none.[2] I suggest you order your men to make camp here; then tomorrow morning after mass draw up your battalions and attack your enemies in the name of God and Saint George, for I'm sure they won't have fled: from what I saw they'll be waiting for you."

The king liked this advice and decided to follow it. He ordered all the banners back, for the English were in position close by and he wanted to camp there till the morning. But none of the French lords was willing to turn back until those ahead of them had done so, and the ones at the front didn't want to at all: they felt it to be shameful. They held their position, unmoving, so those behind kept riding forward – all through pride and envy, and it was to be their downfall. Ignoring the worthy knight's advice, they rode on in all their competitive pride, in no order, one in front of the other, until they saw the English arrayed in three well ordered battalions, waiting for them. Seeing their enemies so near at hand, the French felt the shame of turning back all the more keenly. The officers of the crossbowmen and the auxiliaries and Genoese ordered their men to advance, and to go ahead of the lords' battalions initially and shoot at the English. They advanced so close that they were soon exchanging dense volleys, and it wasn't long before the Genoese and auxiliaries were thrown into disorder by the English archers and started to fly. But the great lords' battalions were so fired by their rivalry with one another that they didn't wait for each other but charged in a jumbled mass, with no order whatever, trapping the Genoese and auxiliaries between themselves and the English, so that they couldn't flee but fell under the charging horses and were trampled by the seething horde behind – they were tumbling over each other like a vast litter of pigs. At the same time the English archers were loosing such awesome volleys that the horses were riddled by the dreadful barbed arrows; some refused to go on, others leapt wildly, some viciously lashed and kicked, others turned tail despite their masters' efforts, and others collapsed as the arrows struck, unable to endure. Then the English lords – who were dismounted – advanced and fell upon these men, as helpless as their horses.

This disaster for the French continued till midnight – it was almost dark when the battle began – and at no point that day did the King of France or his company

---

[1]   Having initially suggested in his edition of Le Bel that this knight was Alard de Bazeilles, Jules Viard later identified him, with extensive explanation, as belonging to 'the renowned Münch or Moine family from the town of Basel in Switzerland'. See *Henri le Moine de Bâle à la bataille de Crécy*, Bibliothèque de l'école des chartes 67 (1906), 489-96.

[2]   The fifth of the canonical hours of prayer, said at the ninth hour, around 3 p.m.

manage to enter the fray.[1] The king was forced to leave, utterly distraught: against his wishes his men – including Sir John of Hainault, retained to preserve the king's life and honour – led him away; and they kept him riding through the night until they reached Labroye. There he stopped to rest, weighed down with grief, and rode next day to Amiens to wait for the rest of his army, or what was left of it. Those of the French who did remain – lords, knights and the various others – had been making their retreat, completely crushed, without knowing which way to go, for the night was very dark and they didn't know the surrounding towns and villages. And they hadn't eaten all day. They wandered in bands, in threes and fours, like lost souls, none of them knowing whether their masters or kinsmen or brothers were dead or had escaped. The catastrophe that befell King Philip and his army that day was the greatest ever visited upon Christian men. It happened in the year of grace 1346, the day after the feast of Saint Bartholomew:[2] it was a Saturday, and began at vespers; and it took place near Crécy in Ponthieu. The French, unaware of the extent of their defeat, spent the whole night in this wretched state.

I've described this as accurately as I can, following the account given to me from his own lips by my lord and friend Sir John of Hainault (God have mercy upon him) and ten or twelve knights and companions of his household; they'd been in the press with the noble and valiant King of Bohemia and had their horses killed beneath them. From the other side I've heard similar accounts from several English and German knights who were there.

Now I shall relate how the noble King Edward had ordered his battalions. The fact is that the valiant King of England was well aware on the Friday evening that King Philip was at Abbeville with a great body of knights. He was elated, and told his men to go and rest, and to pray to Our Lord that he might emerge from this venture with honour and joy, for that ground was his rightful inheritance[3] and he would defend it; he wouldn't move another step forward or backward: if King Philip cared to come there he'd be waiting for him.

Next morning he ordered his men to leave their quarters and arm, and to make a large park near a wood of all the army's carts and wagons, with just one entrance; he had all the horses corralled inside. Then he drew up his battalions in splendid array. He gave the first to his eldest son the Prince of Wales, with twelve hundred men-at-arms, three thousand archers and three thousand Welshmen, placing him in the care of the Earl of Warwick, the Earl of Stafford, the Earl of Kent, Sir Godfrey de Harcourt and a number of others whose names I don't know. The second battalion he gave to the Earl of Northampton, the Earl of Suffolk and

[1]   Literally 'come to this combat'. Other accounts suggest that Philip was caught up in action late on, and indeed was wounded in the face. Le Bel's statement may therefore appear deliberately misleading, another slight against a king he considers so unimpressive; but it may well be that he is quite right, in the sense that, in his view (having heard the authoritative eye-witness report of John of Hainault), the action came to Philip rather than Philip to the action: he failed to make a decisive intervention – he failed to be valiantly proactive in the way that Le Bel would no doubt have expected in the same situation of 'the noble King Edward'.

[2]   i.e. on 25 August.

[3]   See footnote 1, above, p.179.

the Bishop of Durham, with twelve hundred men-at-arms and three thousand archers. The third, to be positioned between the other two, he kept for himself, with sixteen hundred men-at-arms and four thousand archers. All of them were English and Welsh; there weren't even half a dozen German knights[1] – one of them was Sir Races Massures;[2] I don't know the names of the others.

When the valiant king had drawn up his battalions on a fine stretch of ground, clear of any hole or ditch, he went all about, cheerily[3] exhorting each man to do his duty with a will: so winning were his appeals and exhortations that they would have made a coward bold. And he commanded that no man, on pain of hanging, should break ranks or go looking for booty, or plunder the living or the dead without his leave; because if the battle went their way they'd all be pillaging soon enough, and if Fortune turned against them, they wouldn't be worrying about booty.

Once everything was in place he gave them all leave to go and eat and drink until the trumpet sounded, when they were all to return to their positions. He was so loved and feared by all his men that no one would have dared to disobey his order.

At the hour of none[4] the noble king received word that King Philip and his whole army were very near. He immediately ordered the sounding of the trumpet and everyone went straight to his position. They waited there till the French arrived, and then stuck to their task and performed so well that Fortune turned their way.

When the battle was over and darkness had fallen, the king issued instructions that no one was to pursue the enemy or plunder or disturb the dead until he gave permission, so that the bodies could be better identified in the morning. He ordered everyone to return to quarters to rest, but not to disarm, and all the lords to come with him to supper; and he bade the marshals post a good guard and night watch for the army. You can well imagine the great joy in which the noble king and all his lords and barons supped and spent the night, thanking God for their good fortune, that with so small a force they had held and defended the field against the full might of France.

There was a thick fog next morning, and a large English contingent, with the king's permission, ventured into the fields to see if any of the French were regrouping. They found instead large numbers of militia from the cities who'd been sleeping in the woods, in ditches and under hedges,[5] asking each other for news and what they should do – they didn't realise what had happened and had no idea where the king and their lords were. When they saw these English coming they waited to greet them, thinking they were their own side, and the

---

[1]   The MS (surely accidentally) reads 'archiers'.
[2]   'The only surviving indenture of war for the English army in 1346 concerns the service to be provided by a company of about two dozen German men-at-arms headed by a certain "Rasse Mascurel" – clearly Jean le Bel's man.' Andrew Ayton & Philip Preston, *The Battle of Crécy 1346* (Woodbridge, 2005), p.175.
[3]   Literally 'while laughing'.
[4]   About 3 p.m. See footnote 2, above, p.180.
[5]   These are probably troops arriving too late for the battle.

English fell upon them like wolves upon sheep and slaughtered them at will. Another English contingent ventured out and came upon yet more men roaming the fields seeking news of their lords; some were looking for their masters, others their kinsmen or companions;[1] and the English slaughtered them on the spot, wherever they found them.

About the hour of terce[2] they returned to their quarters just after the king and the lords had heard mass, and recounted their adventures. The king then ordered Sir Reginald Cobham, a most worthy knight, to take a herald well versed in arms, and some of the lords and the other heralds, and to go among the dead and record the names of all the knights they could identify, and to have all the princes and magnates carried to one side with each man's name written down and laid upon him. Sir Reginald did as commanded; and it was found that there were nine great princes lying on the field and around twelve hundred knights, and fully fifteen or sixteen thousand others, squires and Genoese and the rest, while the bodies of only three hundred English knights were found.

It's only right that I should record the princes and great barons who were left there dead; I couldn't manage a list of all the others. I shall begin with the noblest and most worthy, and that was the valiant King of Bohemia who, despite his total blindness, was determined to be in the forefront of battle and commanded his knights, on pain of beheading, to lead him forward no matter what, so that he could deliver a sword-blow to an enemy. The greatest prince after him was the Count of Alençon, the King of France's brother. After him was Count Louis of Blois, son of the king's sister.[3] Then the Count of Salm;[4] then the Count of Harcourt; then the Count of Auxerre; then the Count of Sancerre. It was said that not for a long time had anyone heard of so many princes being killed on a single day – neither at Courtrai[5] nor at Benevento,[6] nor anywhere else.

On the Sunday following, the valiant King Edward stayed on the field all day, waiting to see if King Philip would rally his forces. But he didn't reappear; so the valiant king departed with all his army, and had the bodies of his dead carried to a nearby abbey, and sent his marshals to burn and lay waste the surrounding country as they'd done elsewhere. They did so with ease, finding no one to oppose them; and they headed towards Saint-Josse and burned Beaurain and all the land around Montreuil-sur-Mer, and all its suburbs, which were very extensive. Then they left Saint-Josse after setting it ablaze, and did the same to Étaples and Neufchâtel and all the land around Boulogne. Then the noble King Edward laid siege to the city of Calais,[7] considered one of the strongest cities in the world.

---

[1]   These by contrast are presumably survivors of the battle.
[2]   9 a.m. – see footnote 1, above, p.97.
[3]   And husband of John of Hainault's daughter.
[4]   'Saumes en Saumoire'.
[5]   The crushing French defeat at the hands of Flemish rebels in 1302, in which the spurs of so many dead knights were taken after the battle that it became known as the Battle of the Golden Spurs.
[6]   In 1266, when Charles of Anjou defeated Manfred of Sicily with very heavy losses.
[7]   Edward arrived at Calais on 4 September.

Chapter LXXIII

How the King of England with a great army besieged the mighty city of Calais.

The noble king laid siege to the fine, strong city of Calais, and declared that, winter or summer, he wouldn't leave until it was in his hands, unless King Philip came to do battle and defeated him. And because it was so strong and garrisoned with good men he wouldn't allow his troops to attack it, knowing he might well lose more than he gained. Instead he had a lodge made with timber and planks and roofed with straw to house him all that winter, and ordered the building of good earthworks around his army to protect them from attack and harm. All his lords and knights made the best lodges they could, some of wood, some of broom, some of straw, until soon they'd built a strong and substantial town; indeed, you could buy whatever you wanted there at a good price! They had a meat market and a market for cloth and all manner of goods as fine as at Arras or Amiens, for the Flemings were on their side and supplied them with everything they needed. They were well supplied from England, too, by sea – it's only a short crossing at that point – and even more would have come had it not been for Genoese and others who roamed the sea, robbing and wrecking those they met. One of these pirates was named Marant, another Maistrel, and they caused many problems for the English, regularly destroying the supplies that were being sent to the army – much to their displeasure – and they had some fierce encounters, too.

There were frequent clashes around the city also, between the besiegers and defenders; and the marshals would often lead expeditions into the surrounding country in search of adventure, and would return to the army with livestock, large and small, as they burned and pillaged everywhere: the whole county of Guînes and the town and its strong castle were razed to the ground, as was the thriving town of Marck. In short, the whole land was laid waste. Many fine exploits occurred, with gains and losses for one side or the other, as frequently happens during such sieges and campaigns, and it would take too long to recount every incident. I'm going to move on swiftly, though I'll return and tell more of what happened before the city surrendered.

And I don't want to overlook a great act of courtesy performed by King Edward to the city's poor in the course of the siege. When the men of Calais realised King Edward wasn't going to leave that winter, and that their own supplies were short, they sent fully five hundred people out of the city through the English lines. The noble king, seeing these poor folk cast out of their city, summoned them all before him in his great hall and had them all provided with plentiful food and drink. When they'd eaten and drunk their fill he gave them leave to pass through his army, and gave each of them three old[1] English silver pennies for the love of God before seeing them safely escorted far beyond the lines. This should certainly be recorded as a most worthy deed.

---

[1] Emphasising perhaps that this was good coin rather than the debased stuff minted by King Philip: see above, p.154.

But now I shall leave the siege of Calais, for I've said nothing for a long while about the land of Gascony where the Duke of Normandy and the worthy Earl of Derby[1] were not without their battles, or about the valiant Countess of Montfort's continuing resistance [in Brittany], or about King David of Scotland, waging mighty war on the borders of England. One should indeed take note of the great enterprise of a king who was engaged in wars in so many far-flung lands at once. And I shall speak of them all, one after the other: I shall tell first of the Duke of Normandy and his great company outside Aiguillon; then how the worthy Earl of Derby conquered the city of Poitiers and the land of Poitou; and then how the King of Scotland was captured in battle, and then Lord Charles of Blois likewise – all this during the siege of Calais.

Chapter LXXIV

Here we return to Aiguillon, and how the Duke of Normandy and the others
abandoned the siege and went back to the King in France.

The Duke of Normandy had been besieging Aiguillon continuously from the middle of April to the middle of September, and launched assaults in every way imaginable, at great expense; but it was so nobly defended that the least of the men involved should be deemed worthy. While he was there, a knight brought him news that his father the king had been defeated by the King of England near Crécy in Ponthieu, and that the whole of Normandy and all the lands around Beauvais, Amiens, Boulogne and Ponthieu had been ravaged and laid waste, and that, after all that, King Edward had now laid siege to the mighty city of Calais; and he told him of the princes and vast number of dead left on the battlefield.

There's no need to ask if the duke was distressed by the news: it could hardly have been worse; moreover, his father the king and his mother the Queen were summoning him to abandon the siege, come what may, and return to France to defend the kingdom.

His distresses were multiplying. He'd already suffered one when his cousin, the son of his uncle the Duke of Burgundy, the finest young knight in all France and destined to be the richest of princes at his father's death, had recently died there at the siege of Aiguillon through grave misfortune: riding a courser[2] in his eagerness to join an assault upon the castle, the horse had fallen upon him and crushed him so badly that he died. It was a dreadful pity and the Duke of Normandy was distraught, for he'd loved his cousin dearly. The second distress was obviously great: his father's defeat and the deaths of his uncle and cousin.[3] And there was a third: that he had to leave and abandon the siege of Aiguillon without achieving his declared intention; he did this most reluctantly,

---

[1]   As noted above (p.157), Henry of Grosmont was now Earl of Lancaster, but Le Bel contin-
     ues for a while to refer to him as the Earl of Derby.
[2]   See footnote 2, above, p.40.
[3]   i.e. the Count of Alençon and Count Louis of Blois, listed among the dead at Crécy, above,
     p.183.

feeling it was a grave dishonour. Nonetheless he called for his uncle the Duke of Burgundy, his cousin the Duke of Bourbon, the Bishop of Beauvais, the Count of Armagnac, the Count of Lille and the other lords and told them of the news and his father's summons, and asked them to discuss the situation. They were all deeply shocked by the news; and they considered the matter and agreed that it would be more honourable for the duke to return to France, especially in view of the state of the kingdom after the defeat at Crécy, than to stay at Aiguillon and disobey his father. So orders were given for all the troops to pack up and decamp and to follow the banners next day.

They struck camp in the morning; and when the men in Aiguillon saw what was happening, that valiant knight Sir Walter Mauny armed and rode with other good companions over the bridge built by the besiegers and came to their camp and found many who'd not yet left and slaughtered them. Not satisfied with that, the worthy knight ordered his banner onward, and they caught up with the rearguard and launched a vigorous attack. A fine contest followed, but it didn't last long, for the French were so eager to be back in France that few had remained in the rearguard, and they were swiftly overwhelmed and killed or captured. Then Sir Walter and his followers returned to the French camp and found great riches left behind. They joyously carried the spoils back to the castle, leaving the Duke of Normandy to return to France – he didn't stop riding till he reached Paris. But I shan't dwell on the misery of the duke and his fellows: it's easy enough to imagine, so I'll say no more.

When Sir Walter and his companions returned with their prisoners to the castle as you've heard, they asked one captive knight, a kinsman of the duke and a member of his council, why the French army had left. The knight told them exactly what had happened, and of King Edward's great fortune; there's no need to ask if they rejoiced.

Next day the companions divided their booty, and the knight was among the share apportioned by Sir Walter Mauny. The knight offered three thousand écus for his ransom, and I shall tell you now of the noble act performed by the worthy Sir Walter. He said:

"I understand, sir, that you're willing to pay three thousand écus and more for your freedom. I'll tell you what I'll do. As a kinsman of the duke and a member of his council, you'll promise to go to him and acquire for me a letter bearing his seal, fashioned after his father the king's, granting me and just twenty others free passage through the kingdom until I reach Calais: I'll pay my way from town to town. At Calais is the noblest prince ever born of woman! I so desire to see him that, if you can bring me this letter within a month, I'll free you from imprisonment and ransom. And I shan't stay in any town for more than one night: I'll pay my dues and keep riding till I reach Calais. But if you can't secure me safe passage you must return here at the end of the month as my prisoner."

The knight was relieved and delighted by this, and said he would gladly do all he could. He gave Sir Walter his word as a knight, and then left Aiguillon and secured the letter bearing the duke's seal as Sir Walter had requested, and delivered it to him at the end of the month: he was overjoyed and set the knight free. Then that worthy knight Sir Walter Mauny, always more mindful of honour than money, set off on the road through France with just twenty companions, quite openly, trusting in the letters of free passage; and whenever he was stopped and he showed the letters he was immediately allowed to go. He continued his journey until he was near Orléans; but there he was arrested and wasn't released despite the letters; instead he was taken to Paris and imprisoned in the Châtelet, being deeply hated as he was by the French because of his mighty feats of prowess which had earned him great renown.

When the Duke of Normandy learned of this he was very upset, and went straight to his father the king and earnestly begged him to release Sir Walter or he would be dishonoured and people would say he'd betrayed him, for he'd granted him letters of safe passage under his own seal – and he told the king exactly why, just as you've heard. The king refused to respond to any of his son's arguments or entreaties, and had Sir Walter placed in an even more secure prison, in the tower of the Louvre; and there he stayed for a long time. The Duke of Normandy was so upset by this that for as long as the knight remained imprisoned he refused to be part of his father's household. The king was finally persuaded to release the worthy knight from prison and to pay his very substantial expenses; and the duke had him safely escorted to his lord King Edward whom he'd so longed to see. The noble King Edward was overjoyed to see him, and gave him the kind of welcome he'd have given his cousin the Earl of Derby, as did everyone. But I shall leave him now and return to the worthy Earl of Derby.

Chapter LXXV

How the Earl of Derby left Bordeaux and went to Poitou and took Poitiers and Saint-Jean-d'Angély.

You've heard how the worthy Earl of Derby, while the Duke of Normandy and the French lords were besieging the castle of Aiguillon, was based in the city of Bordeaux; he was doing all he could to provide the men in Aiguillon and his other garrisons with victuals and supplies. As soon as he heard that the French had left Aiguillon and were returning to France, he took the lord of Albret, the lord of Lesparre and a great host of other lords, knights and men-at-arms from Gascony and the Bordelais, both mounted and on foot – in all a good thousand or twelve hundred cavalry and a thousand infantry, auxiliaries and archers – and crossed the Gironde estuary to Taillebourg, which he took. Then he advanced into Poitou and took the town of Maillezais,[1] then Surgères and Aulnay; and everything found in every town and village was plundered and pillaged without mercy or pity, and anywhere that failed to surrender immediately was burnt and destroyed. The earl came then to Saint-Jean-d'Angély and besieged the city, attacking it for three days; and the citizens, fearing they would lose their lives and possessions and that their wives and daughters would be raped if the city were taken by force, decided to surrender if their lives and property were spared. So they surrendered the city, and the worthy Earl of Derby accepted their terms.

---

[1] 'Masieres'.

He made a triumphant entry, and installed a garrison on behalf of the King of England, as he did in all the castles and fortified towns he conquered.

Then he left Saint-Jean and headed for Niort. This town was very strongly fortified, and its defenders resisted so well that he couldn't take it no matter how hard he attacked. So he left and carried on towards the city of Poitiers. On the way he took by force the stronghold of Saint-Maixent;[1] there many of the townspeople were killed and some of the women and girls were raped and the whole town was pillaged mercilessly, though it wasn't burnt. The earl made next for Lusignan and took the town, the people saving themselves by surrender and payment; then he took the castle by force and captured the lord, of a great and ancient lineage. He left a strong garrison in the castle and then advanced to Vivonne; but he did no damage there, for the people of the town made terms and paid for their protection.

The earl went next to Montreuil-Bonnin, where a great deal of coin was minted for King Philip of France: he expected to find great riches! A very strong castle stood there, and inside were some three hundred mint-workers who swore they'd mount a stout defence if the English attacked them. The English did so, mightily, but they responded feebly; the castle was taken by storm and many of the mint-workers were killed and others taken prisoner and the town was promptly plundered without mercy.

From there they advanced on Poitiers;[2] it's a great, expansive city, but as soon as they arrived they blockaded it completely, and then went to rest and consider how best to proceed. They delivered their assault at the weakest point, and with too few to defend it the city was taken by storm and more than six hundred men were killed, vintners, butchers and tradesmen of all kinds. The whole city was sacked and looted, churches desecrated, everything destroyed – it was unimaginable;[3] and townswomen were raped: the worthy Earl of Derby was enraged but had been unable to prevent it.

They stayed there for ten days before setting off back to Saint-Jean-d'Angély, so laden with booty that the lowliest fellow in the army had a chest full of florins (they hadn't even bothered with the small stuff). Celebrations greeted their return to Saint-Jean-d'Angély, and the worthy earl gave many fine gifts to the townspeople. Then, after posting a strong garrison in the town, he left there and journeyed on to Bordeaux where he was joyously received; here too he gave many fine gifts to the citizens and to the knights and squires of his company, and rewarded the soldiers so generously that he was extremely popular! But for now I'll say no more about the earl, for not long after this he returned to England before joining King Edward at the siege of Calais.

Now I wish to tell of King David of Scotland, and how in the meantime he'd been faring in his war.

---

[1] 'Saint Maximien'.
[2] It was now 4 October.
[3] The MS reads 'one can well imagine it'. An accidentally omitted negative would seem to make more sense, but perhaps the text is correct and Le Bel (and, he assumes, his audience) has become inured to these levels of destruction.

Chapter LXXVI

How the King of Scotland was captured and defeated in battle
while King Edward had been before Calais, etc.

While the noble King Edward had enjoyed his great good fortune against
the King of France near Crécy and then laid siege to Calais, King David of
Scotland had assembled a huge army to go and ravage and lay waste England,
knowing as he did that King Edward wasn't there. Among them were the Earl
Patrick, the Earl of Moray, the Earl of Orkney, the Earl of Strathearn, the Earl of
Ross,[1] the Earl of Buchan,[2] Sir William Douglas, Simon Fraser and Alexander
Ramsay; they numbered in all three thousand men-at-arms, knights and squires,
and fully forty-three thousand mounted on hackneys, for all the lowly men of
Scotland ride little hackneys when they go to war.

As soon as the Queen of England heard the news she went to Newcastle-upon-
Tyne to give heart to her people there, and summoned the bishops, archbishops
and all the able-bodied men left in England to muster between the city of Durham
and Northumberland, for the King of Scotland was about to invade England with
a great army and burn and lay waste everything. Responding to her summons
came the [Arch]bishop of York, the Archbishop of Canterbury, the new Bishop
of Lincoln[3] and the Bishop of Durham, each of them with all the troops, archers
and foot soldiers he could muster and as well armed and provisioned as he
could manage. Present also were Sir Edward Balliol, the lord Mowbray,[4] the lord
Neville,[5] the lord Percy[6] and so many others that they totalled twelve hundred
cavalry, five thousand archers and a good eight thousand foot. But before they'd
all assembled the Scots had already crossed into Northumberland and burned
and ravaged all the land as far as the River Tyne. Once the English lords had
gathered they came before the Queen, and she prayed and requested them to
fight and to defend the possessions and the honour of the king; and she gave
command of the campaign to four prelates and four knights who most willingly
accepted.

Why should I lengthen the story? They realised that the Scots were burning
the whole land approaching Newcastle, so they headed that way and escorted
the worthy queen into the city. Then they organised four battalions, with one
of the prelates and one of the knights in each. The Scots heard that the English
had gathered to meet them in battle, so they formed their battalions likewise.
The battle[7] was fought on a Tuesday around the hour of terce,[8] and was as fierce
and as mighty as any ever seen, with as many fine feats of prowess and bold

---

[1] 'le conte de Rose'.
[2] 'le conte de Basken'.
[3] John Gynwell (or Gyndell).
[4] 'le sire de Montbrait': John de Mowbray, 3rd Baron Mowbray.
[5] 'le sire de Neufville': John Neville, 3rd Baron Neville de Raby.
[6] Henry Percy, lord of Alnwick.
[7] Neville's Cross, fought on ground to the west of Durham on 17 October 1346.
[8] The third canonical hour, about 9 a.m.

ventures and valiant rescues as ever were made by Roland and Oliver;[1] for the
English, although they were few in number and without their proper lord, strove
to fight with all their might, to win their king's approval, so that even the lowliest
was worth a knight. They fought for each other and vied with each other, with
such spirit that they finally routed their foes. The Earl of Buchan[2] and many
others were killed along with at least three thousand common soldiers; and King
David himself was captured by a valiant squire who took great pains to save
him from being killed by the men of those parts: his name was John Copeland.[3]
The Earl of Moray was taken prisoner, too, and many more whose names I don't
know. When the battle was over, John Copeland summoned his most trusted
companions and mounted his captive King David on a palfrey and took him to a
strong castle he owned called Ogle,[4] which stood on the Tyne some twenty-five
leagues from Newcastle.

As soon as the worthy queen heard that her men had won the battle, and
above all that the King of Scotland had been captured, she was so overwhelmed
with joy that the she came to kiss them all, one after the other.[5] Then the Bishop of
Durham presented her with the Earl of Moray as her prisoner (it was to the bishop
that he had surrendered); but there was no sign of John Copeland delivering the
King of Scotland: he was planning to keep him hidden until someone insisted
otherwise.

The English camped that night on the field of battle, which was fought on
a Tuesday after Michaelmas in the year 1346. The next day they all headed
homeward, jubilant, while the Queen returned to London with her captive
the Earl of Moray, and imprisoned him with the Constable of France and the
Chamberlain de Tancarville. Never did any lady rejoice as much as the Queen
did then, for her lord the king had enjoyed fairer fortune than ever befell any
man, having vanquished in one season the three[6] most powerful kings in the
world. As soon as she arrived in London, she sent a message to her lord the
king, encamped before Calais, informing him of the whole affair, above all the
news that John Copeland had captured the King of Scotland but was making no
sign of delivering him. You can imagine the king's joy at the news; and he sent
messengers and amicable letters to the squire John Copeland, asking him to come
at once and speak with him. The valiant squire went as soon as he could, and
bowed most humbly when he came into the king's presence; the king took him
by the hand and made a great fuss of him, thanking him for the great honour he'd
done him in capturing his enemy the King of Scotland, and thus, by his prowess,
saving his kingdom from burning and destruction. The squire replied, saying:

"Saving your grace, my dear lord, it was not through my prowess; God in
His mercy sent him into my hands and I seized him and made him yield. God,

---

[1]   The heroes of the great French epic *The Song of Roland*.
[2]   '*le conte de Bosquen*'.
[3]   '*messire Jehan de Chappellein*'.
[4]   Le Bel calls it '*le chastel Orguilleux*', a name with a noticeably Arthurian ring. Ogle Castle is
      a fortified manor house near Whalton in Northumberland.
[5]   Queen Philippa was in fact not present at Neville's Cross at all.
[6]   i.e. Philip of France, David of Scotland and, presumably, John of Bohemia.

when He chooses, can send as great a blessing to a poor squire as He can to a high lord."

"Indeed, John," said the noble king, "you're right. But I should love and honour you greatly, and I wish to knight you forthwith, and will grant you a revenue of five hundred pounds sterling in land, right by your home, on condition that you deliver the King of Scotland to London as my prisoner and present him to my queen. And you shall be a member of my household, if it please you."

The valiant squire was overjoyed by these promises, and said he would gladly accept the king's offer. So he was knighted next day, and the noble king held a great court in the new knight's honour. Copeland then set off and returned home, and organised a sufficient escort to take his prisoner safely to London. There he presented him to the Queen, who was delighted: her greatest wish was fulfilled. And she placed him in prison with the Constable of France, the Chamberlain de Tancarville and the others.

After these adventures the valiant queen longed to see her lord the king, and she prepared ships and boats and an escort of men-at-arms and gifts for the knights and other supplies necessary for the voyage, and put to sea despite the grave risk of being captured and lost, and reached the army outside Calais three days before All Saints. The king came to greet her and kissed her joyfully in the presence of all his men, and led her to his hall; and he announced that at All Saints he would hold a great, open court in the Queen's honour. And a great court it was indeed: at least seven hundred knights and others attended – there were too many to serve! – as everyone flocked to see the Queen. The good lady addressed and conversed with her knights so graciously that it was a delight to behold; and she bestowed a great quantity of handsome gifts upon those she deemed most deserving. She spent a long time with the king, and a joyful one; she'd brought with her many ladies and damsels, and it gave the king great pleasure to see the knights and squires revelling in their company.

The siege lasted a very long while, and there were fine feats of prowess performed by both sides, both on land and on sea – too many indeed to recount, and I'll pass over them swiftly for fear of wearying readers and listeners.

The King of France had such good troops – and so many – in all the fortresses around Calais, and so many Genoese and Norman and other mariners out at sea, that the English, who wanted to go foraging over sea or land, had frequent and fierce encounters, sometimes coming off better and sometimes worse. There were so many adventures, on land and sea, that I couldn't relate a tenth of them – and, as always happens, there were a good number killed and wounded and captured. And all the while the noble king and his council were ever contriving new devices to break the city's resistance, but the defenders responded with equal persistence, and the only ones who suffered from these machines and instruments were those who worked them.

But the siege wore on until the men in the city were in such a state that they finally had to surrender: they were starving, as you'll hear in due course. And in all fairness they shouldn't be blamed: they were so tightly blockaded by land and sea that no supplies could get through – though there was one seafarer on their side, the one named Marant, who gave them fine support and brought provisions a number of times, and he was a plague to the English and cost them many lives.

Chapter LXXVII

How King Edward tried to arrange the marriage of his daughter to the young Count of Flanders, but the count would not consent.

The noble king stayed before Calais all that winter, and numerous remarkable adventures occurred.

Now, the noble king had always been keen to nurture his relations with the Flemings, thinking that he could thereby achieve his goals more swiftly. He had sent them frequent embassies, with promises that if he succeeded in his aims he would without doubt deliver Lille and Douai to them.[1] These assurances had prompted the Flemings, while the noble king was advancing into Normandy, to besiege and attack Béthune. But King Philip had such a fine garrison there that the Flemings suffered a fair few losses; moreover, one day while they were burning and ravaging all the land of Artois around Béthune they were challenged by a French force and lost a huge number of men. There's no need to drag the story out: they'd soon had enough of the siege, having no lord to lead them, and abandoned it and went back to their homes.[2]

Nonetheless, when the noble King Edward arrived before Calais he continued to send embassies to the Flemish cities, reiterating his promises as he sought to bind them to him. He was especially intent upon arranging the marriage of his daughter to the noble Count of Flanders,[3] who was not yet sixteen, and in this he gained the complete support of the Flemings. He was convinced that this would secure him Flemish aid in his war, and the Flemings felt likewise that an alliance with the English would help them resist the French. But the young Count of Flanders, who'd been raised with the French royal family, would not consent; on the contrary, with his guardians' encouragement he declared that he would never marry the daughter of the man who'd killed his father.[4]

The fact is that Duke John of Brabant was manoeuvring for the young count to take *his* daughter in marriage, making fulsome promises that he would help him secure the county of Flanders whether the Flemings favoured him or not; and at the same time the duke was assuring King Philip that if this all went to plan he'd win the Flemings over to his side. In the light of these promises King Philip gave his approval to the marriage, and the Duke of Brabant immediately sent grand embassies to the chief cities of Flanders to win their backing and consent, giving so many strong arguments that they were swayed, and sent messages to

---

[1]   The Flemings had long resented French possession of the towns and castleries of Lille and Douai, annexed (along with Orchies) from Southern Flanders in 1304.

[2]   The Flemings ended the siege on 24 August, the very day that Edward and his army crossed the ford at Blanchetaque.

[3]   Louis de Mâle, Count Louis II.

[4]   His father Count Louis I was among the dead at Crécy: it is perhaps surprising that he is omitted from the list above, p.183.

their lord the young count, intimating that if he would come and trust in their counsel they would be his good and faithful subjects and yield to him all the authority and rights enjoyed by his forebears, indeed more than any previously. So the young count came to Flanders[1] and was very warmly welcomed, each city presenting him with handsome gifts.

As soon as the noble king heard about this he sent the Earl of Northampton to Flanders to work upon the commons; he convinced them that they would rather have their count marry King Edward's daughter than the daughter of the Duke of Brabant, and they made heartfelt pleas to their lord, giving such fine arguments that the duke's party were silenced. But nothing anyone could say would change the young count's mind: he insisted that he would never marry the daughter of the one who'd killed his father. When the Flemings heard this, they said that this lord was a Frenchman and ill advised and would never do right by them! So they took him and placed him under house arrest,[2] and said he wouldn't be released until he followed their advice, and that if his father hadn't loved and trusted the French so much he would have been the greatest lord in the world.

Thus matters rested for a time. And all the while the noble king was before Calais. On Christmas Day he held a great court; and after that, around the beginning of Lent, the worthy Earl of Derby arrived to see his lord. God knows he was welcomed with joy and honour: all men are bound to be heartened by the coming of such a prince.

The young Count of Flanders remained confined by his own people for a long while, for he refused to change his mind. But in the end he promised to do whatever they wished if they would just let him go hawking, still under guard, along the river and elsewhere. The Flemings trusted him and allowed him to go; but twenty men followed him constantly, wherever he went – Flemish townsmen they were, who watched him so closely that he could hardly go for a piss. He was allowed the company of only two knights from his council – and they were Flemings.

On the basis of his promise, the Flemings invited the King of England and his queen to meet them at Bergues. The noble king and queen arrived there in state, and were joined there by the Flemings bringing the young count with them. He humbly bowed before the king, and the noble king returned his bow and apologised most graciously for his father's death, but told him that on the day of the battle he hadn't seen or recognised his father, alive or dead. In short, nothing more was said of the matter and promises were duly exchanged, the young count being happily betrothed to the King of England's daughter and the marriage day agreed.

The noble king made sumptuous preparations for this great occasion, acquiring handsome gifts and rich jewels, as did the Queen. And meanwhile the young count continued to go hawking beside the river, escorted by his guards. But on the very eve of his wedding[3] one of his falcons took flight and his falconers

---

[1]   In early November 1346.
[2]   'mirent en prison courtoisement'.
[3]   28 March 1347.

rode after to lure it back. When the young count saw them spurring away he went galloping after them as fast as he could – and never came back for his wedding day to marry his betrothed: he kept galloping all the way to King Philip of France and the Duke of Normandy! And so he made his crafty escape, much to the dismay of the Flemings and the noble king and much to the delight of the French. But it didn't stop the Flemings supporting the noble King Edward; they repeatedly came out to aid the English, and ravaged the country far and wide around Saint-Omer and Thérouanne.

Chapter LXXVIII

How Bishop Engelbert of Liège quarrelled with the people of the region and fought a fierce battle at Vottem and another at Tourinne.

In this same year a great war broke out between the Bishop of Liège, lord Engelbert de la Marck, and the people of the cities of Liège and Huy,[1] prompting the bishop, quite newly appointed,[2] to summon a great gathering of German lords: no greater muster – least of all of foreigners – had ever been witnessed in those parts. Then the bishop advanced upon the city, to a village called Vottem,[3] intending to demand the delivery of certain citizens who were guilty of a crime. But the people of the city were determined to resist, and marched out, all armed, with banners flying, as did the people of Huy. They would never have imagined the bishop to have a twentieth of the men that he did! Out in the fields they took up a position along a big earthwork; this was before they'd seen any of his forces: if they'd known his massive strength they'd have thought twice! And when they saw the mighty army approaching they panicked and took to their heels – not a quarter of them stayed at the earthwork. Seeing this, some of the lords went charging forward instantly, some to chase after those in flight, others to attack those who'd stayed. And they lost a huge number of men-at-arms, knights and squires who foolishly dismounted, while their companions stayed behind on horseback, not helping them in any way but drawing back and stopping to watch. I don't know why this happened, unless it was because they didn't want any of their horses killed. But they outnumbered them by ten to one! So it's baffling that they didn't attack when their brothers and kinsmen and companions were being slaughtered! It's as if they were under a spell: after watching a while they suddenly turned and rode back to their quarters. It's truly an utter mystery.

This outlandish adventure filled the men of Liège with such proud confidence that they would consider no terms of peace; instead they drew all the other cities and the country to their side and waged war all that year. And they fared better than they could ever have hoped: they besieged the castle of Clermont[4] and

---

[1]   The dispute arose over the murder of one of the bishop's subjects by a citizen of Huy.
[2]   Engelbert had succeeded his uncle, Adolph de la Marck, as prince-bishop in 1345.
[3]   Now a northern suburb of Liège.
[4]   Clermont-sur-Meuse.

captured and destroyed it; then they took the castle of Hermalle and destroyed it likewise; and after the feast of Saint John – the year was 1347 – they besieged the mighty castle of Argenteau (a fiefdom held from the Duke of Brabant) and destroyed that, too, taking all its defenders captive and leading them back to prison in Liège.

It was during their siege of Argenteau that Louis, the young Count of Flanders, married the Duke of Brabant's daughter[1] despite his betrothal to the daughter of the King of England (and the duke's other daughter was married to the young Duke of Guelders). At the same time the Duke of Brabant and Bishop Engelbert of Liège agreed to muster all the troops they could and raise the siege, and appealed to all their allies; but the Duke of Brabant spent so long celebrating his daughter's marriage that the castle of Argenteau was taken by storm and destroyed.

On the very day that the castle was captured, the bishop, the Count of Loon and the Duke of Guelders were near the town of Hannut, preparing to burn and lay waste the good land of Hesbaye[2] and to besiege the city of Liège. When the men of Liège learned of their approach they had no intention of holding back; their pride had the better of them, and they sent an urgent appeal to the men of Huy, Dinant and the other major towns, calling them to come out and muster around the towns of Tourinne and Latinne. They deployed there in the fields one Friday, and stood all day, ready to confront the might of all those lords. But the Duke of Brabant had no desire to do battle that day – not that he ever did, anywhere – and he ordered his men to camp in the fields, much to the fury of the bishop and the Count of Loon. It was only about midday, so the men of Liège could easily, and with all honour, have gone home to Liège and the men of Huy to Huy if they'd had the sense and been so inclined. As it was, when they realised that the duke and his army had made camp, they left their position and went to find quarters in villages here and there.

Everyone assumed they'd all gone home; but next morning the bishop and the Count of Loon rose before dawn, went into the fields and saw the men of Liège and their allies already deployed, just as they'd been the day before. They didn't want to risk the Duke of Brabant objecting again, and mounted an attack at once with the forces that they had. They routed the Liégeois with their first charge – though the Duke of Guelders arrived, too, just as the battle was ending – and pursued them across the fields, slaughtering them at will. At least fifteen thousand were left dead and many were taken captive. But the Duke of Brabant and his men didn't show up until the very end. Then the duke went and camped beside the river Yerne above Limont, the bishop at Lamine and the Count of Loon at Remicourt. This was on the eve of the feast of Mary Magdalene, in the year of grace 1347.[3]

They stayed there all next day, and on the Monday went and camped beside the river Geer. Then negotiations began, and peace was made and agreed on the Saturday following, at Waroux; the terms were highly favourable to the Bishop

[1] On 1 July.
[2] See footnote 3, above, p.27.
[3] Le Bel has here described the battle of Tourinne, near Hannut, fought on 21 July.

of Liège. But the Duke of Brabant took no part in this and went destroying far and wide.

But I shall leave this now and discuss another matter which I've left for some while.

Chapter LXXIX

How Lord Charles of Blois was defeated and captured in battle before
La Roche-Derrien in Brittany, and taken to England.

It's a long time since I've spoken about the valiant Countess of Montfort and Lord Charles of Blois, who were still waging a mighty war in Brittany; I wish to return to them now and tell of their adventures.

You heard earlier how the noble King of England sent the worthy Earl of Derby to Gascony, and also sent two knights[1] with a large force of men-at-arms and archers to Brittany to aid the valiant Countess of Montfort; of these two, one was named Sir Thomas Dagworth[2] and the other Sir John Hardeshull.[3] They stayed with her in the city of Hennebont for a long while, frequently clashing with men of Lord Charles of Blois's party, as did other supporters of hers, all (or most) of whom were Breton-speaking Bretons, among them a most valiant knight named Sir Tanneguy du Châtel,[4] who was ever at the lady's side. The country was ravaged and laid waste by both parties, and it was the poor people who paid for it.

One day the three knights named above gathered a great number of men-at-arms and foot soldiers and went to lay siege to a fine and prosperous town with a very strong castle called La Roche-Derrien. They launched vigorous assaults, and the defence wasn't lacking: the castellan was a tough, brave, combative squire named Tassart de Guyenne. But more of the townspeople supported the valiant countess than the other side, and they negotiated successfully with the attackers and on the third or fourth day of the siege surrendered the town and the castle with their lives and possessions guaranteed, and delivered the key to the three knights in the valiant countess's name. The knights left a garrison of men-at-arms and a good body of archers and soldiers to guard the town and castle with the townsfolk and Tassart; then they set off and returned to the countess.

When Lord Charles learned of this he was furious. He summoned all his supporters – knights, Genoese and all the troops available – until he'd mustered fully sixteen hundred cavalry and twelve thousand men on foot; among them were twenty-two or twenty-three bannerets and four hundred knights of one shield.[5] Then he went and laid siege to the castle and town of La Roche-Derrien. But the defenders were undismayed, and sent at once to the valiant countess

---

[1]   To be precise he mentions only Dagworth: above, p.157.
[2]   *'Thomas d'Agorne'*.
[3]   *'Jehan de Articelle'*.
[4]   *'Jehan du Chastel'*.
[5]   A 'knight of one shield' was one who, unlike a banneret, had no other knight serving under him and his banner.

and the three knights, appealing for help. The countess responded with a will, sending urgent messages to all her friends, and soon had a force of a thousand heavy cavalry and fifteen thousand infantry and fifteen hundred archers. She placed them all in the care and command of the three knights, who joyfully and willingly received them and vowed not to return until they'd raised the siege of the town and castle or died in the attempt.

They made their way as swiftly as they could until – why should I lengthen the story? – they were near Lord Charles's army. When they came within two leagues of them Sir Thomas Dagworth, Sir John Hardeshull and the other knights and men-at-arms made camp for the night beside a river, intending to do battle next day. But once they were encamped and settled, the valiant knights took half their army and ordered them to arm and mount quietly, and before midnight they went and launched an attack upon one side of the besieging forces and did much damage, killing a great number; but they stayed so long that the whole of Lord Charles's host was up and armed, and they found themselves locked in combat until so many of the enemy were upon them that it was impossible to escape without grave loss: they were overcome and suffered heavy casualties. Sir Thomas himself was badly wounded and captured along with a score of others, but Sir John, with great difficulty, made it back to their army with two hundred companions who'd escaped with him. They told of the calamity that had befallen them; and at that very moment a valiant knight[1] and a hundred lances arrived as fresh reinforcements, and when he heard the news he proposed that the whole army should arm that instant and go and attack the enemy. Sir John agreed at once, as did they all, and before the sun had risen[2] they met Lord Charles's forces who were already on the alert and out in the field. A fierce and mighty engagement followed, as they fell upon each other immediately and battled long. That small force of English and Bretons had a tough task confronting so many men and lords, you may be sure; they had to fight with the utmost resolve and achieve many feats of prowess and brave recoveries. But they defeated their enemies and won the field. Fifteen bannerets were left dead, and two hundred knights of one shield and four thousand foot soldiers; and Lord Charles of Blois was captured, Sir Thomas Dagworth and all his companions were rescued, and the French tents and pavilions were won. Lord Charles was sent to England as the noble King Edward's prisoner; he spent a long time in prison before he paid a ransom of four hundred thousand old écus.[3]

---

[1] Froissart names him 'Garnier de Cadoudal'; he is perhaps a relation of (or even the same person as) the 'Guillaume de Cadoudal' mentioned several times earlier by Le Bel.

[2] It was the dawn of 20 June 1347.

[3] 'quatre fois cent escus vielx'. The factor of a thousand is clearly missing: four hundred would have been astonishingly cheap! Edward first bought the prisoner from Dagworth for the (still very reasonable) price of twenty-five thousand. The sum of four hundred thousand is confirmed later (below, p.231).

Chapter LXXX

*How the King of France advanced close to Calais to counter the
King of England's siege, but could go no further.*

Now I shall return to the valiant King Edward, who was still before Calais
as he'd been for half a year. Hearing that King Philip had sent a general
summons throughout France for nobles and non-nobles alike to join him at
Amiens around Pentecost to raise the siege of Calais, King Edward began to
consider how to overcome the French and sustain the siege long enough to starve
the city into surrender; for it was clearly so strong and well garrisoned that he
wasn't going to take it by assault or skirmishing, and it grieved him to see his
men pointlessly killed and crippled in attacks. So he ordered the building of a
lofty castle of thick, heavy timber on the sea shore, and filled it with bombards,
springalds and other machines and artillery, and posted forty men-at-arms and
two hundred archers there; and they kept such a close guard upon the harbour
and port of Calais that nothing could sail in or out without being battered and
wrecked. This was a greater blow to the city's resistance than anything else had
been.

Next King Edward persuaded the Flemings to rise and march on Cassel, Aire
and Saint-Omer, burning and destroying the country as they went. So the King
of France headed for Arras and sent most of his men towards Saint-Omer and
Aire, where they had mighty clashes with the Flemings, sometimes winning and
sometimes losing, before the Flemings were finally driven back, whereupon the
French completely laid waste the land called Laleu.[1]

It was while King Philip was at Arras and his men were preparing to do battle
with the Flemings that messengers arrived from Calais begging him to bring
speedy help, as they had no food left. Among those in Calais were two of King
Philip's captains, Sir Jean de Vienne[2] and his companion Sir Jehan de Faerye, and
Sir Arnoul d'Audrehem,[3] a brave and valiant knight, one of the finest in France;
the lord of Beaulot[4] was there, too, and many other good knights whose names
I don't know, and Sir Baulduyn d'Obrecicourt, who died there, shouldn't be
omitted. When King Philip heard this news he was filled with grief and pity, and
he summoned all his men and headed for Hesdin, saying he intended to advance
on the English army and would consider nothing else until he'd raised the siege
of Calais. He left Hesdin the following day and marched to Fauquembergues,
and then made camp around Guînes, which had been razed to the ground and
the surrounding land laid waste; and early next morning he came and camped
on the heights at Sangatte,[5] quite close now to the English army. His forces were
so immense that I can't tell or even guess the number, and when the men of

---

[1] 'La Loye': an area between Arras, Saint-Omer and Ypres.
[2] 'Jean de Vyane'.
[3] 'Arnoul d'Endehen'.
[4] Enguerrand de Beaulo.
[5] 'sur le mont de Sangate': the Mont d'Hubert and the high ground alongside. The French arrived there on 26 July.

Calais saw them on the hill at Sangatte they were overjoyed, feeling sure they were about to raise the siege; but when they saw them making camp their hearts began to sink somewhat.

Now I'll tell you what the noble King Edward did. When he saw King Philip coming with such a mighty host to do battle and raise the siege of Calais, which had cost him so heavily in men and effort and money, just when he had the city under such pressure that it couldn't hold out much longer, he was extremely reluctant to leave. He decided that there were only two ways the French could get to him and the city of Calais: either over the dunes along the sea shore, or by cutting inland over ground littered with bogs and marshes traversed by only one bridge, the bridge of Nieulay.[1] So he ordered all his ships and vessels to go and anchor facing the dunes, arrayed with bombards, springalds and archers so that the French army wouldn't dare to go that way, and sent his cousin the Earl of Derby to camp beside the bridge at Nieulay with a large contingent of men-at-arms and archers, so that the only way the French could cross would be over the marshes, which were impassable. Moreover, there was a tower beyond the hill at Sangatte held by thirty-two Englishmen; they'd strengthened its defences mightily with massive double ditches, and this, too, blocked the way across the dunes. But when the French were encamped on the hill at Sangatte, as you've heard, men from the city [of Tournai][2] attacked this tower; the English used their bows to great effect, but the attackers delivered such a fierce assault that they took the tower and put all its defenders to the sword.

Once the French had made camp, King Philip sent his marshals, the lord of Beaujeu and the lord of Saint-Venant, on a scouting mission to find the best way of approaching the English army. They looked at all the possible paths and returned to the king and told him bluntly that there was no way of approaching the English unless he wanted to suffer greater losses than they'd had at Crécy.

Next morning after mass, King Philip sent high-ranking emissaries to the King of England. They crossed the bridge at Nieulay with the Earl of Derby's leave, and came to the king and told him he'd done great wrong in laying siege to the city of Calais. And they asked him on their king's behalf to allow free passage so that they could meet in battle; if he was unwilling to do that, King Philip would withdraw to suitable ground so that they could do battle there and let God grant victory to one or the other.

When King Edward heard these words he thought for a moment and then said: "Sirs, I understand what your lord – call him what you will – is saying. But he is wrongfully holding my inheritance.[3] Tell him from me that I've been here almost a year, in his full view and knowledge; he could have come much sooner if he'd wanted! But he's let me stay so long that I've incurred great expense! And I believe it will soon have earned me lordship of the fine city of Calais! So I'm

[1] 'Milays'.
[2] The MS simply reads 'les communes'; there is clearly an accidental omission here, and other accounts all refer to the involvement of men from Tournai.
[3] Edward may again be referring to the county of Ponthieu (as above, p.179); but he may be referring more dramatically to the kingdom of France.

not inclined to do anything to please or suit or satisfy your lord; nor do I intend to leave the land I've conquered or mean to conquer, and if he's finding one route difficult he'll have to take another."

The emissaries saw they would have no other response and returned and reported to King Philip. He was dismayed and utterly nonplussed – and no wonder: he'd brought so many noble lords from far-flung lands and realised now that he would have to turn back with nothing done.

It was at this point that two cardinals arrived who'd long been discussing how to make peace between the two kings. They approached King Philip first, asking him to allow a truce of three days to see if they could negotiate some settlement with the King of England; then they came to King Edward and made the same request. He agreed to this, and sent as his delegates the worthy Earl of Derby, the Earl of Northampton, Sir Walter Mauny (in whom he placed great faith) and Sir Reginald Cobham. Representing King Philip came the Duke of Bourbon, Sir John of Hainault, the lord of Beaujeu and Sir Geoffroi de Charny. These lords deliberated throughout the three days, with the two cardinals moving between the parties as mediators, but no agreement could be found. And while they were negotiating the noble king was constantly strengthening his position, building great earthworks in the dunes to prevent any French advance. And the long debate did little to please the people of Calais: it merely extended their fast.

When King Philip saw that no agreement would be reached he decided to head for Arras and leave the people of Calais to make terms with the English. So next day[1] he ordered his army to strike camp. The hardest heart in the world would have wept to see the people of Calais lament and grieve as they watched his army leaving without bringing them aid. As for the English, when they saw the French striking camp, a good number ventured out to attack their tail; they found many abandoned tents and won a load of bread and wine and victuals brought there by tavern-keepers who'd promptly fled at the sight of the English: they plundered and destroyed the whole encampment.

When the people of Calais realised King Philip had gone and all hope was lost, and that they were so stricken with famine that even the strongest could barely go on, they decided it was best to place themselves entirely in the King of England's hands and at his mercy if the only alternative was to starve to death, for most of them were almost deranged with hunger and likely to lose both body and soul. They were all in agreement, and begged their commander Sir Jean[2] de Vienne to open negotiations. He went to the battlements and signalled that he wished to parley. The king immediately sent the Earl of Northampton, Sir Walter Mauny, Sir Reginald Cobham and Sir Thomas Holland, and when they arrived Sir Jean said to them:

"You are very worthy knights, sirs, and you know that the King of France, whom we acknowledge as our lord, sent us here with orders to defend the city and castle to avoid any shame to us and loss to him. We've done this to the best

---

[1]   2 August.
[2]   Despite giving the name correctly earlier (above, p.198), the MS here and throughout the following passage accidentally reads 'Louis'.

of our ability. But now help has failed us, and you've kept us under such close siege that we have no victuals left and will die in agonies of hunger unless the noble king has mercy on us. For pity's sake, dear sirs, beg him to have mercy and allow us to leave, just as we are, and he can take the city and the castle and all its wealth: he'll find plenty!"

Sir Walter Mauny replied, saying: "Sir Jean, we're clear about our lord's intentions because he's made them plain to us. He doesn't intend to let you go as you say; he wants you all to put yourselves entirely at his mercy, and he'll either accept ransoms for those he chooses or put you to death, for you've done him many injuries, caused him great expense and cost him the lives of many of his men: that he is angry is no surprise."

"These terms are too hard to accept!" Sir Jean replied. "We're a small company of knights and squires who've served our lord as faithfully as we could, as you would serve yours in such a case, and we've suffered many hardships; but we'd rather endure the greatest torment ever visited upon man than allow the lowliest fellow in the city to suffer a worse fate than the loftiest! We humbly implore you to beg your king to have pity and accept us at least as prisoners, alive and unharmed."

Sir Walter said they would willingly take this message and do what they could. They told the king all that had been said, but he ignored all pleas and arguments and refused outright to comply with this last request.

"I think that's a mistake, sire," said Sir Walter Mauny. "It wouldn't bode well if you were to send us to one of your strongholds! By holy Mary, we wouldn't be so willing to go if you condemn these people to death as you say, for we'd suffer the same fate in a similar position, even though we were doing our duty."

This reasoning greatly softened the king's heart, and he said: "Fellow lords, I don't wish to be a lone voice in this. Go back and tell them that, for love of you, I shall willingly receive them as prisoners; but I want six of the foremost citizens to come before me in their shifts, pure and simple, with nooses round their necks and the keys of the city in their hands, and I shall do with them exactly as I please."

The lords returned to Sir Jean with this reply and told him it had been hard-won. Sir Jean said that, since there was nothing else for it, he would report to the citizens and his companions. So he left the battlements and gave orders for the bell to be rung to summon the people of the city, men and women alike, who were all desperate to hear good news, tortured by hunger as they were. The knight told them what had happened, whereupon they began to howl and lament most piteously. Then the wealthiest of all the citizens – his name was Eustace de Saint-Pierre – stood up and announced to them all:

"Sirs, it would be a grievous pity and calamity to allow all these people here to die, of famine or otherwise, and if any man could save them it would be a great charity and a most worthy deed in the eyes of Our Lord. For my own part, I have such faith in Our Lord that, if I can save these people through my death, I'm sure I shall have forgiveness for my misdeeds. I shall be the first of the six, and place myself at King Edward's mercy, barefoot and stripped to my shift and with a noose at my neck."

At these words they all worshipped him, overcome with emotion, many men and women falling at his feet – and little wonder, for the agonies of hunger they'd endured for more than six weeks are unimaginable. And after the worthy Eustace had spoken as you've heard, another of the richest citizens stood up likewise and said he would be the second. Then a third citizen stood, then a fourth and a fifth and a sixth. I shan't bother to name them all; but they all declared of their own free will that, to save the rest of the people there, they would place themselves, exactly as he'd demanded, at the mercy of King Edward, deemed the most valiant prince in the world. It was a great pity for them and a great service to the people of the city.

Chapter LXXXI

How six burghers of Calais, stripped to their shifts and with nooses at their necks, delivered the keys of the city to the King of England.

These six burghers, the wealthiest men of the city, wanted to save the rest of the people and fulfil King Edward's demands. They immediately reduced themselves to the demanded state and said to the knights:

"We so much desire to save the people of this city that we've submitted to the required conditions, as you see, and have the keys of the castle and the city with us. Take us to him now, and pray that he may have mercy on us."

The four knights took these six burghers and led them to the king. The whole army was assembled: there was a mighty press, as you may imagine, some saying they should be hanged directly and others weeping for pity. The noble king arrived, accompanied by his earls and barons, and the Queen – who was pregnant – followed after to see what would happen. The six burghers immediately knelt before the king and said:

"Most worthy king, you see before you six citizens of Calais, great merchants and members of its longest established families. We bring you the keys of the city and the castle, and surrender them to your will. And we submit ourselves entirely to your mercy, in the state you see, to save the rest of the people who have suffered many hardships. We beg you, in your great nobility, to have pity and mercy upon us."

Truly, every lord and knight present wept for pity or was moved to do so; but the king's heart at that moment was so hardened by anger that for a long while he couldn't reply. Then he commanded that they be beheaded at once. All the lords and knights, weeping, earnestly begged him to have mercy, but he refused to listen. Then that worthy knight Sir Walter Mauny spoke up, saying:

"Ah, gentle lord! Restrain your heart! You're renowned and famed for all noble qualities: don't do anything now to make men speak ill of you. If you refuse to have mercy everyone will say you have a heart full of cruelty, putting to death these good citizens who've come of their own free will to surrender to you to save the rest of the people."

But the king frowned and replied: "Accept it, Sir Walter: I have made up my mind. Call for the executioner. The people of Calais have cost me the lives of so many of my men that these men, too, must die."

[At that the noble Queen of England, weeping bitterly, fell on her knees before her husband and said:][1] "Ah, my worthy lord! Since I crossed the sea – in great peril, as you know – I've asked for nothing. But now I beg and implore you with clasped hands, for the love of Our Lady's son, have mercy on them."

The worthy king fell silent for a moment; he looked at the Queen on her knees before him, weeping bitter tears, and his heart began to soften a little and he said:

"Lady, I wish you were anywhere but here! Your entreaties are so heartfelt that I daren't refuse you! Though it pains me to say it, take them: I give these men to you."

And he took the six burghers by their halters and handed them over to the Queen, and spared all the people of Calais from death out of love for her. And the good lady bade that the six burghers be freshly clothed and made comfortable.

And so it was that King Edward laid siege to the mighty city of Calais at the end of August in the year of grace 1346, and it surrendered to him in the same month in the year 1347.[2] We must assume he was very determined to win it! For he stayed there a whole year and spent a small fortune in expenses, to pay his troops, to build housing and engines – not to mention the costs he was incurring in Scotland, Gascony, Brittany, Poitou and all the other regions where he was waging war or having it waged on his behalf. I don't believe you'll find that any Christian king in history ever waged war in so many lands at once, or could sustain such costs and expense as he has done thus far; what will happen in the future I don't know. But now I'll return to our story.

After delivering the six burghers to the Queen, the noble king sent his marshals, Sir Walter Mauny and a number of others into the city to take possession and control. He ordered them to take Sir Jean de Vienne and all his fellow knights and send them to England, while all the other soldiers and all the people of the city were to be driven out with nothing more than the clothes on their backs. These commands were duly carried out. And the marshals made the soldiers bring all their equipment to the market place and throw it in a heap. Then they took possession of all the citizens' houses, which they ordered were to be left untouched, on pain of hanging. When all was done the king and the queen entered the city to mighty fanfares of trumpets and clarions, and the king held a great court in the castle. Then he dismissed those of his men he no longer needed, but kept a large number of men-at-arms and stayed in Calais for three weeks to put the city and castle back in good order and to arrange who would remain as its guard and who would now live in the city.

I think it's sad indeed to contemplate what became of those worthy burghers and good ladies of the city – there were many in Calais, of great wealth and rich

---

[1] There is clearly an accidental omission in the surviving MS of Le Bel; all versions of Froissart contain phrases to this effect.
[2] To be precise, the siege began on 4 September and the city surrendered on 3 August.

inheritance – who had to abandon everything they owned and leave the city with nothing but the clothes they wore. It would be a hard-hearted man indeed who felt no pity – not least King Philip, who did nothing to relieve them. At that time he'd withdrawn to Arras, where he gave leave to all his foreign troops and sent large contingents of his best men to guard the frontiers, to prevent further English advances on this side of the sea. It's a clear sign that he'd no intention of trying to do to the English in their land what the King of England had done – and was still doing – to him.

Meanwhile the two cardinals were at work, mediating between the two parties until a truce was agreed: it was to last until the feast of Saint John (which would be the year 1348), and in the meantime each side was to retain the territory it currently held.[1] Once this truce was concluded King Philip disbanded his army and returned to Paris.

For his part King Edward appointed a Lombard as castellan of Calais and installed a large garrison there of fine men-at-arms, along with a great many people who wanted to work and do business in those handsome burghers' houses; and he distributed to the soldiers and men who were to live there all the arms and equipment left behind by the French. Then he and his worthy queen sailed back to England and arrived in London,[2] where they were received with great splendour and joy. You can imagine how highly the king was honoured.

While there, he went to visit his prisoners. He greeted them most courteously and had them dine with him in a full hall. What a fine company of prisoners it was: King Edward had reason to thank God indeed, when he had as captives the King of Scotland and the Earl of Moray who had burnt and ravaged his land, Lord Charles of Blois, Duke of Brittany,[3] who'd been sent to him along with the Constable of France (the Count of Guînes and Eu), the Chamberlain de Tancarville (vicomte de Melun), the captain of Calais Sir Jean de Vienne, and many other knights of one shield[4] and eminent burghers of Amiens and the major towns[5] of Normandy. And meanwhile his enemies held none of his men captive at all![6] In my view – which I share with the world – it should be considered a sign of great honour and a great blessing from God, as indeed it was, that, as

---

[1]   The truce was concluded on 28 September, and was to last until a fortnight after the feast of John the Baptist, 7 July 1348.
[2]   On 14 October.
[3]   Another accidental scribal omission seems probable here. It is highly unlikely that Le Bel would have failed to use a qualifying phrase along the lines of Froissart's 'who called himself Duke of Brittany'.
[4]   See footnote 5, above, p.196.
[5]   The 'bonnes villes': see footnote 4, below, p.232.
[6]   Edward had in fact acquired so many prisoners that the Tower of London couldn't cope! On 2 August 1347 ('the twenty-first year of our reign in England and the eighth in France'), while still besieging Calais, he had to write to his Chancellor complaining that 'because our Tower of London is over-charged with prisoners, we instructed you in our previous letters to divide them up and put them in other places where they can securely stay', and he irritably ordered him to do so then 'without further delay...and if the constables or lieutenants of the said castles are unwilling to obey our orders, have them punished in the appropriate manner'. [The National Archives, C 81/322/18648; printed in Viard and Déprez's edition of Le Bel, Appendix XXIII].

well as this, he and his men had destroyed and laid waste the whole land of Scotland between the city of Perth and the great forest of Jedburgh, and won the city of Berwick and all the surrounding fortresses, and elsewhere his men had ravaged and laid waste most of Gascony almost as far as Toulouse, and, nearer at hand, had ravaged and wasted all of Poitou and won many major towns and strong castles such as Lusignan, Saint-Jean-d'Angély and the city of Poitiers, and likewise the great land of Brittany; and he personally had destroyed and laid waste the lands of the Cotentin and Normandy and the county of Évreux as far as Paris, and crossed the great River Seine at the bridge of Poissy and ravaged and wasted the country around Amiens and Beauvais and the county of Ponthieu, and had then stood arrayed for battle, with a small army in open fields, without ditches or fortifications, to face the entire might of France, and had held the field for two whole days and vanquished, captured and killed all the greatest lords in the kingdom of France, the Empire and Germany, and then laid siege to the mighty city of Calais and stayed there for a year without once returning home, and at the end of that year had taken it as you've heard. It seems to me that such great and lofty exploits are not without high honour, and that one cannot praise, esteem or honour too much the very noble king whom God so clearly wished to help. But I shall say no more of that; I'll return now to our story.

Chapter LXXXII

How bands of brigands assembled and pillaged towns and castles in Brittany and elsewhere.

Throughout the year of the truce the two kings remained at peace with one another; but that didn't stop the valiant knight Sir William Douglas and the wild Scots who were based with him in the forest of Jedburgh from continuing to wage war upon the English and inflicting damage wherever they could – despite the fact that their lord King David was a prisoner of the King of England.

Nor did the truce stop the campaigning of King Edward's men in Gascony and Poitou. King Philip's forces didn't observe the truce, either, and both sides kept capturing strongholds from each other, either by force or subterfuge – often by scaling walls at night, for instance, or through treachery – and many impressive encounters took place, in which honours were shared.

And all the while brigands were on the lookout for chances to pillage towns and castles; they won amazing amounts of loot, some of them becoming so rich that they set themselves up as captains and masters of the others: one of them amassed a fortune of forty thousand écus. Their regular method was to stake out a promising castle or town for a couple of days, after which thirty or forty of them would band together and creep up to the town from more than one direction, make their way in just before dawn, and set fire to one of the houses; the townsfolk would imagine they were an army of a thousand men-at-arms and go rushing off in panic, and the brigands would break into their homes and ransack and pillage everything and then disappear, laden with loot. That's what happened at Donzenac and many other places.

Among these brigands was one who'd been keeping watch on a very strong castle called Comborn, which stands in fine country near Limoges. He took thirty of his companions to the castle and used scaling ladders to enter; they seized possession, and took the lord (named the vicomte de Comborn) in his bed and slaughtered the whole household. They imprisoned the lord in his own castle and kept him there until he paid a ransom of twenty thousand écus. But the brigand retained possession of the castle, put it in fine defensive order, and sold it for thirty thousand écus to King Philip, who also made him one of his personal guards! This brigand, whose name was Bascon,[1] cut a fine figure in Paris and indeed throughout France, always splendidly dressed and mounted.

In the duchy of Brittany likewise towns and castles were pillaged and plundered. Among the brigands here was one called Croquart. All his life he'd been a poor page and servant to the lord of Erkes in Holland, but when he was old enough he took leave of his master and went to the wars in Brittany, where he did so well for himself that before long he was reputed to have forty thousand écus to his name, not to mention a stable of thirty or forty good coursers. He'd earned a reputation, too, as one of the finest fighting men in all the land, and was chosen to be one of the thirty English who did battle against the thirty French in Brittany – you'll hear about this a little later – and was one of those taken captive there. But a great misfortune finally befell him: he was out riding his courser in the fields one day, and in trying to jump a ditch he fell and broke his neck. I don't know who acquired his wealth. As time went on these brigands multiplied to such a degree that they caused much suffering in the lands they haunted.

Chapter LXXXIII

How King Edward personally saved the castle of Calais,
treacherously sold by its castellan to Sir Geoffroi de Charny.

Then came the time, in the year 1348, that Sir Geoffroi de Charny, a most worthy and valiant knight, persuaded the Lombard named Aymery,[2] whom King Edward had trusted so much that he'd made him governor and keeper of Calais castle, to deliver the castle to him under cover of night for the sum of twenty thousand écus. But King Edward somehow learned of the deal (I don't know how), and summoned the Lombard to him and got him to reveal the truth – willingly or otherwise. When the king had heard all the details he pondered a while and then said to the Lombard:

"If you promise to do as I say, I'll forgive you completely and make you a member of my council forever."

The Lombard was only too happy to agree.

[1] Le Bel gives his name as '*Bacon*', but this is almost certainly Jean de Gasnoye, the highly successful independent captain (Le Bel – not, it might be said, without reason – consistently refers to these figures as 'brigands') who called himself *Le Bascon de Mareuil*. He reappears later in the Chronicle, but probably in error: see below, p.253.
[2] Aimeric of Pavia.

"In that case," said the king, "this is what you're to do. I want you to take the money and do as you promised him. Tell him to be ready with plenty of men-at-arms and all the cash! Then do just as you agreed and leave the rest to me. But don't give a hint to any man alive that I know anything about it!"

The Lombard promised not to, and went away delighted that he would have his money with the king's approval – he didn't care what happened next! Back he went to Calais and spoke in secret to Sir Geoffroi de Charny, and they agreed that the plan would go ahead and the Lombard would have the twenty thousand. Then he sent his brother to King Edward as a hostage, to ensure that he faithfully fulfilled his command and to inform the king of the day and time when the plan was to be carried out.

Once the king knew of the time and day he resolved to undertake a bold mission, such a one as no other prince would dare, preferring to risk his own life and his son's than to lose by treachery what had cost him so much to win – and feeling that he was more likely to succeed in the mission than anyone he might send. He arrived in Calais in the middle of the night before the planned day of attack, and he and some of his men took up positions [in towers and chambers of the castle][1] while others hid under cover of tumbled masonry;[2] and they stayed there all the following day, so quietly that no one was aware of their presence. When midnight came[3] Sir Geoffroi arrived with ten thousand foot soldiers and a huge body of men-at-arms, his intention being that, if he captured the castle, he would take the city after. And when the Lombard thought the time had come, he went and found Sir Geoffroi and told him that all was in place if he had the money. Sir Geoffroi replied that the money was ready, but he was going to send two squires ahead with him to make sure it was as he said. This he did. It appeared to the squires that he was telling the truth; they reported as much to their master, and the money was duly handed over. The Lombard took it and carried it off, telling them to follow quietly and avoid making any racket. He passed through the gate and left it open, and slipped into the porter's room. The first band of knights commanded by Sir Geoffroi entered the gate, whereupon the noble king and his son leapt out crying:

"To the death! To the death!"

Their men were right behind them, and the twelve sent forward by Sir Geoffroi were all killed instantly. Then torches were lit in great numbers, and the noble king and his men sallied forth and fell upon Sir Geoffroi and his dumbstruck forces, who thought there were twice as many English as there were! They realised they'd been tricked, and some of them took to flight; but others mounted a vigorous defence and a fearsome battle ensued. That valiant knight Sir Geoffroi fought exceedingly well, as did a good number of squires whose names I don't know; but the one who performed with outstanding valour was Sir Eustace de Ribemont, who fought hand to hand with the king. And a valiant young knight named Sir Henry du Boys was killed there. While the noble king was embroiled

---

1 This phrase, clearly an accidental omission from the MS, is borrowed from Froissart.
2 Literally 'enclosed themselves in old walling'.
3 It was the night of 31 December 1349 – 1 January 1350.

in this mighty combat the people of the town had been roused and taken up arms, and now came running with blazing torches to join the fray. When the French saw this they broke and fled as best they could, but a great many were left there dead; and the fleeing foot soldiers, who couldn't see a thing in the dark, went plunging into a deep river where a huge number drowned.

Such was the daring rescue of Calais castle. And Sir Geoffroi de Charny, who had hatched the whole plot, was taken prisoner along with Sir Eustace de Ribemont and some ten others whose names I don't know.

When the battle was over, the valiant king and his companions returned to the castle with their prisoners and had them disarmed and called for supper to be prepared, while outside, all the people of the town were astounded by the sudden appearance of the king and the extraordinary adventure that had taken place.

When supper was ready the noble King Edward bade all the captive knights sup beside him at his table, treating them with all the honour and respect that were their due. And when supper was over he spoke to them for a fair while about various matters, in the course of which he said to Sir Geoffroi de Charny:

"Sir Geoffroi, I've little cause to love you when you try to steal by night what I bought at such expense and effort! It gives me great satisfaction that I caught you in the act! You planned to have it more cheaply than I, for twenty thousand écus! But God came to my aid and stopped you achieving your goal. And He'll help me again, if it please Him, as surely as He knows that my cause is just and good."

Then he addressed Sir Eustace and said: "I've never seen any knight in all the world assail his enemies more valiantly than you, or defend himself with more skill; nor has any knight in any battle given me a sterner test in fighting man to man. I award you the prize above all others in this day's combat." Then the king took a gorgeous chaplet he was wearing, richly adorned with pearls, and placed it on Sir Eustace's head, saying: "In token of the prize I give you this chaplet, and with all my heart I pray you wear it this whole year whenever you're in the company of lords and ladies and damsels – of whom I understand you're very fond! – and give me your word that you'll tell everyone that I gave it to you, and why. If you promise to do this I'll release you from your imprisonment, for the sake of the ladies and damsels."

When the knight heard this his heart was filled with joy, and little wonder; and he thanked the king most humbly and vowed to do as he'd asked. Then they all went to bed to rest till it was time for mass.

Then the noble king and all the others rose and heard mass before going to dine. After dinner the noble king gave Sir Eustace two horses and twenty écus to provide for his homeward journey; then he boarded ship and took Sir Geoffroi de Charny and his fellow captives with him back to London. They received a splendid welcome, for no one knew what had become of the king. As for King Philip, he was stunned and dismayed by this adventure, and little wonder.

Chapter LXXXIV

How King Philip and his son remarried, and King Philip died soon after and the Duke of Normandy was crowned king.

Not long after the adventure in which King Edward saved the castle at Calais from treachery, the Queen of France – King Philip's wife and sister to the Duke of Burgundy – passed from this world. So too did the lady Bonne, wife of the Duke of Normandy and daughter of the most worthy and noble-hearted king who ever lived, the King of Bohemia. I don't know which of these two ladies died first, though many people say it was lady Bonne – I'm not sure why or if they're right.[1] In any event, the father and son were both widowed fairly soon after each other and remarried equally soon. And the father took a fair young damsel whom his son was keen to have! But he preferred to take her for himself, for she was as gracious and as beautiful as a man could rightly wish – but he was her cousin german.[2] She was the daughter of the King of Navarre who died in Granada during the King of Spain's siege of Algeciras, and the sister of Navarre's present king (of whom you'll hear great wonders in due course). The son meanwhile, the Duke of Normandy, followed his father's advice and married the Countess of Boulogne;[3] she was the widow of his cousin german, the young Duke of Burgundy who had died by great misfortune at the siege of Aiguillon.[4] Both of these marriages were clearly against the commandments of Holy Church, but Pope Clement gave his consent to them, not daring to do otherwise.

In the year of grace 1349 the 'swelling' sickness[5] appeared – physicians call it the epidemic – which led to a great mortality throughout the world, among Saracens and Christians alike; you'll find it referred to earlier. And in July of that year, in great splendour, the King of the Romans, Lord Charles of Bohemia, crowned his second wife.[6]

In the year of grace 1350 King Philip of France died,[7] and his son the Duke of Normandy was crowned at Reims.[8] He was named King John of France, and he immediately chose to debase the coinage, ordering the minting of new écus called *Johannes* of which a third part was copper. And it wasn't long before he went to Pope Clement at Avignon and asked to be granted tithes from his kingdom's clergy and other privileges. When he'd got what he wanted from the Pope he went to Montpellier, and then via Narbonne to Carcassonne where he

---

1   Both died of bubonic plague, Bonne of Luxembourg on 11 September 1349 and the Queen, Jeanne of Burgundy, on 12 December.
2   Philip married Blanche of Navarre on 11 January 1350.
3   John, Duke of Normandy, married Jeanne, Countess of Auvergne and Boulogne, on 9 February.
4   Duke Philippe had died in an accident during the siege in August 1346, as described above, p.185.
5   '*la maladie de la boche*': see footnote 3, above, p.99.
6   The Emperor Charles IV, widowed by the death of his first wife Blanche of Valois, married Anna, daughter of Rudolph II, Duke of Bavaria and Count Palatine of the Rhine, in March 1349; she was crowned at Aachen on 26 July.
7   On the night of 22-23 August.
8   On 26 September.

stayed for a while – I don't know how long – before returning through Gascony and Limousin and Poitou to Paris. And everywhere he found the land burnt and laid waste, and many towns and castles which had once belonged to his kingdom now lost: they were held by the English in determined defiance. He appealed in distress to his knights and barons for advice on what he should do.

They urged him to lay siege to Saint-Jean-d'Angély. To undertake the siege he sent his two marshals, Sir Guy de Nesle[1] and that valiant knight the lord of Beaujeu,[2] with a great force of men-at-arms and Genoese and foot soldiers. In laying siege to the town they exploited two *bastides*[3] which they found just half a league away. It was about the middle of Lent. They mounted constant patrols around the town to stop any supplies getting through, but the defenders boldly resisted any attempted attacks and the French inflicted little damage. About the beginning of May the men in the town sent messengers to the noble King of England to beg and entreat him either to come and raise the siege or to send fresh provisions, for their food was starting to run very short and they couldn't hold out much longer.

Chapter LXXXV

How the English and Gascons defeated the French outside Saint-Jean-d'Angély.

King Edward said he would gladly respond, and without delay, to the plea from Saint-Jean-d'Angély. He sent a most valiant knight, Sir John Beauchamp, and a number of others over the sea to Bordeaux, with instructions to request the lord of Albret, the lord of Pommiers,[4] the lord of Lesparre, Alixandre lord of Chaumont and all his other knights and friends in Gascony to prepare to raise the siege of Saint-Jean-d'Angély, or to replenish its supplies so that it could continue to resist.

Sir John Beauchamp and his companions put to sea and sailed to Bordeaux, where they appealed to the Gascon knights and lords for help as the king had bidden them. They made the best and quickest preparations possible, and had soon mustered six hundred men-at-arms, two thousand archers and a good seven thousand foot soldiers, and amassed a plentiful supply of corn, flour, livestock, salted meat and other provisions which they would drive into Saint-Jean-d'Angély by force if they found they couldn't bring the besiegers to battle: they knew the French were so well fortified inside their *bastides* that there'd be no way of fighting unless they were willing.

They crossed the great Gironde river and advanced into Poitou, heading for Saint-Jean-d'Angély to carry out their mission. The lords besieging Saint-Jean heard the news, and agreed that the lord of Beaujeu should stay before the town with half their forces, while Sir Guy de Nesle, Sir Renault de Pons (another worthy

---

[1]   '*Guy de Noyelle*'.
[2]   '*Beaugny*'.
[3]   Fortified new towns, often built on a grid system rather like a Roman *castrum*.
[4]   '*Pontmers*'.

knight who was there), Sir Arnoul d'Audrehem and several other valiant men should go with the other half of the army to guard the bridge over a major river called the Charente, which the English would have to cross to reach Saint-Jean-d'Angély. It was only five leagues away, and the lords set out from the *bastide* by night and reached the bridge at daybreak. By terce[1] they were encamped there.

The English and Gascon lords came to this river expecting to cross, and were shocked and dismayed to see the French in fine array at the bridge. There was no other possible crossing-place, and if they risked a crossing there they'd be sure to come off worse, for a hundred men on the opposite bank would be worth ten thousand struggling across. They spent a long time in debate, very reluctant to retreat but equally reluctant to place themselves in such obvious danger. And all the while the archers and the Genoese were trading shots, though the river was between them.

They finally decided it was best to turn back, and this they did. But the French lords, seeing them leaving, said they wouldn't return to camp: they'd go and win their supplies! They rode over the bridge and swiftly after them, yelling and bawling, all with shields in position. Seeing them charging in pursuit, the English and Gascon lords said they asked for nothing more! They turned back and prepared to face them. Then a splendid battle began, for all the combatants were the flower of chivalry and élite fighting men. But some from both sides were brought to the ground. The battle raged for a long while, for on neither side were they men to be quickly beaten: it was hand to hand and peer to peer, and you may be sure there were many fine feats of prowess and skill and bold rescues performed by both parties. But it was the French who finally had the worse of it; they were defeated at last, with many killed and wounded. The English and Gascons didn't come off much better, but they won the field and captured the king's marshal, Sir Guy de Nesle, along with Sir Renault de Pons, Sir Arnoul d'Audrehem and a good number of other knights and squires whose names I don't know – fully forty valuable prisoners in all.

They camped that night on the battlefield,[2] and set off next morning back towards Bordeaux with their prisoners and all the provisions, for they couldn't see how to get them through to Saint-Jean-d'Angély while the French had control of the bridge. When they reached Bordeaux and Sir John Beauchamp and his companions had rested, they sailed back with all their prisoners and presented them to the King of England; he was delighted to receive them, for their numbers were ever growing.

But if King Edward was cheered by these events, King John was distressed; and he vowed that, for the soul of the good king his father, he would go in person to Saint-Jean-d'Angély and wouldn't leave, come what may, until the town was in his power. He set off at once,[3] bidding everyone follow.

---

[1]   The third canonical hour, about 9 a.m.
[2]   The battle is thought to have taken place outside the village of Saint-Georges near Saintes on 1 April 1351.
[3]   He didn't leave Paris, in fact, until the second half of August.

While he was on his way, the people and the garrison in the town, seeing there was no chance of receiving victuals and provisions, began to negotiate with their besiegers; and they finally agreed a truce, to last for fifteen days, in which time they were not to attempt to find fresh supplies of food or anything else, but were to send to Bordeaux and England for help; in the event that no help arrived within the fortnight, they would surrender with their lives and possessions spared.

King John reached the besieging army three days after this truce had been agreed, and when the townsfolk learned of his arrival they were afraid he wouldn't approve of the terms, and went to him and humbly begged him, on their knees, to honour the agreement. King John considered the matter, and replied that he would keep the truce his knights had made. He stayed there for the twelve days that were left to run, because if he'd broken the terms of the truce and tried to end the town's resistance, the King of England might have thought he didn't dare wait to do battle with him. And knowing for certain that the defenders were desperate for food, he sent a good quantity of victuals to the town, at a reasonable price, to keep them going for the remaining twelve days.

When the time was up and no one appeared, the people of the town opened the gates and received King John with great joy and acknowledged him as their lord. It was the year of grace 1351, around the month of August,[1] that the town of Saint-Jean-d'Angély was surrendered to King John of France, after his forces had besieged it for seven months. Once he'd installed his garrison, King John made his way back across France.

Chapter LXXXVI

How thirty French agreed to do battle against thirty English and Germans in Brittany, and the English and Germans were defeated.

In this same period, there took place in Brittany an extraordinary deed of arms which should certainly not be forgotten. To make things clear, you need to understand that the war in Brittany was continuing between the rival parties of the two ladies: although Lord Charles of Blois was a prisoner in England, and although there was a truce between the two kings, hostilities continued between the forces of the Countess of Montfort and Lord Charles of Blois's wife.[2]

And one day Sir Jean de Beaumanoir,[3] a most valiant knight of the highest Breton lineage, who was captain of the castle of Josselin and had a mighty company of men-at-arms and squires of his noble line, arrived before the castle of Ploërmel. Its castellan – who was on the Countess of Montfort's side – was a soldier from Germany called Brandebourch,[4] and he had with him a large number

---

[1]   The probable date of the surrender was 31 August.
[2]   Jeanne de Penthièvre.
[3]   *'Robert de Beaumont'*; throughout this passage Le Bel refers to him as 'Sir Robert' and I have corrected it to 'Jean'. Le Bel (or his scribe) may have confused the name with Robert Bramborough: see the next note.
[4]   Other accounts refer to 'Bramborc' and 'Robert Bramborough' (or 'Robert of Bamborough'), an English captain of Ploërmel. German mercenaries were certainly involved and I have

of German soldiers as well as Bretons and English. When Sir Jean saw that none of the garrison would come out, he went to the gate and called for Brandebourch to come and parley; and he asked him if there were two or three knights in the castle who'd be willing to joust – with lances of war[1] – against three of his knights for love of their ladies.

Brandebourch replied that their sweethearts wouldn't want them to get themselves killed as miserably as in a single joust, "for that's a game of chance that's over in moments, and you're more likely to gain a reputation for recklessness and folly than honour and worth! But I'll tell you what we'll do: if it please you, pick twenty or thirty companions from your garrison and I'll do the same from ours, and we'll go to a good field where we won't be troubled or impeded, and command both parties and all those watching, on pain of hanging, that no one is to interfere and either baulk or aid the combatants."

"Thirty against thirty it is!" said Sir Jean. "I swear it, by my faith."

"As do I," said Brandebourch, "for any man who performs well in that contest will earn more honour than in a joust."

And so it was settled, and the day was fixed for the following Wednesday, which was four days later. In the meantime each man chose his thirty as he pleased, and each of the sixty equipped himself as finely as he could.

When the day arrived Brandebourch's thirty companions heard mass and then armed and rode to the appointed place of battle. They all dismounted, and gave instructions to everyone present that no one should be so bold as to intervene, regardless of what befell them. These thirty, whom we'll call English, had to wait a long time for the others, whom we'll call French. When the thirty French arrived they dismounted and, as the English had done, forbade anyone to come to their assistance. Some people say that four or five of the French remained on horseback at the entrance to the field and only twenty-five dismounted like the English; I don't know for certain, as I wasn't there. In any event, all sixty exchanged words for a little and then drew back, one party to one side and the other to the other, and ordered all the people present to stand well away.

Then one of them gave a signal and they instantly attacked and fought all together in one great mass, companions supporting each other most gallantly when they found themselves in trouble. Almost as soon as battle was joined one of the Frenchmen was killed; but that didn't stop the others fighting: rather, both sides conducted themselves as nobly as if they'd all been Roland or Oliver.[2] I couldn't truthfully say if any did better than any other; all I know is that they fought so long that they all ran out of strength and breath, and had no choice but to agree to rest a while. At that stage one of the French was dead and two of the English. Both sides rested for a fair time, some of them drinking a little wine and refastening their battered armour, and cleaning their wounds.

---

retained the name given by Le Bel throughout, but the likelihood is that 'Brandebourch' is indeed Bramborough and that the German nationality given here is the result of a scribal error: the scribe's eye may well have slipped from the words 'un souldoyer d'...' to 'de souldoiers d'Alemaigne' just one line later.

[1] 'de fers de glayves': i.e. not tournament lances.
[2] See footnote 1, p.190.

Once they were sufficiently rested, the first to stand made a signal to recall the others. Then battle resumed, and it lasted a very long time; but finally, as I've heard from those who were there, the English had the worse of it. One of the Frenchmen who'd stayed mounted was giving them a fearful hewing and battering, so much so that their captain Brandebourch was killed along with eight of their companions; and the others, seeing that resistance now was hopeless and they must either yield or die – for they could not and should not flee – surrendered as prisoners. Sir Jean and his surviving companions took them and led them back to the castle of Josselin, jubilant; but they left six of their companions dead on the field, and several more died later from their wounds.

I've never heard of any other battle of this kind being proposed or taking place, and all its survivors should be treated with special honour wherever they go. It happened in the year of grace 1351.[1]

Chapter LXXXVII

How King John of France ordered the beheading of the worthy Count of Eu and Guînes, Constable of France, even though he was a prisoner of the English.

Now I wish to tell what happened in France shortly after the surrender and recapture of the town of Saint-Jean-d'Angély. The Count of Eu and Guînes, the Constable of France, who was so courteous and agreeable in all his ways and loved and respected by great lords, knights, ladies and damsels and everyone (in England as much as in France), agreed to pay King Edward a ransom of sixty thousand écus. He was given leave to sail back to France to raise this sum,[2] failing which he promised to return as the king's prisoner on a certain date.

When he arrived back in France he went to see King John, expecting a fond welcome – he'd loved the count well enough before he became king. The count bowed to him in humble greeting, and expected to be warmly and joyfully received after five years as a prisoner in exile. King John led him into a chamber alone and said:

"Look at this letter. Familiar, is it?"

They say the Constable was utterly dumbstruck when he saw it; and seeing his shock, the king cried:

"Ah, wicked traitor! Death is what you deserve, and you'll have it, by my father's soul!"

And he ordered his guards to seize him there and then and imprison him in the tower at the Louvre in Paris, where the Count of Montfort had been held – and had died, so it's said.[3] Everyone was distressed that the worthy Constable should be so treated, for he was much loved, and no one could understand the king's motives. And next day the king swore to all the Constable's friends who

---

[1]   On 26 March, at the *Chêne de Mivoie* (the 'Halfway Oak') between Josselin and Ploërmel. The site is now marked by a monument.
[2]   In October 1350.
[3]   See footnote 1, above, p.118.

were pleading on his behalf that before he ever slept again he would have him beheaded, and no one would persuade him otherwise. And indeed it was done that very night, in the tower of the Louvre,[1] without any trial or judgement, much to the grief and anger of everyone, and it earned the king great reproach and cost him much love. No one but the king's innermost circle knew why it had happened, but some guessed that the king had been informed of some liaison that had either occurred or been planned between his wife the lady Bonne and the worthy Constable. I don't know if there was any truth in this, but the way in which it happened made many people suspect it.[2]

Chapter LXXXVIII

The reason for the hostility that arose between King John of France and the King of Navarre and his brother.

At this time King John was extremely fond of a worthy knight named Lord Charles of Spain.[3] They'd been raised together as children, and he was his constant companion and most trusted adviser. The king granted his every wish and fancy; but he was generous and courteous towards his fellow knights and a most agreeable companion to them. King John finally appointed him Constable,[4] and granted him land which had long been contested between the late King Philip and the King of Navarre (part of whose kingdom it was considered to be).[5] Great resentment and hostility arose over this disputed territory, between Lord Charles of Spain and King John on one side and the young King of Navarre[6] and his brother on the other. It wasn't long before the King of Navarre and his brother Philip had Lord Charles savagely murdered in a mighty castle at dawn:[7] I won't tell you exactly how it was done, as I wasn't there. From that day forth, despite a series of accords and peace treaties, the two brothers of Navarre were hated by King John of France and there was constant hostility and covert conflict. He lived in permanent fear that they might assist the King of England, and indeed, it was to lead to much trouble for the kingdom of France.

It was at this very time that Pope Clement VI sent the Cardinal of Boulogne to France to negotiate a settlement and peace between the kings of France and England, for he was related to them both. He arrived in greater pomp than Saint Peter, so beloved of God, ever travelled the Earth: it was said he came with seven

---

[1] He was arrested on 16 November and beheaded in the courtyard of the Hôtel de Nesle on the morning of the 18th.

[2] The true reason may have been rather that the Constable had agreed to deliver his castle and county of Guînes to Edward in lieu of the unraisable ransom sum. Although it could be argued that he was entirely within his rights to trade them, their strategic importance so close to Calais made King John regard the deal as treasonous. See Jonathan Sumption, *The Hundred Years War, Vol. 2, Trial by Fire* (London 1999), pp.71-2.

[3] Charles de La Cerda.

[4] He replaced the executed Count of Eu and Guînes in January 1351.

[5] The county of Angoulême, which had belonged to the King of Navarre's mother.

[6] Charles II ('the Bad'); in 1351 he was 19. He was of French royal blood, being the great-grandson of Philip III. He was also John II's son-in-law.

[7] In fact at an inn in the small town of l'Aigle near Évreux, on 7 January 1354.

hundred horses, all paid for by the churches of France. All the same, this cardinal did succeed in securing a truce between the two kings, of what duration I'm not sure;[1] then he stayed in France for a long time – at Paris especially, where King John often revelled and made merry with him.

At the same time, too, King John seized the county of Eu and Guînes after the death of the valiant Constable, and installed a garrison at the castle of Guînes, which is said to be one of the strongest in the world. But Sir John Beauchamp, a most valiant knight appointed by the King of England to be guardian of Calais, negotiated with men at Guînes and secured their promise to surrender the castle to him or his representatives for the sum of thirty-four thousand écus, with their lives and equipment guaranteed along with the lives of the mercenaries in the town.

The day came, the money was paid, the castle was opened at daybreak and the English marched smartly in and found the troops still in their beds. They did them no harm, but said:

"Come on, sirs, up you get! You've slept too long – you're not sleeping here any more!"

The French were utterly horrified – they would rather have been in Jerusalem, and little wonder! Anyway, they armed and left as soon as they could, and carried the news to King John of France, who was filled with rage. He protested to the cardinal, saying the truce had been flouted and broken. The cardinal sent an envoy requesting Sir John Beauchamp to make amends and reverse what he'd done and surrender the castle, or he would consider it a breach and infringement of the truce. The knight replied that he could consider all he wanted: the fact was, he said, that in or out of periods of truce gentlemen could buy and sell, for gold or silver, estates and castles and fortresses and the like without the truce being infringed. And so it was that the mighty castle of Guînes remained in English hands.

Chapter LXXXIX

How King John of France created an order of knights in the manner of the Round Table, and it was called the Company of the Star.

In the year of grace 1352[2] King John of France founded a splendid company, great and noble, modelled upon the Round Table that existed of old in the days of King Arthur. It was to be an order of three hundred of the outstanding knights in the kingdom of France and was to be called the Company of the Star; each knight was to wear at all times a star of gold or gilded silver or pearls as a badge of membership. And the king promised to build a great and handsome house near Saint-Denis,[3] where those companions and brothers who were in the land and had no reasonable impediment would meet at all the most solemn festivals

---

[1]   A truce was agreed on 10 March 1353, but was set to last only until 1 August.
[2]   In fact November 1351.
[3]   At the royal manor of Saint-Ouen.

of the year; it was to be called the Noble House of the Star. And at least once a year the king would hold a plenary court which all the companions would attend, and where each would recount all the adventures – the shameful as well as the glorious – that had befallen him since he'd last been at the noble court; and the king would appoint two or three clerks who would listen to these adventures and record them all in a book, so that they could annually be brought before the companions to decide which had been most worthy, that the most deserving might be honoured. None could enter the Company without the consent of the king and the majority of the companions present, and unless he was worthy and free of reproach.

Moreover, they had to vow never knowingly to retreat more than four *arpents*[1] from a battle: they would either fight to the death or yield as prisoners. They vowed also to help and support each other in all combats, and there were a number of other statutes and ordinances to which they all swore, too. The Noble House was almost built; the idea was that when a knight became too old to travel the land, he would make his home there at the house, with two servants, for the rest of his days if he wished, so that the Company would be better maintained.

But in the year 1353[2] a large English force of men-at-arms came to Brittany to aid and support the valiant Countess of Montfort and to lay waste the region that had sided with Lord Charles of Blois. As soon as the King of France heard the news he sent a great body of men-at-arms to oppose them, including knights from the Company of the Star. But the English, on learning of their approach, sprang such a brilliant trap[3] that all those French who rushed to engage too soon and too recklessly were routed and slaughtered. No fewer than eighty-nine knights of the Star were killed there, and all because of their vow about not retreating: had it not been for that vow, they would have been perfectly able to withdraw. Many others died, too, on their account: men they might well have saved had it not been for this vow of theirs and their fear of reproach by the Company.

This noble order was never spoken of again, and I think it has come to nothing and their House has been left empty. So I'll leave this now and tell of another matter.

Chapter XC

How the King of France made a pact with the King of Navarre, and how King Edward crossed the sea to Calais and ravaged the country.

You've heard of King John of France's intense hatred for the young King of Navarre and his brother Lord Philip following their murder of Lord Charles

---

[1] The *arpent* was a unit of length roughly equivalent, in medieval France, to 70 metres.
[2] In fact in 1352.
[3] At Mauron, on 14 August 1352. Le Bel's phrase here is '*ilz firent sy soubtillement par une embusche qu'ilz firent*', but there is no suggestion in any other account that the French were exactly 'ambushed' at Mauron, and '*embusche*' should probably be understood as a deft tactical ploy. Indeed, the reason why the heavily outnumbered English were victorious at Mauron is not at all clear.

of Spain. This hatred was lodged deep in his heart, however much he might hide it from them, and he was constantly pondering how to cause them harm and shared his wishes with some of his council.

One day he decided to send a message to the King of Navarre bidding him come and speak with him in Paris on a certain day, without fail. One of his privy council revealed this to the Cardinal of Boulogne in the confessional, for he feared great ill would come of it. When the cardinal heard of King John's intent he sent secret word to the King of Navarre, his kinsman, telling him not to come to Paris as King John had bidden, for he feared it would turn out badly, convinced as he was that the king wished him nothing but ill. So the King of Navarre didn't meet King John on the appointed day. He was furious, and suspected that Sir Robert de Lorris, a member of his privy council, had alerted the King of Navarre to something; and such was his hatred of Sir Robert then that he had to leave the country.

When the young King of Navarre and his brother Lord Philip realised that King John meant them ill – they weren't sure why – they garrisoned with men-at-arms and provisioned with the necessary supplies all their castles and strongholds, of which they had (and still have) a good number in the county of Évreux[1] and elsewhere; and at all times they rode armed and with a strong escort.

Matters went from bad to worse, until it was rumoured that the kings of England and Navarre had come to an agreement whereby King Edward would land in Normandy and the King of Navarre would go and join him and lend him aid, along with his brother Philip. And it seems this was the case, because certainly, in the year of grace 1355, the noble King of England organised a great muster of troops and ships and set sail around the month of August and was at sea for a good month or more. King John was well aware of this, and summoned all nobles and non-nobles to come to him at Amiens to defend the kingdom, for King Edward was at sea and about to land in France, though he didn't know where.

Meanwhile some of King John's council learned of the promises which were said to have been exchanged by the kings of England and Navarre, and considered that such a pact might well lead to the kingdom's destruction. They discussed this with King John, and were so persuasive in their arguments that he was forced to accept their advice, contrary to his heart though it was. Negotiations took place and a date was finally fixed for King John and the King of Navarre to meet; the King of France had to leave Paris to speak to him. At this meeting it was agreed that King John would cede[2] to the King of Navarre all the lands he had earlier given to Lord Charles of Spain, whose murder had caused the hostility, along with all the income they had yielded to himself and the late King Philip for the past twenty years: this amounted to some one hundred and fifty thousand écus. In return the King of Navarre was thenceforth to be loyal and faithful to King John of France and withdraw any pledges he might have made to the King of England. Furthermore, the King of Navarre and his brother would

---

[1]   King Charles of Navarre was also Count of Évreux.
[2]   The text reads *'vendi'* (sell), but this is surely a misreading of *'rendi'* (yield / give back).

be entitled to ride freely through the kingdom of France with a hundred lances and bascinets if they wished.[1]

And so the King of England was deceived, and had to turn back with nothing achieved after great expense. He was extremely angry, and has demanded compensation from the King of Navarre ever since. But the noble King Edward had no intention of being idle; he wanted to make use of all his provisions somehow, and told his knights and men who'd been so long at sea and were very weary:

"Go and rest until I call you. But I want all France to know that I'll be coming very soon, and will do battle with King John and ravage the land as far as I can."

The news spread through France, and King John called a general muster. Great lords and knights and commons alike came in astonishing numbers. And he posted Lord Louis of Namur and his marshal Sir Arnoul d'Audrehem at Saint-Omer with three hundred men-at-arms, and installed strong garrisons at Boulogne, at Hesdin, at Montreuil, in the *bastide*[2] outside Guînes, at Ardres, at Aire[3] and in all his fortresses.

For his part, the noble King Edward sent his son the Prince of Wales to Gascony with twelve hundred men-at-arms and four thousand archers, while he himself sailed to Calais about six days before All Saints in the year 1355. He stayed there for about four days to unload the ships and see the horses disembarked; and then, hearing that King John was at Amiens with a mighty army, he said he would head that way and let him see the smoke and flames of his burning country: if he fancied coming to put them out he'd be welcome. So he set out from Calais one day and went to camp between the *bastide* at Guînes and Ardres where King John had garrisons stationed. And truly, I've heard tell from the chevalier de Harduemont[4] and the lord of Bergues[5] and several others that on this expedition King Edward had no more than three thousand cavalry and six thousand archers, yet he wanted to do battle with the King of France and his whole army in his own land. What's more, he'd brought three young children with him – the oldest wasn't yet fourteen – each of them finely dressed and mounted: two were his own and the third was the Countess of Montfort's son who should have been Duke of Brittany and indeed was called so.

Next morning the noble king left this place near Ardres and advanced across the country, burning and laying waste the land, going beyond Saint-Omer to the area around Thérouanne. He made camp near the town; and it was here that a valiant knight came to him, not as a free man but as a prisoner of his, on parole.

---

[1] A treaty between the kings of France and Navarre was signed at Valognes on 10 September 1355.

[2] See footnote 3, above, p.210.

[3] Aire-sur-la-Lys.

[4] Probably Godefroi sire de Harduemont (near Le Bel's home city of Liège), who is mentioned again below, p.249.

[5] 'Berges'.

His name was Sir Boucicaut,[1] and he was the most renowned for prowess in the whole kingdom of France. The noble king greeted him most courteously and asked him news of his lord King John. Sir Boucicaut replied that he thought he was at Amiens.

"Holy Mary!" said the king. "Why is he waiting for me there, when he has a huge army and can see his land being burnt and ravaged by so few?"

"I don't know, sire, truly," said Boucicaut. "I'm not of his privy council."

The king promptly summoned three of his knights and said: "I pray you take Sir Boucicaut to inspect our battalions; he can make a note of what troops we have and go and tell his lord the king."

Sir Boucicaut went with them, and returned to King Edward and said: "You have fine troops, sire, but not as many as I expected."

The king had him stay there with him all that night. Next morning he advanced beyond Hesdin, burning and laying waste, but still had no news of King John.

Next day he took lodging at an abbey and summoned Sir Boucicaut and said: "Sir Boucicaut, do you know what you're to do? I could have more than six thousand écus from you if I wished, I know. But you're to go and tell your lord that I've kept burning his land as far as here because I thought he'd come and put out the fires. Say I'll wait for him here for three days: if he chooses to come he'll find me, but if he doesn't come I'll go back the way I came, because I could easily stay too long and find my return routes rather too constricted. If you promise to take this message, exactly as I've told you, I'll release you from captivity."

The knight humbly thanked him and said he would gladly do this, and that he was his knight in all matters barring opposition to the King of France. Then Sir Boucicaut left King Edward and rode to Amiens to find King John. He delivered his message well and faithfully; but King John had no wish to meet King Edward as proposed.

So King Edward left the abbey and returned by way of Fauquembergues and the county of Boulogne, burning, ravaging and pillaging everything, until he arrived back at Calais on the eve of Saint Martin[2] and gave his knights a joyful supper in honour of the saint. Next day he distributed generous pay to all those who'd been with him and gave pensions, horses and other gifts to many of his knights before granting leave to everyone to go home.

When King John saw the trail of fires lit by the King of England on his return march he decided to follow him. He left Amiens and advanced to Saint-Omer; and his men pillaged and ravaged the land as much as the English had done, except for the burning. On reaching Saint-Omer he sent his marshal Sir Arnoul d'Audrehem and three knights to Calais with a message for the King of England. When they drew near to Calais they sent a herald to tell the king that four knights were coming on behalf of the King of France and would gladly speak with him.

---

[1] Jehan le Meingre, known as Boucicaut, had been captured in Gascony and was on parole – i.e. under oath to remain a non-combatant and to behave as a captive of the English until his ransom was paid. He was the father of a son of the same name who led the French vanguard at Agincourt.

[2] 10 November.

King Edward's cousin the Duke of Lancaster[1] and Sir Walter Mauny were sent to speak to them, for the king said they'd no business entering Calais. So the duke and Sir Walter rode out of the city to meet the knights; they greeted them courteously and asked them what they wanted. They replied that they'd been sent by their lord the King of France to inform the King of England that if he would kindly leave Calais and come to a suitable field he would do battle with him.

The Duke of Lancaster replied that their lord King John had had ample time to come and quench the flames of his burning country if he'd wanted, for he'd seen it ablaze for the last twelve days, and the King of England had waited for him in the field for three days after sending him word. "And on behalf of our lord the King of England, my answer is that he is not inclined to do as you request, for half his men have gone home and the rest are very tired and weary, and it is not in his interests to do battle with the King of France just when it happens to suit him."

Many more proposals and words were exchanged, but I'll say nothing of them, for the simple fact is that no agreement was reached. And the French knights left and returned to Saint-Omer to report the answer to their king. He headed back to Paris crestfallen, while King Edward stayed at Calais for as long as he pleased and then returned to London in England.[2]

Chapter XCI

How King Edward besieged the city of Berwick, captured by
Sir William Douglas and the Scots, and won it back.

No sooner had King Edward arrived back in London than he heard that the valiant knight Sir William Douglas[3] and the other Scots based with him in the great Jedburgh Forest had besieged and taken the city of Berwick. He was as distressed by this news as he'd been cheered by his return.

He hurriedly departed in deepest winter and set out to besiege Berwick, commanding all his forces to follow him. As soon as they joined him he laid siege to the city and stayed there till after Candlemas, and burned and laid waste all the land of Scotland that had rebelled against him.

During this siege of Berwick, the valiant Duke of Lancaster was riding one day past a stronghold captured by the Scots, many of whom were repeatedly harassing the English army. These Scots made a bold sortie and launched a fierce attack upon the duke. A mighty combat ensued, and so many Scots arrived that the duke was forced to retreat to within a league of the king's army. The noise of battle reached the king. He swiftly mounted a courser without waiting for any

---

[1]   Le Bel is now using the new title of Henry of Grosmont, previously the Earl of Derby. Having become Earl of Lancaster on his father's death in 1345, he was created 1st Duke in 1351.
[2]   Edward was at Westminster by 23 November.
[3]   This is the William lord of Douglas (1327-84) who was to become 1st Earl in 1358. He was the nephew of William Douglas of Liddesdale (see above, p.119), and had in fact killed him in 1353.

knight or squire, and headed straight for the commotion. He ordered those who were fleeing to turn back; they all followed him instantly, but before any of them could catch up he was charging into the enemy and performing amazing feats of arms, and he rescued the Duke of Lancaster, who would have been killed (for more and more were flying at him) if he hadn't saved him by his mighty valour and driven back the Scots. He should be credited with high honour for this deed, along with all his others.

It wasn't long after this that the city of Berwick was surrendered to him; he appointed officers and a garrison there before making a joyful return to London in the winter of 1356.[1]

Chapter XCII

How the Prince of Wales led a great and bold expedition[2] through Languedoc, destroying and laying waste the country between Narbonne and Carcassonne.

It's only right that I should tell you how the Prince of Wales fared in Gascony and Languedoc, where his father King Edward had sent him. He gathered to him so many Gascon knights and squires that he had a force of two thousand heavy cavalry, including those he'd brought with him from England, and ten thousand brigandines[3] on foot. He set out from Bordeaux, entered that part of Gascony that supported the French, and advanced right across it, burning and destroying a swathe five leagues wide, until he was almost at the city of Toulouse. He waited there for a day and then crossed the great River Garonne, finding no one to oppose him, despite the fact that the men of Toulouse were so near – and despite the fact that King John had sent his marshal Sir Jean de Clermont there with the Duke of Bourbon, the Count of Armagnac, the Count of Foix, the Count of Forez, and so many knights and squires that they outnumbered the English by four to one.

After crossing the river the Prince's forces formed their battalions and burned all the country right next to Toulouse without anyone leaving the city to defend it. They camped that night at Montgiscard, and advanced next day to Castelnaudary[4] where they captured the castle. Next day, after looting everything, they proceeded to Carcassonne, where they found riches vast beyond all belief; everything was plundered, and fair townswomen and their daughters were raped. They stayed in the lower town for three days to complete their pillage and destruction, but they could do no harm to the mighty citadel above, for its defences are far too strong. On the fourth day[5] they continued their march, setting fire to the fine

---

[1]   Edward was back at Westminster in early March.
[2]   'chevauchée'.
[3]   Just as le Bel refers to heavy cavalry as 'armeures de fer' (see note 4, above, p.25), so he classifies other troops by the armour they wear: in this instance the 'brigandine', the sleeveless padded doublet of canvas or leather, reinforced with small iron plates.
[4]   The text reads 'Chastel Noeuf', but it is surely Castelnaudary, south-east of Montgiscard along the road to Carcassonne.
[5]   6 November.

houses and markets as they left Carcassonne, and made their way to the city of Narbonne, burning and laying waste the land to left and right; and all the while the French lords didn't kill even one of the lowliest fellows – though they were following them, and making camp each day where the English had camped the night before.

On the Prince's army went by way of Lézignan and Capestang, and set ablaze the suburbs of Narbonne. From there they marched to Béziers, and beyond there to Saint-Thibéry. This is five leagues from Montpellier, and they caused such panic that the people of Montpellier set fire to their suburbs so that the English couldn't come and occupy them.

But the English and Gascon lords decided to go no further, feeling they'd gained enough booty and sufficiently destroyed the land. They turned back with all their prisoners and loot; and truly, those captives paid such huge sums in ransom that all the knights and squires were rich with the rings and treasures they received: those still alive are still living off the proceeds, as will their heirs after their deaths. And every foot soldier, even the lowliest fellow, spurned silver coin and cups and goblets and cloths and furs and gowns: they were only interested in good gold florins and rich brooches and jewels.

They marched on until they passed Toulouse and crossed the Garonne once more; and still the French lords followed them but made no attack despite having an army three times as strong, for which they were sorely reproached. I don't know what stopped them attacking the rearguard at the very least, unless they were enchanted or bewitched.

Once they'd crossed the Garonne, the valiant Prince of Wales and the Gascon lords made their way back to Bordeaux. After much celebration their men went their separate ways to their homes in Gascony and elsewhere. The valiant Prince of Wales sent some of his troops back to England, but kept plenty with him and stayed at Bordeaux all that summer, waging a fierce war upon the neighbouring lands that supported the French. I'll leave him for a short while and then return.

Chapter XCIII

How King John, with his own hands, arrested the King of Navarre and the young Count of Harcourt at a castle where they were dining with his son.

King John was furious when he heard that the Prince of Wales had burnt and ravaged such a vast and rich expanse of his land, and that the lords he'd sent to confront him had done nothing. His anger is hardly surprising, and the lords were ashamed and didn't know what to say.

Then one day[1] the King of Navarre, the Duke of Normandy (King John's eldest son), the Duke of Bourbon, the young Count of Harcourt[2] and several other fine young knights were enjoying each other's company at a dinner given by the King

---

[1] 5 April 1356.
[2] Count John VI, who was only 14 in 1356.

of Navarre or the Duke of Normandy, I'm not sure which, at a castle near Rouen. While they were seated at dinner – there were more than thirty of them – King John, who knew of the gathering and had never lost his hatred of the King of Navarre, went there in secret with at least a hundred companions with hidden weapons. He arrived at the castle while they were dining and entered the hall. As soon as the King of Navarre saw him, he and all the others said:

"Sire, sire, come and drink!"

And they all stood, showing him all due and proper respect.

"No, sirs, not a drop!" he said, grim-faced. "Don't move, any of you, on pain of hanging!"

And Sir Arnoul d'Audrehem drew his sword from its scabbard and said: "Anyone who moves is a dead man!"

With that King John launched himself at the King of Navarre, seized him by the neck and dragged him across the table, crying: "Truly, foul traitor, you're going to die!"

"Ah, dear lord!" said the Duke of Normandy. "What are you doing? You can see he's a guest in my house!"

King John told him to put up with it, and kicked him in rage. Then he grabbed the young Count of Harcourt and another knight and had them both beheaded right there and then before everyone in the hall. And he seized a worthy companion of the King of Navarre – his name was Sir Friquet de Fricamp[1] – and had the King of Navarre sent to prison at Château-Gaillard and the knight, Sir Friquet, imprisoned in the Châtelet at Paris. Everyone was bewildered, having no idea why King John had done this. Some were saying he would have Sir Friquet flayed alive and dragged through the streets and hanged at Montfaucon, and the King of Navarre beheaded by night as he'd done to the Count of Guînes; others guessed he would put the king in an iron maiden,[2] which he wouldn't long survive: he would die a swift and hideous death.

When Lord Philip of Navarre heard of his brother's arrest he feared the King of France planned to have him executed as he'd done with the Count of Guînes. He took control of their castles in the county of Évreux[3] and elsewhere and installed strong garrisons with large numbers of men-at-arms in them all. Then he sent a message of defiance to King John of France,[4] declaring that if he put his brother to death there would never be peace between them, and that he shouldn't try to take possession of the county of Évreux or the kingdom of Navarre on the grounds of some trumped-up charge against his brother – as he'd done with the worthy Count of Guînes and Sir Olivier de Clisson in his covetous desire to seize their inheritances. He would never have them! If his brother died, then he, Lord Philip, would be Count of Évreux and King of Navarre! Then he began to wage war upon the kingdom, burning and laying waste the land and slaughtering

[1] 'Frisquet de Frisquan': Jean de Fricamp, nicknamed 'Friquet'.
[2] It isn't clear whether the instrument of torture known as the 'iron maiden' was invented as early as the 14th century, but something very similar seems to be suggested here by 'une estroite chappe de plonc' ('a tight coat of lead').
[3] See footnote 1, above, p.218.
[4] On 28 May 1356, after three requests for his brother's release.

people in the country between Chartres and Paris. King John was incensed, and carried the war to him likewise by burning and ravaging the county of Évreux: half the city of Évreux itself was set ablaze.

Then King John laid siege to the strongest and most handsome castle in the county, named Breteuil;[1] he was stuck there for some time before he took it, and meanwhile Lord Philip of Navarre was campaigning elsewhere, in the Cotentin and Normandy. What's more, he'd secured the support of the valiant Duke of Lancaster, who crossed the sea and landed in the Cotentin; and with the Navarrese and mercenaries assembled by Lord Philip they had an army of almost two thousand six hundred heavy cavalry and a large body of brigandines and other foot soldiers. They marched towards the French host at Breteuil to raise the siege or to do battle, even though they didn't match them in numbers. They advanced, burning and laying waste the land, until they were just four leagues away; but King John wouldn't leave camp and come to engage them or to quench the flames of his burning towns. And the Duke of Lancaster, very astute and experienced in war, considered that the French army was so strong in numbers that they had more to lose than to gain by attacking them; so he advanced no further, and turned back and stayed in Normandy and the Cotentin for a long while, burning and destroying far and wide, until the whole land was laid waste almost as far as Mont Saint-Michel. Meanwhile the defenders of Breteuil, seeing their provisions running out and no help arriving, made terms allowing them to leave in complete freedom. And I've heard there were only twenty-four of them, and of no great status! This was in the month of August in the year of grace 1356.

Chapter XCIV

Of the amazing fortune and adventures of the valiant Prince of Wales who, with only a small army, left Bordeaux in the year of grace 1356 and advanced through Gascony, Limousin and Berry, burning and laying waste the land almost as far as Orléans and Paris; and how King John followed him to Poitiers, where the French were defeated and the said king was captured.

At the same time[2] the Prince of Wales set out from the city of Bordeaux on the Gironde with three thousand heavy cavalry, lords, knights and squires from England and Gascony, and four thousand archers and three thousand brigandines on foot; and they advanced through Gascony and the Agenais, burning and destroying enemy territory, until they came to Poitou and Limousin. They hadn't passed that way before, and they burned and pillaged everything as far as the city of Limoges. I don't know the details of the route they took to Berry, but they burned and laid waste everything as far as the city of Bourges and the outskirts of Issoudun,[3] and then went to besiege the strongly fortified town of Vierzon and

---

[1] 'Berchuel'.
[2] On 6 July.
[3] They reached Issoudun on 25 August; they failed to take the castle but destroyed the town.

took it by storm and razed it to the ground.[1] They planned then to cross the River Loire if they could, at Orléans or Blois or wherever else was possible.

King John was less than happy when he heard the news, you may be sure, and said he would send no one else to confront them: he would go himself. He left Paris and made for Orléans, calling upon all nobles and non-nobles alike to follow him. Anyone would have been ashamed to stay behind when the king was going in person, and so many followed him that before he reached Orléans he had an army big enough to do battle with the rest of the world. He headed for Blois but left a contingent at Orléans, being unsure of the route the English would take; and the lord of Craon and Sir Boucicaut took three hundred men-at-arms and said they would go and have a closer look at the English and see if they could find some adventure. So they rode towards Vierzon; but they were violently repulsed and suffered losses among the less well mounted, and if they hadn't come quickly upon the tower of Romorantin[2] they would all have been killed or captured, but they found the tower in time to take refuge. The English, however, were hot on their heels and besieged them in the tower; they resisted valiantly and avoided being captured that day or the next, but they realised there'd be no speedy help and they had no provisions, and with such a great force besieging them they decided to surrender with their lives guaranteed. They were all taken prisoner and went off with the English, on parole[3] and disarmed.

The English now set fire to the town of Romorantin, and then advanced across the region called Sologne as they headed for the Loire. But when they heard that King John was at Blois they realised they wouldn't be able to cross the river there, so they made for Amboise. King John now made the crossing to meet them, and realising this, they headed for the city of Tours and stayed nearby both that day and the next[4] but then left, realising they wouldn't be able to take control of the city or the bridge; they torched some of the houses in the suburbs and turned back towards Poitou, burning and laying waste as they went.

King John, when he'd seen the English making for Tours, had ordered his whole army to cross the Loire and go after them with all possible speed. The pursuit continued until he camped one night just three leagues from them and five leagues from the city of Poitiers, and his army was ever growing in numbers as men came flocking to him from all sides. When he knew for certain that he was so close to the English, he felt sure they would wait to face him and that he would have to do battle with them next day or the day after. So he held a council of war, to discuss how to order his battalions. The first decision was that they should all fight on foot, for fear of the archers who always killed their horses, as at the battle of Crécy. The next was that the Duke of Athens and the two marshals, Sir Jean de Clermont and Sir Arnoul d'Audrehem, should have command of the first battalion, with six hundred men-at-arms; the Duke of Orléans should have the other, with three hundred; the Duke of Normandy, the

---

[1]   On 28 August.
[2]   'Montmorentin'.
[3]   See footnote 1, above, p.220.
[4]   In fact they were encamped near Tours from 7 to 11 September.

king's eldest son, would command the third, with three thousand men-at-arms; and they would all be accompanied by able captains. The king would command all the remaining men-at-arms and the infantry, of whom there were so many that it was a wonder to behold. In his battalion the king had the Duke of Bourbon and a vast number of knights and lords from Provence, Limousin, Poitou, the Touraine, Berry, Burgundy, Savoy and many other lands, as well as the Count of Nassau with a great contingent of Germans. They were so many that they completely covered the land.

The Prince of Wales and the English and Gascon lords heard the news and realised they must do battle or attempt a very difficult flight. They resolved to stay where they were, a league and a half from Poitiers; they would all risk a good death by selling their lives dearly if that was Our Lord's will. So they drew up their battalions in fine and shrewdly marshalled order.

It was then that the Cardinal of Périgord arrived, and he went between the two armies several times as he strove to secure a peaceful resolution. The Prince of Wales finally offered to relinquish all the towns and castles he'd captured and release the lord of Craon and many more of his fellow prisoners, if King John would let him leave the country; the prince would also swear not to take up arms against the kingdom of France for the next seven years. But no matter what anyone said King John refused to accept this handsome offer. What a mistake it proved to be.

When the valiant young Prince of Wales heard that King John had rejected his offer and wanted the English to place themselves entirely at his mercy, he declared he would rather place himself at the mercy of God, and that he would die but once and preferred to risk all than live in shame. And so it was that early next morning, after hearing mass, the English fearlessly took up their positions and waited for the French battalions to advance.

When King John and his army drew near they all dismounted, except the Marshals and the Constable and some from their battalions who remained on horseback. They made a fine advance towards the English lines, but met with a vigorous response in such an awesome hail of arrows and missiles that this first French battalion was routed. In the midst of this the valiant Duke of Athens, Constable of France, was killed, as were Sir Jean de Clermont, Marshal of France, and more than a hundred knights and squires; and the other Marshal, Arnoul d'Audrehem, was gravely wounded. The English and Gascons now grew in courage and advanced in close and steady order[1] towards the Duke of Orléans's battalion, which was swiftly overcome and took to flight. Then the English regrouped and attacked the Duke of Normandy's battalion, which barely resisted at all but turned and fled towards the king's battalion, so that the English and Gascons, driving on, found themselves confronting the mighty battalion of the King of France. It was broad and very deep, and stood its ground and held firm for a long while. Great numbers were left dead there, most notably Sir Geoffroi de Charny, bearer of the Oriflamme,[2] and many other bannerets

---

[1]   'pas à pas' ('step by step').
[2]   The French royal battle standard.

and countless squires. And King John, who had fought better than anyone, was captured. Taken prisoner alongside him was his young son Lord Philip, only twelve years of age. Also captured were the Duke of Bourbon, the Chamberlain de Tancarville, the Count of Nassau and many other great lords and bannerets and squires whose names I don't know. In all the English and Gascons took fully two thousand valuable prisoners, and killed an incredible number of commoners as they plundered the French carts and wagons and packhorses. The chase and pursuit continued right to the gates of Poitiers, and it was during the chase that most of the prisoners were taken.

This great adventure befell the Prince of Wales in the year 1356, on the day after the feast of Saint Lambert in the month of September.[1] The English and Gascons have every reason to record it in their chronicles, for in all the history of Christendom no adventure so great ever befell so few.

When the battle was won, as you've heard, and the English and Gascons had returned from their pursuit with their prisoners, some with two, some with three and some with four, they went back to their camp at the battlefield and disarmed; the prisoners were theirs and they could do with them as they chose, and they had them disarmed and treated them with all possible honour. You may be sure that the honour – and the profit – won by those who'd taken the prisoners were not small! As for the provisions that they won from the French, they were timely: the English and the Gascons hadn't tasted bread for the past three days. That was why they'd offered the above-mentioned terms: they'd feared being starved by King John more than they'd feared his army.

There's no need to pass lengthy comment. The simple fact is that Fortune wished to raise one side and bring down the other; she couldn't help herself, and kept turning her wheel.

When evening came, the valiant Prince of Wales gave supper in his quarters to the King of France and all the captive knights and squires, treating them as generously as he could to their own victuals – he had no other! He seated the king, the Duke of Bourbon and the Count of Nassau and three other valiant knights at the high table; and throughout the meal he served them, and indeed the other tables, with all possible humility, refusing to sit at the king's table despite all the king's requests, saying he wasn't yet worthy to share the table of such an eminent prince – and such a valiant man, as he had shown himself to be that day. And he stayed kneeling as he spoke to him, saying:

"Don't feel humbled, sire, if God has chosen not to favour you today. I assure you, my father the king will treat you as honourably and as amicably as he can and will agree sensible terms: you will make a lasting friendship. It seems to me you should be of good cheer, even though the battle has gone against you, for you have earned a reputation for high prowess and surpassed the finest of your army in the way you fought today. I'm not saying this to flatter you! All your companions agree with me in awarding you the prize and the laurels[2] if you'll accept them."

---

[1]   i.e. 18 September.
[2]   Literally 'the chaplet'.

At this a general murmur arose, everyone saying that the young prince had spoken most nobly. He had won the respect of them all, and they said that if he was able to continue in that vein he would grow into a man of outstanding wisdom.

After supper everyone returned to his quarters with his prisoners to rest. Many ransomed themselves that night, and truly, the Gascons and the English treated them most courteously, making no stringent demands; they merely asked them to say, on their honour, how much they could afford to pay without ruining themselves, and readily believed what they told them. They required them either to deliver their sums of florins at the city of Bordeaux at the feast of Christmas following, or to return on that date as prisoners. They all said they had no wish to impose such excessive ransom demands that those knights and squires would be unable to serve their lords in a manner befitting their station. This hasn't been the custom hitherto among the Germans! I don't know how they'll behave henceforth, but when the Germans capture Christian men-at-arms they have no more pity or mercy upon them than they do upon dogs.

Next morning after hearing mass they departed. They escorted King John of France and the other lords with great courtesy, letting them ride freely under oath; and day by day, without burning or destroying the land, they made their way back to the city of Bordeaux and arrived to a joyful welcome. They provided the king with very comfortable lodging in an abbey there, but kept him under close guard, needless to say; and with him he still had his son Lord Philip, whom everyone called Sir Philip the Bold.[1] The Prince of Wales redeemed the other lords and bannerets from their captors for a great sum of florins, and allowed them to leave on parole: they undertook to return as prisoners of his father the king at London in England on the day of Candlemas. He would have dearly loved to take King John with him back to England, but the Gascon lords who'd been involved in his capture wouldn't give their consent.

So the Prince stayed at Bordeaux with King John all that winter, and summoned all his minstrels and others who could cheer and comfort him. The Prince and the King held frequent discussions, but they produced no result. Finally, when summer came,[2] King John was taken to England and placed in a handsome castle called Windsor. I don't know how this happened or how the Gascon lords came to give their consent, but King John was still there while these words were being written. And the truth is that many peace negotiations were held between the two kings – the Cardinal of Périgord mediating, along with another who spent nearly a year in England, constantly striving to secure peace – and it was said that they were close to an agreement, the only sticking point being the king's ransom.[3]

In any event, peace was not fully concluded until half way through the year 1358, when the noble King of England held a magnificent feast at Windsor Castle.[4]

---

[1]   The soubriquet he retained when he became Duke of Burgundy.
[2]   The Black Prince and King John left Bordeaux around the middle of May 1357.
[3]   Literally 'the guarantee'.
[4]   A great tournament was held there on St George's Day 1358.

To entertain and honour King John all the more, he invited ladies and damsels, the most beautiful and gorgeously attired in all England, and took part in the jousting himself, followed by his three sons, all in identical arms. It was at this feast that peace was made between the two kings. In the sight of all who wished and were able to see it, they exchanged kisses and promised and vowed to keep the peace securely, and to be good friends forever, giving help and support to each other against all foes. But the exact terms and conditions of the peace were still not generally known when these words were written; I'll say no more about them until they are.

I'll tell now how peace was made with King David of Scotland, and then of the extraordinary events that have taken place in the kingdom of France since the great battle at Poitiers where King John was taken prisoner, as you've heard.

Chapter XCV

How peace was made between the King of England and the King of Scotland, who had been held captive in England for ten years.

You've heard how King David of Scotland was captured in the year 1347,[1] shortly after the battle of Crécy, during the time when King Edward was besieging Calais. You should know that he remained a prisoner in England until the year 1357, when peace terms were agreed between him and King Edward, as I shall now explain according to accounts given to me.

First, he paid homage to the King of England for the entire kingdom of Scotland, except for some islands which he and his forebears had conquered. The Scots never wanted him to consent to this. Next, he undertook to protect the kingdom of England against all his subjects, and to attend four times a year the parliaments customarily held in London; if he was genuinely unable to attend, he would send four of his greatest barons, two prelates of Holy Church and two bannerets. And he would forever relinquish the right he claimed to the city of Berwick, and would guarantee this each year with worthy hostages. Upon these terms peace was agreed between the two kings.

Chapter XCVI

How the Duke of Lancaster besieged and took the city of Rennes in Brittany.

At the time that the battle was fought near Poitiers, as you've heard, the valiant Duke of Lancaster was in the Cotentin and Normandy, waging a fierce war alongside Lord Philip of Navarre. But shortly after, when news of the victory reached him, he moved on past Mont Saint-Michel and into Brittany, to aid the valiant Countess of Montfort and the young count her son, who was claiming his right to the duchy of Brittany as you've heard. Those areas opposed to them

---

[1] Strictly speaking this should be 1346, though it's true that he didn't really become a pris-oner of Edward until some time after his capture at Neville's Cross that October.

he burned extensively, and then went and wasted the country around the city of Rennes, and laid siege to it right through the winter and into the summer without anyone coming to attempt to raise the siege. Lord Charles of Blois was abroad in the country, but it was as a prisoner, forbidden to take up arms, and his ransom had been set at four hundred thousand old écus. He made frequent journeys into France and to Paris to try to raise the sum and to rally support for the relief of Rennes, but he could find no lord willing to assist; and in the end the city was forced to surrender and pay sixty thousand écus to the Duke of Lancaster to compensate him for the costs he'd incurred during the siege.

Chapter XCVII

Of a knight who, after the King of France was captured,
gathered men from every land and plundered Provence.

At the very same time, a knight known as 'the Archpriest' gathered together a great company of men-at-arms from all countries who realised they would have no more pay and wages now that King John was a prisoner. They didn't know where to go to make money in France, so they headed for the county of Provence, where they seized castles and well-fortified towns and plundered far and wide right down to Avignon and beyond, led only by the aforementioned knight.[1] The Pope and all the cardinals residing then in Avignon were in such alarm that they didn't know what to do with themselves, and ordered priests and clerks to arm each night to guard the city against this marauding band. In the end, indeed, the Pope invited 'the Archpriest' to Avignon and treated him with lavish respect, as if he'd been the King of France! It was widely rumoured that the Pope and the College of Cardinals had given him forty thousand old écus to take his company away and guarantee their safety.

But I'll say no more about that; I wish to return to the remarkable events that have taken place in the kingdom of France.

Chapter XCVIII

How the kingdom of France was governed by the three estates, that is to say the
clergy, the nobility and the bourgeoisie, while King John was a prisoner in England.

Now the time has come to tell how the kingdom of France was governed following the capture of King John in Poitou. It was a kingdom that had

---

[1] Arnaud de Cervole, known as '*l'Archieprestre*', terrorised Provence in 1357-8. The reason for his soubriquet is simple: he had been an archpriest. A younger son of a minor Gascon noble family, Cervole had entered the Church and become archpriest of Vélines in the diocese of Périgueux. At some point around 1350 (and before his benefices were taken from him) he had joined the French army, become adept at taking towns and castles by escalade, climbed the social as well as the scaling ladder by marrying a rich widow in Berry, risen through the ranks and fought in the Count of Alençon's battalion at Poitiers (where he was captured). He then realised the rich potential of brigandage.

always been the spring and flower of all the world in learning, chivalry and commerce, the model of all good qualities, of nobility and gentility and honour. But you should know that after the terrible defeat inflicted upon the French in Poitou, the knights who had survived death and capture were held in such contempt by the commons that they hardly dared to enter the towns;[1] and none of them at all, not even the Duke of Normandy (more often called the Dauphin of Viennois)[2] or the Duke of Orléans, attempted to deal with the problems besetting the kingdom.

So it was that all the prelates of Holy Church, bishops and abbots, and all noble lords and knights, the Provost of the Merchants[3] and the burghers of Paris, and aldermen of the other cities and major towns, all assembled one day in Paris to determine how the kingdom would be governed until their lord the king was released. And they wanted to know what had become of the vast sums of money previously raised in tithes, in maletolts, in debasement of the coinage and all the other harsh and questionable impositions upon the land – in return for which the kingdom had been ill defended and its soldiers poorly paid! It was agreed that the prelates should choose twelve good persons who would be authorised to speak on behalf of the clergy in discussing these matters; the lords and the knights would likewise elect twelve representatives, as would the burghers and the commons of the land. These men were to meet in Paris and make rulings on behalf of the three estates: that is, the clergy, the nobility and the *bonnes villes*.[4] They made several which were less than pleasing to the Duke of Normandy: firstly they forbade the continued minting of debased coinage, and seized possession of the dies; they then requested the duke to arrest the royal chancellor,[5] Sir Robert de Lorris,[6] Sir Simon de Bucy, de Poylevilain[7] and the other chief auditors[8] and royal counsellors, and demand that they give a clear account of what sums had been levied at their instigation and what had become of that money. When these chief counsellors got wind of this they made themselves scarce, all leaving the kingdom in various directions: it was a wise move!

After this, the three estates appointed receivers to raise and collect all maletolts, tonnage, tithes and other levies to which the king was entitled, and ordered the minting of fine gold coins which came to be called 'sheep'.[9] They were also keen to see the King of Navarre released from imprisonment, for it seemed to them that the kingdom would be stronger and better defended if he was willing to

---

[1] '*es bonnes villes*': the major towns of the kingdom; see footnote 4 below.
[2] See footnote 1, above, p.104.
[3] Étienne Marcel.
[4] The '*bonnes villes*' of medieval France (of which there were many) were towns enjoying a privileged status which gave them a substantial measure of administrative independence.
[5] The Archbishop of Rouen, Pierre de la Forest.
[6] Chamberlain to King John.
[7] Jean Poilevilain, a key figure in the *Chambre des Comptes*.
[8] '*maistres des comptes*'.
[9] '*moutons*'. These coins, first minted in 1355, bore the figure of a lamb to illustrate an inscription referring to *agnus dei*. It's interesting to wonder whether the nickname was purely playful, or whether the significance was lost on many people and they actually mistook the lamb for a sheep.

be good and loyal; there were, after all, few enough people in the kingdom on whom one could rely: they were all either dead or captive. So they asked the Duke of Normandy to set him free, saying it would be to France's benefit – and in any case they didn't know why he'd been imprisoned and felt he'd been very much wronged. But the duke replied that he didn't dare release him for fear of his father the king, and so the King of Navarre was not set free for the time being.

Chapter XCIX

How robber bands ravaged the kingdom of France, and how the Provost of the Merchants of Paris had two of the Duke of Normandy's counsellors killed.

Meanwhile a company of men-at-arms and brigands from many countries appeared and seized and plundered whatever they found, and ravaged the land between the Seine and the Loire. No one dared travel between Paris and Vendôme, or between Paris and Orléans or Paris and Montargis; and none of the inhabitants stayed in those parts: they all fled to Paris or Orléans. This company had made a man called Ruffin their captain, and knighted him; and he amassed wealth beyond all counting. They terrorised the land close to Paris, and ventured right up to the gates of Orléans and set fire to the suburbs. Every town and village in those parts, no matter how large or populous, was attacked and pillaged: Saint-Arnoult, Gallardon, Bonneval, Cloyes-sur-le-Loir, Étampes, Châtres,[1] Montlhéry, Pithiviers, Larchant, Milly, Château-Landon, Montargis and an amazing number of other substantial towns. They'd roam the land in bands of twenty, thirty, forty, and find no one to oppose them. Elsewhere, along the Normandy coast, there was another even greater company whose leader and captain was Robert Knolles.[2] They likewise took control of the land and destroyed and plundered far and wide. It should be accounted a true wonder that the greatest, most illustrious land in the world should have been wasted and pillaged thus, in the very heart of the kingdom.

And let me tell you, this Robert Knolles I mentioned had worked in the cloth trade when these wars began! And then he became a foot soldier in brigandine.[3] But now this German[4] had done so well for himself – by a mixture of luck and guile – and won so many castles in Saintonge, Poitou and Brittany, by force and otherwise, that he had a revenue of forty thousand écus and, it was said, had amassed property worth one hundred thousand. He plundered and conquered

---

[1] '*Castres*'; presumably Châtres-sur-Cher.
[2] '*Robert Canolle*'.
[3] '*brigand et soldoyer à pyé*'. This could be interpreted as a blunt statement that he became 'a brigand and a mercenary', but elsewhere (see footnote 3, p.222), Le Bel uses '*brigand*' in reference to the brigandine as he classifies troops by their armour, and Le Bel seems here to be emphasising Knolles's low status, with implicit dismay that one of his origins should acquire power and wealth.
[4] The surprising '*Alemand*' may well be simply a scribal slip (for an intended '*Angloys*'): a few lines later Le Bel seems perfectly aware of Knolles's English connection. He came from Cheshire.

ceaselessly with the mercenaries he kept in his pay; and he made it clear that he wasn't fighting for the King of England but for himself and in his own name, and he paid his soldiers well with his own money.

Meanwhile the prelates of Holy Church and the nobles were beginning to distance themselves from the actions of the three estates, and left matters to the Provost of the Merchants of Paris,[1] feeling the estates might go further than they'd intended. And then one day the Duke of Normandy was in the Palace at Paris with a great company of knights and nobles and prelates, and the Provost of the Merchants gathered a big crowd of Parisian ruffians[2] who sided with him and shared his views and came to the Palace; and in harsh terms he asked the duke to take responsibility and start sorting things out so that the kingdom – which would eventually be his – was properly defended to stop these bands of robbers roaming the land. The duke replied that he would gladly do so if he had the wherewithal, but that the provost, who'd taken control of levying the taxes due to the king, would have to do it and should get on with it if he was so keen. I don't know exactly how it happened or who was most to blame, but the exchange became so heated that two of the duke's counsellors were killed beside him – his gown was spattered with their blood – and he might well have been killed, too, if he hadn't been pulled clear of the fray. One of the dead knights was named Sir Robert de Clermont, a valiant and most accomplished gentleman; I don't know the name of the other, but he was a lawyer of knightly rank.[3]

It was after this[4] that a knight named Sir Jean de Picquigny and others, at the prompting of the Provost of the Merchants and the aldermen of the *bonnes villes*, went to the castle where the King of Navarre was and took him into custody and led him to Paris.[5] Everyone was delighted by this, wanting to know his state of mind and exactly where his heart lay. When he arrived in the city he called together all manner of people, clerics, nobles and lay, and addressed them most eloquently, complaining of the injustices and wrongs he'd suffered and assuring them that they had nothing to fear from him: he wished to live and die defending the kingdom of France, as was his duty, for he was descended from French royalty on both his father's and his mother's side, and he set forth a number of reasons why, if he chose to claim the crown, he would be found to be nearer in line in several respects than either the one currently a prisoner in England or the English king.

He then used his powers of persuasion to earn the full support of the Provost of the Merchants, until he had total command in all matters and the approval and favour of most of Paris, of Rouen and Amiens and Beauvais and the other

[1] Étienne Marcel, still not named by Le Bel – in fact he never is.
[2] Another use of the word *'brigans'*. The incident Le Bel is about to describe took place on 22 February 1358.
[3] *'chevalier en loys'*. There is a confusion here. Along with Robert de Clermont, Marshal of Normandy, the other knight killed was the Marshal of Champagne, Jean de Conflans. But there was a 'knight in law' – i.e. a prominent lawyer – lynched by a mob outside the palace: Regnaut d'Acy, who was beaten to death as he fled into a baker's shop.
[4] Le Bel's chronology is not quite right. He is about to describe events of three months earlier, in November 1357.
[5] On 29-30 November.

bonnes villes. At the same time word came that peace had been agreed between King Edward and King John if the French concurred and were willing to send worthy hostages by way of guarantee. But the Provost of the Merchants and those collecting the maletolts and the other royal taxes sought constant delay and every opportunity to prevent agreement being reached. And so it was that peace wasn't confirmed until the month of May 1358, when it was agreed as you heard earlier. But the Provost and his fellows would not observe it and sought every possible means of obstructing it: they didn't want King John to return or they'd be held to account and deprived of their offices. Nor did the King of Navarre want him back, fearing very much his return.

Chapter C

How there was a rising of leaderless men bent on killing noblemen,
ladies and damsels, and of the atrocities they committed.

When news reached France that the two kings had reached an accord and formed an alliance against all others, the Provost of the Merchants was more alarmed than ever, knowing as he did how deeply he was hated by the Duke of Normandy, who complained to everyone about the offence he'd suffered at his hands in the Palace at Paris. In urgent need of support, the Provost arranged a meeting with the King of Navarre; and when he arrived, the Provost and the burghers of Paris secured his solemn promise[1] to remain their staunch ally against all men, barring none, not even the king, which astonished many people.

It was not long after this, around Pentecost, that a terrible upheaval struck many parts of the kingdom, around Beauvais and Amiens, in Brie, in Perthois, in the Île-de-France and in Valois as far as Soissons. Inhabitants of the country towns – initially fewer than a hundred – started gathering in villages everywhere, led by no one; and they declared that the nobles, knights and squires were a disgrace and bringing the kingdom to ruin, and that it would be a good deed to destroy them all. They all cried: "It's true! It's true! Curse anyone who stands in our way!"

The first band set off without further debate, armed only with cudgels and knives, and broke into the home of a knight and murdered him and his wife and children and set fire to the house. From there they moved on to a strong castle and did still worse: they seized the knight and bound him tightly to a stake and raped his wife and daughter before his very eyes; then they killed them both – and the wife was with child – before slaughtering the knight and all his children and setting the castle ablaze. They did the same in many castles and fine houses, and by now they numbered six thousand: everywhere they went their numbers grew as everyone of a like mind flocked to join them. Knights and ladies, squires and damsels fled to take refuge wherever they could, often carrying their little children on their shoulders for ten or twenty leagues as they abandoned their manors and castles. And so they went on, these bands of leaderless men, burning

---

[1] On 15 June 1358.

and looting and murdering gentlemen and noble ladies and their children and raping ladies and maidens without any mercy whatever.

Truly, in neither the Christian nor the Saracen world has such a chaotic madness ever taken hold – nor one so diabolical, for those who committed the foulest deeds and the greatest number, such deeds that no human being should conceive without shame and horror, were the most esteemed among them. I wouldn't dare recount or record the monstrous outrages perpetrated upon ladies; but among the other vile, base deeds, they killed a knight and stuck him on a spit and roasted him in front of his wife and children; and after ten or twelve had raped the lady they tried to force her to eat his flesh before they killed her horrifically.

In the Beauvaisis they burned and destroyed more than sixty fine houses and strong castles, and if God in His mercy hadn't intervened, the chaos would have grown until these commoners had utterly destroyed the nobility and Holy Church and the rich in every part of the land, because the same thing was happening in Brie and in Perthois, along the River Marne; and all the nobles, knights and squires and ladies and damsels who managed to escape had to flee, one after the other, to Meaux in Brie, some of them dressed only in their shifts.

It was the same in Normandy, and between Paris and Noyon and Paris and Soissons, towards the land of the lord of Coucy; in these parts they destroyed more than eighty castles, fine houses and notable manors belonging to knights and squires. And everywhere they slaughtered and laid waste everything; but as you'll hear in due course, God in His mercy intervened, for which all good people should give Him thanks.

It's truly bizarre that these wicked people were gripped by the same fever in many different, far-flung places all at the same time, unless it was instigated by some of those controllers and collectors of taxes who didn't want to see peace take hold in the kingdom and thereby find themselves kicked out of office. Some people suspected the involvement of the Bishop of Laon[1] (ever a devious man) and the Provost of the Merchants, being of one mind as they were and colluding with the King of Navarre. I don't know whether they truly were to blame, but I'll move on now and tell of the remedy sent by God.

Know, then, that the lords of the region around Beauvais and Corbie, seeing their homes destroyed and their loved ones wickedly murdered, appealed for help from their friends in Flanders, Poitou and elsewhere. Then they attacked these pernicious bands from every side, and killed them and hung them from the nearest trees; and when they asked them why they'd behaved in this appalling way they said they didn't know, except that they'd seen others do it and decided to do the same, and really thought they could wipe out the gentry. There were some who admitted being involved in rape – some of six ladies, others of seven or eight or nine or ten or twelve: they'd even killed them when they were with child.

---

[1]   Robert le Coq.

As soon as the foreign rescuers appeared in the Beauvaisis and won their first victory, these miscreants were beside themselves with alarm and terror; and the men-at-arms went through the country from town to town until they came to Creil, which they thought was the rebels' home town, and there they burned and plundered indiscriminately, not bothering to stop and ask questions.

It's inconceivable, especially in the kingdom of France, that the commons would ever have dared embark upon this devilry without the encouragement of others. And when the lord of Coucy, summoning help from wherever he could find it, attacked the mob in his region and destroyed them and hanged and butchered so many that it would be amazing to relate, the captain of these miscreants, a perfect villain known as Jimmy Goodfellow,[1] tried to suggest that the Bishop of Laon had put him up to it, because he was one of his men. And indeed, the lord of Coucy was no friend of the bishop.

Chapter CI

How knights and squires who had taken refuge at Meaux in Brie killed a great number of the commons.

Now I wish to return to the people who, as you've heard, had taken refuge in the city of Meaux. The Count of Foix and the Duke of Orléans were there with some two hundred men-at-arms, knights and squires and three hundred ladies and their children. They'd taken shelter in the market; they'd seen their homes destroyed and their towns in flames across the country, but didn't dare go out to defend them.

When news reached Paris that these noble ladies and gentlemen were at Meaux and afraid to leave, bands of men slipped out of Paris, gathered together in a prearranged place – fully six thousand of them – and headed for Meaux.[2] They halted for a moment outside the gate; and when the noble lords and ladies and damsels saw the size of the mob they were terrified and didn't know what to do or which way to turn. Some proposed they should escape through the other gate, but others said they had nowhere to flee and would just as soon die now as later; so they hurriedly armed and went to defend the market entrance. The wicked townspeople wouldn't refuse entry to the Parisians; they opened the gates, and the mob swarmed in unopposed and charged towards the market like men possessed, intent on slaughter. But when they found the entrance to the market barred and men-at-arms ready to fight, they were sobered somewhat. Some went forward and started hurling missiles, but not for long: before you could say a Hail Mary they were turning back in stampeding flight, tumbling over each other in panic; and the men-at-arms surged forward and slaughtered them like pigs, in heaps. So great was the slaughter and so narrow were the

---

[1] Their leader was Guillaume Cale. 'Jimmy Goodfellow' ('*Jacques Bonhomme*') was a contemptuous nickname given by the nobles to the peasants – hence the name 'Jacquerie' usually applied to this revolt of 1358 (and to others subsequently).

[2] It was 9 June 1358.

streets that the way was blocked, and many of the Parisians were able to escape from the city and get back into the open fields. And the men-at-arms, after killing every one of them they could find, turned back and set fire to the city, burning everything as far as the market and plundering everything they found, because it seemed the people of the city were against them, having let the Parisians in.

The lords and ladies and damsels stayed in the market for a long time, and in much discomfort, after this mighty adventure. But it had turned out well for them and for all Christendom, for if Fortune had turned against them there, the mob would have been unstoppable: their daring and their devilry would have carried on growing and their assaults upon the nobility would have intensified by the day, and if God in His holy mercy hadn't intervened, they would have risen up everywhere until France in particular was destroyed.

When the news reached the Provost of the Merchants and his fellows they feigned outrage; but not a single one of those involved was censured or punished in any way.

Chapter CII

How the Duke of Normandy laid siege to Paris and the Provost was killed inside the city, which prompted the King of Navarre to defy Paris and wage war upon the kingdom.

Immediately after this, the Duke of Normandy sent out a call to all the nobles of the kingdom. A good number came also from the bishopric of Liège, from Lorraine and Hainault and other lands, and he finally had an army of six thousand men-at-arms. He went and laid siege to the city of Paris on the Saint-Antoine side, his men quartering at Saint-Maur[1] and the other villages thereabouts, around the Bois de Vincennes, foraging and plundering supplies of food from the surrounding country and burning five hundred townships and more, assuming them to be on the side of the wicked mob. They stayed there outside Paris for three weeks.

Meanwhile the King of Navarre had come from another direction with large bodies of horse and foot – and some English archers, too – and was lodging in the abbey and the town of Saint-Denis. Everyone thought he'd come to the aid of the people of Paris, since he'd vowed to support them, rightly or wrongly, against anyone who threatened them. He sent an embassy to the Duke of Normandy asking his intentions, for he, the King of Navarre, had a good two or three hundred archers in Paris – English archers, notably – paid for by the Parisians. Negotiations continued until the King of Navarre went to the duke's army in person[2] and spoke to him most graciously, excusing himself and finally promising to side with the duke for good or ill. He'd thus given the same undertaking to both sides.

---

[1]   Saint-Maur-des-Fossés, to the south-east of Paris.
[2]   On 8 July.

He now began to mediate between the duke and the people of Paris. Lengthy talks were held, until he was able to inform the duke that the Parisians would make amends for the wrong they'd done in killing his knights at his side, likewise for the offences committed by the mob who'd attacked Meaux; such reparations would be determined by four arbitrators, of whom the King of Navarre would be one. And at the same time the duke would select twelve burghers of Paris who would be judged and sentenced by the peers of France.

On the understanding that this would happen, the Duke of Normandy dismissed his men and headed for Meaux[1] to join his wife the duchess and all the nobles who'd taken refuge there. Meanwhile the King of Navarre returned to Paris, where he was locked in frequent talks behind closed doors with the Bishop of Laon and the Provost of the Merchants. No one knew what they were discussing so secretly, and everyone was very perplexed, because it was perfectly clear that nothing was being done about the terms agreed with the Duke of Normandy. They didn't know what was going on, and were anxious for a settlement to be reached, because they could see the English and the others who'd been in their pay now working against them, pillaging the land around Paris day by day in ever-increasing numbers. Some of the citizens now suspected that some treachery was afoot; but no one dared say a word, because the Provost of the Merchants had built such support for himself throughout the city: he'd bewitched the people and had them as much under his thumb as Jacob van Artevelde had once had the Flemings. His word was final in all matters, and no one dared raise a voice against him.

But finally God would not tolerate such proud rule, and roused some of the burghers by inspiring their suspicions that treachery was planned. Among them was one named Jean Maillard, more astute than all the rest. He rallied a party of those more inclined towards the Duke of Normandy than the King of Navarre, and came with them, fully armed, to confront the Provost of the Merchants, and demanded to know what he was planning as he was convinced he was up to no good. The Provost's reply wasn't to Jean Maillard's liking, and the argument got out of hand: the Provost was killed on the spot along with eight other members of his party and his household.[2] Then Maillard and his company ran through the town searching out the Provost's supporters, and they killed a great number; and sixty they arrested and imprisoned in the Châtelet so that they could find out more and confirm their suspicions.

They now sent a grand embassy to the Duke of Normandy to beg him to come to Paris, for the whole city was ready to obey his commands in all matters. The duke duly came and received a stately welcome; and he immediately pardoned them for the killing of the Provost and his companions. And then the truth was revealed: the Provost and his party had been planning to bring all the English and the men-at-arms at Saint-Denis – they numbered a good eight thousand – into Paris where they were to put to the sword all who sided with the Duke of Normandy and didn't want to obey the King of Navarre.

---

[1] On 20 July.
[2] The provost Étienne Marcel was killed on 31 July.

You should know that the King of Navarre was in Paris when the Provost was killed, but the moment he heard the news he jumped on a horse and rode to Saint-Denis, where he openly sided with the forces there and declared his defiance to the people of Paris.[1] He and his army started burning and laying waste all the land around the city, and when everything was destroyed between Paris and Senlis he headed towards Creil and Pont-Sainte-Maxence and then started campaigning around Beauvais and Compiègne and Noyon. His men won a number of castles and major towns, including a mighty castle called Mauconseil which belonged to the Bishop of Noyon; they turned this into a stronghold from which they conquered the whole region.

And so it was that the noble kingdom of France, the noblest of the noble, which had always been a sanctuary of peace and security, was now a lawless, confounded ruin.

When the Duke of Normandy, at Paris, heard that these men were destroying and laying waste the land with the support of the King of Navarre, he summoned all the *bonnes villes* of France to send troops, both horse and foot, to oppose this ravaging army. The towns responded readily, each to its capacity. When the forces were all assembled they were sent towards Noyon where the enemy was known to be, and they laid siege to the castle of Mauconseil, held by the English. They maintained the siege for many days; among their number were the Bishop of Noyon, Sir Raoul de Coucy, Le Flamenc de Canny and a great many men-at-arms: in all they numbered ten thousand horse and foot.

Then one day Sir Jean de Picquigny and other knights and squires on the King of Navarre's side assembled a great company of men-at-arms to go and help the English besieged at Mauconseil. They set out from Creil by night and attacked the French army at dawn. They routed them utterly, taking captive those they wished and killing a huge number: of the eight hundred sent by the city of Tournai not half escaped, and the same was true of the other towns. And the Bishop of Noyon, Sir Raoul de Coucy and Le Flamenc de Canny were taken prisoner along with many more whose names I don't know. This was in the year of grace 1358, on the Tuesday after the feast of Our Lady in August.[2]

After this, the Navarrese and English rode in bands across the country around Beauvais and Compiègne and the Vermandois, plundering whatever they wanted, unopposed, and burning and holding towns to ransom. They found no lords from the *bonnes villes* or anywhere else to resist them; each town protected itself as best it could and left the country to be pillaged and destroyed. And they lived in constant fear of betrayal, everyone suspecting everyone else; that's why the knights and nobles of the kingdom kept their heads down and didn't dare stir: they feared that, if anything misfired, they'd instantly be suspected of treacherous intent. The French, then, were all locked in spellbound terror of each other, and that includes the Duke of Normandy (heir to the kingdom after his father King John), his brother the Count of Poitiers,[3] his uncle the Duke of

---

[1]   On 3 August.
[2]   21 August.
[3]   John, later to be Duke of Berry.

Orléans and many other great lords and barons. They were all generally sitting quiet in the city of Paris, and letting the kingdom go to wrack and ruin. And when foreign lords and troops appeared they eagerly hired them with offers and promises of bountiful payment and reward, but when it came to it they didn't pay at all, so their dishonour steadily deepened while their enemies grew ever stronger.

It was at this time that the noble abbey of Ourscamps was taken, burnt and destroyed by pillagers from the castle of Mauconseil near Noyon, which was a grievous shame.

And then Sir Jean de Picquigny, on the King of Navarre's side, formed a close alliance with citizens of Amiens – burghers for the most part, but commoners, too – and one day,[1] with their complicity, he came with eight hundred lances and entered the suburbs and started putting them to the torch with a great deal of violence and commotion. The fire spread to the rest of the city, which would have been taken by force if the Count of Saint-Pol hadn't come to the rescue: when Sir Jean and his company became aware of his arrival they retreated. But later the burghers' treachery was revealed and fourteen of the most eminent were executed and disembowelled in public, because it was discovered that they'd concealed large numbers of men-at-arms in their cellars to support Sir Jean and let him into the suburbs.

At Laon, too, six of the wealthiest burghers suffered a similar fate, accused of having plotted to betray the city for money. I don't know whether they were guilty or not, but I find it hard to believe that good and honourable citizens would commit such a craven act. Mutual distrust was rampant between the great and the humble, the nobles and the commons. Such was the level of order and government in the kingdom of France.

All this while the Duke of Normandy and his brother were residing in Paris, where no merchant dared leave the city or venture abroad because the King of Navarre and his brother Lord Philip, with strong forces, were based on the Seine upriver at Melun and downriver at Mantes. Because of this, nothing could reach Paris at all. It was an expensive time: a barrel of herrings cost thirty or forty écus, and firewood and salt were entirely controlled by the duke: he'd requisitioned everything, and was forcing the clerks and all the other citizens to buy it at the price he set, to raise more money for himself; he was finding it hard to cover his costs from the current yield of the crown's usual revenues. There was deep discontent among the burghers of Paris, and the majority supported the King of Navarre; so the duke didn't dare leave the city, fearing that if he did, it would be placed in the king's hands. So he and his brother and all his friends stayed put in Paris all that winter and into the following summer, right up to Pentecost; and in all that time they did nothing, much to the disgust of all the people.

---

[1]   16 September.

Chapter CIII

Of the terrible plunder committed by robber bands in the most noble kingdom of France, and how they were finally destroyed.

At this time there was a Franciscan friar of great learning and intellect in the papal curia at Avignon;[1] but Pope Innocent VI had had him imprisoned in the nearby castle of Bagnols[2] because of his prophecies of future wonders, due to befall especially the prelates of Holy Church, the kingdom of France and the mightiest lords of Christendom. He claimed convincing proof in the Apocalypse and the Prophets and the ancient scriptures, and uttered his prophecies in dark and troubling words by the grace of the Holy Spirit; and several, hard though they were to believe, were seen to come true at the very time and day he'd predicted. And when he was asked how he came to make these pronouncements, he said they weren't prophetic utterances but things he knew from the ancient scriptures and by the grace of God and the Holy Spirit, who'd visited him one day when he was deep in contemplation while imprisoned in a filthy hole; Our Lord had opened all five of his natural senses and revealed to him the meaning of these ancient prophecies, so that he could announce to all Christian people the times and places where they would occur. He committed his prophecies to a number of authoritative and eloquent books, one of which, begun in the year of grace 1345, included predictions of so many wonders to occur between 1356 and '70 that it would take too long to record them all. But among many others, when asked what would become of the war with the English he said that what had been seen so far was nothing compared with what was still to come, for there would be no peace until every part of the kingdom of France had been destroyed. And indeed, this has come true in large measure since the year of '56, when the King of France and all his barons (the greatest of them at least) were routed, killed and captured, as you've heard.

It's now become clear that the kingdom had been – as it still is – so battered and crushed in every region that none of its princes, barons and lords had the courage to oppose those men of low estate, thronging together from every country, who had spread across the kingdom of France to burn, destroy and pillage. These bands of men, termed robbers and pillagers, had supreme captains in charge of them in all parts of the realm, so powerful that all the people of the kingdom obeyed their rule. And all who joined their companies and were in their pay were obliged at all times to give them everything they'd won – both plunder and prisoners for ransom – no matter how they'd got it; it's no wonder these captains amassed the wealth they did, wealth so great that they didn't know the worth of all their loot.

Of these captains I want to record the names of some who operated in the marches this side of Paris and the River Seine, so that they're not forgotten. The

---

[1]   Jean de Roquetaillade.
[2]   Bagnols-sur-Cèze.

richest (and the one who'd been at it longest) was named Robert Knolles.[1] He
finished up with around two hundred thousand high-quality florins[2] and some
sixty fine castles at his command; and he'd captured the fine city of Auxerre[3]
and pillaged and held to ransom all the surrounding country within a two- or
three-day ride in every direction, as far as Tonnerre and Vézelay, and the whole
length of the River Loire from Nevers to Orléans, and burnt and destroyed all the
suburbs of Orléans right up to the city gates, and won the noble house known as
Châteauneuf-sur-Loire and installed his own garrison there. When he wanted
he had an army of three thousand lances or three thousand horse and foot in his
pay and at his command.

Elsewhere, around Nogent and Pont-sur-Seine in Brie, and along the River
Marne and around Troyes and Provins in Champagne, were based other bands
of pillagers and robbers who had several captains. One was an English knight
named Sir Peter Audley, a great and experienced fighter, and another was a knight
from Hainault called Sir Eustache d'Auberchicourt;[4] there was also a squire from
Germany by the name of Albrecht.[5] On any given day these commanders could
call upon at least a thousand or twelve hundred fighting men, and they were
terrorising the whole region, ransoming, looting and destroying without mercy.
They'd captured and destroyed Damery, Épernay, the town of Vertus and all the
land along the Marne as far as Château-Thierry; they'd done the same around
the city of Troyes and right across Champagne as far as Rethel and Bar-sur-Aube.
They'd taken the town of Rosnay and the castle of Hans in Champagne, and
looted and stripped them utterly, and burnt and destroyed the surrounding
towns and fortresses, except the strongholds and castles they wanted to keep
for their own use, such as Lucy, Saponay, Troissy, Nogent, Pont-sur-Seine and
several more I couldn't name.

Elsewhere, around Soissons and between Laon and Reims, other robber bands
held sway, holding the entire region to ransom from Aubenton in Thiérache to
Châlons in Champagne, and all the land of the lord of Coucy and the county
of Roucy except for the fortresses still held by those two lords. For a long time
these pillagers were based at Vailly-sur-Aisne, and had greatly strengthened its
fortifications; there were six or seven hundred of them, under the command of
a captain who hired Germans and all manner of men: he was an Englishman
named Rabigot Dury.

There was another with him who set himself up as a great figure, called Robert
Scot.[6] At the feast of Christmas this Robert led a savage attack on the castle of

[1] 'Robin Canolle', as above, p.233.
[2] 'florins au mouton': see note 9, above, p.232.
[3] On 10 March 1359.
[4] 'Eustace d'Obrechicourt'. Auberchicourt's family had a long connection with England,
     and Eustache may well be the 'Sauchet' d'Auberchicourt who appears in the records as a
     founder member of the Order of the Garter.
[5] 'd'Albreke'. Jonathan Sumption has suggested that 'Albrecht was probably the same person
     as Albert Sterz, a brutal professional commander who later became famous as a soldier of
     fortune in Italy and died on the scaffold at Perugia in 1366'. Sumption, *The Hundred Years
     War, Vol. 2, Trial by Fire* (London, 1999), p.406.
[6] 'Robin l'Escot'.

Roucy, and took captive the rightful count and his gentle wife and daughter[1] and everyone within. After plundering the whole town this Robert placed a strong garrison in the town and castle, from which they caused the surrounding country endless grief; and he ransomed the count, the countess and their daughter for twelve thousand florins but kept possession of the castle throughout that winter and the following summer of '59, and the count had to go and stay at Laon and wherever else he chose.

Just after Easter, the robber bands at Roucy and Vailly went and took the town of Sissonne and garrisoned it well; one of their captains called himself Frank Hennequin[2] and was said to be from Cologne. This garrison at Sissonne inflicted great misery upon the country, destroying and demanding ransoms everywhere: any towns that couldn't provide ransom money they put to the torch. Then one day the count (who'd already been ransomed), seeing his land being devastated, decided to take revenge and trust to Fortune. He gathered together a band of knights and squires and rode from Laon with thirty or forty mounted companions. He finally managed to raise a good sixty; and early one morning he came upon the Sissonne garrison burning a town and launched a spirited attack. The combat was very fierce, and those Germans from Sissonne would have been outfought had it not been for some of the Laon company who fled at the first clash; because of them the count and all his companions were defeated, and he was taken prisoner for a second time and sorely wounded, too. Also captured in that battle were the lord of Montigny-en-Austrevant (a knight banneret), Sir Gérard de Chauvency[3] and the Count of Porcien, who was handed over to Sir Rabigot Dury (he'd been newly knighted) and Robert Scot. They led him away to imprisonment at Roucy. He was still there at the time of writing, in the month of May 1359.

Not long after this, Sir Rabigot left Vailly, putting part of it to the torch as he did so, and headed for Pont-Arcy to take the castle there; but it was so ably defended that he failed. Immediately afterwards the people of Soissons went and burnt the rest of Vailly so that the robbers wouldn't reuse it as a base.

In the year of grace 1359, around the feast of Saint John,[4] the Duke of Normandy for an agreed sum of florins secured the services of a valiant knight, a fine and experienced fighter named Sir Brocard de Fénétrange, and five hundred mounted lances. Sir Brocard led his men first to Champagne, and with the aid of a number of knights from Châlons and the county of Rethel he laid siege to the castle of Hans, recently captured by the English and Navarrese. After a fierce assault that lasted all day the castle was taken by storm, despite the spirited resistance of the English and Navarrese, none of whom escaped. They had a captain named Jacques Senak who offered an immediate ransom of sixteen thousand écus, but his eighty companions were all either killed or taken prisoner.

---

[1] It is hard in modern English to convey Le Bel's typically respectful 'madame sa femme et madamoiselle'.
[2] 'Hanequin Françoys'.
[3] 'Gerard de Chavechy'.
[4] i.e. late June.

Not long after this the men of Cormicy and the county of Rethel and the city of Reims laid siege to Sissonne and took it by storm on the third day, and all the defenders were either killed or captured.

In the same week the Bishop of Troyes, Sir Jean de Chalon, the Count of Vaudémont and Sir Brocard de Fénétrange mustered a large force to go and lay siege to Pont-sur-Seine or Nogent, where pillaging bands were based led by Sir Eustache d'Auberchicourt from Hainault, the Englishman Sir Peter Audley and the German called Albrecht. When they heard of this gathering of troops, they sent word to their fellow brigand garrisons at Saponay and Crécy-sur-Serre and had soon raised a good six or seven hundred mounted lances. They took to the field to do battle with the lords, but were mistaken about the numbers they'd confront: it was a much stronger force than they'd expected. But they dismounted nonetheless and took up a position on foot.[1] When the lords saw their intentions they formed three battalions and launched well-directed attacks from three sides; they won a speedy victory, leaving a huge number dead and capturing the rest, and Sir Eustache was gravely wounded. But that man Audley was nowhere to be found. Rumour had it he'd sold three of his castles and disappeared to Mechelen or Sluys to look after the sixty thousand 'sheep'[2] he'd got for them! Others said he was sick in bed and died soon after. God forgive him for all his foul deeds – his fellow villains too!

Meanwhile the Duke of Normandy set out from Paris with a great company and went to lay siege to Melun. He was there till August: the siege was still continuing as I was writing this, and I'll say no more until we see the outcome.

Elsewhere, in Ponthieu and around Beauvais and Amiens and along the coast around Boulogne, there was similar strife, with brigands destroying and laying waste the whole land. Their biggest garrison was in the town of Creil, where the captain was an English knight named Sir John Fotheringhay;[3] he had five hundred mounted lances in his pay, and archers in addition. There was another large garrison at the castle of Poix.

In overall command of these garrisons was Sir Jean de Picquigny – the one who'd taken charge of the King of Navarre and released him from custody[4] – and he'd drawn to his side many knights and squires of those parts, some by coercion, others out of fear; and from oppressing and holding the country to ransom he'd amassed gold and silver beyond counting. But almighty God finally demonstrated his miraculous powers as Sir Jean was seized by a hideous madness, gnawing insanely at his own hands and throttling his chamberlain, a man of the noblest family in Picardy.

Another knight of his persuasion was likewise stricken and lost his mind: his name was l'Ours de Briquisy. He was with the aforementioned Peter Audley and Albrecht when they and all their company broke into a town called Rosnay[5] and

---

1   The battle took place near Bray-sur-Seine on 23 June 1359.
2   See note 9, above, p.232.
3   'messire Fodrigand'.
4   To bring him to Paris, above, p.234.
5   'Renay': Rosnay-l'Hôpital.

started a free-for-all looting of the place. And while the people were at mass and the priest was about to raise the precious body of Our Lord, this wretch[1] burst in and tore the chalice from his hands along with the corporals and the most holy sacrament and stuffed the lot down his tunic, and struck the priest across the ear with his iron gauntlet when he tried to stop him. And what was his reward? When the whole town had been plundered and everyone was leaving with his loot, the wretch mounted his horse and rode off with the others; but he hadn't gone far, not a quarter of half a league, before both he and his horse went demented and started attacking each other's throat so hideously that all the companions who saw the sight fled in all directions: there was none brave enough to go near them until they were stone cold dead. God always delivers his punishments in time, even if he sometimes waits.

Not long after this, about the middle of August in the year 1359, the men of the city of Reims and Champagne and all the surrounding country, supported by the men of the county of Rethel, knights, squires and others of all classes, took the castle of Roucy after a three-week siege. The defenders surrendered with their lives and safety guaranteed – they were allowed to leave with their horses and all their equipment – but most of them were killed by the commons in defiance of the lords' agreed terms. And taken prisoner was Frank Hennequin, who'd committed so many wicked deeds: burning towns, destroying castles, plundering and extorting; and he'd abducted and raped good ladies and worthy women and then murdered them or held them to ransom; his crimes were so many and so foul that I'd be ashamed to commit them to writing. He was rightfully nothing more than a poor fellow from Germany, but so great was his profit from plunder that he'd bought the castle of Roucy, while it was in the hands of Rabigot Dury and Robert Scot, for the sum of seven thousand florins.[2] Now the people led Hennequin away to Reims for execution, in defiance of the lords; but the lords, to honour their promise, finally forced them to release him, much against their will. It was a great shame and pity that all the men found in the castle didn't die a foul death or lose their minds at God's hand; for no men, Saracens or Christians, ever committed so many monstrous deeds as they had in that land – and whoever committed the most was the most esteemed among them. What's more, quite unbelievably, when they realised they were besieged and had no way of escape or of ransoming their host of prisoners, they forced those worthy captives, men and women alike, to climb on to the walls stark naked and dealt them two or three sword-blows to send them plummeting down.

Meanwhile news came that the King of Navarre had made terms with the Duke of Normandy while he was besieging the town and castle of Melun. The king surrendered the place completely; and though no one knew the exact nature of their agreement they entered Paris together in apparent accord, much to the astonishment of many people after all that had happened: there was great doubt

---

[1]   The MS reads 'a wretch', but the passage is surely Le Bel's description of how the second knight he mentioned, l'Ours de Briquisy, 'lost his mind', rather than an account of a third.

[2]   'florins au mouton': see note 9, above, p.232.

that there would ever be real trust between them. And at no time since has either of them made any move to trouble the kingdom's enemies.

At the very same time Sir Brocard de Fénétrange, the knight who, along with Sir Jean de Chalon, had been supporting the Duke of Normandy against the English and Navarrese, had not received his promised pay. So he defied the Duke of Normandy and the whole land of France, and proceeded to inflict as much harm upon Champagne and the surrounding country as the robber bands had done. He and his accomplices were based at a castle called Conflans. After he'd wasted the country far and wide the people answered his demands, but the damage had already been done. He returned then to his own land, but some of his men, eager to continue their pillage and destruction, stayed on at the castle, and one day they stormed into the suburbs of Châlons and plundered at will and took a huge number of prisoners.

At the same time, too, Robert Knolles was sweeping through Berry and Auvergne and Limousin with three thousand lances, all in his own pay, and won the undisputed control and obedience of the whole region from Orléans to Notre Dame du Puy and from there to Limoges. He then returned to Brittany and Poitou, where he'd won more than twenty castles (with all their lands and rents), and left great numbers of his men up and down the country in the strongholds he'd won and brought into subjection.

But I wish to leave him and all the other robbers and plunderers, and the great iniquities and wonders that have befallen the kingdom of France, and return to my principal subject: the noble King Edward and the Prince of Wales.

Chapter CIV

How peace was agreed and sealed by the kings of France and England, but the French would not observe it, so the King of England made ready to come to France once more.

It's high time I returned to the story of the noble King Edward, of whom I've said nothing for a good while. He had King John of France and the greatest of the French nobility as his prisoners, and was letting the brigands terrorise and wreck the whole kingdom as you've heard, in the hope that it would either bring the war to a successful end or peace on his terms.

Now, around Pentecost in the year 1359, the two cardinals sent to England by the Pope to broker peace between the kings, from whose conflict the whole of Christendom had suffered, left England with nothing achieved – even though they'd been there for two years and more in great comfort and at vast expense. But the two kings then met privately in the city of London, accompanied only by King Edward's eldest son the Prince of Wales and the valiant Duke of Lancaster, and drew up a treaty[1] sealed with their respective seals; then they sent it to the princes and barons and all the cities of France, carried by the Chamberlain de

[1] Dated 24 March 1359.

Tancarville, vicomte de Melun, and by Sir Arnoul d'Audrehem, considered the finest knight in France, both of whom were prisoners of King Edward.

These two gentlemen arrived in France just as the Duke of Normandy and the King of Navarre had made a pact and returned from Melun to Paris, as you've heard. At the request of the two knights they summoned all the barons and nobles and representatives of the *bonnes villes*; and when they were assembled the knights delivered their message, the letters they'd brought being read aloud, setting forth all the peace-terms willingly agreed between the two kings. After it had all been read the assembly launched into a very long debate. They didn't approve of what they'd heard, for to some it seemed that the peace-terms were too onerous for the kingdom of France in many respects; and they would rather endure their present troubles and their King John's present plight and await the will of God, than consent to the noble kingdom being diminished and divided by the proposed peace. When the knights heard this they took their leave and returned to England and reported to the two kings what they'd found.

The noble King Edward was enraged by the response, and declared, loud enough for all to hear, that before August was out he would come to the kingdom of France in such force that he would stay until the war was decisively won or peace terms were secured that were honourable for him. And he began to make the greatest preparations ever seen in that land or any other. Word of this spread far and wide through Germany and Brabant and Hainault, and knights and squires started preparing horses and equipment and all the trappings of war, and made their way to Calais to await the King of England's arrival. They were all expecting to gain so much from joining him that they would never be poor.

So many flocked to Calais from every direction that there was nowhere left to take lodging, and bread and oats and victuals became so dear that no one could afford them. They were constantly being told that the king would be there next week; but in the end, all these men from Germany, the Hanse, Hesbaye,[1] Brabant, Flanders and Hainault, rich and poor, waited for King Edward from the end of August to the feast of Saint Rémy,[2] at great expense, in great difficulty and poverty, until many were compelled to sell their horses; and if the noble king had arrived, there would have been nowhere for him to lodge – and it was very much feared that no one would have persuaded these gentlemen at Calais to leave unless they were compensated in full.

The noble King Edward, meanwhile, had been unable to raise troops and supplies to the extent he would have wished, but had had full reports of the multitude awaiting him at Calais and expecting favours and rewards – even though he hadn't summoned a quarter or a fifth of them: most had come of their own volition to enhance their honour or for material gain. The news worried him, and he wisely decided to send his cousin the Duke of Lancaster to Calais ahead of him to apologise to them for his delay. So the duke prepared a great, strong company, and arrived at Calais with three hundred men-at-arms and two thousand Welsh archers to a splendid reception. With typical eloquence he made

[1] See footnote 3, above, p.27.
[2] 1 October.

the most courteous apology to the gathered lords for the noble King Edward's delay; then he had the horses and equipment brought ashore and told the lords there was no point in waiting: it was better to venture into France; he asked them to go with him, and he would give each of them a certain sum of money to cover modest expenses.

So he gathered them together and they set out from Calais in noble array, and within two days had reached Saint-Omer. There might have been as many as two thousand men-at-arms, not to mention the archers and infantry. Next day they marched by way of Béthune and the city of Arras before coming to a fine abbey called Mont-Saint-Éloi, where they stayed for four days to rest and recover,[1] for they found the place well provisioned and they certainly needed sustenance, having tasted neither bread nor wine for the previous four days: they'd suffered much hardship despite their stripping and plundering of towns and villages.

After staying there for four days and wasting the country all around, they headed towards the River Somme and Péronne, burning and ravaging all the way, and came to the walled town of Bray.[2] They launched a major attack, but suffered considerable losses and set off again along the line of the river, short once more of bread and wine. But they came then to Cerisy[3] where they found plenty of victuals and were able to cross the river as the bridge had not been destroyed. They spent the day of All Saints there.

It was then that word reached the valiant duke that King Edward had arrived at Calais[4] and was summoning him to return with all his company. Everyone rejoiced at the news and the prospect of money, of which they'd all run short; so they crossed the river again and made their way back to Calais.

Taking part in this expedition were Sir Henry of Flanders[5] with two hundred men-at-arms from that land; from Brabant came Sir Henry of Boutersem,[6] lord of Berghes, Sir Gerard van der Heyden[7] and Sir Frank van Hale;[8] from Hainault, Sir Walter Mauny, the lord of Commines and a fine company; from Hesbaye, Sir Godefroi de Harduemont and his son Sir Jehan and his cousin Sir Watier de Hastepem, Sir Jehan de Duras, Sir Tierry de Seraing and his young brother Sir Watier, Sir Rasse de Jemeppe, Sir Gile Surles, Sir Jean de Bernalmont[9] and Sir Renault de Berghes; and there were many more from Germany and Meissen and Holland and Burgundy and Savoy and so many other lands that I couldn't name them all.

As the Duke of Lancaster and his splendid force approached Calais to find the eagerly-awaited King Edward, they met him along the way, four leagues from the city, and with him so great a company that the whole land was covered with

---

[1] The text reads 'aviser' (to take stock), which could be right, but in context is more likely to be a misreading of 'aisier' (to relax).

[2] Bray-sur-Somme.

[3] 'Cressy'.

[4] Edward landed there on 28 October.

[5] Grandson of Count Guy.

[6] 'Bautresem'.

[7] 'Gerard de le Heyde'.

[8] 'Francq de Halle'.

[9] Le Bel's own nephew.

men. It was a glorious sight to behold, with armour shining, banners flying and trumpets and clarions ringing. When the lords came before the king they made their bows, and he greeted them most courteously and gave them gracious thanks for having coming to serve him of their own free will. The men from Germany, from the marquisate of Meissen, from Hesbaye and from Brabant promptly made plain to the king, with due humility, how much in want they were, explaining that while waiting for him they'd spent all they had and even sold their gear and horses, so that they were left barely able to be of service to him or to make their way home! They begged him, out of nobility and humanity, to provide them with what they needed.

The king, on his horse there in the open field, considered this for a moment and then said: "I'm not quite in a position to reply, and in any case I think you're weary; go and rest and refresh yourselves in Calais for two or three days, and overnight I'll consider your request and send you my answer."

For the time being it was the only response these foreigners were going to get, so they carried on to Calais to await a better one, which they hoped would involve money. They hadn't gone half a league before they came upon the grandest baggage train they'd ever seen, piled high with all manner of provisions. And behind it they met the noble Prince of Wales, so splendidly armed, as were all his men, that they were a joy to behold; and they were all riding in time with each other and arrayed as if ever ready for combat, a league or two beyond the army of his father the king, so that the baggage train and their provisions were constantly between the two bodies of men. The foreign lords were mightily impressed by this arrangement.

After observing their fine conduct the foreign lords presented their humble greetings to the noble prince; he bade them a typically courteous welcome, and they explained their needs to him and begged him to give them aid and assistance. Then they carried on to Calais to rest and find refreshment.

On the second day of their stay, the noble King Edward sent two or three knights to them with his response: that he hadn't brought enough money from England to give them what they'd asked, for he needed every penny he'd got to accomplish what he planned; if they wanted to take a chance with him, and if Fortune smiled upon them, he was happy that they should share in future gains; but they weren't to ask for compensation for past expenses, and there was no question of their horses or lost equipment being replaced, as he'd brought enough men with him for his campaign.

The foreign lords were less than pleased by this reply; they'd toiled hard and endured great want and hunger, as you've heard. But they were each advanced a sum of money to see them home, though it was very small. And back they went, some poorly mounted, others on foot; some sold their equipment or the clothes off their backs, or pawned their other baggage with the people who'd given them lodging: they were truly in a wretched state. I've heard it said that the Margrave of Meissen[1] had spent so much that he'd no way of getting home, so decided to

---

[1]   'Mise'.

follow the noble King Edward and risk either losing all or gaining a little, and he set off with the noble Prince of Wales to do the best he could.

But I'll say no more about this expedition by the Duke of Lancaster, who had so shrewdly led the foreigners out of Calais so that the king would be able to find lodging when he arrived, fearing as he did that they'd have refused to budge unless they were reimbursed for their expenses. I'll return now to the noble King Edward.

Chapter CV

How King Edward entered France with a greater force than ever before, determined to secure an honourable peace or never to return to England.

It should now be known that when the Duke of Lancaster, as you've heard, sailed from England to meet the foreign lords at Calais, the noble King Edward prepared to achieve his aims in France with the greatest expedition ever seen; and he divided his prisoners – the most eminent of French barons – and sent them to his strongest castles, guarded by large garrisons. He placed King John in one of the strongest of all,[1] and denied him most of his pleasures, having him kept under closer guard than before.

He then instructed all who meant to join him to head for Dover, where he would be supplying a fleet of ships and vessels. And everyone made ready to go: no knight or squire or man of honour between the ages of twenty and forty remained in England (any who did felt shame at doing so) when they saw that the noble king their lord was returning in such force to France. Every prince and baron and knight and squire, and men of every degree, followed the king to Dover, each equipped to the very best of his ability. When the muster was complete the king called the entire company together in one place, and told them plainly that he meant to go once more to the kingdom of France and never to return or sail back across the sea unless he'd brought the war to a successful end or secured peace decisively to his honour, or died in the attempt. If any among them didn't share his resolve, he bade them return home; but truly, they were all of one mind with their king, and joyously embarked in the name of Saint George and Saint Nicholas, and set sail and arrived at Calais two or three days before All Saints in the year 1359.

When King Edward landed with the Prince of Wales and his two brothers he gave orders for immediate disembarkation and commanded everyone to make ready to march; he'd no intention of staying there: he wanted to go after his dear cousin the Duke of Lancaster and find out how he was faring. So he set out from Calais next day, with the finest supply train ever seen: it was said there were six thousand handsomely fitted wagons, all brought over from England. And he ordered his battalions so splendidly that they were a pleasure to behold: he commanded his Constable, whose title was the Earl of March,[2] to ride half a league

---

[1]   Somerton Castle in Lincolnshire.
[2]   *'monseigneur de la Marche'*: Roger Mortimer, 2nd Earl.

ahead of him with six hundred heavy cavalry, the most splendidly accoutred in the army, and a thousand archers; next he formed his own battalion with three thousand cavalry and five thousand archers, and followed his marshal in battle array, ever ready to fight if the need arose; behind this great battalion came the baggage train, stretching fully two French leagues,[1] carrying everything needed for camp or combat, including hand-mills and ovens for baking bread in case they found that all the ovens and mills in the country had been destroyed; and behind the train rode the Prince of Wales and his brother the Earl of Richmond[2] (recently married to the Duke of Lancaster's daughter): in their battalion they had two thousand five hundred heavy cavalry, superbly mounted and richly armed, and four thousand archers and as many brigandines forming the rearguard. They didn't allow a single fellow to fall behind: they'd wait for any straggler; so they couldn't cover more than three leagues in a day. And let me tell you, it rained both day and night, which was a misery for men and horses alike. And they found the entire land laid waste, so you can imagine that all, of every degree, were in great want of bread and wine and meat; but worst of all was the foul weather.

The noble King Edward rode on until he neared Cambrai, where he found the land in a somewhat better state. So he let his men stay there for four or five days before setting out towards Saint-Quentin. He advanced right through the Vermandois with his battalions arrayed as I've described, and crossed the Somme, the Oise and the Aisne and then quartered his army in the area around the city of Reims, at Saint-Thierry and Pontfaverger and thereabouts. He stayed there from the feast of Saint Andrew until five weeks after Christmas,[3] which should be counted as the year 1360 from the Incarnation. And throughout that time it rained incessantly.

Meanwhile his men ventured this way and that, wherever they thought might be profitable: into the county of Rethel, for instance, as far as Warcq and Mézières and Donchery and Mouzon, camping in the country for two or three days and looting and laying waste the land. But King Edward had commanded, on pain of hanging, that no one was to set fire to any town, except for the odd house or two to make it easier to extract ransom for the rest. One band fell upon Attigny, well fortified though it was, and here they found abundant stocks of wine; they drank their fill of it before distributing some to the gentlemen of the army. The captain of this company was a valiant knight from Hainault named Sir Eustache d'Auberchicourt:[4] he was in command of all those who went raiding through the county of Rethel, and they'd taken the town of Rethel below the castle and also the town of Le Chesne.[5] Other companies who'd ridden towards Laon and Soissons had taken the town of Cormicy below the castle. Meanwhile the noble

---

[1] The league in France was a distance of ten thousand feet: just over two miles. The 'English league' was a somewhat vague distance closer to three.

[2] John of Gaunt.

[3] To be precise, Edward was outside Reims from 4 December 1359 to 11 January 1360.

[4] i.e. the same knight who had earlier been the captain of a band of 'pillagers and robbers' in Champagne, above, pp.243, 245.

[5] 'Chayne Poullieux'.

king and his sons stayed put with the rest of their army; they went hunting along the river when they wished – but never set a watch by night, no matter how far they'd gone.

Chapter CVI

How the King of Navarre hatched a plot in Paris to have the Duke of Normandy murdered by a knight, who was executed for it.

While the King of England and all his forces were quartered around Reims as you've heard, with instructions not to storm any town or fortress because he was reluctant to see his men lost or putting their lives in such blatant danger, rumours spread of a most treasonous plot hatched in Paris. The King of Navarre, as explained above, had made a pact with the Duke of Normandy and was residing in Paris and often in his company, though the people had no great faith in their alliance. Now, some men of the king's household had gained the duke's confidence and would frequently go hunting with him in the woods and along the river; and they plotted together and with some burghers of Paris to murder the duke while he was out hunting with his inner circle. But by the grace of God it transpired that just as he was about to set out on this hunt the planned treachery was revealed, and the knight at the centre of the plot was seized at once. Without any coercion he confessed to it immediately and exposed his fellow conspirators, and he was executed in Paris on Christmas night. His name was Le Bascon de Mareuil,[1] and he was said to be one of the King of Navarre's principal chamberlains. As soon as it happened the King of Navarre withdrew to Saint-Denis and declared for the English again and defied the duke and his brothers.

Shortly after hearing this news[2] King Edward left the environs of Reims, where he'd spent seven weeks of the winter, and marched on through Champagne. He passed by way of Châlons, where he found it easier to support his army, and then carried on towards the city of Troyes. But he'd left strong garrisons in the country around Reims with Sir Eustache d'Auberchicourt in command, and he and his two thousand troops plundered and ravaged far and wide. But no one could think what the king's intentions were in marching across Champagne.

This knight Sir Eustache and his companions did fearful damage to the country around Reims, especially the county of Rethel around Mézières, mercilessly killing men, women and children if they couldn't pay a ransom. It's impossible to calculate how much they made from extorting ransoms from captives and protection money from towns, for they would stay in each place for two or three

---

[1] '*Le Bascoux de Morrely*'. Le Bascon, according to Jean de Venette, was killed at the battle of Cocherel in 1364. Le Bel is surely referring here to the plot by the eminent Parisian Martin Pisdoé (who was executed for it on 30 December), and his confusion is probably explained by the fact that Le Bascon, who had become one of the King of Navarre's officers, was a key figure in the plot against Charles de La Cerda ('Charles of Spain', Constable of France) and his brutal assassination in 1354.

[2] On 11 January.

days, unchecked and unopposed. The noblemen and others of the region kept sending threats that they would come and confront them; but at the time of writing they've made no move at all, which has shocked many people, who've reproached them strongly and accused them of cowardice, especially when they could see that these plunderers would have no help from the King of England if they were attacked but were becoming ever more ready and able to withstand a siege.

And then, in the year '60, about five days after Easter,[1] while these empty threats to attack them were being made, they came by night to a well-fortified town by the name of Pierrepont, in the Laonnais near Montaigu. It was surrounded by dense marshland, and the people of those parts, nobles and others, had stowed all their belongings there. As soon as the companions sensed that the watch was asleep they ventured into the marshes, greedy for booty, crept up to the walls, broke into the town and set about their looting unopposed; they plundered at will, and found more riches there than anywhere else they'd been. Then they returned to Attigny with all their spoils, not to mention a good three hundred prisoners and thirty fair damsels (and other women, too) to do with as they wished and pleased.

Chapter CVII

Here you can see which parts of the kingdom of France the King of England wasted and held to ransom, and how long he stayed there unchallenged.

Now I shall return to King Edward, who was advancing through Champagne after ravaging the country around Reims. He came then into Burgundy, which he found so well stocked with all commodities that he stayed there from Christmas till the middle of Lent in one place and another. He wasted all the open land, though he never burned more than one house in a town; and he stayed in that fine country for fully ten weeks without any opposition, and won a hoard of booty beyond all belief. After he'd wasted the whole land the Duke of Burgundy was very happy to give him two hundred thousand florins[2] to make him leave and agree a three-year truce.[3]

Then the noble king moved on, leading his army through the counties of Nevers and Auxerre and holding the land to ransom, amassing in the process incalculable sums. He headed then towards Montargis where he stayed for three days, and then passed through Gastinois and finally appeared before Paris. All the noble barons of France were gathered there, and he would gladly have done battle with them if only they'd come out. He stayed there for six days, waiting to see what they would do; then, seeing they had neither the mind nor the courage to come and fight, he made for Chartres and sent his son the Prince of Wales towards Rouen in Normandy. The Abbot of Cluny had been moving frequently

---

[1]   Easter fell on 5 April that year.
[2]   '*florins au mouton*': see note 9, above, p.232.
[3]   Le Bel is referring to the Treaty of Guillon, 10 March 1360.

between the king's army and Paris, trying to broker a peace,[1] but I'll tell of that at the appropriate time.

When King Edward left Burgundy, a number of knights and squires and others from foreign parts who'd joined him as volunteers – men of Lorraine, for instance, and Savoy and Upper Burgundy[2] – took their leave of him and returned to their own lands, riding together to make their way out of France in greater safety. When they reached the duchy of Bar they found great bands of men wasting and ravaging all the land; and they heard also that the Duke of Bar[3] was making mighty preparations to raise men from Reims and the county of Rethel to besiege the English based at Attigny. So they made an agreement with the men of the duchy of Bar, who were in opposition to their duke, that they'd go and keep him occupied and stop him attacking their allies at Attigny. They joined forces and marched to Saint-Mihiel,[4] the finest city in the duchy of Bar, and wasted all the surrounding land. Their numbers were ever growing as men flocked to them from every direction, and it was said they had fifteen thousand combatants, three thousand of them mounted. And they had so many abducted women riding with them that it was quite amazing. After wasting the whole land they headed for Pont-à-Mousson and invested the town and ravaged the surrounding country.

It's quite true that the Duke of Bar, supported by the city of Metz, had mustered forces to confront these men; but when he drew near he found them in such good order that he wasn't inclined to attack them and made a pitiful retreat with all his troops, leaving his opponents all the more assured. They became even better organised, appointing captains to command and impose discipline; then they all advanced into the rich and fertile valley of Metz.

It wasn't long before the Count of Salm,[5] the Duke of Lorraine, the Duke of Bar and the men of Metz, seeing the enemy strengthening daily and capable of destroying them if they didn't take steps to stop them, sent word to the Duke of Luxembourg and Brabant, who was in the full flower of youth,[6] telling him that these people would lay waste Luxembourg unless he came to defend it; but if he would come with an army they would do all in their power to assist him: all the people of the great city of Metz in particular would rally to his side. As soon as the Duke of Luxembourg heard this news he summoned troops from Brabant, Liège and other marches, and called upon friends such as my lord of Liège[7] who sent him a hundred lances, and his brother Lord Louis who brought a hundred companions with him. But when he arrived in Luxembourg he found that the lords who'd begged him to come were ill prepared to do as they'd said, and that the townsmen of Metz had cooled or were no longer in agreement. He was aghast and dismayed: he didn't know what to do; he revoked his order and

---

[1]   Unsuccessful negotiations were held on Good Friday (3 April) and 10 April.
[2]   'Haute Bourgogne'.
[3]   Robert I, not yet 16 years old.
[4]   'Saint Mehu'.
[5]   'Sames en Samoys'.
[6]   Wenceslaus of Luxembourg, also Duke of Brabant through his marriage to Joanna, was 23.
[7]   i.e. the Prince-Bishop.

dismissed his troops. The situation now was worse than ever, their enemies in even better heart. And truly, it was a great disgrace for the lords and the people of Metz.

And as his troops departed a great misfortune occurred; it was a shame and a pity indeed. The young Count of Mons, the eldest son and heir of the Duke of Jülich, in the full flower of youth, went to dine at the castle of his cousin, the lord of Scleyde. While he was seated at dinner, a knight called the lord of Gerarstene arrived outside the town with a large force and started driving off the cattle. The commotion reached the castle, and the lord of Scleyde and his brother and his men hurriedly armed and ran to try and rescue the herd. When the noble young count saw this he declared that, since his path had brought him there, he'd behave as if he were the castle's lord. The lord of Scleyde and his companions begged him to stay, saying it wasn't fitting for a prince of his rank to risk his life to rescue cattle; but no one's entreaties would stop the noble count from mounting his courser, and he was the first to overtake the enemy and the first to be killed. It was a grievous pity that such a prince, who surpassed all others of his age in grace and prowess, should have met such a tragic death, and there was the deepest, most piteous mourning throughout Germany and every land where he was known. But it so happened that in this fray the knight who'd led the expedition, known as the Provost of Gerarstene, was also killed: a squire, seeing his lord the count struck down, risked his life, on foot though he was, and managed to thrust his sword through the knight's thigh and up into his belly. But the squire himself was so badly wounded that he had to be rescued with the utmost difficulty and carried back to the castle.

But I shall leave this now and return to the noble King Edward, to tell how he left France following a peace settlement negotiated by the Abbot of Cluny between Chartres and Paris in the month of May 1360.

Chapter CVIII

How peace was made between the two kings, and how King Edward returned to England and sent home King John of France.

Firstly you should know that the noble King Edward crossed the sea to France, as I've told you, in the year 1359, three or four days before All Saints, and stayed there till the end of May without encountering any opposition or impediment. He went wherever he liked and took victuals at will, except in the strongest walled towns; indeed he never suffered shortage or discomfort for more than three days, except from rain and bad weather while they were wintering around Reims. And you should know that the noble king and his men had a train of between ten and twelve thousand wagons brought over from England, each with a team of three horses, on which the lords carried tents and pavilions, and forges and ovens to make whatever was needed, fearing as they did that they'd find the land completely wasted and ruined; and they had a fair number of dinghies and boats of boiled leather, good enough to take three men to fish in pools and rivers if they wished, so that the lords and men of rank had plenty of fish during Lent – though the commoners made do with what they could get. What's more, the noble king had a good thirty falconers with a fine stock of birds, and some sixty pairs of great dogs and just as many greyhounds with which he went hunting every day.

The army was divided into three, each division always marching on its own and each with an advance guard and a rearguard, and they would camp a league apart; the Prince of Wales commanded one, the Duke of Lancaster another and King Edward the third. On they marched in this manner until they arrived before Paris to offer battle, as you've heard, and then headed for the city of Chartres, always seeking out the most plentiful country, and then made for Bonneval and the march of Vendôme. It was now that the noble king, at the request of the Abbot of Cluny, turned back to Chartres and stayed there for twenty-one days negotiating a peace, which was concluded and agreed on the following terms.

Namely: the noble King Edward and his successors were to have and to hold forever, freely and in peace, unreservedly and without holding them in fief from the King of France or anyone else, all the following lands and territories: La Bigorre, the Agenais, Quercy, Périgord, Rouergue, Poitou, La Rochelle, Limousin, Saintonge, the county of Angoulême, the fiefdoms of Thouars and Belleville, along with the whole duchy of Guyenne to its full former extent; and in the marches of Picardy he was to have and to hold forever, unreservedly and without liege dependency, the city and castle of Calais and all its appendages, the land of Marck and the whole county of Guînes to its full extent, including its towns and castles. If he wished, he was also to have all the county of Ponthieu, which had been given to the Queen of England his mother at her marriage, though if he wished to have this, he was to hold it in fief from the King of France as his father had done. Moreover, he was to receive, by way of expenses and damages, three million old florins[1] – that is, thirty times one hundred thousand florins – to be paid in six instalments. The first payment was due three weeks after the feast of Saint John in the year 1360 and the remainder was to be paid within the next three years, a third of it each year. And all the ransoms he'd taken from lands, towns, houses and prisoners he was to keep quite freely. As security, the French were to send good and worthy hostages, the most eminent in the kingdom, to remain at Calais until these terms had been fully met.

For his part, King Edward undertook and promised to take King John of France back to Calais by Saint John's Day, and to keep him there for three weeks at his own expense, within which time the French were to have fulfilled the above-mentioned conditions and placed the noble King Edward's men in peaceful possession of all the castles, towns, lands and territories which he was thenceforth to hold and own unreservedly. If the terms had not been fully met, King John of France and all the hostages were to stay in Calais for three months and pay thirty thousand florins for their board and expenses, and the English would remain in possession of all the castles and fortresses they'd won in the kingdom of France, though they were not to pillage or make war.

---

[1] 'flourins à l'escu Philippus': old florins of higher quality than more recent, debased coin.

Furthermore, the young Count of Montfort was to have free lordship of the county of Montfort, along with a portion of the duchy of Brittany: how much of the latter should be rightfully his would be determined by the two kings once they'd heard and considered the arguments of Lord Charles of Blois on the one hand and of the count on the other; and he would hold all his lands in fief from the King of France.

Once all had been settled, King John was to be peacefully escorted back to Paris with just sixteen of his fellow captives, those to be agreed by the two kings. So that all this might be better accomplished, a truce was agreed,[1] to be observed in all parts until Michaelmas[2] in the following year; and the French were to conduct King Edward peacefully through France to Calais, which they duly did.

In return for all this, the King of England was to renounce the right and title he claimed in France.

When all these issues had been settled and agreed, the Duke of Normandy, as first in line to the kingdom of France, promised to maintain and observe them; he made his vow in the presence of the Prince of Wales, the Duke of Lancaster and a number of English barons as King Edward's representatives.[3] Several lords of France who were present made the same vows, and King Edward's proxies made theirs in return. Then the noble king sent four knights to the palace at Paris to confirm the vows in public, much to the joy of all; churchmen and laymen alike came through the gates to meet them in a glorious procession, with the bells ringing on every side and all the streets of Paris bedecked. Everyone followed them to the palace, where they made the aforesaid oath. They were nobly welcomed by the Duke of Normandy and all the lords, and led into the beautiful chapel[4] where they were shown the most wondrous relics and jewels in the world, notably the holy crown with which God was crowned at His most holy Passion, from which the Duke of Normandy gave each knight one of the longest thorns: the knights were overwhelmed. Then the duke had each of them presented with the finest courser to be seen or found anywhere, and many more magnificent gifts, before they were taken back with a mighty escort to the English forces waiting for them at Palaiseau.

The two Marshals of France rode with them to King Edward, who was waiting for the Marshals to conduct him back through France as agreed; and when the English knights came before him they told him of the honour and courtesy with which the French had treated them: he was delighted, and entertained them and the French lords splendidly.

Next morning the king and all his forces set out peacefully and in good order towards Normandy and Pont-de-l'Arche to make the crossing of the Seine. Everywhere they passed along the way they found the towns open and a reasonable supply of all provisions on sale, for as soon as peace was made it had been proclaimed throughout the kingdom. And the noble king had his knights

[1]   At Brétigny near Chartres on 7 May 1360.
[2]   i.e. the end of September.
[3]   The duke ratified the Treaty of Brétigny on 10 May at the Hôtel de Sens in Paris.
[4]   The Sainte-Chapelle.

constantly ride at the rear of the army to ensure that his troops did no one any harm or offence. They quartered at Pont-de-l'Arche and then, next morning, the noble king set off with a small company to the port of Harfleur and sailed back to England, while his men as agreed went peacefully on to Picquigny in Picardy where they crossed the Somme and made their way to Calais. There the French took leave of them, and the English prepared to take passage home, each as best he could.

As soon as the noble king and his company arrived in London and he'd been welcomed by the Queen, he went straight to King John and escorted him back to London, where he was entertained by the Queen, the Prince of Wales (who harboured only good feelings towards him),[1] the Duke of Lancaster and a number of other lords with all possible honour and warmth. This feasting and open court lasted for fifteen days.

When all was done and the King of France had been provided with the noble apparel befitting his station, King Edward and his children and all the other lords escorted him to the sea at Dover. King Edward sent his son and a great company of lords with him to Calais as he'd promised.[2]

But they waited a long while at Calais for the French lords who, according to the terms agreed, were due to bring six hundred thousand florins and then remain as hostages. When they'd waited long enough and it was clear that neither the money nor the hostages were ready, they took their leave of King John and returned to England; but they left him and his young son Lord Philip in the custody of four knights and other very able men who provided them with all the comfort they reasonably could, and allowed French knights of his choosing to converse with him at dinner and supper, and took him on frequent excursions to hunt and so forth, all the while waiting for the promised sum of money to be delivered to Saint-Omer. But the French were reluctant to deliver it until all the hostages had arrived – and not without good reason; for if the florins had been handed over but the hostages had refused to surrender as promised, then the money would have been lost, the peace broken and King John taken back to England. And so it was that the King of France and his youngest[3] son were stuck at Calais for a long time, let down by the high peers and barons of France who were loath to surrender as hostages to release their king. In the end and with great reluctance most of them said they were ready and prepared to be hostages, but would do so only if the king's two sons, the Count of Anjou and the Count of Poitiers, offered themselves first, since they were more obligated than anyone. This was by no means unjustified, for the two counts appeared to be putting up more resistance than anybody else, and all the others named as hostages had arrived at Saint-Omer a fortnight before them.

---

[1]   'pas ne le hayoit': literally 'didn't hate him'. This phrase, using a negative as a positive, is not uncommon in medieval French; the implication is that he 'didn't dislike him in the least – in fact was really very fond of him'.

[2]   King John arrived back in Calais on 8 July.

[3]   The text reads 'aisné' ('eldest') but, if referring to Philip, should read 'mainsné'.

Eventually, around the feast of All Saints, the agreed sum of six hundred thousand florins was delivered to Calais along with all the hostage knights, amid much celebration. Then King John left the city, the Prince of Wales and the Duke of Lancaster escorting him as far as Saint-Omer where the king held a great court at All Saints. The prince and the duke and their companions were richly entertained there throughout the three days, and then the English lords departed and made a joyful return to England.[1] King John now made for Arras, and from there rode from town to town until he arrived at Paris just before Christmas, where he and all the princes with him spent the whole winter. Everywhere he passed he was showered with handsome, splendid gifts, but not a word of thanks ever crossed his lips.

It was at this time that a great company appeared in Burgundy and Champagne who were known as the Latecomers.[2] They'd taken possession and control of the castle of Joinville, and of all the treasure amassed within it for supposed safe keeping: a vast pile of inestimable worth. And then around Christmas this company, having ravaged and wasted the whole region, headed for Avignon and promptly captured the stronghold called Pont-Saint-Esprit,[3] taking captive a large number of fine men-at-arms who were stationed there to guard it, raping girls and women of the town, plundering everything they found and laying waste the whole of the surrounding land on every side as far as Avignon, much to the terror of the Pope and his cardinals. This company had appointed a captain who signed all his letters with the name by which he wished to be known: 'God's Friend and the World's Enemy'.[4]

In many parts of France at this time there were hordes of bandits and robbers wasting the land – Englishmen and others – and they still had possession of a huge number of castles and fortresses, so that few people dared travel across country, especially in Champagne and Brie and between Paris and Orléans and Paris and Chartres, despite the fact that peace had been made and King John and all his greatest barons were back together in Paris. But when they heard the news that this great company had taken the stronghold of Pont-Saint-Esprit and thought they'd soon conquer Avignon and the whole of Provence, all these brigands decided to go and join them, which they did: some sold the castles and fortresses they held to their rightful owners, or to other local men, and the rest went scurrying after.

The Pope and his cardinals held urgent talks, and declared a Crusade against the wicked Christians who were remorselessly ruining the country and Christendom and murdering men, women and children without mercy, and raping women and girls. The Pope and cardinals issued a decree that all who committed themselves to destroying these wicked men would be given absolution for their sins and remission from Purgatory. As commander of this Crusade they appointed the Cardinal of Ostia, and he set out swiftly from Avignon with such men as he had

---

[1]   Edward left Calais with the hostages and returned to England on 31 October.
[2]   'les Tart Venus'.
[3]   On 28 December.
[4]   'amy de Dieu et anemy de tout le monde'.

to await the arrival of those who would come to earn their pardons by joining him. A good number of knights and squires came, expecting great rewards from the Pope besides the promised indulgences; but no one was interested in giving them a thing, so off they went, some back home and some to Lombardy – and others indeed to join the wicked band that was steadily growing by the day: captains and companies were springing up everywhere.

Chapter CIX

How the Marquis of Montferrat led the Great Companies into Lombardy.

Seeing this, the Pope, terrified and helpless, sent for the Marquis of Montferrat, an outstanding soldier who had long been at war against the lords of Milan, and commissioned him to negotiate with the Great Companies; and in return for a huge sum of money paid to each one, they left the country around Avignon and Pont-Saint-Esprit and promised to go with the marquis to Lombardy to fight the Milanese.

But that's not all: the Pope also gave them pardon for all their misdeeds and absolution and remission from Purgatory.

This was in the year of grace 1361, in the month of April.

Index

Aachen, 99, 101
Aardenburg, 86
Abbeville, 177, 179, 181
Abu Al-Hasan, *king of Tlemcen*, 95, 96
Abu Umar, *sultan of the Benimerines*, 95-7
Affligem, 102
Afonso IV, *king of Portugal*, 96
Agen, 166
Agenais, 225, 257
Aigimont, Louis d', 92
Aiguillon, 158-67, 185-7
Airaines, 176-7, 179
Aire-sur-la-Lys, 88, 198, 219
'Albrecht' (Albert Sterz?), 243, 245
Albret, Bernard-Aiz, lord of, 187, 210
Alcalá, 98
Alfonso XI, *king of Castile*, 95-8, 156
Alfonso, *nephew of Louis of Spain*, 139, 143
Algeciras, 98, 156, 209
Alençon, Charles, Count of, 90, 92, 99, 115, 170, 183
Almonses, Liebert d', 91
Amboise, 226
Amiens, 168, 175-7, 184, 185, 198, 204, 205, 218-20, 234, 235, 241, 245
Anderlecht, 102n
Ancenis, 115
Angers, 115, 151
Angoulême, 160-3, 257
Anjou, Louis, Count of, 259
Anor, 94
Antenis, 162, 163, 164
Antioch, 164
Antoing, Henry d', 35
Antwerp, 71-2, 76, 94, 103, 107
'Archpriest, the': see Cervole
Ardres, 219
Argenteau-sur-Meuse, 57, 195
Armagnac, John, Count of, 90, 92, 186, 222
Arques, 75
Arras, 89, 184, 198, 200, 204, 249, 260
Arteine, Robert d', 164
Artevelde, Jacob van, 69, 70, 82, 86-8, 157-8
Arthur, King, 22, 39, 45, 63, 65, 132, 153, 216
Artois, 36, 192
Artois, Mahaut, Countess of, 55
Artois, Robert of, 56-8, 60, 65, 88, 147-9, 155
Arundel, Richard Fitzalan, Earl of, 28, 29
Asse, Henry d', 91
Ath, 107n
Athens, Walter of Brienne, [titular] Duke of, 90, 226
Attigny, 252, 254, 255

Aubenton, 83, 243
Auberchicourt, Eustache d', 243, 245, 252, 253
Auberchicourt, Sauchet d', 243n
Audley, Peter, 243, 245
Audrehem, Arnoul d', 198, 211, 219, 220, 224, 226, 227, 248
Aulnay, 187
Aumale, Catherine, Countess of, 178
Auray, 112, 132-3, 136, 138
Auxerre, 243, 254
Auxerre, Jean de Chalon, Count of, 138, 161, 170, 183
Avesnes-sur-Helpe, 82
Avignon, 51, 209, 231, 242, 260-1
'Aymery' (Aimeric of Pavia), 206

Bagnols-sur-Cèze, 242
Baileux, 83
Bailleul, Robert de, lord of Fontaine-l'Évêque and Morialmé, 35
Balliol, Edward, 189
Balliol, Robert, 147
Bannockburn, 22n, 35n
Bar, 255
Bar, Robert, Duke of, 57, 89
Bar-sur-Aube, 243
'Barbevair', *pirate*, 77, 83
Barfleur, 170
Bascon de Mareuil, Le, 206, 253
Basle, le Moyne de, 180
Baume, Galoys de, 116
Bavaria, William, Duke of, 99, 107
Bavay, 84
Bayonne, 157-8
Beaucaire, seneschal of, 162
Beauchamp, John, 210, 211, 216
Beaujeu, lord of, 199, 200, 210
Beaulot, lord of, 198
Beaumanoir, Jean de, 212
Beaumanoir, Robert de, 145
Beaumont, 83, 94
Beaumont, Jean de : see Hainault, John of
Beaumont, John, 2nd Baron, 78, 88, 147
Beaurain, 183
Beauvais, 175, 185, 205, 234-6, 240, 245
Beauvais, bishop-count of, 23n, 90, 161, 162, 186
Belleville, 257
Benevento, battle of, 183
'Benmarin, King' : see Abu Al-Hasan
Bergerac, 158
Berghes, Henry of Boutersem, lord of, 249
Berghes, Renault de, 249

Bergues, 193
Bergues, lord of, 219
Berkhampstead, 59n
Bernalmont, Jean de, 249
Berry, 161, 225, 227, 247
Bertrand, Robert, 87, 133, 172
Berwick, 22, 24, 60-5, 119, 122, 146-7, 205, 221-2, 230
Béthune, 192, 249
Béziers, 223
Bigorre, La, 257
Binche, 102
Blanche, *daughter of Charles IV of France*, 55n
Blanche of Navarre, *2nd wife of Philip VI of France*, 209
Blanche Lande (Blanchland), 45
Blanchetaque, 99, 178-9
Blaye, 160
Blise, Daynals de, 91
Blois, 226
Blois, Charles of, 108-9, 113-8, 128-38, 142-5, 231, 258
Blois, Louis, Count of, 90, 99, 108, 170, 183, 196-7, 204, 212
Bohemia, King John of, 33, 55-7, 68, 79-80, 89, 92, 98-9, 169, 181, 183, 190n, 209
Bois-le-duc, 103
Boneffe, 105
Bonn, 99
Bonne, *daughter of John of Bohemia, wife of John II of France*, 68n, 104, 209, 215
Bonneval, 233, 257
Bordeaux, 103, 147, 157, 158, 160, 187, 188, 210, 211, 212, 222, 223, 225, 229
Bornem, 107
Boroughbridge, battle of, 24n
Boroughmuir, battle of, 64
Bouchain, 84
Boucicaut, Lord (Jehan le Meingre), 84, 220, 226
Bouillon, 90, 91
Bouillon, Godfrey of, 164
Boulogne, 168, 183, 185, 219, 220, 245
Boulogne, cardinal of, 215, 218
Boulogne, Count of: see Burgundy, Philip of
Boulogne, Jeanne, Countess of, 209
Bourbon, Pierre, Duke of, 115, 128, 132, 160, 162, 186, 200, 222, 223, 227, 228
Bourbourg, 56n
Bourg, 160
Bourges, 225
Boutillier, Jehan le, 139, 140, 143
Bove, Jehan de la, 83
Boys, Henry du, 207
Brabant, 27, 35, 36, 57, 60, 76, 89-91, 100, 101-7, 248, 249, 250, 255
Brabant, John III, Duke of, 57, 66-8, 71-9, 82, 85-8, 92-4, 101, 192, 195-6
Bramborough, Robert: see 'Brandebourch'
'Brandebourch', 212-4
Brandenburg, Marquis of, 99
Branquebierge, lord of, 36

Bray-sur-Seine, 245n
Bray-sur-Somme, 249
Brech, 132n, 151n
Brest, 109-11, 132n, 151n
Bret, Gérard de la, 147
Breteuil, 225
Brétigny, Treaty of, 257-8
Brie, 235, 236, 243, 260
Briffeuil, Alard de, 35
Briquisy, L'Ours de, 245
Bristol, 28-31
Brittany, 108-118, 128-57, 196, 206, 212, 217, 230, 233, 247, 258
Brittany, Arthur II, Duke of, 108n
Brittany, John III, Duke of, 108
Bruce, Robert, king of Scotland, 24, 34, 40, 52
Bruges, 34, 56, 70, 88, 158n,
Brussels, 72, 94-5, 102-3, 105
Brusto, Jehan de (John Briscoe?), 160
Buchan, Earl of, 189-90
Buironfosse, 80-1
Burgundy, 227, 249, 254, 255, 260
Burgundy, Eudes IV, Count of, 55n, 90, 115, 128, 160, 186
Burgundy, Jeanne, Countess of, 56n
Burgundy, Philippe I, Duke of, 254
Burgundy, Philip of, 162, 185, 209
Bury St Edmunds, 28
Bucy, Simon de, 232

Cadoudal, Guillaume de, 129-30, 139, 197n
Cadzand, 86
Caen, 169, 172
Cahors, 166
Calais, 175, 183-209, 215, 216, 219-21, 248-51, 257-60
Cale, Guillaume, 237n
Cambrai, 73, 76-9, 252
Cambrai, bishop of, 84
Canny, Le Flamenc de, 240
Canterbury, archbishop of, 189
Capelle, La, 80-1
Carcassonne, 166, 209, 222-3
Cardueil, 39, 123n
Carhaix, 113, 138, 141, 142, 145
Carlisle, 39, 43, 52, 123
Carquefou, 116
Cassel, 56, 88, 198
Castelmoron-sur-Lot, 159
Castelnaudary, 222
Castelsagrat, 159
Castile, 95
Castile, king of: see Alfonso XI
Castle of the Maidens, 63
Castle Rising, 59n
Cateau-Cambrésis, 83-4
Cayeu, lord of, 87
Cerisy, 249
Cervole, Arnaud de, 'the Archpriest', 231

Chalon, Jean de (Jean II de Chalon-Arlay), 245, 247
Châlons, 243, 244, 247, 253
Champagne, 243-4, 246-7, 253, 254, 260
Champtoceaux, 116, 128
Chappelle, Godefroy de la, 36
Charente, river, 211
Charlemagne, 24, 164
Charles IV, king of France, 23, 55
Charles of Bohemia, the Emperor Charles IV, 99-106, 169, 209
Charny, Geoffroi de, 87, 200, 206-8, 227
Charterhouse, 52n
Chartres, 225, 254, 256, 257, 260
Chastebercke, Jehan de, 36
Chastel, Philippe du, 34
Château-Gaillard, 55, 57n, 224
Château-Landon, 233
Châteauneuf-sur-Loire, 243
Château-Thierry, 243
Châtel, Tanneguy du, 196
Châtelet, 83, 123, 187, 224, 239
Châtres-sur-Cher, 233
Chaumont, Alixandre, lord of, 159, 164, 210
Chauvency, Gérard de, 244
Chepstow, 30n
Cherbourg, 170
Chesne, Le, 252
Chimay, 83, 94
Chinon, 57n
Choisy, 87
Christopher (English ship), 83, 86
Clement VI, Pope, 99-100, 209, 215
Clermont, 98, 194
Clermont, Jean de, 222, 226, 227
Clermont, Louis de, 90
Clermont, Robert de, 234
Clisson, Amaury de, 129, 134, 139, 144
Clisson, Garnier de, 109, 110
Clisson, Olivier de, 110, 149, 151-3, 224
Clisson, Olivier de (2), 112
Cloyes-sur-le-Loir, 233
Cluny, abbot of, 254, 256-7
Cobham, Reginald, 21, 78, 183, 200
Coke, Thomas, 159, 161
Cologne, 244
Cologne, archbishop of, 57, 67, 68
Comborn, 206
Compiègne, 87, 240
Condé-sur-l'Escaut, 33
Condroz, 90, 98
Conflans, 247
Conflans, Jean de, 234n
Conquest, castle, 136
Conrard, bishop of Liège's cook, 91
Copegueule, 176
Copeland, John, 190-1
Coq, Robert le: see Laon, bishop of
Corbie, 236
Cormicy, 245, 252
Cornet, Castle, 169

Coteberque, Gille de, 36
Cotentin, 169-72, 174, 205, 225, 230
Coucy, lord of, 236, 237, 240, 243
Coudenberg, 102, 103
Courtrai, battle of, 183
Courtrai, Siger de, 70
Coutances, 172
Craon, lord of, 226, 227
Crécy (-en-Ponthieu), battle of, 179-83, 226
Crécy-sur-Serre, 80, 245
Creil, 237, 240, 245
Crèvecoeur, 73
Croix, Waflard de la, 90
Croquart, brigand, 206
Crotoy, Le, 179

Dagworth, Thomas, 157, 196-7
Damazan, 160
Damery, 243
Dargies, 176
David II, king of Scotland, 23, 52, 54, 60-1, 74-5, 90, 119-28, 148, 189-90, 230
Denis, Gerard, 158
Derby, Earl of: see Lancaster, Henry of Grosmont, Earl, then Duke of
Despenser, Hugh the Elder, 24, 28-31
Despenser, Hugh the Younger, 24-6, 29-31
Diest, 75, 103
Dinant, 95, 195
Donchery, 252
Donzenac, 205
Doria, Ayton, 116, 138, 149
Dordrecht, 27, 30
Douai, 82-4, 87, 89, 192
Douglas, James ('The Black'), 40, 47-8, 52-4
Douglas, William, lord of Liddesdale, 63-4, 119-21, 123, 127, 189, 205
Douglas, William, his nephew, later 1st Earl, 221
Dover, 32, 34, 35, 50, 251, 259
Duffle, Henri Berthout, lord of, 36
Dunfermline, 53n
Dunkirk, 25n, 56n
Duras, Jehan de, 249
Durham, 39, 49-50, 63, 119, 122-3, 125, 189
Durham, bishop of, 122, 182, 189-90
Dury, Rabigot, 243-4, 246

Edinburgh, 64n, 119-21
Edward I, king of England, 22
Edward II, king of England, 22-31
Edward III, king of England, 21-2, 24-5, crowned king 33, first campaign against the Scots 34-50, marries Philippa of Hainault 50-1, claims French crown 58, 65-6, second war with Scotland 59-65, first campaign against the French 66-93, appointed Vicar of the Empire 75-6, assumes arms of France 82, at La Capelle 80-2, at Sluys 85-6, siege of Tournai 88-92, at Esplechin 93, third war with the Scots 119, 124-8, with the Countess of

Salisbury 125-7, 153-6, *in Brittany* 149-51, *his Round Table* 153, 157, *the Crécy campaign* 167-83, *siege of Calais* 184, 198-205, *saves Calais Castle* 206-8, *ravages Picardy* 219-21, *recaptures Berwick* 221-2, *last campaign in France* 248-59
Edward the Black Prince: see Wales, Prince of
Eleanor of Woodstock, 23
Enghien, Gauthier d', 35 , 37
Enghien, Gérard de, castellan of Mons and lord of Havré, 35
Engloye, Watyer, 94
Engloye, Renier, 94
Épernay, 243
Erkes, lord of, 206
Escaudoeuvres, 84
Esplechin, 92
Étampes, 233
Étaples, 183
Eu, Raoul, Count of, 57, 87, 115, 128, 167, 169, 172, 204, 214-5
Évreux, 174, 205, 218, 224-5
Évreux, Louis d', 55

Faerye, Jehan de, 198
Fagnolle, Hugues, lord of, 35
Faouët, Le, 140-3
Fauquembergues, 198, 220
Fauquemont: see Valkenburg
Fay, Godemar du, 87, 177-8
Fénétrange, Brocard de, 244-5, 247
Fexhe, Henry de, 91
Fexhe, Ogier de, 91
Fitzwaren, William, 66n
Flamengrie, La, 80-1
Flanders, 35, 69-70, 82, 86-90, 107, 157-8, 192-3, 236, 248
Flanders, Louis I, Count of, 56, 70, 90, 92, 99, 108, 170
Flanders, Louis II, Count of, 101-8, 192-5
Fleming, Malcolm ('Sir Richard the Fleming'), 121
Foix, Count of, 98, 222, 237
Fontaine-sur-Somme, 177
Fontenelle, 92
Forest, La, *castle*, 113
Forest, Pierre de la, archbishop of Rouen, 232
Forez, Count of, 222
Fortune, 22, 44, 80n, 81, 182, 228, 238, 244, 250
Fotheringhay, John, 245
Franck, 56
Frankfurt, 99
Fraser, Simon, 119-20, 189
Fresnay, Hubert de, 130, 139-40, 143
Freypont, Colin, 91
Frisia, 101, 106
Fricamp, Fri(s)quet de, 224
Froidchapelle, 83

Gallardon, 233
Garonne, river, 159, 164-5, 222, 223

Gascony, 38, 88, 93, 98, 108, 147, 153, 157-67, 185, 187, 205, 210, 219, 222-3, 225
Gastinois, 254
Gaunt, John of: see Richmond
Gavere, Raes van, 36
Geer, river, 195
Gembloux, 104
Geneva, Count of, 89
Gerarstene, lord of, 256
Ghent, 56, 69-70, 86, 88, 102, 158
Ghistelles, Wulfart de, 36
Gironde, 147, 158, 160, 187, 210, 225
Glay, Guy de, 141
Glay la Forest, *castle*, 141-2
Gloucester, Hugh de Audley, 1st Earl of, 78, 88, 147
Granada, 63, 113, 143, 173, 209
Granada, sultans of: see Muhammed IV, Yusuf I
Grandvilliers, 176
Grandmont, 107
Grimaldi, Carlo, 116, 149
Guelders, 66n
Guelders, Edward of, 23
Guelders, Reginald III, Duke of, 23, 101, 195
Guelders, Reginald II, Duke of, 23, 57, 67, 68, 71, 73-4, 85, 87, 88, 92
Guémené-sur-Scorff, 129n, 133, 136-7, 140-1, 150
Guérande, 136, 137, 139
Guernsey, 169, 171
Guildford, 58n
Guînes, 184, 198, 215n, 216, 219, 257
Guînes, Count of, 87, 115
Guingamp, 145
Guingant, castellan of, 129, 131, 133, 134, 139, 144
Guingant, Regnault de, 134, 137
Guyenne, 257
Guyenne, Tassart de, 196
Guzman, Eleanor of ('La Riche Donerde'), 97n

Hainault, 27, 35, 67, 72, 75, 78-9, 82-5, 90-1, 100, 108, 238, 243, 245, 248, 249, 252
Hainault, Albert, Duke of
Hainault, John of, 26-7, 29-38, 50-1, 56, 57-8, 66-8, 71, 77, 80, 83-5, 87, 92, 93-5, 170, 181, 200
Hainault, Philippa of: see Philippa
Hainault, William I, Count of, 25n, 27, 33, 50-1, 56-8, 66-8, 70, 73
Hainault, William II, Count of, 73, 79, 81, 83-5, 87-8, 92, 93, 95, 101, 106, 147
Hainault, William III, Count of, 106, 107-8
Hale, Frank van, 21, 157, 161, 164, 166, 249
Halle, 72, 130n
Hannut, 104, 195
Hans, 243, 244
Hanse, 248
Harcourt, John IV, Count of, 90, 169, 170, 183
Harcourt, John V, Count of, 223-4
Harcourt, Godfrey de, 169, 171, 175, 181
Hardeshull, John, 196-7

Harduemont, Godefroi, lord of, 219n, 249
Harduemont, Jehan de, 249
Harfleur, 259
Harlebecque, 'the three brothers of', 36
Hastepem, Watier de, 249
Hastings, Ralph, 161
Havré, lord of: see Enghiem, Gérard
Hebden, Richard, 161
Hemiksem, 72n
Hennebont, 112, 118, 130-44, 157, 196
Hennequin, Frank, 244, 246
Henry of Flanders, 249
Henry of Luxembourg (the Emperor Henry VII), 55
Henselode, lord of, 36
Hercs, Gillebert de, 36
Hereford, 31
Hermalle, 195
Hesbaye, 27, 35, 36, 57, 90, 91, 98, 195, 248, 249, 250
Hesdin, 198, 219, 220
Heusden, 106
Heyden, Gerard van der, 249
Holland, 27, 30, 50, 66n, 108, 206, 249
Holland, Thomas, 173, 200
Huldenbergh, Gauthier de, 36
Huntingdon, William Clinton, Earl of, 66n
Huy, 91, 98, 194-5
Hyerclais, Evrard, 94-5

Île-de-France, 235
Innocent VI, Pope, 231, 242, 247, 260-1
Isabella, queen of England, mother of Edward III, 23-33, 36, 38, 50-1, 58-9
Issoudun, 55, 225

Jeanne, 3rd wife of Charles IV of France, 55
Jeanne, Countess of Burgundy, 56
Jeanne of Burgundy, wife of Philip VI, 209
Jeanne de Valois, abbess of Fontenelle, wife of William I of Hainault, 92-3
Jedburgh, 118-9, 121, 125, 127, 205, 221
Jehanne of Brabant, wife of Wenceslaus of Luxembourg, 101, 107
Jemeppe, Rasse de, 249
Jerusalem, 53, 164, 216
Joan of Bar, 34
Joan of Navarre, 23n
Joan of the Tower, 23
Jodoigne, 104
John of Eltham, 23, 58
John II, king of France, *as Duke of Normandy* 84, 90, 104, 106, 115-6, 128, 151, *in Gascony* 160-5, 185-7, *crowned king* 209, *pact with King of Navarre* 217-9, *captured at Poitiers* 227-9, *his release* 257-9
Joinville, 260
Josselin, 212, 214

Jülich, Guillaume, Margrave (later Duke) of, 36, 57, 67, 68, 71, 73-5, 85, 87-8, 92, 102, 256
Juliers: see Jülich
Jupeleu, Loys de, 91
Jupleu, Bureau de, 105

Kenilworth, 31n
Kent, Edmund of Woodstock, Earl of, 23-6, 34, 50, 58-9
Knolles, Robert, 233, 243, 247
Koblenz, 76n, 99
Kraainem, Louis of, 71, 76, 79

Labbel, 73
Labroye, 181
La Haze, Jean, 130, 135, 139
La Haze, Louis, 130, 135, 139
Laleu, 198
Lamine, 195
Lancaster, Henry of Grosmont, 4th Earl, then 1st Duke of (previously Earl of Derby), 21, 28, 52, 78, 86, 88, 98, 147, 153-4, 157-61, 187-8, 193, 196, 199-200, 221-2, 225, 230-1, 247-52, 257-9
Lancaster, Thomas, 2nd Earl of, 24, 28
Lancaster, Henry, 3rd Earl of, 28, 30n, 50, 78, 147
Lande-Halle ('the two Lande-Halle brothers'), 130, 135, 139, 157
Landen, 104
Landreman, lord of (Galeran de Landreman), 129, 131, 134-5, 139, 144
Lanvaux, 113n
Laon, 241, 243, 244, 252, 254
Laon, bishop-duke of, 236, 237, 239
Larchant, 233
Latinne, 195
Le Bel, Henry (the author's brother), 36
Le Bel, Jean (the author), canon of Liège, 36
Léon, bishop of, 129, 131, 134, 136, 138
Léon, Hervé de, 109, 110, 112, 113, 117, 129, 131, 133, 134, 136, 138, 141, 149, 151-3
Lesparre, lord of, 187, 210
Leuven, 74-6, 94, 102-5
Libine, Jehan de, 36
Liège, 60, 71, 85, 98, 100, 102, 107, 194-5, 238, 255
Liège, Adolph de la Marck, bishop of, 57, 67-8, 79-80, 89-91, 92, 98
Liège, Engelbert, bishop of, 105-7, 194-5, 255
Lille, 82-3, 87, 90, 123, 192
Lille, Count of, 186
Limburg, John of Brabant, duke of, 67n
Limoges, 109, 114, 206, 225, 247
Limont, 195
Limousin, Walter de, 119
Lincoln, bishop of, 147-8, 189
Lisle, John de, 161, 164
Llantrissant, 30n
Loire, river, 226, 233, 243
Lombardy, 101, 136, 260-1
Lonchiens, Connars de, 91

London, 22, 31-3, 35, 51, 59-63, 67, 119, 122, 129, 146, 155-6, 169n, 190-1, 204, 208, 221, 222, 229, 247, 259
Long-en-Ponthieu, 177
Longpré, 177
Longré-les-Corps-Saints, 177
Loon, *county*, 75, 104
Loon, Godefroy de, 98
Loon, Thierry de Heinsberg, Count of, 36, 57, 85, 102, 104, 106, 195
Lorraine, John, Duke of, 255
Lorraine, Raoul, Duke of, 89, 99, 170
Lorris, Robert de, 218, 232
Lot, river, 159
Louis X, king of France, 23
Louis of Bavaria, Emperor, 98
Louvain: see Leuven
Louviers, 174
Louvre, 118, 128, 187, 214-5
Lucy, 243
Lusignan, 188, 205
Luxembourg, Wenceslaus, Duke of, 101-6, 255

Maastricht, 75, 106
Maillard, Jean, 239
Maillezais, 187
Maistrel, *pirate*, 184
Malain, Gérard de, 133-4, 137, 140-1
Malain, Renier de, 140-1
Malestroit, Geoffroi de, 112, 129, 133, 138, 139, 152
Malestroit, Henry de, 152
Malestroit, Treaty of, 151n
Malines: see Mechelen
Mantes, 174, 241
Marant, *pirate*, 184, 191
Marcel, Étienne (*never named*), provost of Paris merchants, 232, 234-6, 238-40
Marchiennes, 87
Marck, 184, 257
Marck, Adolph de la: see Liège, bishop of
Marck, Engelbert, Count of La: see Liège, bishop of Mareuil, 177
Mareuil, Le Bascon de: see Bascon
Marle, 80
Marmyon, Robert, 84
Marne, river, 236, 243
Marque, river, 90n
Massures, Races (Rasse Mascurel), 182
Mauconseil, 240-1
Mauny, Walter, 21, 51, 52n, 61-2, 78, 84, 86, 130, 135-7, 139-42, 144, 147, 157, 161, 164-6, 186, 200-3, 221, 249
Mauron, 217
Meaux, 236-7, 239
Mechelen, 75, 77, 78, 101-2, 104, 105-7, 245
Meilhan-sur-Garonne, 159
Meingre, Jean le: see Boucicaut
Meissen, 249, 250
Meissen, Frederick, margrave of, 250

Melun, 241, 245-6, 248
Metz, 105-6, 255-6
Metz, bishop of, 89
Meule, Gossuin de, 36
Meuse, river, 95
Mézières, 252, 253
Milan, 101, 169, 261
Milhy, Hugue de, 139
Milly-sur-Thérain, 175-6, 233
Miramont, 160, 161-2, 163
Mohalt, Thierry de, 91
Moncheaulx, Race de, 91
Mondrepuis, 94
Mons, 84, 95
Mons, castellan of: see Enghien, Gerard d'
Mons, Count of, 102-4, 106, 256
Monségur, 159, 164
Montagu, William, *nephew of the Earl of Salisbury of the same name*, 123-5
Montaigu, 254
Montargis, 233, 254
Montbéliard, Count of, 89
Montebourg, 170
Montfaucon, 151, 224
Montfaucon, Girard de, 87, 89
Montferrat, John, Marquis of, 101, 261
Montfort, John Count of, 108-118, 128-9
Montfort, John Count of (his son), 129, 219, 230
Montfort, Jeanne de Flandre, Countess of, 118, 128-37, 140, 142-8, 152, 157, 196-7, 212, 217, 230
Montgiscard, 222
Montgomery, John, 159, 164
Monthalt, 90
Montigny, Jean de, 35
Montigny-en-Austrevant, lord of, 244
Montjoye, 176
Montlhéry, 233
Montmorency, lord of, 162
Montpellier, 209, 223
Montpezat, 159
Montreuil-Bonnin, 188
Montreuil-sur-Mer, 183, 219
Mont-Saint-Eloi, abbey of, 249
Mont-Saint-Jean, abbey of, 80
Mont-Saint-Martin, abbey of, 80n
Mont-Saint-Michel, 225, 230
Moray, 121
Moray, John Randolph, Earl of, 63-4, 119, 122, 128, 189-90, 204
Moray, Thomas Randolph, Earl of, 40, 53
Moret, Jehan de, 83
Morillon, Thibault de, 152
Mortimer, Roger, 25-6, 34, 50, 58-9
Mouzon, 252
Mowbray, John 3rd Baron, 189
Muhammed IV, king of Granada, 54

Nagor, lord of, 152
Namur, 57, 91, 94-5, 106
Namur, Guy of, 63-4

Namur, John, Count of, 57, 63-4
Namur, Louis of, 219
Namur, William, Count of, 104-6, 170
Namur, Philip of, 63-4
Nantes, 109, 112-4, 116-8, 128-9, 150-1
Narbonne, 209, 223
Narbonne, Aimery of, 87
Nassau, John, Count of, 227-8
Navarre, Charles II, King of, 215, 217-9, 223-4, 232-6, 238-41, 246, 248, 253
Navarre, Philip III, King of, 90, 98
Navarre, Lord Philip of, 215, 217-8, 224-5, 230
Nesle, Guy de, 210-1
Neufchâtel, 183
Nevers, 243, 254
Neville, John, 3rd Baron de Raby, 189
Neville's Cross, battle of, 189-90
Newcastle-upon-Tyne, 39, 43, 61, 63, 122, 189
Nieulay, 199
Niort, 188
Nivelles, 78, 103, 104
Nogent, 243, 245
Norfolk, Thomas of Brotherton, Earl of, 23, 39
Normandy, John, Duke of: see John II of France
Normandy, Duke of, Charles, John II's eldest son, 104, 223-4, 226-7, 232-5, 238-41, 244-7, 253, 258
Northampton, William de Bohun, Earl of, 66n, 78, 88, 147, 181, 193, 200
Northumberland, 39, 119, 122, 189
Norway, 122
Norwich, John of, 162-4, 166
Noyelles, 178
Noyers, lord of, 90
Noyon, 236, 240, 241
Noyon, bishop-count of, 240
Nuremberg, 74

Obrécicourt, Bauldwyn d', 198
Ogle Castle, 190
Ohay, Huars d', 36
Oise, river, 80, 252
Oisemont, 177
Origny-Sainte-Benoîte, 80
Orkney, Earl of, 122, 189
Orléans, 160, 187, 226, 233, 243, 247, 260
Orléans, Philip, Duke of, 226, 232, 237, 241
Orwell, 71n
Ostia, cardinal of, 260
Oupey, Lambert d', 36
Ourscamps, abbey, 241
Ourthe, river, 39
Oxford, John de Vere, Earl of, 147, 148, 157, 159

Panetier, Colart le, 91
Paris, 25, 55, 67, 93, 94, 104, 108, 110, 113-5, 118, 128, 151, 154, 168-9, 174-6, 186-7, 204, 214, 216, 218, 221, 226, 231, 232-41, 245-6, 248, 253-5, 257, 258, 260

Patrick, 'the Earl Patrick', Patrick of Dunbar, 9th Earl of March, 119-20, 189
Pembroke, Lawrence Hastings, Earl of, 147-8, 157, 161, 164
Percy, Henry, lord of Alnwick, 189
Percy, Richard de, 152
Périgord, cardinal of, 227, 229
Péronne, 79-81, 249
Perrers, Alice, 146n
Perth, 119n, 121n, 205
Perthois, 235, 236
Philip IV, king of France, 23
Philip V, king of France, 23
Philip VI, king of France, 23, 55-8, 65, 67, 71, 73, the campaign ending at La Capelle 79-95; 174-6, at Crécy 178-83; 192, 194, at Calais 198-200; 204, 206, 208, death 209
Philip, son of John II of France, (later Philip the Bold, Duke of Burgundy), 229, 259
Philippa of Hainault, wife of Edward III [named only as 'queen of England'], 25n, 51, 74-6, 189-91, 193, 202-4, 259
Picardy, 146, 257
Picquigny, 176n, 259
Picquigny, Jean de, 234, 240-1, 245
Pierrepont, 254
Pisdoé, Martin, 253n
Pithiviers, 233
Ploërmel, 138, 212
Poissy, 174-5, 176, 205
Poitiers, 103, 188, 205, 226-8
Poitiers, Aymard de, 87
Poitiers, John, Count of, 240, 259
Poitou, Jourdain de Loubert, seneschal of, 87
Poix, 176, 245
Pommiers, lord of, 210
Pons, Renault de, 210-1
Pont-à-Mousson, 255
Pont-Arcy, 244
Pont-de-l'Arche, 258-9
Pontfaverger, 252
Ponthieu, 25n, 176, 179n, 185, 199n, 205, 245, 257
Pont-Rémy, 177
Pont-Sainte-Maxence, 240
Pont-Saint-Esprit, 260-1
Pont-sur-Seine, 243, 245
Poperinghe, 88
Porcien, Gaucher de Châtillon, Count of, 170, 244
Porteboeuf, Pierre, 134, 137, 141
Port Sainte-Marie, 164
Portsmouth, 149n
Portugal, king of: see Afonso IV
Pourelach, Gautier de, 91
Poylevilain, Jean, 232
Provence, 227, 231, 260
Provins, 243
Prussia, 173
Pyliser, Jean, 36
Pypempoys, Willaume, 91

Quarick, de ('the two de Quarick brothers'), 129
Quercy, 257
Quesnoy, Le, 81, 84
Quiéret, Hugues, 77, 83, 86
Quimper, 118n, 139
Quimperlé, 139, 143

Ramsay, Alexander, 119-20, 189
Redon, 113, 140
Reims, 55, 209, 243, 245, 246, 252-6
Remicourt, 195
Rennes, 111-2, 118, 128-30, 133, 140, 142, 150, 152, 230-1
Réole, La, 159
Rethel, 243, 244, 245, 246, 252, 253, 255
Rhine, river, 38, 68, 99
Ribemont, Eustace de, 207-8
Richmond, earldom of, 58, 60
Richmond, John of Gaunt, Earl of, 252
Rio Salado, battle of, 97
Robechies, 83
Roche-Derrien, La, battle of, 196-7
Rochefort, Gerard de, 145
Rochelle, La, 257
Roche-Périou, La, 112, 134, 140-2
Roche-Tesson, lord of La, 152
Rodes, Jehan de, 36
Roeulx, Fastré du, 35
Rohan, Alain, viscount of, 115, 133, 136, 138
Roland, *hero of 'The Song of Roland'*, 190, 213
Rome, 101, 103, 169
Romorantin, 226
Roquetaillade, Jean de, 242n
Rosnay-l'Hôpital, 243, 245
Ross, Earl of, 189
Roucy, 243-4, 246
Roucy, Robert, Count of, 170
Rouen, 172, 224, 234, 254
Rouergue, 257
Roxburgh, 119, 122, 128, 146, 147
Ruffin, 233

Saarbrücken, 89
Saarbrücken, John, Count of, 170
Saint-Amand-les-Eaux, 87
Saint-Antoine, 238
Saint-Arnoult, 233
Saint-Cloud, 174
Saint-Denis, 216, 238-40, 253
Saint-Germain, 175n, 176
Saint-Jean-d'Angély, 187-8, 205, 210-2, 214
Saint-Josse, 183
Saint-Lô, 172, 174
Saint-Maixent, 188
Saint-Mathieu, Finistère, 139
Saint-Maur-des-Fossés, 238
Saint-Mihiel, 255
Saint-Omer, 69, 88-9, 168, 194, 198, 219-21, 249, 259

Saint-Ouen, 216n
Saint-Pierre, Eustace de, 201-2
Saint-Pol, Guy, Count of, 170, 241
Saint-Quentin, 252
Saint-Servais, Baldwin de, 91
Saint-Servais, John de, 91
Saint-Thibéry, 223
Saint-Thierry, 252
Saint-Vaast-la-Hougue, 169n, 171, 174
Saint-Venant, 199
Sainte-Bazeille, 158
Saintonge, 93, 108, 128, 146, 152, 153, 233, 257
Saissignies, Gérard de, 84
Salisbury, Catherine Montagu, Countess of, 123-7, 146-7, 154-6
Salisbury, William Montagu, 1st Earl of, 62, 78, 80, 98, 123, 128-9, 146-8, 155-6
Salles, 83
Salm, Simon, Count of, 170, 183, 255
Sancerre, John, Count of, 170, 183
Sandwich, 158n, 169n
Sangatte, 198-9
Saponay, 243, 245
Savoy, 227, 249, 255
Savoy, Amadeus, Count of, 89
Scheldt, river, 85, 87, 89
Scheut, battle of, 102
Scleyde, lord of, 256
Scot, Robert, 243-4, 246
Seine, river, 174-5, 205, 233, 241, 258
Senak, Jacques, 244
Senlis, 240
Seraing, Tierry de, 249
Seraing, Watier de, 249
Sirehoude, Alain de, 130, 139
Sissonne, 244-5
Sluys, 50, 53-4; *battle* 86; 157, 245
Soissons, 235, 236, 243, 244, 252
Sologne, 226
Somerton Castle, 251n
Somme, river, 176, 177, 249, 252, 259
Sorre, Jehan de, 91
Spain, king of: see Alfonso XI
Spain, Lord Charles of, 215, 218, 253n
Spain, Lord Louis of, 115, 128, 132-45, 149-50, 161
Spinefort, Henry de, 111-2, 133, 138, 139
Spinefort, Olivier de, 129, 133, 138
Stafford, Ralph de, 1st Earl of, 78, 147-8, 152, 157, 170, 181
Stanhope Park, battle of, 47
Star, Company of the, 216-7
Staveren, battle of, 101n, 106n
Stirling, 22, 24, 35, 119, 128
Straten, Guillaume de, 36
Strathearn, Earl of, 189
Surgères, 187
Surles, Gile, 249
Surrey, John de Warenne, Earl of, 34n
Sweden, 122
Swinford, Norman, 161

Taillebourg, 187
Tancarville, Jean de Melun, lord of, Chamberlain
    of Normandy, 167, 172-3, 190-1, 204, 228, 248
Tarifa, 95
Teba, battle of, 54
Thiérache, 80, 83, 94, 243
Thouars, 257
Thouars, Louis, viscount of, 90
Thun-l'Évêque, 84-5
Tillemont, 103
Tombey, Stephen, 161
Tonneins, 160
Tonnerre, 243
Toulouse, 159, 165-6, 205, 222-3
Tourinne, battle of, 195
Tournai, 87, 89-90, 92-4, 98, 108, 199, 240
Tours, 226
Trésiguidi, Yves de, 112, 129, 131, 134-5, 139
Tressin, 90n
Troissy, 243
Troyes, 243, 253
Troyes, bishop of, 245
Tunis, king of, 97
Tuscany, 101
Tuwegnies, Robert de, 91
Tyne, river, 39, 41-2, 52, 119, 122-3, 189, 190
Tyre, 164

Vadencourt-et-Bohéries, 80
Vailly-sur-Seine, 243-4
Valerant, brother of Margrave of Jülich, 68
Valencia, 54
Valence, Louis, Count of, 138
Valenciennes, 27, 51, 66-8, 70-1, 84
Valkenburg, Thierry, lord of, 57, 67-8, 71, 84-5,
    87-8
Valognes, 170, 219n
Valois, 235
Vannes, 112, 133-4, 138, 142, 149-50, 152
Vans, 88
Vaudémont, Henry of Joinville, Count of, 245
Vendôme, 233, 257
Ventadour, Bernard, viscount of, 90
Vernon, 174
Vermandois, 79, 84, 240, 252

Vertus, 243
Veurne, 56n
Vézelay, 243
Vienne, Jean de, 198, 200, 203, 204
Vierzon, 225-6
Vilains, Hector, 36
Villefranche-de-Lonchat, 161
Villefranche-du-Queyran, 159
Villers-la-Tour, 83
Vilvoorde, 76-7, 78, 86, 105
Vimeu, 177-8
Vivonne, 188
Vottem, battle of, 194

Wake, Thomas, 29, 31, 34
Walcourt, Thierri de, 36
Wales, Prince of (Edward the Black Prince), 103,
    157, 169, 171, 181, 219; in Languedoc 222-3; at
    Poitiers 225-9; 247, 250-2, 254, 257-9
Walhain, Jehan de, 91
Wallingford, 58n
Warcq, 252
Warenne, Countess of: see Joan of Bar
Wargny, Jehan de, 91
Wark Castle, 123, 125, 127, 155
Waroux, 195
Warwick, Thomas de Beauchamp, 11th Earl of, 78,
    88, 147, 170, 181
Wavre, 95
Wildeberg, lord of, 36
Winchekus, rector of, 91
Winchester, 58n
Windsor, 59n, 153, 156n, 157, 229
Wissant, 32, 35, 37, 50

Yerne, river, 195
York, 35-8, 50, 63, 120-1, 123, 125, 148
York, bishop of, 189
Ypres, 56, 70, 88
Yusuf I, king of Granada, 95-7, 156

Zuaure, Clays, 94-5

Printed and bound by CPI Group (UK) Ltd, Croydon, CR0 4YY

09/06/2025

14685695-0002